The Stability of Input–Output Dynamical Systems

This is Volume 168 in
MATHEMATICS IN SCIENCE AND ENGINEERING
A Series of Monographs and Textbooks
Edited by RICHARD BELLMAN, *University of Southern California*

The complete listing of books in this series is available from the Publisher upon request.

The Stability of Input–Output Dynamical Systems

C. J. HARRIS
*Department of Electrical and
Electronic Engineering
Royal Military College of Science
Shrivenham
U.K.*

J. M. E. VALENCA
*Matematica
Universidade do Minho
Braga
Portugal*

1983

ACADEMIC PRESS

A Subsidiary of Harcourt Brace Jovanovich, Publishers

London   New York
Paris   San Diego   San Francisco
São Paulo   Sydney   Tokyo   Toronto

ACADEMIC PRESS INC. (LONDON) LTD.
24/28 Oval Road
London NW1

United States Edition published by
ACADEMIC PRESS INC.
111 Fifth Avenue
New York, New York 10003

British Library Cataloguing in Publication Data

Harris, C. J.
  The stability of input–output dynamical systems.—
  (Mathematics in science and engineering ISSN 0076–
  5392)
  1. System analysis   2. Stability   3. matrices
  I. Title   II. Valenca, J.M.E.   III. Series
  515'.35   QA402

  ISBN 0-12-327680-2

Filmset and printed in Northern Ireland at The Universities Press (Belfast) Ltd.,
and bound at William Brendon & Son, Ltd. Colchester.

Preface

The determination of the stability of dynamical feedback systems from open loop characteristics is of crucial importance in control system design, and its study has attracted considerable research effort during the past fifty years. Those stability criteria which have a simple graphical interpretation such as the Nyquist criterion have become popular with design engineers because extensions that include nonlinearities in the feedback loop are readily incorporated in the same graphical method via frequency domain methods such as the circle or Popov criteria. Until the early 1960s almost all these methods were for scalar input–output feedback systems; however, the rapid developments in the state-space representation of dynamical systems and their realizations from transfer functions led to an equally important development in stability criteria for multivariable feedback systems. Much of this early work attempted to establish generalizations of the Nyquist, Popov and circle criteria by utilizing an extended version of the mathematical structures used for establishing scalar results. It is becoming increasingly clear to the authors that such system representations are inadequate for the analysis of generalized multivariable operators in feedback systems, and an alternative mathematically rigorous approach based upon the systems input–output spaces is required. Thus the definitions of system, system stability used in this book are based entirely upon input–output properties. The only systems representation admissible *a priori* is the description of the properties of the input–output map which defines the system. The existence of every other representation (including the representation by a transfer function) are therefore deduced from these properties. For this reason this book develops the necessary and sufficient conditions for input–output stability (which are implementable in a graphical form similar to the classical Nyquist criterion) by establishing the existence of a space of transfer functions which are in a one-to-one correspondence with the family of input–output maps which define stable systems. Various spaces of transfer functions in the complex domain (with their respective Principle of the Argument and Nyquist criterion) which are isomorphic with the algebra of multipliers in the time domain (for example, for linear time-invariant operators defined on L_2^n) are developed in this book. This radical approach to the representation of multivariable feedback systems

forms the basis of the development of readily implementable graphical
stability criteria for both linear and nonlinear systems in the remainder of
the book. Many results of the book are entirely new, some integrate
previously derived stability criteria, and some previously known results
are included to both unify the theory and place in context the most
significant results.

The mathematical approach adopted in the book is that of topological
vector spaces, and Chapter One contains the necessary mathematical
preliminaries of topology to ensure that the book is essentially self
contained. This introductory chapter, which may be omitted by readers
conversant with elements of functional analysis and measure theory,
contains only those proofs which are germane to the subject development.

In the development of frequency domain stability criteria for multivariable feedback systems, the single most important result in establishing
generalized type Nyquist criteria is the Principle of the Argument. In
Chapter Two a variety of local and generalized Principles of the Argument for complex polynomials with singular points (such as poles and
zeros) and the associated encirclement conditions are derived for multivariable systems. The concepts of this chapter rely on the properties of
Riemann surfaces and the concept of homotopic triviality as found in
algebraic topology. These basic concepts are also established in Chapter
Two.

In Chapter Three the fundamental question of the representation of
linear time invariant operators is addressed such that a one-to-one
correspondence between the concept of a multiplier (a linear,
continuous—or sequentially continuous time-invariant operator) and the
concept of a transfer function is established. For the spaces L_2^n and X_2^n we
derive a space of transfer functions which are isomorphic with the space
of multipliers; this is essentially a representation theory for linear time-
invariant operators and forms the basis of stability studies of linear
feedback systems. For the important spaces L_1^n, L_∞^n, X_1^n and X_∞^n a full
representation theory is shown not to be possible, however, we estab-
lished a multiplier in these spaces which has a transfer function in some
space of complex functions. Chapter Three also contains the theory of
multipliers and the conditions for invertibility of linear time-invariant
operators, which are essential in establishing closed loop stability conditions from open loop considerations.

Chapter Four establishes a family of generalized Nyquist stability
criteria for linear feedback systems with operators defined on the spaces
L_p^n and X_p^n by utilizing the results of Chapters Two and Three. The lack of
a full representation theory for systems defined upon L_1^n, L_∞^n and X_∞^n
spaces ensures that it is not possible to state, in similar terms to L_2^n and X_2^n

spaces, necessary and sufficient conditions for closed loop stability. However, by imposing some structural conditions at least necessary conditions for closed loop stability for these spaces can be determined.

The concepts of input–output stability are essentially based upon the existence of operators defined on Banach spaces. However, many dynamical systems are frequently open loop unstable and function spaces which grow without bound are not contained within Banach spaces, so some mathematical description of unstable operators is necessary if feedback stability is to be interpreted from open loop system descriptions. This is achieved in Chapter Five by setting up the problem in extended spaces which contain well behaved as well as asymptotically unbounded functions. These generalized extended spaces contain all functions that are integrable or summable over finite intervals. A close relationship is established between extended spaces and locally convex spaces equipped with a projective limit type of topology. The concepts of causality, passivity, positivity and sectoricity are introduced in this chapter as a preliminary to their practical application in Chapters Six and Seven. Finally an introduction is given to the theory of multipliers and the multiplier factorisation theorem, which are utilized in the development of the various off-axis multivariable circle stability criteria.

The final two chapters are concerned with establishing graphical conditions for the stability of nonlinear multivariable feedback systems. In Chapter Six we develop a series of interconnected multivariable on-axis circle type stability criteria that are based upon the various small gain theorems and the loop transformation theorem. Chapter Seven utilizes the concepts of sectoricity, multipliers and passivity to derive a series of new and powerful off-axis circle stability criteria and a Popov criterion for nonlinear multivariable feedback systems.

This book is the result of a collaborative effort between the authors at the University of Oxford, University of Minho and the Royal Military College of Science, and the authors wish to acknowledge their debt to these institutions for their support and the provision of facilities to carry out this work. A major debt of gratitude is owed to the Science and Engineering Research Council for the financial support of this work. A special vote of thanks must be given to Dr R.K. Husband of Oxford University whose inspiration, and collaboration with the authors, resulted in the multivariable off-axis circle criteria of Chapter Seven. Finally, personal thanks are given to Mrs J.D. Swann whose excellent typing turned an untidy and complex manuscript into the final version of this book and to Mrs S.J. Prescott for the tracing of the figures.

February 1983   *J.M.E. Valenca*
                                                                   C.J. Harris

Contents

Chapter One

Mathematical Preliminaries

1.1 INTRODUCTION

This chapter provides an introduction to the fundamental topological and functional analytic concepts used extensively in this book. Input–output stability is essentially a topological concept defined on spaces of time functions which have various properties including those of linear topological spaces. Thus in Section 1.2 the concept of linear spaces and various topological notions associated with linear spaces are introduced. In Section 1.3 we develop generalized topological vector spaces with particular structural forms of metric spaces, inductive and projective limits, and Banach and Hilbert spaces. Various results in Chapters 5 and 6 depend upon the fixed-point theorems introduced in Section 1.4. The majority of time functions of interest in this book are L_p spaces and are reviewed as part of Section 1.5 on measures and function spaces. Finally in Section 1.6 the concepts of functionals and dual spaces are developed.

1.2 BASIC TOPOLOGICAL NOTIONS

1.2.1 Linear topological spaces

A set E is called a *linear space* over a field K when:

  (i) An operation $+$ is defined on E and with this operation E is an abelian group; that is whenever $x, y, z \in E$
  (a) $x + y = y + z$,
  (b) $(x + y) + z = x + (y + z)$
  (c) There exists an identity $0 \in E$ such that $0 + x = x + 0 = x$
  (d) There exists an $x' \in E$ such that $x + x' = 0$

  (ii) A scalar multiplication is defined which assigns any pair $(\alpha, x) \in K \times E$ to $\alpha x \in E$; furthermore the following properties are verified

1

for all $\alpha, \beta \in K$ and $x, y \in E$

(e) $\alpha(x + y) = \alpha x + \alpha y$

(f) $(\alpha + \beta)x = \alpha x + \beta x$ and $(\alpha . \beta)x = \alpha(\beta x)$

(g) $1 . x = x$ where 1 denotes the unit element of the multiplication in K

Throughout K is either the field of real numbers R^1, in which case E is said to be a real linear space, or the field C^1 of complex numbers, when E is said to be a complex linear space. Frequently the designation of vector space will be used as synonymous of linear space.

Example 1.1   Consider the linear space $C(R_+)$ defined as the space of all continuous time functions $t \mapsto f(t)$ defined on the half real line, $R_+ = [0, \infty)$, with addition and scalar multiplication defined by

$$(f+g)(t) = f(t) + g(t)$$
$$(\alpha f)(t) = \alpha f(t)$$

The degree of proximity between two points in a linear space E can be expressed in terms of sets which are generalizations of the familiar balls in R^n. Let x be arbitrary in E and let $B(x) = \{U\}$ be a family of subsets of E satisfying

B.1   Every element of $B(x)$ contains x

B.2   The intersection of two elements of $B(x)$ is an element of $B(x)$

B.3   For every $U \in B(x)$ and every $y \in U$ there exists a $V \in B(y)$ contained in U

The collection $B(x)$ is called a *base of open neighbourhoods of the point* x. Any set $W \subset E$ which contains some $U \in B(x)$ is called a *neighbourhood* of x. Axioms B.1 − B.3 induce the following properties in the family $N(x)$ of all neighbourhoods of x.

N.1   Every $U \in N(x)$ contains x

N.2   Every set which contains an element of $N(x)$ is itself an element of $N(x)$

N.3   The intersection of a finite collection of elements of $N(x)$ is an element of $N(x)$.

N.4   Each $U \in N(x)$ contains some $V \in N(x)$ such that U is a neighbourhood of every point of V

Example 1.2   In $C(R_+)$ define

$$B(\xi) = \{f : \sup_{t < \infty} |f(t)| < \xi, \xi > 0\} \tag{1.1}$$

Each $B(\xi)$ is called an open ball in $C(R_+)$. It is trivial to show that the collection $B(f) = \{f + B(\xi)\}_{\xi > 0}$ is a base of neighbourhoods of the point $f \in C(R_+)$. In particular, to show B.3, consider $g \in f + B(\xi)$; then the quantity $\xi' = \xi - \sup_{t < \infty} |f(t) - g(t)|$ is non-zero positive. Clearly $g + B(\xi')$ is contained in $f + B(\xi)$.

When a class of neighbourhoods is defined for every point of a space E, then a topology is defined in E. Let τ represent such a topology; the pair (E, τ), called a *topological space*, is represented by $E[\tau]$.

Frequently, when E is a linear space, the neighbourhoods of an arbitrary point x take the form $x + U$, where U is a neighbourhood of the origin. In these circumstances, the base of neighbourhoods of the origin defines completely the topology of the space. Such a space is called a *linear topological space*.

Given a topological space E, whose topology is defined by families of a base of neighbourhoods of its points, an *open set* is defined as any set which contains a neighbourhood of each of its points. Note that B.3 implies that every set in a base of neighbourhoods is an open set. A *closed set* is defined as the complement of an open set.

The following properties of open sets are readily proved:

O.1 The empty set and the set E are open sets
O.2 An arbitrary union of open sets is an open set
O.3 An arbitrary finite intersection of open sets is an open set

The concept of topology has been defined through axioms B.1–B.3 and the concept of a neighbourhood; alternatively it is possible to define topology through a definition of open sets which takes O.1–O.3 as axioms. In this alternative definition, a neighbourhood of a point x is defined as any set containing an open set which contains x. Properties N.1–N.4 can easily be established. (The equivalence of these two alternative definitions of topology is given in Kothe (1969).)

It is possible to define several topologies on the same space, the question now arises of relating these topologies. Let τ_1 and τ_2 be two topologies on the same space E. The topology τ_1 is said to be *stronger* (or *finer*) than the topology τ_2, when for any $x \in E$ the collection of all neighbourhoods of x defined by τ_1 contains the collection of all neighbourhoods of x defined by τ_2, here τ_2 is *weaker* (or *coarser*) than τ_1. Clearly τ_1 coincides with τ_2 when it is both weaker and stronger than τ_2.

Example 1.3 The topology $C(R_+)$ defined by the collection of open balls (1.1) is called the *uniform* topology. Other topologies are sometimes useful in $C(R_+)$: consider a finite collection of points $0 < T_1 < T_2 < \ldots < T_n$ and a collection of positive numbers $0 < \xi_1 < \xi_2 < \ldots < \xi_n$. Let U be

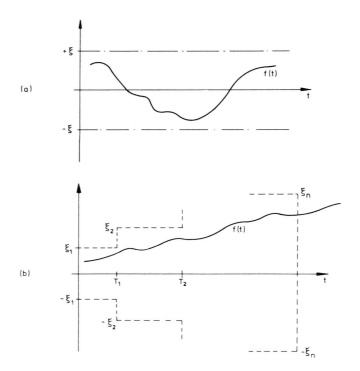

FIG. 1.1   Illustration of Example 1.8 for extended space topologies

defined as

$$U = \{f : \sup_{t \leq T_i} |f(t)| < \xi_i, \ i = 1, 2, \ldots, n\} \tag{1.2}$$

The elements of an open ball $B(\xi)$ can be visualized as functions which lie on an infinite strip bounded by $+\xi$ and $-\xi$ (Fig. 1.1a). The elements of U are functions which are bounded by $\pm\xi_i$ only in the interval $[0, T_i]$. Therefore for $t > T_n$, the set of all possible values for $f(t)$ (with $f \in U$) is not bounded (Fig. 1.1b).

For any $x \in E$, the collection $\{x + U\}$, where the totality of sets U is obtained by taking in (1.2) all possible finite selections of points $T_1 < T_2 < \ldots < T_n$ and numbers $\xi_1 < \xi_2 < \ldots < \xi_n$, satisfies axioms B.1–B.3 and therefore defines a base of open neighbourhoods of x. The topology thus defined is called the *topology of the extended space*; we now relate this topology to the uniform topology.

We can state that the uniform topology is stronger than the extended space topology. In fact, given a neighbourhood V of a point x in the extended space topology, it must contain a set of the form $x + U$ (for U given by (1.2)); but U always contains an open ball $B(\xi)$ provided that $\xi < \xi_i = \min_i \xi_i$. Thus V contains $x + B(\xi)$, and therefore it is a neighbourhood of x in the uniform topology. Conversely we can prove that the topology of the extended space is always weaker than the uniform topology because we can find neighbourhoods of x in the uniform topology which are not neighbourhoods of x in the extended space topology. For example the neighbourhood $x + B(\xi)$ is not a neighbourhood of x in the extended space topology because it is not possible to find any U of the form (1.2) contained in $B(\xi)$; in fact, even if $\xi > \xi_n = \max_i \xi_i$, it is always possible to find some $f \in U$ such that $\sup_{t > T_n} |f(t)| > \xi$. We conclude that the uniform topology is stronger than the extended space topology and that the two topologies do not coincide.

Of particular interest are those topologies which separate points; a topology is said to separate points in the space E when two distinct points of E lie in disjoint open sets. Equivalently a topology separates points when the intersection of all closed neighbourhoods of a point x coincides with x itself. The topology that satisfies this property is called a Hausdorff topology.

Example 1.4   We can show that the extended space topology and the uniform topology in $C(R_+)$ are both Hausdorff topologies. Taking the extended space topology, consider the intersection of all closed neighbourhoods of a point $f_0 \in C(R_+)$. We need to show that an arbitrary $g \neq f_0$ is not a point in this intersection. Since g and f_0 are distinct there exists a $T > 0$ and $\xi > 0$ such that

$$\sup_{t \leq T} |f_0(t) - g(t)| > \xi. \quad \text{Defining} \quad U = \{f : \sup_{t \leq T} |f(t)| \leq \xi\}$$

then $f_0 + U$ is a closed neighbourhood of f_0 which does not contain g. The extended space topology is therefore an Hausdorff topology. Since the uniform topology is stronger than the extended space topology (see Example 1.3) then it must also be a Hausdorff topology.

If F is a subspace of a topological space $E[\tau]$ a topology is defined in F if we consider as neighbourhoods of the point $x \in F$ all the sets of the form $U \cap F$, where U is a neighbourhood of x in E, such a topology is called the topology *induced* in F by the topology of E.

1.2.2   Sequences, nets and continuity

Possibly the most important of all topological concepts are the concepts of limit and continuity. A *sequence* in a topological space E is defined as any map from the set of natural numbers Z into E; it will be represented by $\{x_n\}_Z$ or simply as $\{x_n\}$. If Γ is an arbitrary totally ordered set, we define a *net* in E as any map of Γ into E.

A subset $I \subset Z$ is called a *cofinal* set when for each $n \in Z$, there exists an $m \in I$ such that $m \geq n$. Given a sequence $\{x_n\}_Z$ its restriction to a cofinal set I is represented by $\{x_n\}_I$ and is called a cofinal subsequence of $\{x_n\}_Z$. Identically we can define a cofinal subnet.

A point x_0 is said to be an *adherent point* of a net $\{x_a\}_\Gamma$ when any neighbourhood of x_0 contains a cofinal subnet. The point x_0 is said to be the *limit* of the net $\{x_a\}_\Gamma$, when for each neighbourhood U of x_0 there exists an $a \in \Gamma$ such that the subnet $\{x_a\}_{a \geq a}$ is contained in U. In a Hausdorff space the limit of a net is unique (provided that it exists); moreover it is also the unique adherent point.

Of special interest in linear topological spaces are the Cauchy nets; a net $\{x_a\}$ is a Cauchy net when given any neighbourhood of the origin U there exists a γ such that for all $\alpha, \beta \geq \gamma$, $x_\alpha - x_\beta \in U$. A linear topological space in which every Cauchy sequence has a limit is said to be *complete*.

Given a subset F of a topological space E, we define the *closure* of F (represented by $\bar{F}$) as the set of all limits of convergent nets of F. The closure $\bar{F}$ is the intersection of all closed sets which contain F. If $\bar{F}$ coincides with E then F is said to *dense* in E.

Example 1.5   Consider the space C_0 of all functions $f \in C(R_+)$ which satisfy $\lim_{T \to \infty} \sup_{t \geq T} |f(t)| = 0$. Consider also the space C_{00} of all functions in $C(R_+)$ which vanish outside some finite interval $[0, T]$. We wish to show that the closure $\bar{C}_{00}$ of C_{00} coincides with C_0.

Consider first an arbitrary convergent sequence $\{f_n\}$ in C_{00} and let f be its limit. For any $\xi > 0$ there must exist an n such that for all $m \geq n$, $\sup_{t < \infty} |f(t) - f_m(t)| < \xi$. Let T_m be such that f_m vanishes outside $[0, T_m]$. Then $\sup_{t \geq T_m} |f(t)| < \xi$, which illustrates that f lies in C_0. Thus $C_0 \supset \bar{C}_{00}$.

Conversely let f be arbitrary in C_0 and let $\{\phi_n\}$ be a sequence in C_{00} satisfying:

(i) $\phi_n(t) \in [0, 1]$ $\forall\, t < \infty$

(ii) $\phi_n(t) = 1$ $\forall\, t \leq n$

Define $f_n(t) = f(t)\phi_n(t)$, then

$$\limsup_{\substack{n \to \infty \\ t < \infty}} |f(t) - f_n(t)| \leq \limsup_{\substack{n \to \infty \\ t < \infty}} |f(t)| \cdot |1 - \phi_n(t)|$$

$$\leq \limsup_{\substack{n \to \infty \\ t > n}} |f(t)| = 0$$

Consequently $\bar{C}_{00} \supset C_0$, therefore the closure $\bar{C}_{00}$ of C_{00} must coincide with C_0.

Given two topological spaces E and F and a map $A : E \to F$; A is said to be continuous in a point $x_0 \in E$ when, given any neighbourhood U of $A(x_0)$, there exists a neighbourhood V of x_0 such that $A(V) \subset U$. If A is continuous at every point of E, then A is continuous. Equivalently, A is continuous when, given any open set O in F, $A^{-1}(O)$ is open and, given any closed set C in F, $A^{-1}(C)$ is closed.

    If given any convergent sequence $\{x_n\}$ in E we have $\lim_n A(x_n) = A(\lim_n x_n)$, then A is said to be *sequentially* continuous; every continuous map is sequentially continuous.

    Let A be a one to one map from a topological space E into a topological space F; then if both A and A^{-1} are continuous, we say that A is a *homeomorphism*.

1.2.3   Convex and compact sets

A subset F of a linear topological space E is *absorvent* when, for any $x \in E$, there exists a $\rho > 0$ such that $\rho x \in F$. The set F is *circled*, when for any complex number a, $ax \in F$ whenever $x \in F$ and $|a| \leq 1$. F is said to be *absolutely convex*, when for any $a, b \in C^1$ which satisfy $|a| + |b| \leq 1$, we have $ax + by \in F$ whenever $x, y \in F$. The set F is *bounded* if, given any neighbourhood of the origin U, there exists a $\rho > 0$ such that $F \subset \rho U$.

Example 1.6   Consider an arbitrary open ball $B(\xi)$ in $C(R_+)$. For any $f \in C(R_+)$, either $f = 0$, in which case $f \in B(\xi)$, or $f \neq 0$, in which case for

$$\rho < \frac{\xi}{\sup_{t < \infty} |f(t)|}$$

we have $\rho f \in B(\xi)$. Thus $B(\xi)$ is absorvent. Moreover, given any $f, g \in B(\xi)$ we have

$$\sup_{t < \infty} |af(t) + bg(t)| \leq \xi(|a| + |b|)$$

Thus, provided that $|a| + |b| \leq 1$, then $af + bg \in B(\xi)$, and $B(\xi)$ is absolutely convex. Taking the special case $b = 0$ we see that $B(\xi)$ is circled. Finally given any neighbourhood U of the origin in the uniform topology, let $B(\xi')$ be an open ball contained in U. For any $\rho > \xi/\xi'$ we have $B(\xi) \subset \rho B(\xi')$, thus $B(\xi)$ is bounded.

A subset M of a Hausdorff topological space E is *compact* when every net in M has an adherent point in M. Compactness can be recognized in various alternative forms. The equivalence between some of these forms is stated in:

PROPOSITION 1.1   *If M is a subset of a Hausdorff space E, then the following statements are equivalent*:

   (i)   *M is compact*
   (ii) *Every cover of M by open sets contains a finite subcover*
   (iii) *Every collection of closed sets in M with empty intersection contains a finite subcollection with empty intersection*

Compact spaces have special significance in the study of topological spaces of time functions, we therefore state some of its properties:

PROPOSITION 1.2   *Let M be a compact subset of a topological space E. Then*:

   (i)   *M is closed and bounded*
   (ii) *Every closed subset of M is compact, and every open subset of M is relatively compact (that is, its closure is compact)*
   (iii) *Any continuous image of M is also compact*
   (iv) *The union of finitely many compact sets is compact*

A Hausdorff space is *locally compact* if every neighbourhood of an arbitrary point x is relatively compact. Classical examples of locally compact spaces which are not compact are R^n and C^n. A very important property of these spaces is expressed in:

THEOREM 1.1: ALEXANDROFF'S THEOREM   *Every locally compact space E which is not compact can be enlarged with the addition of one point to give a compact space, called the one-point compactification of E. Moreover such a compactification is unique up to a homeomorphism.*

Example 1.7   Consider the space $R^1 = (-\infty, \infty)$. With the addition of *one* point at infinity we can enlarge R^1 into a compact space $R^c = [-\infty, \infty]$, where the points $+\infty$, $-\infty$ are the same point. The neighbourhoods of infinity are sets of the form $(T, +\infty]$ or $[-\infty, T)$. The space $C(R^c)$ of all continuous bounded functions in R^c can be obtained from $C(R^1)$ by taking all functions $f \in C(R^1)$ for which $\lim_{t \to +\infty} f(t)$ and $\lim_{t \to -\infty} f(t)$ exist and coincide; the value of $f(\cdot)$ in the point of compactification is defined as this limit.

Identically we can enlarge the complex plane C^1 with a compact space C^c by the addition of *one* point at infinity. The neighbourhoods of infinity are sets of the form $U = \{\sigma : |\sigma| > \xi\}$. We can define a space $C(C^c)$ of all continuous bounded functions in C^c by taking the limit of $C(C)$ formed with all functions which converge uniformly at infinity to same limit.

We have seen that every compact space is bounded and closed; the converse is not in general true. As an example, consider a bounded closed ball in $C(R_+)$

$$B = \{f : \sup_{r < \infty} |f(t)| \le \xi\}$$

Although we cannot show that B is compact, the following result (a consequence of the Ascoli–Arzlea theorem) recognizes a compact subset of B.

PROPOSITION 1.3 *A subset $B' \subset B$ is compact if it lies in $C(R_+^c)$ where R_+^c is the one-point compactification of R_+, and is equicontinuous, that is, given any increasing homeomorphism $\rho : [0, \infty] \to [0, 1]$ and any $\xi > 0$, there exists a $\delta > 0$ such that $\rho(|t - t'|) < \delta$ implies*

$$\sup_{f \in B'} |f(t) - f(t')| < \xi \quad \text{for all} \quad t, t' \in R_+^c.$$

1.3 TOPOLOGICAL VECTOR SPACES

1.3.1 General topological vector spaces

Let E be a Hausdorff linear topological space; if the maps $(x, y) \mapsto x + y$ from E^2 into E, and $(x, \alpha) \mapsto \alpha x$ from $E \times C^1$ into E, are continuous then E is called a *topological vector space*. The following theorem identifies a linear space as a topological vector space.

THEOREM 1.2 *Let E be a linear space. The following statements are equivalent*:

  A *E is a topological vector space*

  B *There exists a family $N = \{U_a\}$ of absorvent circled subsets of E which satisfy*

      (i) *the intersection of any two elements of N is an element of N*

(ii) *The intersection $\bigcap\limits_{a} U_a$ of all sets in N coincides with the singleton $\{0\}$*

(iii) *For every $U \in N$ there exists a $V \in N$ such that $V + V \subset N$*

When a topological vector space has a base of neighbourhoods of the origin consisting of absolutely convex sets, the space is said to be a *locally convex space*. This type of space is the more general form of topological vector space used in this book; it can be identified through the following theorem.

THEOREM 1.3   *Let E be a linear space. Then the two following statements are equivalent*:

A   *E is a locally convex space.*

B   *There exists a family $N = \{U_\alpha\}$ of absolutely convex absorvent subsets of E satisfying*;

(i) *The intersection of any two elements of N is an element of N*

(ii) *The intersection $\bigcap\limits_{\alpha} U_\alpha$ of the totality of elements of N coincides with the singleton $\{0\}$*

(iii) *For any $U \in N$ and any $\rho > 0$ the set ρU lies in N*

Example 1.8   Consider the space $C(R_+)$ equipped with the extended space topology, and let us consider the collection $N = \{U\}$ of all sets of the form

$$U = \{f : \sup_{t \leq T_i} |f(t)| < \xi_i, i = 1, \ldots, n\}$$

with

$$T_n > T_{n-1} > \ldots > T_1 > 0 \quad \text{and} \quad \xi_n > \xi_{n-1} > \ldots > \xi_1 > 0$$

Clearly every U is absolutely convex and absorvent. Conditions B(i) and B(iii) of Theorem 1.3 are obvious; condition B(ii) was proved in Example 1.4. Thus $C(R_+)$ with the extended space topology is a locally convex space. Identically we can show that equipped with the uniform topology, $C(R_+)$ is still a locally convex space.

Locally convex spaces are closely related to finite semi-normed spaces which are defined as follows:

Let E be a linear space and $\rho : E \to R_+^c$ a positive function in E. The function $p(\cdot)$ is called a *semi-norm* when

s.1   For all $x \in E$ and complex numbers α,

$$p(\alpha x) = |\alpha| p(x)$$

s.2   For all $x, y \in E$

$$p(x + y) \leq p(x) + p(y)$$

If in addition the following is satisfied

s.3 $p(x) = 0$ if and only if $x = 0$

then $p(\cdot)$ is called a norm and is usually represented by $\|\cdot\|$.

A finite semi-norm space is a space where the range of every semi-norm is restricted to R_+, that is $p(x) < \infty$ for all $x \in E$. In similar manner we define a finite normed space.

The relationship between circled, absolutely convex subsets of E and semi-norms is explored in the following result.

PROPOSITION 1.4

A   *A finite semi-norm defines a family $N = \{U_\xi\}$ of absolutely convex absorvent subsets through*

$$U_\xi = \{x \in E : p(x) < \xi, \, \xi > 0\}$$

Moreover the intersection of any two elements of N is an element of N

B   *An absorvent absolutely convex set M defines a finite semi-norm through $p(x) = \inf \{k > 0 : x \in kM\}$*

The relationship between finite semi-normed spaces and locally convex spaces is established in:

THEOREM 1.4   *Let E be a linear space. Then the two statements are equivalent*:

A   *E is a locally convex space.*

B   *There exists a collection $\{p_a(\cdot)\}$ of finite semi-norms in E with the property that for each non-zero $x \in E$, there exists one semi-norm $p_a(\cdot)$ such that $p_a(x) \neq 0$.*

A stronger result can be proved for finite normed spaces:

THEOREM 1.5   *If E is a linear space equipped with a finite norm $\|\cdot\|$, then E is a locally convex space and its topology is generated by a family of open balls, $B(\xi) = \{x \in E : \|x\| < \xi, \, \xi > 0\}$.*

Example 1.9   Consider in $C(R_+)$ the positive function defined by

$$\|f\| = \sup_{t < \infty} |f(t)|$$

Clearly $\|\cdot\|$ is a finite norm, moreover the open balls generated by this norm coincide with the open balls (1.1) in Example 1.2. Then the topology generated by this norm coincides with the uniform topology.

For the extended space topology (Example 1.3) we consider the family of positive functions defined for all $T > 0$

$$p_T(f) \triangleq \sup_{t \leq T} |f(t)|$$

Clearly every $p_T(\cdot)$ is a semi-norm and given any $f \neq 0$ there exists some $T > 0$ such that $\sup_{t \leq T} |f(t)| > 0$; consequently given any $f \neq 0$ there exists a semi-norm $p_T(\cdot)$ such that $p_T(f) \neq 0$. Thus the family of semi-norms $\{p_T(\cdot)\}$ define in E a locally convex space topology (Theorem 1.4). To see that this topology coincides with the extended space topology we note that the generic neighbourhood of the origin contains a set of the form

$$U = \{f : p_{T_i}(f) < \xi_i ; i = 1, 2, \ldots, n\}$$

which coincides with the generic set (1.2) in Example 1.3.

Let $p(\cdot)$ be an arbitrary finite semi-norm in a linear space E. Although $p(\cdot)$ is not necessarily a norm we can introduce a space where $p(\cdot)$ induces a norm. Let $N \subset E$ be the null space of $p(\cdot)$, that is $N = \{x \in E : p(x) = 0\}$. It is simple to show that N is a linear proper subspace of E, and unless $p(\cdot)$ is a norm, N is distinct from the singleton $\{0\}$. It is now possible to define the quotient space (Kothe, 1969), E/N. To each $x_0 \in E$ there is assigned an element $[x_0] \in E/N$, called the N-coset of x_0, which is the set of all $x \in E$ such that $x - x_0 \in N$. Thus we can represent $[x_0]$ as the set $x_0 + N$. The map $A : x_0 \to [x_0]$ is called the *canonical mapping*. The zero element of E/N is the N-coset of zero and is therefore in the set $0 + N \equiv N$. E/N can be identified with a linear space by defining $[x] + [y] \triangleq [x + y]$ and $a[x] = [ax]$; although these definitions seem to depend on the particular values of x and y chosen, its coherence results from the fact that given any $x' \in x + N$ and $y' \in y + N$, we have

$$(x' + y') - (x + y) = (x' - x) + (y' - y) \in N$$
$$(ax') - (ax) = a(x' - x) \in N$$

The canonical mapping A, is as a consequence of this definition a linear map.

We can define a positive map $\|\cdot\| : E/N \to R_+$ through

$$\|[x]\| = p(x)$$

This definition is also independent of the point $x \in [x]$ chosen, since given any $x' \in x + N$, we have $|p(x') - p(x)| \leq p(x' - x) = 0$, which implies that $p(x') = p(x)$. It is straightforward to show that $\|\cdot\|$ is a semi-norm; moreover if $\|[x]\| = 0$ then $p(x) = 0$ for all $x \in [x]$, which means that $[x] \equiv N \equiv [0]$. Therefore $\|\cdot\|$ is a norm in E/N. We have now shown:

THEOREM 1.6   *Let $p(\cdot)$ be a finite semi-norm in a linear space E. If N represents its null space, then E/N is a finite normed locally convex space. Moreover, every open ball $\hat{U} \subset E/N$ is of the form $\hat{U} = A(U)$ where A is the canonical mapping and $U = \{x \in E : p(x) < \xi, \xi > 0\}$.*

If E and F are two normed spaces and $A : E \to F$ is a linear, onto map such that $\|Ax\| = \|x\|$ for all $x \in E$, then we say that E and F are *isometrically isomorphic spaces*. The map A is obviously a homeomorphism. As an example of isometrically isomorphic spaces we consider the following:

Example 1.10　Let $C_e(R_+)$, or simply C_e, be the space of all continuous, but not necessarily bounded, functions with domain in $[0, \infty)$.

Let $p_T(\cdot)$ be the semi-norm defined in Example 1.9

$$p_T(f) \triangleq \sup_{t \leq T} |f(t)|$$

Let N_T be the null space of this semi-norm. We wish to show that the space $C([0, T])$, or simply C_T, of all continuous functions defined in the interval $[0, T]$, is isometrically isomorphic with C_e/N_T, we consider C_T equipped with the uniform norm.

Let $P_T : C_e \to C_T$ be the linear map defined as

$$(P_T f)(t) = f(t) \qquad \forall\, t \in [0, T].$$

$P_T f = 0$ if and only if $f \in N_T$; moreover for all $f \in C_e$, $\|P_T f\| = p_T(f)$. Let $\hat{P} : C_e/N_T \to C_T$ be defined as $\hat{P}[f] \triangleq P_T f$. The coherence of these definitions result from the fact that, given any $f' \in f + N_T$, $P_T f' = P_T f + P_T(f - f') = P_T f$. The map $\hat{P}$ is clearly linear and onto; moreover

$$\|[f]\| = p_T(f) = \|P_T f\| = \|\hat{P}[f]\|$$

Hence $\hat{P}$ is an isometric isomorphism.

1.3.2　Metric spaces

As a generalization of the concept of distance in a space E let $d(\cdot, \cdot)$ be a positive real function in $E \times E$ which satisfies:

M.1　$d(x, y) = d(y, x)$ 　　　　　　　　$\forall\, x, y \in E$

M.2　$d(x, y) = 0$ 　　　　　　　if and only if $x \equiv y$

M.3　$d(x, y) \leq d(x, z) + d(z, y)$ 　　$\forall\, x, y, z \in E$

The function $d(\cdot, \cdot)$ is called a *metric* in E, and the space E is called a metric space. A metric space is a topological space if we define as base of neighbourhoods of a point $x \in E$, the family of open balls

$$U_\xi(x) = \{y \in E : d(y, x) < \xi, \xi > 0\}$$

Form axiom M.2, this topology is a Hausdorff topology.

One of the most usual examples of a metric is defined in finite normed spaces through $d(x, y) \triangleq \|x - y\|$. Thus we can state that every finite normed space is *metrizable.* In these cases the topology defined by the metric coincides with the topology defined by the norm. Some other locally convex spaces can also be metrizable, consider the space $C_e(R_+)$ (Example 1.10) of all continuous but not necessarily bounded functions with domain in $R_+ = [0, \infty)$. Define the following family of semi-norms

$$p_T(f) = \sup_{t \leq T} |f(t)|, \qquad T > 0$$

As was shown in Example 1.9, this family of semi-norms defines a locally convex topology in $C_e(R_+)$. We call $C_e(R_+)$, the extended version of $C(R_+)$. Although it is not possible to define a finite norm in $C_e(R_+)$ we can define a metric as follows. For an unbounded increasing sequence $T_1 < T_2 < \ldots < T_n < \ldots$ and a sequence of positive numbers $c_1 > c_2 > \ldots > c_n > \ldots$ such that

$$\sum_{i=1}^{\infty} c_i < \infty$$

then

$$d(f, g) = \sum_{i=1}^{\infty} c_i p_{T_i}(f - g)(1 + p_{T_i}(f - g))^{-1}$$

defines a metric in $C_e(R_+)$.

The basic topological notions take a more familar appearance when expressed in terms of metrics, thus

(i) A map $T:(E, d) \to (E, d')$ between two metric spaces is continuous at a point $x_0 \in E$ when, given any $\xi > 0$, there exists a $\delta > 0$ such that $d(x, x_0) < \delta$ implies $d'(T(x), T(x_0)) < \xi$.

(ii) A sequence $\{x_n\}$ in metric space (E, d) is said to converge to a point x_0 when, given any $\xi > 0$, there exists an order N such that, for all $n \geq N$, $d(x_n, x_0) < \xi$.

(iii) A point x_0 is said to be a closure point of a subset F of a metric space (E, d) when, for all $\xi > 0$, there is a point $x \in F$ such that $d(x, x_0) < \xi$.

(iv) A subset F of a metric space (E, d) is compact if, given any $\xi > 0$, there exists a finite collection of points $x_1, x_2, \ldots x_n$, such that for all $x \in F$, $\min_{i \leq n} d(x, x_i) < \xi$.

We now introduce a new concept; a map T from a topological space (E, d) into a topological space (F, d') is *uniformally continuous* when, given any $\xi > 0$, there exists a $\delta > 0$ such that $d'(T(x), T(y)) < \xi$ whenever $d(x, y) < \delta$, $x, y \in E$. If E is compact, then every continuous operator $T:(E, d) \to (F, d')$ is uniformly continuous.

Two metrics d and d' in the same space E are *equivalent* when the identity operator as a map on (E, d) into (E, d') and as a map on (E, d') into (E, d), is uniformly continuous. Consequently, if d and d' are equivalent metrics, given any $\xi > 0$, there exists a $\delta > 0$ such that

(i) $d(x, y) < \delta$ implies $d'(x, y) < \xi$

and

(ii) $d'(x, y) < \delta$ implies $d(x, y) < \xi$.

Clearly, equivalent metrics define the same topology in the space E.

1.3.3 Inductive and projective limits of normed spaces

Although normed spaces are the most frequent of locally convex spaces used in stability studies, our studies will require more general topological vector spaces which can be seen as limits of normed spaces.

Suppose that to each $a > 0$ we associate a finitely normed space E_a; let $\|\cdot\|_a$ represent the norm in E_a. Let us also assume that $E_a \supset E_b$ if $b > a$. We can define a vector space E as

$$E = \bigcup_{a > 0} E_a \qquad (1.3)$$

which is called the *inductive limit* of the spaces E_a (for a more general definition see Kothe section 19 (1969)). From this definition we see that for $b > a > 0$

$$E \supset E_a \supset E_b$$

Let $I_a : E_a \to E$ represent the embedding of E_a in E, and let $I_{ab} : E_b \to E_a$ represent, for $b > a$, the embedding of E_b in E_a, clearly $I_b = I_a I_{ab}$. The inductive limit E is frequently represented by

$$E = \varinjlim I_{ab}(E_b)$$

We can define a base of absolutely convex neighbourhoods of the origin in E by considering the convex covers of sets of the form $U = \bigcup_{a > 0} U_a$ where U_a is an absolutely convex neighbourhood of the origin in E_a (the convex cover of U is the intersection of all absolutely convex sets containing U). If such a topology, denoted by τ, is Hausdorff we say that $E[\tau]$ is the topological inductive limit of the spaces E_a.

THEOREM 1.7   *The space $E = \bigcup_a E_a$ is the topological inductive limit of the spaces E_a if and only if, for $b > a$, the topology induced in E_b by the topology of E_a is weaker than the original topology of E_b. In these circumstances, the absolutely convex neighbourhoods of the origin in E are* *the sets* $U = \bigcup_a U_a$, *with* U_a *an absolutely convex neighbourhood of the origin in* E_a.

In a family of normed spaces $\{E_a\}_{a>0}$ where $E_a \supset E_b$, for $b > a$, the requirements of Theorem 1.6 are equivalent to the requirement that $\|x\|_a \leq \|x\|_b$ for all $x \in E_b$.

We now consider the relationship between E and the inductive limit $\tilde{E}$ generated when we consider a cofinal subset of $(0, \infty)$. Let Γ be a subset of $(0, \infty)$ such that, for all $a > 0$, there exists a $\gamma \in \Gamma$ such that $\gamma < a$, and let the inductive limit be generated by $\tilde{E} = \bigcup_{\gamma \in \Gamma} E_\gamma$. Then

PROPOSITION 1.5   *Under the above conditions, if E is a topological inductive limit, so is $\tilde{E}$ and the two spaces are topologically isomorphic.*

As a consequence of Proposition 1.5, consider any sequence $\{a_n\}$ in $(0, \infty)$ such that $\lim_n a_n = 0$, and if E_n represents E_{a_n}, then

$$E_1 \subset E_2 \subset \ldots \subset E_n \subset \ldots$$

and the topological inductive limit E can be identified with the limit

$$\bigcup_{n=1}^{\infty} E_n.$$

Example 1.11   Let $\|\cdot\|_a$, $a > 0$, be a norm defined in $C(R_+)$ by

$$\|f\|_a = \sup_{t < \infty} \exp(at) |f(t)|$$

Clearly $\|f\|_a \leq \|f\|_b$, for $b > a$ and all $f \in C(R_+)$. Let C_a represent the set of all $f \in C(R_+)$ for which $\|f\|_a$ is finite, then the space $\tilde{C}(R_+) = \bigcup_{a>0} C_a$ can be identified with the topological inductive limit of the spaces C_a (Theorem 1.6).

Frequently the properties of topological inductive limits are insufficient for stability studies; a stronger concept is required.

Let E be the topological inductive limit of a countable family of spaces,

$$E_1 \subset E_2 \subset E_3 \ldots \subset E_n \subset \ldots$$

and assume that the topology induced in E_n by the topology of E_{n+1} coincides with the topology of E_n. Then E is called the *strict inductive limit* of the spaces E_n. The equivalence between the normed topologies of E_{n+1} and E_n exists if and only if there exist positive constants $\delta, \rho > 0$ such that

$$\rho \|x\|_{n+1} \leq \|x\|_n \leq \delta \|x\|_{n+1} \qquad \forall \, x \in E_n$$

The two following results establish the *raison d'être* of strict inductive limits

THEOREM 1.8   *If* $E = \bigcup_{n=1}^{\infty} E_n$ *is the strict inductive limit of the spaces* E_n, *then a set B is bounded in E if and only if there exists some n such that B is contained in* E_n *and is bounded in the topology of* E_n.

THEOREM 1.9   *If* $E = \bigcup_{n=1}^{\infty} E_n$ *is the strict inductive limit of the spaces* E_n, *then a sequence* $\{x_k\}$ *converges in E to a limit* $x_0 \in E$ *if and only if there exists some n such that both the sequence and the limit are contained in* E_n *and* $\{x_k\}$ *converges to* x_0 *in the topology of* E_n.

Although we can define strict inductive limits when we have a non-countable family of spaces $\{E_a\}_{a>0}$, it is not possible to prove results of the nature of Theorems 1.8 and 1.9 for these spaces. Therefore, as such, they are of little practical value in stability studies.

As a consequence of Theorems 1.8 and 1.9 the following result can be proved:

PROPOSITION 1.6   *Let T be a continuous linear mapping from a finitely normed space F into a strict inductive limit* $E = \bigcup_{n=1}^{\infty} E_n$. *Then there exists some n such that* E_n *contains* $T(F)$.

Consider again a family $\{E_a\}$ of finitely normed spaces defined for all $a \geq 0$. Suppose there exists a family $\{P_{ab}\}$ of linear onto maps, $P_{ab} : E_b \to E_a$ defined for all $b > a$ such that

$$P_{ab} P_{ac} \equiv P_{ac} \qquad \forall\, c > b > a$$

Consider the topological product space $\hat{E} = \prod_a E_a$; $\hat{E}$ is the space of all functions $x(a) = x_a \in E_a$. Each $\hat{x} \in \hat{E}$ is represented as (x_a) and $x_a \in E_a$ is called the component of $\hat{x}$ in E_a. Let $\hat{P}_a : \hat{E} \to E_a$ be the map which assigns $\hat{x} \in \hat{E}$ to its component x_a in E_a. The mappings $\hat{P}_a$ are called *projections*. The space $\hat{E}$ is a linear space under the obvious definitions of sum and product by a scalar: $(x_a) + (y_a) = (x_a + y_a)$, $\alpha(x_a) = (\alpha x_a)$. We can define in $\hat{E}$ a topology, called the product topology, by constructing a base of absolutely convex neighbourhoods of the origin which are finite intersections of sets of the form $\hat{P}_a^{(-1)} B_a$, where B_a is an open ball in E_a.

$$U = \bigcap_{i=1}^{n} \hat{P}_{a_i}^{(-1)} \{ x_{a_i} \in E_{a_i} : \|x_{a_i}\| < \xi_i \} \qquad (1.4)$$

With such a topology, $\hat{E}$ is a locally convex space.

The projective limit of the spaces E_a, represented by $E = \varprojlim P_{ab}E_b$, is defined as the subspace $E \subset \hat{E}$ formed with all elements $\hat{x} = (x_a)$ which satisfy

$$x_a = P_{ab}x_b \qquad \forall \, a < b \qquad (1.5)$$

In E the families of maps $\{P_{ab}\}$ and $\{\hat{P}_a\}$ are related by

$$\hat{P}_a = P_{ab}\hat{P}_b \qquad \forall \, a < b \qquad (1.6)$$

When E is equipped with the topology induced by the product topology we say that E is the topological projective limit of the spaces E_a.

Example 1.12   Consider the space C_e (see Example 1.10) equipped with the extended space topology (Example 1.9), and the family $\{C_T\}_{T>0}$ (see also Example 1.10). We now show that C_e can be identified with the topological projective limit of the spaces C_T.

Let $P_T : C_e \to C_T$ be the family of maps defined in Example 1.10. Given $S > T$ and any f_S, we see that $P_T f = P_T f'$ for any pair $f, f' \in P_S^{(-1)} f_S$ (see Fig. 1.2). Hence a linear onto map $P_{TS} : C_S \to C_T$ is defined for all $S > T$, as

$$P_{TS} \triangleq P_T P_S^{(-1)}$$

Obviously $P_{TR} = P_{TS}P_{SR}$ for all $R > S > T$. It is therefore possible to define the topological projective limit of the spaces C_T.

Let $\hat{C}$ be such a limit. We need to establish that C_e and $\hat{C} = \varprojlim P_{TS}C_S$ are topologically isomorphic.

Let $\hat{P} : C_e \to \hat{C}$ represent the map which assigns $f \in C_e$ to $(f_T) \in \hat{C}$ when $f_T = P_T f$, since $f_T = P_{TS}f_S$ the element (f_T) lies in $\hat{C}$. The map $\hat{P}$ is onto, since given any $(f_T) \in \hat{C}$ it is possible to define an $f \in C_e$ such that $\hat{P}f = (f_T)$, indeed it is only necessary to set

$$f(t) = f_T(t) \quad \text{for any} \quad T \geq t$$

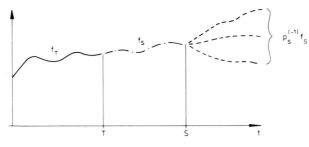

FIG. 1.2

The coherence of this definition follows from the equivalence $f_S(t) \equiv f_T(t)$ for all $S > T$. Finally $\hat{P}$ is one-to-one since $\hat{P}f = 0$ means that $P_T f = 0$ for all $T > 0$ and therefore $f(t) \equiv 0$. As vector spaces we can then conclude that C_e and $\hat{C}$ are isomorphic. Let us now compare topologies.

In C_e the generic element of the base of neighbourhoods of the origin is a set U of the form

$$U = \{f \in C_e : P_{T_i}(f) < \xi_i, \, i = 1, \ldots, r\}$$

which can be rewritten as

$$U = \bigcap_{i=1}^{n} \{f \in C_e : \|P_{T_i}f\| < \xi_i\}$$

$$= \bigcap_{i=1}^{n} C_e \cap P_{T_i}^{(-1)} B_{T_i}(\xi_i)$$

where $B_{T_i}(\xi_i)$ is the open ball in C_{T_i} of radius ξ_i. Then

$$\hat{P}(U) = \bigcap_{i=1}^{n} \hat{P}(C_e) \cap \hat{P}P_{T_i}^{(-1)} B_{T_i}(\xi_i)$$

Noticing that $\hat{P}_T$, the projection of $\hat{C}$ into C_T, can be expressed as $P_T \hat{P}^{(-1)}$ and that $\hat{P}(C_e) = \hat{C}$:

$$\hat{P}(U) = \hat{C} \cap \bigcap_{i=1}^{n} \hat{P}_{T_i}^{(-1)} B_{T_i}(\xi_i)$$

The second member above is the generic set in the base of neighbourhoods of the origin which define the topology of the projective limit, consequently $\hat{C}$ and C are topologically isomorphic.

The above example introduced two important concepts: first, it introduced an alternative means of defining the projective limit; secondly it established the equivalence between a locally convex space and a projective limit. These results are generalized in the next two theorems.

THEOREM 1.10   *Let $\{E_a\}$ be a family of finitely normed spaces and assume the existence of a linear complete topological space F and a family of linear operators $\{P_a\}$ such that*

(i) *$P_a F \supset E_a$ and the map $P_a : P_a^{(-1)} E_a \to E_a$ is continuous*

(ii) *$P_a^{(-1)} E_a \supset P_b^{(-1)} E_b$ for all $a < b$*

(iii) *$P_b(x) = P_b(x')$ implies $P_a(x) = P_a(x')$ for all $a < b$ and all $x, x' \in F$*

(iv) *$P_a x = 0$ for all a, implies $x = 0$*

Then it is possible to define the projective limit of the spaces E_a, and the space $E = \bigcap_{a>0} P_a^{(-1)} E_a$ can be identified with such a limit.

Proof The proof follows similarly to the technique used in Example 1.12. Define $P_{ab} : E_b \to E_a$ as $P_{ab} \triangleq P_a P_b^{(-1)}$; this is possible since, from conditions (ii), (iii), given any $x_b \in E_b$ and any pair $x, x' \in P_b^{(-1)} x_b$ we have

$$P_a x = P_a x' \in E_a$$

Clearly $P_{ab} P_{bc} = P_a P_b^{(-1)} P_b P_c^{(-1)} = P_{ac}$, hence it is possible to define the projective limit $\hat{E} = \varprojlim P_{ab} E_a$. Let $\hat{P}_a : \hat{E} \to E_a$ be the projection which assigns $\hat{x} \in \hat{E}$ to its complement x_a.

Consider now the map $\hat{P} : E \to \prod_a E_a$, which assigns $x \in \bigcap_{a>0} P_a^{(-1)} E_a$ to $\hat{x} = (x_a)$ with $x_b \triangleq P_b x$. Applying P_{ab} to x_b we have $P_{ab} x_b = P_a P_b^{(-1)} P_b x = P_a x = x_a$, for any $a < b$. Hence $x_a = P_{ab} x_b$ for all $a < b$ and therefore $\hat{P} x$ is always an element of the projective limit $\hat{E}$. The operator $\hat{P}$ maps E into $\hat{E}$, and from condition (iv) we see that $\hat{P}$ is one to one. To show that it is onto, consider any $\hat{x} = (x_a) \in \hat{E}$ and the set $0 = \bigcap_a 0_a$, with $0_a = P_a^{(-1)} x_a$. Notice that every $0_a = P_a^{(-1)} x_a$ is a closed set as P_a is continuous. Moreover, since $x_a = P_a P_b^{(-1)} x_b$ we have $x_a = P_a 0_b$ and therefore $0_a \supset 0_b$. As a consequence, $0 = \bigcap_a 0_a$ is the intersection of a decreasing net of closed complete non-empty sets, hence 0 is a closed non-empty set. Furthermore, for any $x \in 0$ we have $P_a x = x_a$ for all $a > 0$; hence $0 \subset \hat{P}^{(-1)} x$ and $\hat{P}$ is onto, thus $\hat{P}$ is an isomorphism.

Applying the projection $\hat{P}_a$ and the definition of $\hat{x}$ we have on noting that $\hat{P} x = \hat{x}$

$$\hat{P}_a \hat{x} = x_a = P_a x = \hat{P}_a \hat{P} x$$
$$P_a = \hat{P}_a \hat{P} \Rightarrow \hat{P}_a = P_a \hat{P}^{(-1)} \tag{1.7}$$

The topology in $\hat{E}$ is defined by a base of neighbourhoods of the origin whose generic element is

$$\hat{U} = \hat{E} \cap \bigcap_{i=1}^{n} \hat{P}_{a_i}^{(-1)} B_{a_i}$$

where B_{a_i} is an open ball in E_{a_i}. Hence

$$\hat{U} = \hat{P}(E) \cap \bigcap_{i=1}^{n} \hat{P} P_{a_i}^{(-1)} B_{a_i} \tag{1.8}$$

We can therefore identify $\hat{U}$ with the set $P(U)$ where

$$U = E \cap \bigcap_{i=1}^{n} P_{a_i}^{(-1)} B_{a_i} \tag{1.9}$$

It is natural to define the topology in $E = \bigcap_a P_a^{(-1)} E_a$ by a base of absolutely convex neighbourhoods of the origin whose generic element has the form (1.9). In these circumstances $\hat{P}$ is a topological isomorphism.

□

In each application of Theorem 1.10 it is important to see how large the space $E = \bigcap_{a \geq 0} P_a^{(-1)} E_a$ is; it may happen that E is reduced to the single point $\{0\}$. Consider for example a space F of left continuous functions, defined in R_+, which have at most a countable number of discontinuities: assume that F is equipped with the extended uniform topology. Let $E_a \equiv C([0, a])$, $a > 0$, and let P_a be the truncation operator,

$$(P_a f)(t) = \begin{cases} f(t) & \text{for} \quad t \leq a \\ 0 & \text{for} \quad t > a \end{cases}$$

Clearly the conditions of Theorem 1.10 are all satisfied. We can now see that $\bigcap_{a \geq 0} P_a^{(-1)} E_a$ is the subspace of F formed by all continuous functions.

A case of special importance arises when the mappings P_a are into E_a; that is, P_a maps F into E_a. Under these conditions the maps P_a are also onto (condition (i), Theorem 1.10) and consequently $P_a^{(-1)} E_a \equiv F$. Therefore $E = \bigcap_{a > 0} P_a^{(-1)} E_a$ coincides with F, and the space F is isomorphic with the projective limit $\varprojlim P_{ab} E_b$. This result is used in the following theorem:

THEOREM 1.11 *Every complete locally convex space is topologically isomorphic with a topological projective limit of complete finitely normed spaces.*

The proof follows the arguments used in Example 1.12. Whilst not intending to repeat the arguments here, we want to show how to construct the complete finitely normed spaces referred in the theorem. Take the family $\{P_a(\cdot)\}$ of finite semi-norms which define the topology in E and order it by taking $a \leq b$ when $P_a(x) \leq P_b(x)$ for all $x \in E$. Let N_a be the null space of P_a. Then $E_a \triangleq E/N_a$ is a finitely normed space (Theorem 1.6). It is a simple exercise to show that the family of canonical mappings $A_a : E \to E/N_a$ satisfies each of the conditions of Theorem 1.10.

1.3.4 Banach spaces and Hilbert spaces

A complete finitely normed space is called a *Banach space*. Because of their simple topological structure, Banach spaces are frequently utilized in stability studies.

Example 1.13 The space $C(R_+)$ is a Banach space. To prove this statement we need only show the completeness of $C(R_+)$ under the uniform topology. Consider a Cauchy sequence $\{f_n\}$ in $C(R_+)$ clearly, for each $t \in R_+$, the complex numbers $\{f_n(t)\}$ form a Cauchy sequence in C^1. A function $t \mapsto f(t)$ can then be defined where $f(t)$ is the pointwise limit of $\{f_n(t)\}$. For any $t \in R_+$ and any f_m, f_n

$$\|f_n(t) - f(t)\| \le \|f_n - f_m\| + \|f_m(t) - f(t)\|$$

Taking the limit as $m \to \infty$ and then the supremum for all t

$$\|f_n - f\| \le \lim_{m \to \infty} \|f_n - f_m\|$$

Therefore since $\{f_n\}$ is a Cauchy sequence

$$\lim_n \|f_n - f\| \le \lim_{n,m} \|f_n - f_m\| = 0$$

It follows that $\{f_n\}$ converges to f in the uniform topology and therefore f is an element of $C(R_+)$.

A Banach space is called a Hilbert space, *HS*, when there exists a complex function $\langle \cdot, \cdot \rangle : HS^2 \to C^1$, called an *inner product*, which satisfies

(i) $\|x\|^2 = \langle x, x \rangle \qquad \forall\, x \in HS$

(ii) $\langle x, y \rangle = \langle y, x \rangle^* \qquad \forall\, x, y \in HS$

where x^* denotes the complex conjugate of x.

(iii) $\langle \alpha y + \beta z, x \rangle = \alpha \langle y, x \rangle + \beta \langle z, x \rangle \qquad \forall\, \alpha, \beta \in C^1, x, y, z \in HS$

PROPOSITION 1.7: SCHWARTZ INEQUALITY *For all* $x, y \in HS, |\langle x, y \rangle| \le \|x\| \cdot \|y\|$.

Two elements x, y of a Hilbert space are said to be orthogonal when $\langle x, y \rangle = 0$. Given a subset $M \in HS$, we define $M^\perp$ as the orthogonal complement of M, given by the set of all vectors $x \in HS$ which are orthogonal to every vector in M.

THEOREM 1.12 *If HS is a Hilbert space and M is a linear closed subspace of HS, then HS can be decomposed in the direct sum $HS = M \oplus M^\perp$.*

This theorem illustrates the closeness between an arbitrary Hilbert space and the well-studied cases of R^n and C^n. The theorem says that every $x \in HS$ has a unique decomposition

$$x = x' + x''$$

with $x' \in M$ and $x'' \in M^\perp$.

THEOREM 1.13   *Let* $f : HS \rightarrow C^1$ *be an arbitrary linear, continuous, complex valued function in a Hilbert space HS. Then there exists a unique* $y \in HS$ *such that*

$$\text{(i)} \quad f(x) = \langle x, y \rangle \qquad \forall\, x \in HS$$

$$\text{(ii)} \quad \|y\| = \sup_{\|x\|=1} |f(x)|$$

An important aspect of Hilbert spaces is illustrated in Theorem 1.13; in Section 1.6 it is shown that a linear, continuous, complex valued function that satisfies the conditions of Theorem 1.13 is called a *functional* and that the space of all functionals of a space E is called the dual space of E. Theorem 1.13 says in this context that the dual space of a Hilbert space coincides with the Hilbert space itself.

1.3.5   Operators in Banach spaces

Let E and F be Banach spaces equipped with norms $\|\cdot\|_E$ and $\|\cdot\|_F$ respectively. A linear continuous operator $A : E \rightarrow F$ is said to be *compact* or *completely continuous* when, given a sphere S in E, the closure of its image $A(S)$, under A, is compact in F.

One of the most frequent uses of compact operators is in the characterization of integral operators. For example, consider an arbitrary compact interval I of the extended real line and the space $C(I)$. Given a complex, continuous valued function $g : I^2 \rightarrow C^1$, then the operator $G : C(I) \rightarrow C(I)$ defined as

$$(Gf)(t) = \int_I g(t, s) f(s)\, ds$$

can easily be shown to be compact.

An operator $A : E \rightarrow F$ is *Lipschitz continuous* when there exists a positive real $\gamma > 0$ such that

$$\|A(x) - A(y)\|_F \leq \gamma \|x - y\|_E \tag{1.10}$$

for all $x, y \in E$. Obviously any Lipschitz continuous operator is also continuous but the converse is not generally true. The infimum of all γ which satisfy (1.10) is called the *Lipschitz norm* or the *incremental norm* (or *gain*). It is important to note that, except in special circumstances, the incremental norm is not a norm in the strict sense; this term is, however, used for convenience.

If there exists a $\gamma > 0$ such that $\|A(x)\|_F \leq \gamma \|x\|_E$ for all $x \in E$, the operator A is said to be *bounded*. The infimum over all values of γ which satisfy this inequality is called the *bound* of A. If in addition $A(0) = 0$ (that is, the operator A is unbiased) then A is bounded if it is Lipschitz continuous, and the bound on A is inferior to the incremental norm.

Let us represent by $B(E, F)$ the space of all Lipschitz continuous operators $A : E \to F$ which satisfy $A(0) = 0$; under these conditions:

THEOREM 1.14   *In the space $B(E, F)$ the incremental norm is a norm in the strict sense, and with this norm the space $B(E, F)$ is a Banach space.*

A Banach algebra is a Banach space where the operation of multiplication is defined such that $\|x \cdot y\| \le \|x\| \cdot \|y\|$ for all x, y in the algebra. If we consider a Banach space E, the space $B(E, E)$ can be seen as an algebra if multiplication is defined as the composition of operators. Moreover:

COROLLARY 1.14 $B(E, E)$ *is a left distributive Banach algebra.*

If we take the subspace $L(E, F)$ formed by all linear operators which are elements of $B(E, F)$, then

THEOREM 1.15 $L(E, F)$ *is a Banach space.*

COROLLARY 1.15 $L(E, E)$ *is a linear Banach algebra.*

1.4   FIXED-POINT THEOREMS

Fixed-point theorems are widely used in the study of equations where it is necessary to establish the existence of a solution, and as such they have a particular significance in determining the stability of dynamical systems.

Given a subset M of a locally convex space E and an operator $T : M \to E$, we say that a point $x_0 \in M$ is a *fixed point* of T in M if it is invariant under the application of T; that is, $T(x_0) = x_0$. The subset M is said to have the fixed-point property when every continuous operator which maps M into itself has, at least, one fixed point in M.

The following two theorems allow us to identify those spaces with the fixed-point property.

THEOREM 1.16: BROUWER FIXED-POINT THEOREM   *The closed unit ball in R^n has the fixed-point property.*

A more general result which includes the above as a special case is

THEOREM 1.17: SCHAUDER–TIKHONOV THEOREM   *Any absolutely convex compact subset of a locally convex space has the fixed-point property.*

COROLLARY 1.17   *Every compact operator $T: E \to E$ which maps a sphere $S \subset E$ into itself has at least one fixed point in S.*

An operator $T: E \to E$ is said to be *affine* when it can be written as

$$T(x) = A(x) + T(0)$$

where $A: E \to E$ is a linear operator.

THEOREM 1.18: MARKOV–KATUTANAI THEOREM   *Let E be a topological vector space and M an absolutely convex compact subset of E. Let $\{T_a\}$ be a family of affine mappings satisfying:*

(i) $T_a(M) \subset M$, $\forall\, a$

(ii) $T_a T_b \equiv T_b T_a$, $\forall\, a, b$

Then there exists a point $x_0 \in M$ which is a fixed point of every map T_a.

A Lipschitz continuous operator in a Banach space, $A: E \to E$ is called a *contraction* when its incremental norm $\|A\|$ is inferior to the unit. Given a subset M of E such that $A(M) \subset M$, the operator A is called a *local contraction* in M, if $\|A(x) - A(y)\| \leq \gamma \|x - y\|$ for all $x, y \in M$, for some $\gamma < 1$. Local contractions provide the method frequently used for establishing the existence of a fixed point.

THEOREM 1.19: CONTRACTION MAPPING THEOREM   *Let E be a Banach space and let M be a closed subset of E. Assume that $T: E \to E$ is a local contraction in M, then there exists a unique fixed point of T in M. Moreover such a fixed point can be calculated as the limit of the sequence $\{x_n\}$ defined recursively as $x_{n+1} = T(x_n)$ with $x_0 \in M$. Finally, for all n*

$$\|x_n - \bar{x}\| \leq \frac{\|T\|^n}{1 - \|T\|} \cdot \|T(x_0) - x_0\|$$

where

$$\|T\| = \sup_{\substack{x, y \in M \\ x \neq y}} \frac{\|T(x) - T(y)\|}{\|x - y\|}$$

Proof   Consider the sequence $\{x_n\}$ defined recursively as

$$x_{n+1} = T(x_n), \qquad x_0 \in M$$

Clearly as $T(M) \subset M$, the sequence is contained M, we have

$$\|x_{n+1} - x_n\| = \|T(x_n) - T(x_{n-1})\| \leq \|T\| \cdot \|x_n - x_{n-1}\|$$

Hence

$$\|x_{n+1} - x_n\| \leq \|T\|^n \|T(x_0) - x_0\|$$

For any $m > n$,

$$x_m - x_n = \sum_{i=n}^{m-1} (x_{i+1} - x_i)$$

$$\|x_m - x_n\| \leq \sum_{i=n}^{m-1} \|T\|^i \cdot \|T(x_0) - x_0\|$$

$$\|x_m - x_n\| \leq \frac{(\|T\|^n - \|T\|^m)}{1 - \|T\|} \|T(x_0) - x_0\| \qquad (1.11)$$

Since $\|T\| < 1$, then $\lim\limits_{m,n} \|x_m - x_n\| = 0$, hence $\{x_n\}$ is a Cauchy sequence.

Because the space E is complete, the sequence has a limit $\bar{x}$; moreover since M is closed, $\bar{x}$ must lie in M. Taking the limit in m in inequality (1.11)

$$\|\bar{x} - x_n\| = \lim_m \|x_m - x_n\| \leq \frac{\|T\|^n}{1 - \|T\|} \cdot \|T(x_0) - x_0\|$$

To show that $\bar{x}$ is a fixed point of T we use the continuity of $T(\cdot)$ and have

$$T(\bar{x}) = T(\lim_n x_n) = \lim_n T(x_n) = \lim_n (x_{n+1}) = \bar{x}.$$

Finally we can show that $\bar{x}$ is unique in M by considering some point $x \in M$ such that $x = T(x)$:

$$\|\bar{x} - x\| = \|T(\bar{x}) - T(x)\| \leq \|T\| \cdot \|\bar{x} - x\|$$

but since $\|T\| < 1$ this inequality can only hold if $x = \bar{x}$.   □

1.5   MEASURES AND FUNCTION SPACES

1.5.1   Measures and integrals on the positive real line

A σ-algebra is a collection of subsets of a space X, which includes X and the null set $\varnothing$, and is closed under countable unions of its elements. In this work we restrict our study to the smallest σ-algebra of subsets of the extended real line, $R^e = [-\infty, \infty]$, or the extended half real line $R^e_+ = [0, \infty]$, which contain every open set. Let B represent such a σ-algebra; its elements are called Borel sets. It can be shown that every bounded interval on the real line is a Borel set and that every compact set is also a Borel set.

Let A be a σ-algebra of subsets of the space X. A function $\mu : A \to R^e_+$

is called a finitely additive, positive measure, or simply a measure, if $\mu\left(\bigcup_{k=1}^{n} A_k\right) = \sum_{k=1}^{n} \mu(A_k)$ for any finite collection of pairwise disjoint $A_k \in \mathbf{A}$.
If in addition, $\mu\left(\bigcup_{k=1}^{\infty} A_k\right) = \sum_{k=1}^{\infty} \mu(A_k)$, for any countable collection of pairwise disjoint $A_k \in \mathbf{A}$, then $\mu(\cdot)$ is said to be a countably additive measure. The triplet $(X, \mathbf{A}, \mu)$ is called a measure space.

Throughout this work, X is restricted to either R_+^e or R^e and $\mathbf{A}$ is the σ-algebra of Borel sets. Also we restrict measures to those defined in $\mathbf{B}$, which take finite values when applied to an arbitrary compact set $C \subset R$; such measures are called Borel measures.

A Borel measure μ is *regular* when for each set $E \in B$ for which $\mu(E) < \infty$, we have

$$\mu(E) = \inf \mu(0) = \sup \mu(C)$$

where the infimum is taken over all open sets O containing E, and the supremum is taken over all compact sets C contained in E.

Example 1.14   Let $F: R_+ \rightarrow R_+$ be a monotone increasing positive function, continuous everywhere except perhaps in a countable set which is only left continuous. Consider the collection of all semi-open intervals of the form $[a, b)$ and define

$$\mu([a, b)) = F(b) - F(a)$$

For an arbitrary Borel set E define

$$\mu(E) = \inf \sum_{k=1}^{n} \mu(I_k)$$

where the infimum is taken over all finite unions $I = \bigcup_{k=1}^{n} I_k$ of semi-open intervals $I_k = [a_k, b_k)$ such that $I \supseteq E$. It can be shown (Barra, Chapter 9, 1974) that $\mu(\cdot)$ is a regular Borel Measure, $\mu(\cdot)$ is called the Lebesgue–Stieltjes measure with respect to $F(\cdot)$. In particular the measure generated by the function $F(x) = x$ is called the Lebesgue measure.

A function $f: R_+ \rightarrow R$ is said to be Borel measurable, or simply measurable, when for each $c > 0$, the set $\{t: R_+ : f(t) > c\}$ is a Borel set. Clearly if f is measurable, then $|f|$ is also measurable; moreover the space of all measurable functions is a linear space. A linear space of functions which, like the space of all measurable functions, is closed under the operation of taking absolute values, is called a linear lattice.

Given two elements ϕ, ψ of a linear lattice of functions we can define the operations $\vee$ and $\wedge$ through

$$\phi \vee \psi = \max\{\phi, \psi\} \triangleq \tfrac{1}{2}(\phi + \psi) + \tfrac{1}{2}|\phi - \psi|$$

$$\phi \wedge \psi = \min\{\phi, \psi\} \triangleq \tfrac{1}{2}(\phi + \psi) - \tfrac{1}{2}|\phi - \psi|$$

Clearly a linear lattice is closed under the operations $\vee$ and $\wedge$. A subspace of the space of all measurable functions which is itself a linear lattice is the space of simple functions in B, represented by $S(B)$. Let χ_E represent the characteristic function of a set E

$$\chi_E(t) = \begin{cases} 0 & \text{if} \quad t \notin E \\ 1 & \text{if} \quad t \in E \end{cases}$$

A simple function is any function ϕ of the form $\phi = c_1\chi_{E_1} + c_2\chi_{E_2} + \ldots + c_n\chi_{E_n}$ where the c_i are all real, non-zero constants and the E_i are pairwise disjoint relatively compact Borel sets. It is obvious that $S(B)$ is a linear lattice, since $|\phi| = \sum_{i=1}^{n} |c_i| \chi_{E_i}$, and that every ϕ is measurable. Note that $\{t : \phi(t) \neq 0\} \equiv \bigcup_{i=1}^{n} E_i$; we can therefore say that ϕ is concentrated in $\bigcup_{i=1}^{n} E_i$.

PROPOSITION 1.8   *Every positive measurable function* $f : R_+ \to R_+$ *can be expressed as the limit everywhere of an increasing sequence of positive simple functions.*

Proposition 1.8 is fundamental in the following definition of an integral. Let μ be a Borel measure; we can define in $S(B)$ a positive linear functional $\hat{\mu} : S(B) \to R$ through

$$\hat{\mu}(\phi) = c_1\mu(E_1) + c_2\mu(E_2) + \ldots + c_n\mu(E_n)$$

for

$$\phi = c_1\chi_{E_1} + \ldots + c_n\chi_{E_n}$$

Clearly if $\phi \geq 0$, then $\hat{\mu}(\phi) \geq 0$; therefore $\hat{\mu}$ is a positive functional. Conversely, let $\phi = c_1\chi_{E_1} + c_2\chi_{E_2} + \ldots + c_n\chi_{E_n}$ be such that $\phi \geq 0$ and $\hat{\mu}(\phi) = 0$. Since every c_i is non-zero, positive, and every $\mu(E_i)$ is also positive, then $\mu(E_i) = 0$ for all $i = 1, 2, \ldots, n$. $\hat{\mu}(\phi) = 0$ implies that ϕ is concentrated in a set whose measure μ is zero; such a function and associated set are called respectively a μ-null function and a μ-null set.

We can now extend the positive functional $\hat{\mu}$ to a positive measurable function f. Let ϕ_n be an increasing sequence of positive simple functions converging pointwise to f everywhere, such a sequence, by Proposition 1.8, always exists. Then the positive numbers $\hat{\mu}(\phi_n)$ form an increasing sequence; if such a sequence is bounded, we say that f is μ-integrable and we define $\hat{\mu}(f)$ as $\lim_n \hat{\mu}(\phi_n)$. The positive functional $\hat{\mu}$ is called the μ-integral and $\hat{\mu}(f)$ is more usually represented as $\int f\, d\mu$.

Although there may be an infinity of different increasing sequences of simple functions converging to f, it can be shown that the limit $\lim_n \hat{\mu}(\phi_n)$ is independent of the particular sequence chosen and hence the above definition of the μ-integral is consistent.

If f is a positive μ-null function (that is, the set $\{t:f(t)>0\}$ is μ-null) then every simple function $\phi\leq f$ must also be μ-null; consequently $\int f\, d\mu = 0$. Conversely if $f\geq 0$ and $\int f\, d\mu = 0$, then for any $\phi\leq f$, $\int \phi\, d\mu = 0$. Thus every simple function which satisfies $\phi\leq f$ must be μ-null, and therefore $\{t:f(t)>0\}$ must be a μ-null set. Hence if f is a μ-integrable positive function, we have $\int f\, d\mu = 0$ if and only if f is μ-null.

1.5.2   The function spaces L_p

Define, $L^{inc}(\mu)$ as the space of all positive μ-integrable functions. If two positive μ-integrable functions f and g satisfy $f+n_f = g+n_g$, where n_f and n_g are positive μ-null functions, then we can associate f and g with the same element of $L^{inc}(\mu)$. Under these conditions the integral $\int d\mu$ vanishes only on the zero elements of $L^{inc}(\mu)$.

Define $L_1(\mu)$ as the space of all measurable functions $f: R_+ \to R$ which can be written as

$$f = g - h \tag{1.12}$$

with $g, h \in L^{inc}(\mu)$. We extend the integral $\int d\mu$ to $L_1(\mu)$ by defining

$$\int f\, d\mu = \int g\, d\mu - \int h\, d\mu \tag{1.13}$$

There are an infinity of pairs $g, h \in L^{inc}(\mu)$ which satisfy (1.12); however, the value of the integral (1.13) is independent of the pair chosen. Of all partitions one has special importance: define $f_+ = f\vee 0$ and $f_- = (-f)\vee 0$. Clearly $f = f_+ - f_-$ and $|f| = f_+ + f_-$, with $f_+, f_- \in L^{inc}(\mu)$. Therefore $L_1(\mu)$ is a linear lattice and

$$\int |f|\, d\mu = \int f_+\, d\mu + \int f_-\, d\mu \tag{1.14}$$

Since the μ-integral vanishes only in the zero of $L^{inc}(\mu)$, then if $\int |f|\, d\mu = 0$ we must have $f_+ = f_- = f = 0$.

It can now be seen that the function $\| \cdot \| : L_1(\mu) \to R_+$ defined by

$$\|f\| = \int |f| \, d\mu$$

is a norm in $L_1(\mu)$ and that with the topology defined by such a norm, the space $L_1(\mu)$ is a Banach space.

A more general definition of an integral can be made in an arbitrary measure space (X, A, μ). The space of all μ-integrable real valued functions thus defined is represented by $L_1(X, A, \mu)$, we see that $L_1(\mu)$ is an abbreviation of $L_1(R_+, B, \mu)$. In particular, when μ is the Lebesgue measure we shall represent this space simply as L_1.

For any $1 \le p < \infty$ we define $L_p(\mu)$ as the space of all measurable functions $f : R_+ \to R$ such that $|f|^p \in L^{\mathrm{inc}}(\mu)$. As in $L_1(\mu)$ and $L^{\mathrm{inc}}(\mu)$ we can identify with some element of $L_p(\mu)$ any two functions which differ by a μ-null function. The norm in $L_p(\mu)$ is defined as

$$\|f\|_{L_p} = \left\{ \int |f|^p \, d\mu \right\}^{1/p}$$

With the topology defined by such a norm, $L_p(\mu)$ is a Banach space. As with $L_1(\mu)$ we represent by L_p the particular case when μ is the Lebesgue measure, and by $L_p(X, A, \mu)$ in the more general case when we consider integration in the general measure space (X, A, μ).

To define the $L_\infty(\mu)$ space, we introduce the set $V(f)$ for any positive measurable function f defined by

$$V(f) = \{\alpha \ge 0 : \mu(\{t : f(t) > \alpha\}) > 0\}$$

If $V(f)$ is unbounded, we say that the *essential supremum* of f, represented by ess sup f, is infinite. If $V(f)$ is bounded, the essential supremum of f is the least upper bound on $V(f)$.

We shall define $L_\infty(\mu)$ as the space of all measurable functions $f : R_+ \to R$ such that ess sup $|f| < \infty$ and define $\|f\|$ as the value of this essential supremum. We identify with the same element of $L_\infty(\mu)$, two functions which differ by a μ-null function. The space $L_\infty(\mu)$ is also a Banach space.

The space $L_2(\mu)$ is of particular significance since we can define an inner product. Given $f, g \in L_2(\mu)$, then

$$|fg| \le \tfrac{1}{2}(|f|^2 + |g|^2)$$

hence the integral $\int fg \, d\mu$ is well defined. It is easy to show that

$$\langle f, g \rangle \triangleq \int fg \, d\mu,$$

defines an inner product and so the space $L_2(\mu)$ is also a Hilbert space.

So far we have only considered real valued functions, but our definition of an integral can be readily extended to complex valued functions, so $f: R_+ \rightarrow C^1$ is measurable (respectively, integrable) if both its imaginary and real parts are measurable (respectively, integrable) functions. The space $L_p(\mu)$, $1 \leq p \leq \infty$ can be defined as the space of all measurable functions $f: R_+ \rightarrow C^1$ such that $|f|^p$ lies in $L^{\text{inc}}(\mu)$. The inner product in $L_2(\mu)$ is now defined by

$$\langle f, g \rangle = \int f^* g \, d\mu$$

1.5.3 Real and complex measures

Until now we have considered only positive measures. The concept of a measure can be extended to real valued measures, also called signed measures, by considering set functions of the form $\mu = \omega - \gamma$ with ω, γ positive measures,

$$\mu(E) \triangleq \omega(E) - \gamma(E) \qquad \forall E \in B$$

Clearly there exists an infinity of pairs γ, ω which generate the same signed measure μ. One of these pairs of particular importance: if we define

$$\mu_+(E) = \sup_{A \subset E} \mu(A)$$

$$\mu_-(E) = \sup_{A \subset E} - \mu(A)$$

then μ_+ and μ_- are positive measures such that $\mu = \mu_+ - \mu_-$. The measures μ_+ and μ_- are called the Jordon decomposition of μ. An important property of this decomposition is that the positive measure $\mu_+ + \mu_-$ is the smallest measure which satisfies

$$|\mu(E)| \leq \mu_+(E) + \mu_-(E) \qquad \forall E \in B$$

The measure $\mu_+ + \mu_-$ is called the *total variation* of μ and is represented by $|\mu|$. We then have

$$|\mu(E)| \leq |\mu|(E) \qquad \forall E \in B$$

Complex measures are set functions of the form

$$\mu(E) \triangleq \mu_R(E) + j\mu_I(E)$$

where μ_R and μ_I are signed measures. The total variation of μ, represented by $|\mu|$, is defined as

$$|\mu| = |\mu_R| + |\mu_I|$$

Moreover the total variation is the smallest measure which satisfies

$$|\mu(E)| \leq |\mu|(E) \qquad \forall E \in B$$

1.5.4 Indefinite integrals

Let λ represent the Lebesgue measure, and let μ be a finite measure that vanishes at every λ-null set. The measure μ is then said to be absolutely continuous with respect to the measure λ. If in addition μ is regular and countably additive, then a famous theorem specifies an explicit form for μ.

THEOREM 1.20: RADON–NYKODYM THEOREM   *Under the above conditions there exists a unique $f \in L_1(\lambda)$ such that*

$$\mu(E) = \int_E f \, d\lambda \qquad \forall E \in B \tag{1.15}$$

Conversely any integral of the form of (1.15) defines an absolutely continuous, regular, countably additive Borel measure.

Note   For an alternative statement of this theorem, see Section 3.3.

Consider now some positive $f \in L_1$, then for any $x \geq 0$ we can define

$$F(x) = \int_{[0, x]} f \, d\lambda + F(0) \tag{1.16}$$

A function $F(\cdot)$ of this form is called an indefinite integral. Clearly $F(x) = \mu([0, x]) + F(0)$, where $\mu(\cdot)$ is defined by (1.15).
   For any interval $[a, b)$ we have

$$\mu([a, b)) = F(b) - F(a)$$

therefore $\mu(\cdot)$ is a Lebesgue-Stieltjes measure with the characteristic that $F(\cdot)$ is both left and right continuous everywhere. As $\mu(\cdot)$ is absolutely continuous, then for any $\xi > 0$ there exists a $\delta > 0$ such that $\sum_i (b_i - a_i) < \delta$ implies that

$$\sum_i F(b_i) - F(a_i) < \xi \tag{1.17}$$

for $[a_i, b_i)$ disjoint intervals. Notice that $\sum_i (b_i - a_i)$ is the Lebesgue measure of the set $\bigcup_i [a_i, b_i)$ and that $\sum_i (F(b_i) - F(a_i))$ is the μ-measure of the same set. A function $F(\cdot)$ which satisfies (1.17) is called an absolutely continuous function. Because $f \in L_1$ was defined to be positive, $F(\cdot)$ is monotonically increasing. For a more general real valued function $x \mapsto F(x)$ we say that $F(x)$ is absolutely continuous when, for any $\xi > 0$, there exists a $\delta > 0$ such that $\sum_i (b_i - a_i) < \delta$ implies

$$\sum_i |F(b_i) - F(a_i)| < \xi$$

for $[a_i, b_i)$ disjoint intervals.

Consider then a generic real valued $f \in L_1(\lambda)$ and define

$$F(x) = F(0) + \int_{[0, x]} f \, d\lambda \qquad (1.18)$$

for any $b > a$

$$F(b) - F(a) = \int_{[a,b)} f \, d\lambda = \mu([a, b))$$

where $\mu(\cdot)$ is defined as in (1.15). Hence

$$|F(b) - F(a)| = |\mu([a, b))| \le |\mu|([a, b))$$

If μ, defined by (1.15), is absolutely continuous, so is its measure $|\mu|$ and so

$$|\mu|(E) = \int_E |f| \, d\lambda.$$

Hence if

$$I = \bigcup_{i=1}^{n} [a_i, b_i) \quad \text{and} \quad \lambda(I) \to 0, \quad \text{then} \quad |\mu|(I) \to 0$$

Therefore $\sum_{i=1}^{n} |F(b_i) - F(a_i)| \le |\mu|(I) \to 0$ as $\lambda(I) \to 0$ and so $F(\cdot)$ is absolutely continuous.

We have seen how every indefinite integral generates an absolutely continuous function. The converse is also true; however, before we state this result we require some additional definitions.

Let $F: R_+ \to R$ be a continuous function and let $C \subset R_+$ be a compact set. The *total variation* of F in C, represented by $V_C(F)$ is defined by

$$V_C(F) = \sup \sum_{i=1}^{n} |F(a_i) - F(b_i)|$$

where the supremum is taken over all finite unions $\bigcup_{i=1}^{n} [a_i, b_i)$ of disjoint intervals contained in C. The total variation of F in R_+, represented by $V_\infty(R_+)$, is $V_\infty(R_+) = \sup V_C(F)$, where the supremum is taken over all compact sets $C \subset R_+$.

Every absolutely continuous function has finite total variation in any compact set but not necessarily in R_+. If F is absolutely continuous and has finite total variation in R_+, then F is represented by an indefinite integral of the form

$$F(x) = F(0) + \int_{[0,x]} f\, d\lambda \qquad (1.19)$$

where f is an element of L_1. Moreover

$$V_\infty(F) = \int |f|\, d\lambda$$

Every absolutely continuous function F (even when it does not have finite total variation in R_+), can be represented by an integral of the form of (1.19), where f is now a function such that for every compact set $C \subset R_+$, the function $f_C \triangleq f \cdot \chi_C$ is an element of L_1. In these circumstances $V_C(F) = \int |f_C|\, d\lambda$.

1.6 DUAL SPACES

In Section 1.5 it was shown that integrals are special forms of a more general concept—a functional. Given a locally convex space E, a *functional* in E is any linear, continuous, complex valued function in E. The zero functional is identified with the function which assigns zero to every $x \in E$; two functions f, g, such that $f(x) = g(x)$ for all $x \in E$, are considered to be the same functional in E.

The space of all distinct functionals in E is called the dual space of E and is represented by E'. Under the definition

$$(\alpha f + \beta g)(x) \triangleq \alpha f(x) + \beta g(x), \qquad \alpha, \beta \in C^1; \qquad f, g \in E'$$

the space E' is clearly a linear space.

PROPOSITION 1.9   *Let* $\{p_\alpha\}$ *be a collection of semi-norms defining the topology in a locally convex space E. For any $f \in E'$ there exists a finite collection* $\{p_{\alpha_i}\}_{i=1}^n$ *of these semi-norms and a collection* $\{\rho_i\}_{i=1}^n$ *of positive numbers such that*

$$|f(x)| \le \max_i \rho_i p_{\alpha_i}(x), \qquad \forall\, x \in E \qquad (1.20)$$

Proof   Given any $\xi > 0$, let $\{p_{\alpha_i}\}$ be a finite collection of semi-norms and let $\{\xi_i\}$ be a collection of positive numbers such that $p_{\alpha_i}(y) < \xi_i$, $i = 1, 2, \ldots, n$ implies $|f(y)| < \xi$; such collections must exist since $f(\cdot)$ is continuous. Defining $\rho_i = \xi_i/\xi$ and $p(y) = \max_i \rho_i p_{\alpha_i}(y)$; the above statement can be written as $|f(y)| \geq 1$ implies $p(y) \geq 1$. For any x in the null space of $f(\cdot)$, (1.20) is obviously true, if $f(x) \neq 0$ let $x = |f(x)| \hat{x}$ where $\hat{x} \triangleq x/|f(x)|$. Note that $|f(\hat{x})| = 1$, so $p(\hat{x}) \geq 1$. And clearly since $p(\cdot)$ is a semi-norm then $p(x) = |f(x)| p(\hat{x})$ and therefore, $p(x) \geq |f(x)|$ for all $x \in E$. Consequently

$$|f(x)| \leq \max_i \rho_i p_{\alpha_i}(x), \qquad \forall\, x \in E. \qquad \qquad \square$$

In a finitely normed space E, the topology is defined by a unique semi-norm (which is the norm itself); then as a consequence of Proposition 1.5. given $f \in E'$ there exists a $\rho > 0$ such that $|f| \leq \rho \|x\|$ for all $x \in E$. The infimum of all such ρ is represented by $\|f\|$ and we have

$$\|f\| = \inf \{\rho > 0 : |f(x)| \leq \rho \|x\|\}, \qquad \forall\, x \in E$$

$$= \sup_{\|x\|=1} |f(x)|$$

(1.21)

It is straightforward to establish:

PROPOSITION 1.10 *If E is a finitely normed space, the positive function defined in E' by (1.21) is a finite norm and, equipped with the topology thus defined, the space E' is a Banach space.*

The topology defined in E' by the norm (1.21) is called the *strong topology*; E' equipped with this topology is called the strong dual and is generally represented by E^*.

Let B be the unit closed ball in the finite normed space E; then (1.21) can be written as $\|f\| = \sup_{x \in B} |f(x)|$. A similar relationship can be obtained even when E is an arbitrary locally convex space. Consider an arbitrary bounded set B in the locally convex space E and let $f(\cdot)$ be a functional in E. Since $f(\cdot)$ is continuous $f(B)$ is bounded. A positive finite valued function $p_B : E' \rightarrow R_+$ can be defined as

$$p_B(f) = \sup_{x \in B} |f(x)|$$

which is a semi-norm in E'. Consider now a B spanning all the bounded sets of E; we then obtain a family of finite semi-norms $\{p_B(\cdot)\}$ in E'. These semi-norms define a topology in E'. To see this consider Theorem 1.4: it is only necessary to show that for any $f \neq 0$ in E' there exists a B such that $p_B(\cdot) \neq 0$. This is true since $f \neq 0$ implies that for some $x_0 \in E$, $f(x_0) \neq 0$; as the singleton $\{x_0\}$ is a bounded set, the conditions of Theorem 1.4 are satisfied. The topology defined in E' by this family of semi-norms is called the *strong topology*. When E is a finitely normed space, the topology generated by the semi-norms $\{p_B(\cdot)\}$ coincides with the topology generated by the norm (1.21). As in the case of the normed space, the dual space equipped with the strong topology is called the *strong dual* and is represented by E^*.

Consider now arbitrary finite collections of single points in E, $I = \{x_1, x_2, \ldots, x_n\}$. These are particular cases of bounded sets, and they include the single point sets. Therefore the family of semi-norms $\{p_I\}$, generated when I spans all the finite collection of points in E, also defines a locally convex topology in E'. It is called the *weak topology*. Since the collection $\{p_I(\cdot)\}$ is a sub-collection of $\{p_B(\cdot)\}$, the weak topology is weaker than the strong topology: hence its name! The generic elements of the bases of neighbourhoods of the origin in the strong dual and in the weak topologies are then, respectively,

$$U_s = \{f \in E' : \sup_{x \in B_i} |f(x)| < \xi_i, i = 1, \ldots, n; \xi_i > 0 \quad \text{and} \quad B_i \quad \text{bounded}\}$$

$$U_\omega = \{f \in E' : |f(x_i)| < \xi_i, i = 1, 2, \ldots n; \xi_i > 0 \quad \text{and} \quad x_i \in E\}$$

Let E and F be locally convex spaces and $A : E \to F$ a linear continuous operator; for any $f \in E'$ define a linear continuous map $e \in E'$ through

$$e(x) = f(A(x)) = f \otimes A(x) \qquad \forall x \in E \tag{1.22}$$

where $\otimes$ represents the composition of operators. Hence a map $A^* : F' \to E'$ is defined which assigns $f \in F'$ to $e \in E'$ through (1.22). The map A^*, which is linear and continuous, is called the strong dual of A (if E' and F' are equipped with strong topologies). If E and F are finitely normed spaces, we also have $\|A\| = \|A^*\|$ (Yosida, 1971).

Having defined general dual spaces, we now consider explicit forms for the duals of some spaces of time functions used in this work.

Consider the L_p spaces. Theorem 1.13 shows that the strong dual of any Hilbert space, HS, is isometrically isomorphic with itself. In particular, if μ is any positive Borel measure, the space $L_2(\mu)$ is a Hilbert space and therefore $L_2^*(\mu) \equiv L_2(\mu)$. Any $\hat{f} \in L_2^*(\mu)$ can be written as

$$\hat{f}(\phi) = \int f\phi \, d\lambda \qquad \forall \phi \in L_2(\mu)$$

for some $f \in L_2(\mu)$.

The duals of $L_p(\mu)$ spaces, $1 < p < \infty$, are spaces of the same type, and it can be shown that:

PROPOSITION 1.11   *The space $L_p^*(\mu)$, $1 \leq p < \infty$, is isometrically isomorphic with the space $L_q(\mu)$, where q satisfies $p^{-1} + q^{-1} = 1$. Any $\hat{f} \in L_p^*(\mu)$ is* *uniformly determined by some* $f \in L_q(\mu)$ *such that*

$$\hat{f}(\phi) = \int \phi f \, d\mu \qquad \forall \, \phi \in L_2(\mu)$$

The dual of $L_\infty(\mu)$ cannot be expressed as one of the spaces $L_p(\mu)$. In the appendix to Chapter 3 we refer to results which show that L_α^* contains a space of the form $L_1(\lambda)$ but also contains a space of measures which are strictly not countably additive.

An important space which is loosely related with L_∞ is the space $C(X)$ of all continuous bounded functions in the set $X \subset R_+$. Assume that X is a compact space, then

PROPOSITION 1.12   *If* $X \subset R_+$ *is compact then* $C^*(X)$ *can be identified with the space of all countably additive, regular, bounded measures in the* σ-*algebra* $B \cap X$, *(where* B *denotes the class of all Borel sets in* R_+*). Any* $f \in C^*(X)$ *is uniquely represented by such a measure* μ *and*

$$f(\phi) = \int \phi \, d\lambda$$

This Theorem, called the Riesz's representation theorem, illustrates how the measure $\mu(\cdot)$ is constructed from a functional f. We have assumed that f is real and positive; however, the extension to arbitrary complex functionals is straightforward.

Let $O \subset X$ be any open set and define

$$\mu(O) = \sup f(\phi) \qquad (1.23)a$$

where the supremum is extended to all $\phi \in C(X)$ which satisfies $\phi \leq \chi_0$. For any set $A \subset X$ we define

$$\mu(A) = \inf \mu(O) \qquad (1.23)b$$

where the infimum is extended to all open sets O containing A. The set function defined by (1.23) is not necessarily a measure if we consider the σ-algebra formed by all subsets of X. However, if we restrict the applicability of $\mu(\cdot)$ to Borel sets contained in X (that is, sets of the form $B \cap X$), it can be demonstrated that $\mu(\cdot)$ is a countably additive, regular, bounded measure. It is important to note that $\mu(\cdot)$ is such a well-behaved measure only in the σ-algebra $B \cap X$. It may happen that $\mu(\cdot)$ can be extended to a set function in the whole B which has neither of the attributes of $\mu(\cdot)$ in $B \cap X$.

PROPOSITION 1.13   *Let* $E = \bigcup_{n=1}^{\infty} E_n$ *be the topological strict inductive limit of*

*a countable family $\{E_n\}$ of finitely normed spaces. Then the strong dual E^*
can be identified with a topological projective limit of the strong duals of the
spaces E_n.*

Proof For each $f \in E'$ define $f_n \in E'_n$ as the restriction of f to E_n, let
$R_n : E' \to E'_n$ be the map which represents such a restriction. Identically,
for $m > n$, let $R_{mn} : E'_m \to E'_n$ represent the map which assigns $f_m \in E'_m$ to
its restriction in E_n; clearly $R_n = R_{nm} R_m$ for $m > n$
  For any $f_n \in E'_n$ we have for some $k_n > 0$,

$$|f_n(x)| \leq k_n \|x\|_n, \qquad \forall\, x \in E_n$$

Since the topology induced in E_n by the topology E_m, $m > n$, coincides
with the topology of E_n, then the norms $\|\cdot\|_n$ and $\|\cdot\|_m$ are equivalent in
E_n and there exists a $\delta > 0$ such that

$$\|x\|_n \leq \delta \|x\|_m \qquad \forall\, x \in E_n.$$

So $|f_n(x)| \leq k_n \delta \|x\|_m$ for all $x \in E_n$. Utilizing the Hahn–Banach theorem
(Kothe, section 17.6, 1969), the functional f_n can be extended to a
functional $f_m \in E'_m$ such that $R_n R_m f_m = f_n$. As a consequence the family of
maps $\{R_{nm}\}$ are always onto. Moreover if $f \in E'$ is such that $R_n f = 0$, for
all n, then for any $x \in E$ there exists E_n which contain x and therefore
$f(x) = (R_n f)(x) = 0$; thus $R_n f = 0$, for all n, implies $f = 0$. It now follows
from Kothe (section 19.7(8), 1969) that the maps $R_n : E' \to E'_n$ are onto.
Thus using Theorem 1.10, it follows that as a vector space

$$E' \equiv \varprojlim R_{nm}(E'_m)$$

To compare the topology of E^* with the topology of the projective
limit, consider an arbitrary semi-norm $p_B(\cdot)$ of the family which defines
the topology in E^*. B is a bounded set in E so, utilising Theorem 1.8,
there exists some E_n which contains B and in which B is a bounded set,
thus B is contained in some closed ball $B_n = \{x \in E_n : \|x\|_n \leq \xi_n\}$. Therefore

$$p_B(f) = \sup_{x \in B} |f(x)| \leq \sup_{x \in B_n} |R_n f(x)| = \xi_n \|R_n f\|_n^*,$$

where $\|\cdot\|_n^*$ denotes the norm in E_n^*. Thus any neighbourhood $U =
\{f \in E^* : p_B(f) < \xi\}$ contains a neighbourhood of the form $R_n^{(-1)}\{f \in
E_n^* : \|f\|_n^* < \xi \xi_n^{-1}\}$; therefore U is a neighbourhood in the topology of the
projective limit. Conversely, any neighbourhood in the topology of the
projective limit is also a neighbourhood in the strong topology of E^*, thus
the two topologies coincide.

1.7 NOTES

The basic topological concepts introduced in Section 1.2 can be found in Kothe (1969) sections 1–3, together with the associated proofs. The definitions and results produced in Section 1.3.1 are as given in Valenca (1978). An exhaustive study on the properties of inductive and projective limits can also be found in Kothe, section 19 (1969). The example in Section 1.3.3 and Theorem 1.10 were introduced as a preliminary to the study of extended spaces in Chapter 5, the operators P_a (referred to in Theorem 1.10) are in the majority of applications truncation operators. The results of Sections 1.3.4 and 1.3.5 on Banach and Hilbert spaces can be found in Yosida (1971) and Valenca (1978). The proofs of the Brouwer and Schauder–Tikhonov fixed-point theorems can be found in Dunford and Schwartz (1957); the proof of the Markov–Katutanai theorem can be found in Larsen (1973). The approach to measure and integration theory adopted in this book is similar to that of Halmos, (1950), Hewitt and Ross (1979), Hewitt and Stromberg (1965) and Barra (1974), the presentation of these concepts follows that of Weir (1974). The analysis of the spaces L_p of indefinite integrals is based upon the approach of Hewitt and Stromberg (1965), where the reader may also find the detailed proofs of Propositions 1.11 and 1.12.

REFERENCES

Barra, G. (1974). "Introduction to Measure Theory". Van Nostrand Reinhold, New York.

Dunford, N. and Schwartz, J. (1957). "Linear Operators" Part I. Interscience, New York.

Halmos, P. R. (1950). "Measure Theory". Van Nostrand, New York.

Hewitt, E. and Ross, K. A. (1979). "Abstract Harmonic Analysis", I, Band 115, 2nd Edition. Springer Verlag, New York.

Hewitt, E. and Stromberg, K. (1965). "Real and Abstract Analysis", Graduate Texts in Mathematics, **25.** Springer Verlag, New York.

Kothe, G. (1969). "Topological Vector Spaces", I, Band 159. Springer Verlag, New York.

Larsen, R. (1973). "Functional Analysis". Marcel Dekker Inc, New York.

Valenca, J. M. E. (1978). "Stability of Multivariable Systems". D.Phil. Thesis, Oxford University.

Weir, A. J. (1974). "General Integration and Measure". Cambridge University Press, Cambridge.

Yosida, K. (1971). "Functional Analysis", Band 123. Springer Verlag, New York.

Chapter Two

Riemann Surfaces and the Generalized
Principle of the Argument

2.1 INTRODUCTION

In the development of frequency domain stability criteria for multivariable feedback systems, the single most important result in establishing generalized Nyquist criteria is the Principle of the Argument. In this chapter a variety of local and generalized Principles of the Argument for complex polynomials with singular points (including multiple poles and zeros) and the associated encirclement conditions are derived. The concepts of this chapter rely on the properties of Riemann surfaces and the concept of homotopic triviality as found in algebraic topology (Massey, 1967; Hilton and Wylie, 1960).

Associated with every analytic function there exists a Riemann surface which has the property that the image of a simply connected region in the complex plane X is simply connected on the Riemann surface. The Principle of the Argument and Nyquist criterion in such cases are trivial. However, for algebraic functions whose Riemann surfaces are multiple connected, the extension of the Principle of the Argument is non-trivial, since the Principle of the Argument must hold for a region of the Riemann surface which is non-simply connected and whose boundary surface is composed of distinct closed contours. Riemann surfaces were originally introduced to solve the problem of a multivalued complex function such as $s^{1/2}$. The extension of the Principle of the Argument for general multiple valued analytic functions has only been considered by Evgrafov (1978), Postlethwaite and MacFarlane (1979), and Valenca and Harris (1980). The approach in Section 2.5 consists in replacing a complex region X with a surface Σ (whose topological properties are closely related to X) and multivalued functions on X by single valued functions on Σ. By this mechanism Cauchy's theorem can be restated for homotopically trivial loops in some subset of Σ. Cauchy's residue theorem

40

is directly instrumental in establishing the Principle of the Argument in Section 2.6.

To derive the generalized Principle of the Argument we present the theory of covering spaces (Section 2.3) and minimum contours (Section 2.4). The essence of this approach is that Nyquist criteria are shown to be just aspects of homotopy theory. Homotopy is introduced in Section 2.1.2 as a relationship of equivalence in quotient spaces or in the fundamental group of a topological space. Indeed it is shown that a path Γ in a complex region X does not encircle the -1 point if and only if Γ is homotopic to a point in $X-\{-1\}$; such a path Γ is called homotopically trivial. Conversely Γ encircles -1 if and only if Γ cannot continuously be deformed to a point in $X-\{-1\}$. This simple analysis shows that the Nyquist encirclement condition is fundamentally a homotopy concept (see Decarlo and Seaks, 1977).

Multiple singular points of complex polynomials are considered in Section 2.6; by identifying these points with punctures on simple regions we can define an algebroid Riemann surface Σ over simple regions with punctures. Finally by defining a minimum contour generated in Σ by the boundary loop of a bounded simple region of the complex plane the generalized Principle of the Argument and encirclement conditions are established.

2.1.1 Paths in topological spaces

Let I and I_1 be arbitrary intervals of the extended real line of the form $[a, b]$, $-\infty \leq a < b \leq \infty$, and let X be a topological space. Identify any continuous function $f: I \rightarrow X$ with any function $f_1: I_1 \rightarrow X$ when there exists an increasing isomorphism $h: I \rightarrow I_1$ such that both h and h^{-1} are absolutely continuous and $f(t) = f_1(h(t))$ for all $t \in I$, that is $f = f_1 \circ h$. It is clear that such an identification defines an equivalence relationship in the space of X valued continuous functions of a real variable with connected compact support. Each equivalence class is called a *path* in X. When no ambiguity arises the same symbol will be used to represent both a continuous function $f: I \rightarrow X$ and the class of equivalence to which it belongs. When in addition X is a region in the complex plane and $f: I \rightarrow X$ is absolutely continuous, the path defined by f is *rectifiable* or that it is an *arc*. The variation of f in I, represented by $l(f)$ is called the length of f. It is well known (Hewitt and Stromberg, 1965, p. 283) that $t \mapsto f'(t)$ can be identified with an element of $L_1(I)$ so that the variation of f in I coincides with $\int_I |f'(t)| \, dt$.

Because a path is defined as a class of equivalence in a space of continuous functions, it is necessary to establish the consistency of the definition of an arc and its length. Consider then $f_1 = f \circ h$ with h an absolutely continuous homeomorphism of I_1 into I. Then $f_1(s)$ is also differentiable almost everywhere such that

$$\frac{df_1(s)}{ds} = \left(\frac{df}{dt}\right)_{t=h(s)} \frac{dh}{ds}$$

From Corollary (20.5) of Hewitt and Stromberg (1965) we have

$$\int_I \left|\frac{df(t)}{dt}\right| dt = \int_{I_1} |f' \circ h(s)| . |h'(s)| \, ds = \int_{I_1} \left|\frac{df_1(s)}{ds}\right| ds,$$

and therefore $f_1(\cdot)$ is also absolutely continuous and its variation in I_1 coincides with the variation of f in I.

Given a path $f : I \to X$ it is always possible to define a homeomorphism $h : [0, 1] \to X$ such that f and $f \circ h$ are equivalent. Hence it is always possible to think of a path in X as being defined by a function whose domain is $[0, 1]$. In this work, unless otherwise stated, it is assumed that a path is defined by a function $f(\cdot)$ whose domain is $[0, 1]$. The point $f(0)$ is called the *origin* of the path (represented by $0(f)$) and the point $f(1)$ is called the *extremity* (represented by $e(f)$). If in a path f the origin and the extremity coincides then the path is *closed*. A closed rectifiable path is called a *loop*. If a path is defined by a constant function it is said to be *trivial*. Finally a *contour* is a finite sequence $\{f_i\}$, $i = 1, 2, \ldots, n$, of closed paths, clearly any finite sequence of contours is also a contour.

2.1.2   Homotopy

Definition 2.1   Let X be a topological space and f and g be two paths in X. The two paths are said to be homotopic to each other (that is $f \sim g$) when $f(0) \equiv g(0)$, $f(1) \equiv g(1)$ and there exists a continuous function $H : [0, 1] \times [0, 1] \to X$ such that:

(a) $f(0) = g(0) = H(0, s)$ and $f(1) = g(1) = H(1, s)$ $\forall \, s \in [0, 1]$
(b) $f(t) = H(t, 1)$ and $g(t) = H(t, 0)$ $\forall \, t \in [0, 1]$

A closed path in X is said to be *homotopically trivial* when it is homotopic to a trivial loop. Any path f has an inverse (represented by $\bar{f}$) and defined by the function $t \mapsto f(1-t)$. Given two paths f and g which satisfy $g(0) = f(1)$ a third path h can be defined by the function

$$h(t) = \begin{cases} f(2t) & \text{for} \quad t \in [0, \frac{1}{2}] \\ g(2t - 1) & \text{for} \quad t \in [\frac{1}{2}, 1] \end{cases}$$

The path h is said to be the *concatenation* of f and g and is represented by

$$h = f \oplus g$$

Consider for example the path $f \oplus \bar{f}$, the function

$$H(t, s) = \begin{cases} f(2st) & \text{for} \quad t \in [0, \tfrac{1}{2}] \\ f(2s(1-t)) & \text{for} \quad t \in [\tfrac{1}{2}, 1] \end{cases}$$

demonstrates that $f \oplus \bar{f}$ is always homotopically trivial.

An important result on homotopically trivial paths is:

PROPOSITION 2.1   *Let f be a path in X and let g_1 and g_2 be homotopically trivial closed paths which satisfy, respectively, $g_1(1) = f(0)$ and $g_2(0) = f(1)$. Then both $g_1 \oplus f$ and $f \oplus g_2$ are homotopic to f.*

Proof   Let $G_1(t, s)$ and $G_2(t, s)$ be the continuous functions which establish respectively the homotopy of g_1 to $g_1(1)$ and the homotopy of g_2 to $g_2(0)$. The functions

$$H_1(t, s) = \begin{cases} G_1(2t, s) & t \in [0, 1], \quad s \in [0, 1] \\ f(2t-1) & t \in [\tfrac{1}{2}, 1] \end{cases}$$

and

$$H_2(t, s) = \begin{cases} f(2t) & t \in [0, \tfrac{1}{2}] \\ G_2(2t-1, s) & t \in [\tfrac{1}{2}, 1], \quad s \in [0, 1] \end{cases}$$

establish then respectively the homotopy between f and $g_1 \oplus f$ and the homotopy between f and $f \oplus g_2$.   □

Definition 2.2   A contour $C = \{f_i\}$, $i = 1, 2, \ldots, n$, in a topological space X is said to be homotopically trivial when there exists a point $x_0 \in X$ and arcs ϕ_i in X such that

(i) $0(\phi_i) \equiv x_0$ and $e(\phi_i) \equiv 0(f_i)$ $\forall\ i = 1, 2, \ldots, n$ (2.1)

(ii) $\tilde{C} \triangleq (\phi_1 \oplus f_1 \oplus \bar{\phi}_1) \oplus (\phi_2 \oplus f_2 \oplus \bar{\phi}_2) \oplus \cdots \oplus (\phi_n \oplus f_n \oplus \bar{\phi}_n)$

is a homotopically trivial loop in X. Any loop $\tilde{C}$ of the form (2.1) is called an *associated* loop of the contour C.

Let $\sigma(X, x_0)$ represent the set of all closed paths in X with origin x_0. It is now easy to show:

PROPOSITION 2.2   *Let $f_1, g_1, f, g \in \sigma(X, x_0)$ satisfy $f \sim f_1$ and $g \sim g_1$, then $f \oplus g \sim f_1 \oplus g_1$*

Proof   Let $F(t, s)$ and $G(t, s)$ be the functions defining the homotopy between f and f_1 and between g and g_1 respectively; then the function

$$H(t, s) = \begin{cases} F(2t, s) & t \in [0, \tfrac{1}{2}], \quad s \in [0, 1] \\ G(2t-1, s) & t \in [0, \tfrac{1}{2}], \quad s \in [0, 1] \end{cases}$$

establishes the homotopy between $f \oplus g$ and $f_1 \oplus g_1$.   □

The concept of homotopy clearly defines a relation of equivalence in $\sigma(X, x_0)$. The quotient space thus defined is called the *fundamental group* of X and is represented by $\pi(X, x_0)$. The group operation is the operation induced in $\pi(X, x_0)$ by the concatenation of loops in $\sigma(X, x_0)$; that is if $f, g \in \sigma(X, x_0)$ and $[f]$, $[g]$ represent respectively the class of equivalence containing f and g, $[f]+[g]$ is defined as the class of equivalence which contains $f \oplus g$. Proposition 2.2 illustrates the mathematical consistency of this definition. The identity element (represented by 0) is defined as the class of all homotopically trivial loops. Proposition 2.1 shows that $0+[f]=[f]$ and that $[f]+0=[f]$, proving that 0 is a unit element. Since $f \oplus \bar{f}$ is always homotopically trivial, the inverse of $[f]$, represented by $-[f]$, can be defined as the class of equivalence which contains $\bar{f}$; in this case $[f]+(-[f])=0$. Finally it is clear that $f \oplus (g \oplus h) = (f \oplus g) \oplus h$ for any f, g, $h \in \sigma(X, x_0)$. Consequently the operation $+$ is associative and is therefore a group operation.

There exists sets, X, for which the fundamental group has a particularly simple and useful form. Consider, for example, the unit disc in the complex plane $D\ \{z : |z| \le 1\}$ and a collection $\{z_1, z_2, \ldots, z_n\}$ of n distinct interior points of D. A region, X, of the complex plane which is homeomorphic with $D - \{z_1, z_2, \ldots, z_n\}$ is called a simple region with n punctures. If $n = 0$, X is called a *simple region*, for these regions the following holds:

THEOREM 2.1 (Hilton and Wylie, p. 242, (1960))   *Let X be a simple region with n punctures and let $x_0 \in X$, then $\pi(X, x_0)$ can be identified with a free abelian group of n generators.*

Theorem 2.1 establishes that $\pi(X, x_0)$ is isomorphic with Z^n, where Z represents the abelian group defined by the integers, furthermore in a simple region every loop is homotopically trivial.

Finally to complete this section it is convenient to present a result which relates the fundamental groups of the two topological vector spaces X and Y.

PROPOSITION 2.3 (Hilton and Wylie, pp. 234–235, 1960)   *Let $h : X \to Y$ be a continuous map, then h induces a homomorphism*

$$h^* : \pi(X, x_0) \to \pi(Y, h(x_0))$$

by assigning the class of equivalence, which contains the path f in X to the class of equivalence which contains $h \circ f$. Moreover if $h(\cdot)$ is a homeomorphism, h is an isomorphism.

2.2   COMPLEX INTEGRATION AND CAUCHY'S THEOREM

Let X be a region in the complex plane and let $H(X)$ represent the set of all complex functions which are analytic in some open set containing X. Let $z \mapsto F(z)$ be an element of $H(X)$ and f an arc in X. Since $t \mapsto F(f(t))$ is bounded and $t \mapsto f(t)$ is absolutely continuous, the integral

$$\int_0^1 F\{f(t)\}f'(t)\,dt \qquad (2.2)$$

is well defined. Note that $t \mapsto f'(t)$ can be identified with an element of $L_1[0, 1]$.

Suppose now that $g:[a, b] \to X$ is equivalent to f and that the homeomorphism $h:[a, b] \to [0, 1]$ establishes such an equivalence, then $g = f \circ h$. By hypothesis h and h^{-1} are both absolutely continuous, so from Hewitt and Stromberg (corollary 20.5 (1965)),

$$\int_0^1 (F \circ f)(t)f'(t)\,dt = \int_a^b \{F \circ f \circ h\}(s)\{f' \circ h\}(s)h'(s)\,ds$$

$$= \int_a^b (F \circ g)(s)g'(s)\,ds$$

Hence the value of (2.2) is independent of the particular function $f : I \to X$ which defines the arc, and depends only on $F(\cdot)$ and on the arc. We represent (2.2) by

$$\int_f F(z)\,dz$$

Consider now two arcs f and g in X such that $f(1) = g(0)$; the elementary properties of the Riemann integral (Hille, (1959)) and the definition of concatenation of paths produces immediately:

PROPOSITION 2.4

$$\int_{f \oplus g} F(z)\,dz = \int_f F(z)\,dz + \int_g F(z)\,dz$$

Now follows one of the most important theorems in analysis:

THEOREM 2.2 (Fundamental theorem of plane topology)   *Let X be a*

region in the complex plane and f and g two homotopic arcs in X. For any
$z \mapsto F(z)$ *in* $H(X)$

$$\int_f F(z)\, dz = \int_g F(z)\, dz$$

Proof For proof see Springer (1957, p. 157). A direct consequence of this theorem is Cauchy's theorem:

THEOREM 2.3 (Cauchy's theorem in the plane) *Let X be a simple region and* $z \mapsto F(z)$ *a complex function analytic in an open set containing X. If C is a loop in X, then*

$$\int_C F(z)\, dz = 0$$

LEMMA 2.1 *Let X be a simple region,* x_0 *an interior point of X and f a path in* $X - x_0$. *There then exists an arc* f^* *which is homeotopic to f in* $X - x_0$.

Proof Since $t \mapsto f(t)$ is continuous and $[0, 1]$ is closed

$$d \triangleq \inf_{t \in [0,1]} |f(t) - x_0|$$

is non-zero. Moreover, since $[0, 1]$ is compact, $t \mapsto f(t)$ is uniformly continuous and there exists a $\delta > 0$ such that

$$\sup_{t \in [0,1]} \sup_{|s-t| < \delta} |f(t) - f(s)| < d \qquad (2.3)$$

Consider the finite partition of $[0, 1]$, $o = t_0 < t_1 < \ldots < t_n = 1$ satisfying $t_i - t_{i-1} < \delta$, $i = 1, 2, \ldots, n$, and define

$$f^*(t) = f(t_{i-1}) + (t - t_{i-1})(t_i - t_{i-1})^{-1}(f(t_i) - f(t_{i-1})) \qquad (2.4)$$

for

$$t \in [t_i, t_{i-1}].$$

then

$$|f^*(t) - x_0| \ge |f(t_{i-1}) - x_0| - |f(t_i) - f(t_{i-1})| > d - d,$$

so $t \mapsto f^*(t)$ defines a path in $X - x_0$. Furthermore $t \mapsto f^*(t)$ is differentiable everywhere except in a finite set, therefore f^* is an arc.

Consider now the function

$$H(t, s) = sf(t) + (1 - s)f^*(t), \quad \text{for} \quad t \in [t_i, t_{i-1}]$$

$$|H(t, s) - f(t_{i-1})| \le s\,|f(t) - f(t_{i-1})| + (1 - s)\,|t - t_{i-1}|\,(t_i - t_{i-1})^{-1}$$
$$\times |f(t_i) - f(t_{i-1})|$$
$$< sd + (1 - s)d = d. \qquad (2.5)$$

Consequently $H(t, s)$ lies in $X - x_0$, for any $(t, s) \in [0, 1]^2$. Moreover $H(\cdot, \cdot)$ satisfies the remaining conditions of definition 2.2 of homotopy, therefore f and f^* are homotopic. We can now establish the following theorem:

THEOREM 2.4   Let X be a simple region and x_0, z_0 interior points of X, then any $F \in H(X - z_0)$ defines a homomorphism $m : \pi(X - z_0, x_0) \to C^1$ as

$$m : f \mapsto \int_f F(z)\, dx \qquad (2.6)$$

where f is an arbitrary loop in the class of equivalence $\underline{f}$. Moreover either $m \equiv 0$ or $m(\cdot)$ is one-to-one.

Proof   From Lemma 2.1, any closed path has a loop with origin x_0 to which it is homotopic every equivalence class $\underline{f} \in \pi(X - z_0, x_0)$ contains a loop. For such a loop $\int_f F(z)\, dz$ is well defined, furthermore from the fundamental theorem of plane topology the value of $\int_f F(z)\, dz$ is independent of the particular loop chosen in $\underline{f}$. In consequence the map (2.6) is well defined and a homomorphism (see Proposition 2.4).

Finally suppose that for some $\underline{f_0} \neq 0$ we have $m(\underline{f_0}) = 0$. Since $\pi(X - z_0, x_0)$ can be identified with a free abelian group of one generator (Theorem 2.1) then there exists a non-zero integer n_0 such that $\underline{f_0} = n_0 \underline{g}$, where $\underline{g}$ represents the generator of the group. Then $m(\underline{f_0}) = n_0 m(\underline{g}) = 0$ and hence $m(\underline{g}) = 0$; consequently $m(\underline{f}) = 0$ for an arbitrary $\underline{f} \in \pi(X - z_0, x_0)$ since $\underline{f} = n\underline{g}$ for some n. Clearly $m(\cdot)$ is identically zero, therefore if $m \neq 0$, then $m(\underline{f}) = 0$ if and only if $\underline{f} = 0$. □

Example 2.1   Consider the function

$$F(z) = \frac{1}{2\pi j} \frac{1}{(z - z_0)}$$

For an arbitrary circle C with centre z_0, then

$$\int_C F(z)\, dz = 1 \neq 0$$

Consequently, using Theorem 2.4, it follows that

$$m : \underline{f} \mapsto \frac{1}{2\pi j} \int_f \frac{dz}{(z - z_0)} \qquad (2.7)$$

defines an isomorphism between $\pi(X - z_0, x_0)$ and $m\{\pi(X - z_0, x_0)\}$.
Given an arc f (not necessarily closed) which does not contain z_0, it is

well known (Springer, 1957) that

$$\Delta(f) \triangleq \frac{1}{2\pi j} \int_f \frac{dz}{(z - z_0)}$$

represents the increase in the argument of $(z - z_0)$ when z describes f and that $\Delta(f)$ is called the *index* of f with respect to z_0. When f is closed, $\Delta(f)$ gives the number of anticlockwise encirclements of z_0 by the loop f. Therefore the contradomain of $m(\cdot)$ is a subset of Z.

For $\varepsilon > 0$ sufficiently small the loop

$$f_\xi(t) = z_0 + \xi \exp(j2\pi t)$$

lies in $X - x_0$. If g is the class of equivalence containing f_ξ then $m(g) = 1$. Since $m : \pi(X - z_0, x_0) \mapsto Z$ is obviously onto (given $n \in Z$ there always exists an $f = ng$ such that $m(f) = n$) and is one-to-one, then $m(\cdot)$ establishes the isomorphism between $\pi(X - z_0, x_0)$ and Z. Moreover since $m(g) = 1$, g must be the generator of $\pi(X - z_0, x_0)$.

2.3   RIEMANN SURFACES

This introduction to Riemann surfaces is based upon the concept of a *covering space*:

Definition 2.3   A topological space E is a covering space of a topological space X when a continuous onto map $p : E \to X$ exists such that every $x \in X$ has an open neighbourhood which satisfies

(a) $p^{-1}(X)$ is a disjoint union of open sets s_i in E
(b) For each i, $p|_{s_i}$ defines a homeomorphism between s_i and X

The sets s_i are called the *sheets* of X, and p is called a *covering*; X is said to be *evenly covered*. Throughout this section it will be assumed that the space X is pathwise connected, that is, given two points $x_0, x_1 \in X$ there exists a path in X with origin x_0 and extremity x_1. Our use of the concept of covering space is based upon the following two theorems:

THEOREM 2.5 (Unique Lifting Theorem, Greenberg (1967))   *Let* $p : E \to X$ *be a covering*, f *a path in* X, *and* e_0 *a point of* $p^{-1}\{0(f)\}$. *If there exists a path* $\hat{f}$ *in* E *with origin* e_0 *satisfying* $p \circ \hat{f} = f$, *such path is unique.*

The path $\hat{f}$ is called a *lifting* of f.

THEOREM 2.6 (Homotopy Lifting Theorem, Greenberg (1967))   *Let* $p : E \to X$ *be a covering*, f *a path in* X, *and* e_0 *a point of* $p^{-1}\{0(f)\}$. *If* f *has* *a lifting $\hat{f}$ and g is a path in X homotopic to f, then g has a lifting $\hat{g}$ which is homotopic to $\hat{f}$.*

An immediate consequence of Theorem 2.6 is that $p : E \rightarrow X$ induces a monomorphism $p_* : \pi(E, e_0) \rightarrow \pi(X, p(e_0))$. To prove this we need only note that p_* defines a homomorphism (Proposition 2.3) and that $p \circ f$ is homotopically trivial if and only if f is homotopically trivial (Theorem 2.6).

Remark Given a closed path of f in X, it is important to note that even if a lifting $\hat{f}$ of f exists, such a lifting is not necessarily closed (as in the case of Riemann surfaces). However, the point $e(\hat{f})$ lies in $p^{-1}\{0(f)\}$, as $0(f) \equiv e(f)$ and $f = p \circ \hat{f}$. Moreover this point depends only on the class of equivalence to which f belongs (Theorem 2.6). Suppose now that E and X are such that every path in X has a lifting in E, then a map $\hat{e} : \pi(X, x_0) \rightarrow p^{-1}(x_0)$ is well defined as

$$\hat{e} : [f] = e(\hat{f}),$$

where $[f]$ is the class of equivalence which contains f and $\hat{f}$ is the lifting of f.

Consider now a connected complex region X with non-empty interior and let $H(X)$ represent the ring of all complex functions which are analytic in some open set containing X. Let $\phi[\lambda]$ represent an irreducible monic polynomial of degree n over $H(X)$ such that

$$\phi[\lambda] = b_0 + b_1\lambda + \ldots + b_{n-1}\lambda^{n-1} + \lambda^n$$

with $b_i \in H(X)$, $i = 0, 1, \ldots, n-1$.

Let $\phi_s[\lambda]$ be the polynomial over C^1 obtained from $\phi[\lambda]$ by replacing each coefficient $b_i \in H(X)$ by the complex number $b_i(s)$; finally let $\hat{\phi}(\lambda; \cdot)$ represent the element of $H(X)$ obtained from $\phi[\lambda]$ by assigning complex number λ to the indeterminate variable of the polynomial.

It is assumed that the following holds:

HYPOTHESIS 2.1 *The region X is such that for each $s \in X$ the polynomial $\phi_s[\lambda]$ has n distinct roots.*

Now let s_0 be an interior point of X and λ_0 one of the roots of $\phi_{s_0}[\lambda]$, then for appropriate $\alpha_i \in H(X)$.

$$\phi_s[\lambda] = \alpha_0(s) + \alpha_1(s)(\lambda - \lambda_0) + \ldots + \alpha_{n-1}(\lambda - \lambda_0)^{n-1} + (\lambda - \lambda_0)^n$$

with $\alpha_0(s)_0 = 0$ and $\alpha_1(s_0) \neq 0$. Selecting a sufficiently small ρ_0, the disc $|s - s_0| < \rho_0$ is contained in X and every $\alpha_i(\cdot)$ has a Taylor's series expansion in this disc. From Theorem 4.5.1 (Hille, 1959), there exists a

$\rho \leq \rho_0$ and a power series

$$\theta(s) = \sum_{k=0}^{\infty} a_k (s - s_0)^k \qquad (2.8)$$

which is convergent in the disc $\{s : |s - s_0| < \rho\}$ such that $\phi_s[\theta(s)] = 0$ for every s in this disc and such that $\theta(s_0) = a_0 = \lambda_0$. A power series of the form (2.8) is called a *function element*. The point s_0 is called the *centre* of the function element θ and is represented by $z(\theta)$. The largest value of ρ for which (2.8) converges in the open set $|s - s_0| < \rho$ is called the *radius of convergence* of θ and is represented by $R(\theta)$.

The function element $\theta(\cdot)$ is well determined if the point s_0 and the root of $\phi_{s_0}[\lambda]$ which coincides with $\theta(s_0)$ are well specified (any one of the remaining roots of $\phi_{s_0}[\lambda]$ could have been specified). Therefore each $s_0 \in X$ determines n function elements θ, all with centre s_0, each function element being associated with a particular root. Two function elements θ and θ' are not distinct when $z(\theta) = z(\theta')$ and when in some disc with centre $z(\theta)$, $\theta(s) \equiv \theta'(s)$. Thus every $s_0 \in X$ determines n distinct function elements; moreover these n function elements are the only function elements which have centre s_0, consequently the set formed by these elements can be represented as $z^{-1}(s_0)$.

By forcing s_0 to describe the whole of X, Σ can be defined as the set of all function elements thus defined, that is $\Sigma = \bigcup_{s_0 \in X} z^{-1}(s_0)$. The map $z : \Sigma \to X$ is now an onto map and for each $s \in X$, $z^{-1}(s)$ is formed with exactly n points of Σ.

Having defined Σ, the next step is to define a topology in Σ; to begin with, the concept of *immediate continuation* needs to be developed. Let θ_0 be arbitrary in Σ and let s_0 be the centre of θ_0. For any $s' \neq s_0$ in the disc $|s - s_0| < R(\theta)$,

$$\theta_0(s) = \sum_{k=0}^{\infty} a_k (s - s_0)^k = \sum_{k=0}^{\infty} a_k [(s - s') + (s' - s_0)]^k.$$

By expanding $[(s - s') + (s' - s_0)]^k$ via the binomial expansion the above becomes

$$\theta_0(s) = \sum_{k=0}^{\infty} a_k (s - s_0)^k = \sum_{k=0}^{\infty} a_k' (s - s')^k$$

The power series $\theta_1(s) = \sum_{k=0}^{\infty} a_k' (s - s')^k$ has centre s' which is distinct from s_0. However, in the intersection of the regions of convergence, $\{s : |s - s_0| < R(\theta)\}$ and $\{s : |s - s'| < R(\theta')\}$, the two power series take the same values (note that $R(\theta')$ cannot be inferior to $R(\theta_0) - |s_0 - s'|$)

Definition 2.4   Any function element $\theta \in \Sigma$ which like θ_1 satisfies

(a) $|z(\theta) - z(\theta_0)| < R(\theta_0)$

(b) For any s satisfying $|s - z(\theta_0)| < R(\theta_0)$ and $|s - z(\theta)| < R(\theta)$, we have $\theta(s) = \theta_0(s)$, is called the immediate continuation of θ_0. And the set of such immediate continuations is represented by $S(\theta_0)$.

Definition 2.5   The base of the neighbourhoods of the point $\theta_0 \in \Sigma$ is defined as the collection of all sets U of the form

$$U = \{\theta \in S(\theta_0) : |z(\theta) - z(\theta_0)| < \xi\}$$

for some $0 < \xi < R(\theta_0)$. U is called the *parametric disc* with centre θ_0 and radius ξ. It is a straightforward exercise to demonstrate that all parametric discs satisfy the axioms used in the definition of the base of neighbourhoods (Section 1.2.1).

THEOREM 2.7 $z : \Sigma \rightarrow X$ *is a covering*

Proof   It has already been established that $z(\cdot)$ is onto. Let V be an open disc in X with centre s_0 and radius $0 < \xi < \min\limits_{\theta \in z^{-1}(s_0)} R(\theta)$, such that

$$V = \{s : |s - s_0| < \xi\}$$

Let $\theta_1, \theta_2, \ldots, \theta_n$ be the elements of $z^{-1}(s_0)$ and consider the n parametric discs

$$U_i = \{\theta \in S(\theta_i) : |z(\theta) - s_0| < \xi\}$$

Let λ_i be defined as $\theta_i(s_0)$, that is $\lambda_1, \lambda_2, \ldots, \lambda_n$ form the collection of the n roots of $\phi_{s_0}[\lambda]$.

By defining

$$d \triangleq \min\limits_{i \neq j} |\lambda_i - \lambda_j| > 0$$

ξ can be chosen sufficiently small such as to ensure that

$$\max\limits_i \sup\limits_{|s - s_0| < \xi} |\theta_i(s) - \lambda_i| < \frac{d}{2}$$

So for an arbitrary $s \in V$

$$|\theta_i(s) - \theta_j(s)| > |\lambda_i - \lambda_j| - |\theta_i(s) - \lambda_i| - |\theta_j(s) - \lambda_j|$$

$$> d - \frac{d}{2} - \frac{d}{2}$$

therefore for any $i \neq j$ for any $s \in V$, $\theta_i(s) \neq \theta_j(s)$.

Let θ be arbitrary in U_i and θ' be arbitrary in U_j. If $z(\theta) \neq z(\theta')$ it follows that $\theta \neq \theta'$. Suppose that $s = z(\theta) = z(\theta')$; since θ is an immediate continuation of θ_i and θ' is an immediate continuation of θ_j, then $\theta(s) = \theta_i(s)$ and $\theta'(s) = \theta_j(s)$. So $\theta \neq \theta'$ and therefore $U_i \cap U_j = \phi$, $i \neq j$.

Consider now an arbitrary $s \in V$. For each $i = 1, 2, \ldots, n$ it is always possible to find an immediate continuation of θ_i with centre s. Let $\hat{\theta}_i$ be such a function element, then $\hat{\theta}_i \in U_i$ and since $U_i \cap U_j = \phi$ it follows that $\hat{\theta}_i \neq \hat{\theta}_j$ for $i \neq j$. In conclusion given any $s \in V$ there are n distinct elements of $z^{-1}(s)$, each of which are contained in its associated parametric disc U_i. Since $z^{-1}(s)$ contains exactly n-distinct elements, it follows that $z^{-1}(s)$ is contained in $\bigcup\limits_{i=1}^{n} U_i$; moreover for each i, $z(U_i) \equiv V$ and so

$$z^{-1}(V) = \bigcup_{i=1}^{n} U_i$$

Finally it is necessary to show that the map z restricted to U_i is an homeomorphism. It has already been shown that given an arbitrary $s \in V$ there exists one and only one function element in U_i whose centre is s, consequently $z : U_i \to V$ is an isomorphism.

Let Θ be an arbitrary neighbourhood in U_i of some $\theta \in U_i$, such that

$$\Theta = \{\alpha \in S(\theta) \cap U_i : |z(\alpha) - z(\theta)| < \delta\}$$

for some $\delta < \xi - |z(\theta) - z(\theta_i)|$. Then

$$z(\Theta) = \{s \in V : |s - z(\theta)| < \delta\}$$

and $z(\Theta)$ coincides with a neighbourhood of $z(\theta)$ in V, proving that $z\,|_i$ and its inverse are continuous. In conclusion it was first established that there exists a neighbourhood V of a point s_0 and a collection of n parametric discs U_i such that

(a) $z^{-1}(V) = \bigcup\limits_{i=1}^{n} U_i$

(b) $U_i \cap U_j = \phi$, $i \neq j$

(c) $z : U_i \to V$ is a homeomorphism.

Consequently z is a covering.   □

Definition 2.6   The topological space $\Sigma = \bigcup\limits_{s_0 \in X} z^{-1}(s_0)$ is called the *algebroid Riemann surface* generated by the region X and by the polynomial

$$\phi[\lambda] = \sum_{i=0}^{n} b_i \lambda^i \qquad b_i \in H(X)$$

A direct consequence of Theorem 2.7 and the homotopy lifting theorem is:

THEOREM 2.8   *The map* $z : \Sigma \rightarrow X$ *induces a monomorphism*

$$z^* : \pi(\Sigma, \theta) \rightarrow \pi(X, z(\theta))$$

COROLLARY 2.1   *If X is a simple region with punctures, then* $\pi(\Sigma, \theta)$ *is an abelian group.*

Proof $\pi(X, z(\theta))$ is a free abelian group and $\pi(\Sigma, \theta)$ can be identified with a subgroup of $\pi(X, z(\theta))$, hence it must be an abelian group.   □

It has been shown that Σ is a set of power series, as a consequence all properties of the space (including its topology) are defined locally, that is, they are defined in a small region around each point of the space. An important problem that now arises is how to find a global structure for the space? To achieve this the concept of *analytic continuation* is used.

Let θ_0 be arbitrary in Σ and let f be a path in X whose origin coincides with $z(\theta_0)$. Due to the continuity of $t \mapsto f(t)$ there exists a t_1 such that $f(t_1)$ lies in the circle of convergence of θ_0. Therefore there exists a unique $\theta_1 \in z^{-1}\{f(t_1)\}$ which is an immediate continuation of θ_0. For sufficiently small t_1.

$$|f(t_1) - f(0)| < \tfrac{1}{2} R(\theta_0)$$

But since $R(\theta_1) \geq R(\theta_0) - |f(t_1) - f(0)|$, θ_0 lies in the disc of convergence of θ_1 and must therefore be an immediate continuation of θ_1.

We now proceed by induction; consider a sequence of points in $[0, 1]$

$$0 = t_0 < t_1 < \ldots < t_k < \ldots \leq 1$$

and a sequence of points in Σ, $\theta_0, \theta_1, \ldots, \theta_k, \ldots$ such that

(a) $z(\theta_i) = f(t_i)$

(b) θ_i is an immediate continuation of both θ_{i-1} and of θ_{i+1}.

Suppose that the sequence $t_0 < t_1 < \ldots < t_i < \ldots$ reaches 1 in a finite number of steps; that is there exists a partition of $[0, 1]$ such that

$$0 = t_0 < t_1 < \ldots < t_m = 1$$

and a sequence of function elements $\theta_0, \theta_1, \ldots, \theta_m$ which satisfy conditions (a) and (b) above. Then it is said that the *analytic continuation* of θ_0 along f is possible and that θ_m is the analytic continuation of θ_0 along f. Such an operation on θ_0 is represented as

$$\theta_m = \xrightarrow[f]{} \theta_0$$

Note that although θ_m was obtained for a particular partition of $[0, 1]$, it can be shown (Bers, 1958) that the function element θ_m is independent of the particular partition used.

Let $W(\theta_0)$ represent the set of all analytic continuations of a function element θ_0 along paths in X with origin $z(\theta_0)$. $W(\theta_0)$ is a subset of Σ and is called a *complete analytic function* in the sense of Weierstrass. Notice that $W(\theta_0)$ is defined in a space of power series which are not necessarily derived from a space of roots of a polynomial over $H(X)$. Furthermore through the device of analytic continuation, function elements which are not immediate continuation of each other can be related (that is $W(\theta_0)$ has a global structure). An important question with respect to the global structure of Σ is whether $W(\theta_0)$ is a proper subset of Σ.

THEOREM 2.9 (Bers, 1957) *Let $\phi[\lambda]$ be an irreducible polynomial of degree n over X such that for every $s \in X$, $\phi_s[\lambda]$ has n distinct roots. Then the algebroid Riemann surface Σ thus generated is a complete analytic function in the sense of Weierstrass. Conversely, given any complete analytic function W in the sense of Weierstrass such that for all $\theta \in W$, $z^{-1}\{z^{-1}\{z(\theta)\}$ has exactly n function elements, then there exists an irreducible polynomial $\phi[\lambda]$ over H(X) of degree n such that the algebroid Riemann surface generated by X and $\phi[\lambda]$ coincides with W.*

Let f be an arbitrary path in X. For an arbitrary $T \in [0, 1]$ let $f_T(t) \triangleq f(tT)$, then f_T defines a path such that $0(f_T) \equiv 0(f)$ and $e(f_T) \equiv f(T)$. Let $\hat{f}(T) \in \Sigma$ be defined as $\xrightarrow[f_T]{} \theta$. Using the definition of analytic continuation it follows immediately that $T \to \hat{f}(T)$ is continuous. So $\hat{f}$ defines a path in Σ, furthermore

$$(z \circ \hat{f})(T) = z\{\hat{f}(T)\} = z\left\{\xrightarrow[f_T]{} \theta\right\} = e\{f_T\} = f(T)$$

that is $z \circ \hat{f} \equiv f$. Consequently $\hat{f}$ is a lifting of f, and because $z : Z \to X$ is a covering (Theorem 2.7), $\hat{f}$ is the unique lifting with origin θ (Theorem 2.5). We have now established the first part of

THEOREM 2.10 *Let f be an arbitrary path in X and θ an arbitrary element of $z^{-1}\{0(f)\}$. Then there exists a unique path $\hat{f}$ in Σ which is a lifting of f and whose origin is θ. Moreover if g is homotopic to f, the lifting $\hat{g}$ of g which has origin θ is homotopic to $\hat{f}$.*

Proof The second part of the theorem follows from the homotopy lifting theorem.   □

COROLLARY 2.2 *Let f and g be two homotopic paths in X and let $\theta \in z^{-1}\{0(f)\}$, then $\xrightarrow[f]{} \theta \equiv \xrightarrow[g]{} \theta$.*

Proof Let $\hat{f}, \hat{g}$ be the liftings of f and g respectively; since f and g are homotopic, $\hat{f}$ and $\hat{g}$ are also homotopic and consequently $\xrightarrow{f} \theta = e(\hat{f}) = e(\hat{g}) = \xrightarrow{g} \theta$. $\qquad\qquad\qquad\qquad\qquad\qquad\qquad\qquad\qquad\qquad\qquad\square$

2.4 MINIMUM CONTOURS AND ALGEBROID RIEMANN SURFACES

In the remainder, X is assumed to represent a simple region with punctures. Let $\phi[\lambda]$ be an irreducible polynomial of degree n over $H(X)$ satisfying Hypothesis 2.1, and let Σ be the algebroid Riemann surface thus generated. Let f be an arbitrary closed path in X: the lifting $\hat{f}$ of f, already noted, is not necessarily closed. In general we can only state that the extremity of $\hat{f}$ has the same centre as the origin of $\hat{f}$, that is

$$e(\hat{f}) \in z^{-1}[z\{0(f)\}]$$

However, if f is concatenated with itself a certain number of times, the lifting of the resultant path is closed. Formally setting

$$\underbrace{f \oplus f \oplus \ldots \oplus f}_{m \text{ times}} = f^m$$

If $[f] \in \pi(X, 0(f))$ is the homotopy class containing f, then, as $\pi(X, 0(f))$ is a free abelian group (Theorem 2.1), $[f^m] = m[f]$, and so

PROPOSITION 2.5 *Let f be a closed path in X and θ be arbitrary in $z^{-1}\{0(f)\}$. Then there exists an $m \le n$ such that $\theta \equiv \xrightarrow{f^m} \theta$, where n is the degree of $\phi[\lambda]$.*

Proof Let $\theta' \ne \theta$ be another element of $z^{-1}\{0(f)\}$. The following $\xrightarrow{f^m} \theta' \ne \xrightarrow{f^m} \theta$ must be true, otherwise $\xrightarrow{\bar{f}^m}\{\xrightarrow{f^m}\theta'\} = \theta$, and since $\bar{f}^m \oplus f^m$ is homotopically trivial, it is necessary that $\theta' = \theta$. If for all $m \le n$, $\theta \ne \xrightarrow{f^m} \theta$, then the $n+1$ function elements

$$\theta, \xrightarrow[f]{} \theta, \xrightarrow[f^2]{} \theta, \ldots, \xrightarrow[f^n]{} \theta$$

would all be distinct and there would be $n+1$ distinct function elements in $z^{-1}\{0(f)\}$ (which is not possible). $\qquad\qquad\qquad\qquad\qquad\square$

Similarily the following may be derived:

PROPOSITION 2.6 *Let f be a path in X, and let $\theta, \theta' \in z^{-1}\{0(f)\}$ be such that $\theta' \ne \xrightarrow{f^k} \theta$ for any integer k. Then for any integers $m, k, \xrightarrow{f^m} \theta \ne \xrightarrow{f^k} \theta$.*

Now consider an arbitrary closed path f in X. Let θ_1 be arbitrary in $z^{-1}\{0(f)\}$, and represent the lifting of f with origin θ_1 as $\xrightarrow{f} \theta_1$. Let $m_1 \leq n$ be the smallest integer which satisfies

$$\theta_1 = \xrightarrow{f^{m_1}} \theta_1$$

Then the path Γ_1 defined by

$$\Gamma_1 = \xrightarrow{f^{m_1}} \theta_1$$

is closed.

If $m_1 = n$, define a contour C in Σ as Γ_1. Suppose that $m_1 < n$ and define $\textcircled{+}_1$ as

$$\textcircled{+}_1 = \left\{ \theta_1, \xrightarrow{f} \theta_1, \dots, \xrightarrow{f^{m_1}} - 1\theta_1 \right\}.$$

This is the set of all function elements whose centre coincides with the centre of θ_1, which can be reached from θ_1 by analytic continuation along some multiple of the closed path f.

Since $m_1 < n$, $z^{-1}\{0(f)\} - \textcircled{+}_1$ is non-empty. Let θ_2 be an element of this set and m_2 be the smallest integer satisfying $\xrightarrow{f^{m_2}} \theta_2 = \theta_2$. Another closed path Γ_2 can be defined as

$$\Gamma_2 = \xrightarrow{f^{m_2}} \theta_2.$$

On defining $\textcircled{+}_2 = \{\theta_2, \xrightarrow{f} \theta_2, \dots, \xrightarrow{f^{m_2}} - 1\theta_2\}$, Proposition 2.6 shows that the sets $\textcircled{+}_1$ and $\textcircled{+}_2$ are disjoint. Continuing in this manner form N closed paths $\Gamma \triangleq \xrightarrow{f^{m_i}} \theta_i$ until every function element of $z^{-1}\{0(f)\}$ is contained in some loop. Therefore the union of all sets $\textcircled{+}_i = \{\theta_i, \xrightarrow{f} \theta_i, \dots, \xrightarrow{f^{m_i-1}} \theta_i\}$ contains $z^{-1}\{0(f)\}$.

The contour C in Σ defined by the sequence of closed paths $\{\Gamma_i\}_{i=1}^N$ is called a *minimum contour* generated in Σ by the path f. A simple analysis shows that the minimum contours generated by the same closed path differ only in the choice and order of origins $0(\Gamma_i)$.

Let $C = \{f_i\}_{i=1}^m$ be a contour in X and F_i be a minimum contour generated in Σ by f_i. The contour $\hat{C} = \{F_i\}_{i=1}^m$ is said to be a *minimum contour generated by the contour C*.

THEOREM 2.11   *Let $C = \{f_i\}_{i=1}^m$ be a homotopically trivial contour in X. Then every minimum contour generated in Σ by C is homotopically trivial.*

The proof of the theorem is a consequence of the following lemmas:

LEMMA 2.2   *Let f be a closed path in X and $F = \{\Gamma_i\}_{i=1}^N$ a minimum* *contour generated in Σ by f. Then if $\underline{F}$ is any associated closed path of F, $z \circ \underline{F}$ is homotopic with f^n.*

Proof Given the contour $F = \{\Gamma_i\}_{i=1}^N$, let $\theta_i = 0(\Gamma_i)$. For an arbitrary $\theta \in z^{-1}\{z(\theta_i)\}$ let ϕ_i be the closed path in X which satisfies

$$\theta_i = \xrightarrow[\phi_i]{} \theta, \, i = 1, 2, \ldots, N$$

and let $\underset{\sim}{\phi}_i$ be defined as $\xrightarrow[\phi_i]{} \theta$

An associated path $\underline{F}$ is constructed as

$$\underline{F} = \bigoplus_{i=1}^N \phi_i \oplus \Gamma_i \oplus \underset{\sim}{\bar{\phi}}_i$$

so

$$z \circ \underline{F} = \bigoplus_{i=1}^N \phi_i \oplus z \circ \Gamma_i \oplus \underset{\sim}{\bar{\phi}}_i$$

Since $\Gamma_i = \xrightarrow[f^{m_i}]{} \theta_i$, $z \circ \Gamma_i = f^{m_i}$. Noting that ϕ_i and $\bar{\phi}_i$ are both closed paths with origins $z(\theta)$ and that $\pi(X, z(\theta))$ is a commutative group (it is an abelian group since by hypothesis X is a simple region with punctures), then $\phi_i \oplus z \circ \Gamma_i \oplus \bar{\phi}_i$ is homotopic with $z \circ \Gamma_i$. And so $z \circ \underline{F}$ is homotopic with $\bigoplus_{i=1}^N f^{m_i}$. Utilizing the fact that $\pi(X, 0(f))$ is a commutative group, then $z \circ \underline{F}$ is homotopic, with $(f)^{m_1+m_2+\ldots+m_N}$, however, in constructing a minimum contour $m_1 + m_2 + \ldots + m_N = n$, and so $z \circ \underline{F}$ is homotopic with f^n.   □

Proof of Theorem 2.11 Let $\underline{F}_i$, $i = 1, 2, \ldots, m$ be an associated loop of a minimum contour F_i generated by f_i, also let θ_i be the origin F_i and suppose that $z(\theta_i) \equiv 0(f)$. Let s be arbitrary in X, θ arbitrary in $z^{-1}(s)$, and let ψ_i be a path in X satisfying $\theta_i = \xrightarrow[\psi_i]{} \theta$

Finally let $\underset{\sim}{\psi}_i$ be the lifting of ψ_i; then an associated contour of C is of the form

$$\underline{C} = \bigoplus_{i=1}^m \psi_i \oplus F_i \oplus \underset{\sim}{\bar{\psi}}_i$$

so that

$$z \circ \underline{C} = \bigoplus_{i=1}^m \psi_i \oplus z \circ F_i \oplus \underset{\sim}{\bar{\psi}}_i$$

From Lemma 2.2, $z \circ \underline{F}_i \sim f_i^n$, but

$$\psi_i \oplus f_i^n \oplus \bar{\psi}_i \sim (\psi_i \oplus f_i \oplus \bar{\psi}_i)^n$$

so

$$z \circ \underline{C} \sim \bigoplus_{i=1}^m (\psi_i \oplus f_i \oplus \bar{\psi}_i)^n$$

And since the fundamental group of X is commutative, then

$$z \circ \underset{\sim}{C} \sim \left(\bigoplus_{i=1}^{m} \psi_i \oplus f_i \oplus \bar{\psi}_i \right)^n$$

Now, $\bigoplus_{i=1}^{m} \psi_i \oplus f_i \oplus \bar{\psi}_i$ is an associated loop of the contour $C = \{f_i\}_{i=1}^{m}$
which by hypothesis is homotopically trivial. So $z \circ \underset{\sim}{C}$ is homotopically trivial and therefore $\underset{\sim}{C}$ is also homotopically trivial (see Theorem 2.8). $\square$

2.5 ANALYTIC FUNCTIONS AND INTEGRATION IN ALGEBROID RIEMANN SURFACES

Riemann surfaces were originally introduced (Springer, 1957) to solve the problem of multivalued complex functions such as $s^{1/2}$. The approach consists in replacing a complex region X with a surface Σ (whose topological properties are closely related with X) and the multivalued function $h : X \to C'$ by a single-valued function $\hat{h} : \Sigma \to C'$. The function h can be made single valued if its domain is restricted to a sufficiently small region U, for example $s^{1/2}$ can be made single valued if its domain is restricted to a region which does not contain the origin. The function $\hat{h}$ must retain this characteristic and for a sufficiently small region $\hat{U}$ in Σ, and in some sense the two functions h, $\hat{h}$ must coincide.

To formalize these considerations, consider an algebroid Riemann surface Σ generated by a region X and a polynomial $\phi[\lambda]$ of degree n over $H[X]$. Let G be an open set in Σ, and let $F : G \to C'$ be a complex valued function in G.

If U is an arbitrary parametric disc

$$U = \{\theta \in S(\theta_0) : |z(\theta) - z(\theta_0)| < \xi\}$$

then the map $z : \Sigma \to X$ restricted to $U(z|_U)$ defines a homeomorphism between U and $z(U) : \{s : |s - z(\theta_0)| < \xi\}$. The function F is said to be analytic in G when for any $\theta_0 \in G$ and for any parametric disc U with centre θ_0, the complex function $s \mapsto F\{(z|_U)^{-1}(s)\}$ is analytic in the disc $z(U) = \{s : |s - z(\theta_0)| < \xi\}$. An analytic function of special importance in algebroid Riemann surfaces is the centre function $\theta \mapsto z(\theta)$. Now, any such θ can be expressed as a power series

$$\theta = \sum_{k=0}^{\infty} a_i [s - s_0]^k, \qquad s_0 = z(\theta)$$

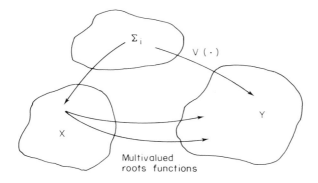

$$\Sigma_i$$

$$V(\cdot)$$

$$Y$$

$$X$$

Multivalued
roots functions

FIG. 2.1

so that by defining the so called *value function* $V:\Sigma \to C^1$ as

$$V(\theta) = a_0$$

and recalling the definition of Σ, then a_0 is the root of the complex polynomial $\phi_{s_0}[\lambda]$ around which the power series for θ was constructed.

Let Y be the complex region formed with all roots of the complex polynomial $\phi_s[\lambda]$ when s described X. Graphically the relationships between the spaces X, Σ and Y are represented in Fig. 2.1. The multivalued function which assigns each $s \in X$ to the roots of $\phi_s[\lambda]$ can be written as $V \circ z^{-1}$. The multivalued character of the roots function is then absorbed in z^{-1} leaving $V(\cdot)$ as a single valued function which will be shown to be analytic. The practical advantage of this approach is not immediately clear, since the usual problem is to relate a complex region X with the image of X under the roots function, and the difficulty of this problem lies in the multivalued character of such a map. It is not apparent how this difficulty is resolved by introducing the single valued function $V(\cdot)$, since it requires the introduction of an abstract space Σ and furthermore the multivalued character is simply transformed to z^{-1}. The answer to these questions lies in:

(a) The multivalued character is associated with z^{-1} for many multivalued maps in X, that is, a large number of multivalued maps in X can be written as $F \circ z^{-1}$ where $F:\Sigma \to C'$ is a single valued function. Had Σ and z not been introduced, the complex process of investigating each multivalued function in turn would be necessary.

(b) Although Σ is an abstract surface, its topological properties are very closely related with the topological properties of X (see

Sections 2.3 and 2.4). Therefore, to relate the topological properties of X and Y, it is natural to achieve it through Σ, since the
topological properties of X and Σ are closely related, and because
$V : \Sigma \to Y$ is single valued, it is likely that there exists a simple
relationship between the topological properties of Σ and Y.

Following this digression it is now shown that the value function
$V : \Sigma \to C^1$ is an analytic function. Let U be a parametric disc with centre
θ_0, for any $s \in z(U)$, $(z|_U)^{-1}(s)$ is the function element with centre x,
which is an immediate continuation of θ_0. Let $s_0 = z(\theta_0)$ and suppose that
θ_0 is the power series

$$\theta_0(w) = \sum_{k=0}^{\infty} a_k(w - s_0)^k$$

Since θ is an immediate continuation of θ_0, then

$$\theta(w) = \sum_{k=0}^{\infty} a_k'(w - s)^k = \sum_{k=0}^{\infty} a_k\{(w - s) + (s - s_0)\}^k$$

for any w in the intersection of the disc of convergence of both series. In
particular for $w = s$,

$$V(\theta) = \theta_0(s) = \sum_{k=0}^{\infty} a_k(s - s_0)^k \tag{2.9}$$

Consequently for any $s \in z(U)$, $s \mapsto V\{(z|_U)^{-1}(s)\}$ is given by the series

$$\sum_{k=0}^{\infty} a_k(s - s_0)^k$$

and therefore must be analytic.

Let $F : \Sigma \to C'$ be an analytic function in some open set $G \subset \Sigma$, then for
any parametric disc U the complex function $s \mapsto F[(z|_U)^{-1}(s)]$ is differen-
tiable. Let $f'(s)$ be such a derivative, then $s \mapsto f'(s)$ is analytic and
furthermore

$$f'(s_0) = \lim_{s \to s_0} \frac{1}{(s - s_0)} \{F[(z|_U)^{-1}(s)] - F[(z|_U)^{-1}(s_0)]\}$$

Let $\theta_0 = (z|_U)^{-1}(s_0)$ and $\theta = (z|_U)^{-1}(s)$, so

$$f'(s_0) = \lim_{\substack{\theta \in S(\theta_0) \\ z(\theta) \to z(\theta_0)}} \left\{ \frac{F(\theta) - F(\theta_0)}{z(\theta) - z(\theta_0)} \right\}$$

The derivative of an analytic function in Σ can now be defined as

$$F'(\theta_0) = \lim_{\substack{\theta \in S(\theta_0) \\ z(\theta) \to z(\theta_0)}} \left\{ \frac{F(\theta) - F(\theta_0)}{z(\theta) - z(\theta_0)} \right\} \tag{2.10}$$

This derivative is well defined and is such that

$$F'\{(z\mid_U)^{-1}(s)\} = \frac{d}{ds}F\{(z\mid_U)^{-1}(s)\} \tag{2.11}$$

Hence $\theta \mapsto F'(\theta)$ is also an analytic function in G. Identically derivatives of higher order can be defined, for example from (2.9) and (2.11)

$$V^{(k)}(\theta_0) = k!\, a_k$$

Let $\hat{f}$ be a path in Σ; $\hat{f}$ is said to be rectifiable when the path $z \circ \hat{f}$ is rectifiable. Also the *length* of $\hat{f}$ is defined as the length in X of the path $z \circ \hat{f}$. Similar to the definitions for paths in the complex plane, an arc in Σ is a rectifiable path and a loop is a closed arc.

Given an open set G in Σ, an analytic function $F : G \to C'$ and an arc $\hat{f}$ in G, the integral $\int_f F(\theta)\, dz(\theta)$ is defined as

$$\int_f F(\theta)\, dz(\theta) = \int_0^1 F\{f(t)\}\, dz\{f(t)\} \tag{2.12}$$

THEOREM 2.12 (Springer, 1957)   *Let F be an analytic function in open set G of Σ. If f and f' are homotopic in G, then*

$$\int_f F(\theta)\, dz(\theta) = \int_{f'} F(\theta)\, dz(\theta)$$

COROLLARY 2.3 (Cauchy's theorem)   *If $F : G \to C'$ is an analytic function in an open set G of Σ and f is a homotopically trivial loop in G, then*

$$\int_f F(\theta)\, dz(\theta) = 0$$

Let $C = \{f_i\}_{i=1}^N$ be a contour in an open set $G \subset \Sigma$ formed by loops. Let $\theta \mapsto F(\theta)$ be analytic in G and define

$$\int_C F(\theta)\, dz(\theta) = \sum_{i=1}^N \int_{f_i} F(\theta)\, dz(\theta)$$

Also set $\underset{\sim}{C}$ be an associate loop of C, then for appropriate arcs ϕ_i,

$$\underset{\sim}{C} = \bigoplus_{i=1}^N (\phi_i \oplus f_i \oplus \bar{\phi}_i)$$

Hence

$$\int_{\underset{\sim}{C}} F(\theta)\, dz(\theta) = \sum_{i=1}^N \int_{\phi_i} F(\theta)\, dz(\theta) + \int_{f_i} F(\theta)\, dz(\theta) + \int_{\bar{\phi}_i} F(\theta)\, dz(\theta)$$

But since

$$\int_{\phi_i} F(\theta)\, dz(\theta) = -\int_{\bar{\phi}_i} F(\theta)\, dz(\theta)$$

then

$$\int_C F(\theta)\, dz(\theta) = \int_C F(\theta)\, dz(\theta)$$

And so the integral of F along any associated loop of the contour C coincides with the integral along the contour.

2.6 SINGULAR POINTS

Consider a compact simple region Ω in the complex plane and an irreducible polynomial $\phi[\lambda]$ over $H(\Omega)$. It has been assumed throughout that for each $s \in \Omega$, $\phi_s[\lambda]$ has n distinct roots. This restriction is now removed by allowing points $s_0, s_1, \ldots, s_k, \ldots$ in Ω for which the complex polynomials

$$\phi_{w_k}[\lambda] = a_0(w_k) + a_1(w_k)\lambda + \ldots + a_{n-1}(w_k)\lambda^{n-1} + \lambda^n$$

have multiple roots. The points $s_0, s_1, \ldots, s_k, \ldots$ are called *singular points*.

Suppose that for each $s \in \Omega$ the n roots $\lambda_i(s)$, $i = 1, 2, \ldots, n$ (not necessarily distinct) of $\phi_s[\lambda]$ are known. And define the complex number $D(s)$ as

$$D(s) = \prod_{k=1}^{n} \prod_{j<k} [\lambda_j(s) - \lambda_k(s)]^2 \tag{2.13}$$

which is clearly symmetrical in the roots $\lambda_i(s)$. It can be shown (Hille, 1962) that $s \mapsto D(s)$ defines an analytic function in some open set containing Ω. The function $D(s)$ is called the *discriminant* of $\phi[\lambda]$.

Now, since $s \mapsto D(s)$ is analytic in an open set containing the compact set Ω, there are at most a finite number of zeros of $s \mapsto D(s)$ and at most a finite number of singular points of $\phi[\lambda]$ in Ω. Let $s_1, s_2, \ldots, s_m$ be the collection of all such singular points; the region $X = \Omega - \{s_1, s_2, \ldots, s_m\}$ is now a simple region with m punctures and satisfies Hypothesis 2.1. Hence an algebroid Riemann surface Σ can be generated by X and by $\phi[\lambda]$. The relationships between the function elements $\theta \in \Sigma$, whose centres $z(\theta)$ are in a neighbourhood of the singular points s_k, are now explored.

Consider an arbitrary point s_0 in the collection of singular points. Let

λ_0 be a multiple root of $\phi_{s_0}[\lambda]$ and let $N < n$ be its multiplicity. For appropriate analytic functions $s \mapsto \alpha_k(s)$,

$$\phi_s[\lambda] = \alpha_0(s) + \sum_{k=N}^{n} \alpha_k(s)(\lambda - \lambda_0)^k \qquad (2.14)$$

with $\alpha_0(s_0) = \alpha_1(s_0) = \ldots = \alpha_{N-1}(s_0) = 0$, $\alpha_N(s_0) \neq 0$ and $\alpha_n(s) = 1$. The function $s \mapsto \alpha_0(s)$ coincides with $s \mapsto \phi_{\lambda_0}(s)$ and is shown in the following section to be of particular significance. Let M be the multiplicity of the zero s_0 of such a function; in a neighbourhood of s_0, $\alpha_0(s)$ can be written as

$$\alpha_0(s) = \frac{(s - s_0)^M}{M!} \alpha_0^{(M)}(s) + 0[(s - s_0)^{M+1}] \qquad (2.15)$$

where $0[x^m]$ represents an infinitesimum in x of order at least m.

In a region $D \times U$ of $C \times C^1$ where

$$\begin{aligned} D &= \{s : 0 < |s - s_0| \leq \xi\} \\ U &= \{\lambda : 0 < |\lambda - \lambda_0| \leq \delta\} \end{aligned} \qquad (2.16)$$

The function $(s, \lambda) \mapsto \phi_s[\lambda]$ can be written as

$$\phi_s[\lambda] = \alpha_0^{(M)} \frac{(s - s_0)^M}{M!} + \alpha_N(s_0)(\lambda - \lambda_0)^N + \Delta(\lambda - \lambda_0, s - s_0) \qquad (2.17)$$

where $\Delta(\lambda, s)$ is of the form

$$\Delta(\lambda - \lambda_0, s - s_0) = 0[(s - s_0)^{M+1}] + 0[(\lambda - \lambda_0)^{N+1}] + 0(s - s_0)0[(\lambda - \lambda_0)^N]$$

If $\phi_s[\lambda] = 0$, then

$$(\lambda - \lambda_0)^N = a(s - s_0)^M - \frac{1}{\alpha_N(s_0)} \Delta(\lambda - \lambda_0, s - s_0) \qquad (2.18)$$

where

$$a = -\frac{\alpha_0^{(M)}(s_0)}{M! \, \alpha_N(s_0)}$$

From Theorem 9.4.2 (Hille, 1959) the following proposition holds:

PROPOSITION 2.7 *For sufficiently small ξ and δ in 2.16 and for each $s \in D$ there exists exactly N distinct roots $\lambda_1(s), \lambda_2(s), \ldots, \lambda_N(s)$ of 2.14 in U. Each root tends to λ_0 when s tends to s_0. Moreover $\lambda_1(s), \lambda_2(s), \ldots, \lambda_N(s)$ are also roots of a polynomial*

$$\psi[\lambda] = b_0(s) + b_1(s)(\lambda - \lambda_0) + \ldots + b_{N-1}(s)(\lambda - \lambda_0) + (\lambda - \lambda_0)^N \qquad (2.19)$$

of degree N whose coefficients $s \mapsto b_k(s)$ are analytic functions in D and tend to zero when $s \mapsto s_0$.

For sufficiently small ξ, every singular point of $\phi[\lambda]$ can be excluded from D. Therefore each $s \in D$ and for each of the N roots of $\lambda_k(s)$, there exists a unique function element $\theta_k \in z^{-1}(s)$ for which $V(\theta_k) = \lambda_k$. Let Σ_0 be the subspace of Σ formed with all such function elements, that is, Σ_0 is the set of all $\theta \in \Sigma$ such that $z(\theta) \in D$ and $V(\theta) \in U$, or in simple terms, Σ_0 is the set of Σ defined by the roots $\lambda(s)$ of (2.14) which are close to λ_0 when s is close to s_0.

Heuristically (2.18) can be written as

$$(\lambda - \lambda_0)^N \simeq a(s - s_0)^M \qquad (2.20)$$

Hence for a given $s \in D$, the N function elements θ with centre s which lie in Σ_0, are precisely those for which

$$V(\theta) - \lambda \simeq [a(s - s_0)^M]^{N^{-1}}$$

each one being specified by one of the N determinations of $[a(s - s_0)^M]^{N^{-1}}$.

Various questions arise concerning the global structure of Σ. Is it connected? If not, what are the relationships between its elements? To begin with, consider the second part of Proposition 2.7: suppose initially that the polynomial $\psi[\lambda]$ is irreducible in D; then D and $\psi[\lambda]$ will generate an algebroid Riemann surface Σ' which is connected and a complete analytic function in the sense of Weierstrass (Theorem 2.9). Let $z':\Sigma' \to D$ and $V':\Sigma' \to U$ be respectively the centre function and the value function in Σ'. From Theorem 2.8 it can be shown that for each $s \in D$ and $\theta \in z^{-1}(s)$ there exists one and only one $\theta' \in (z')^{-1}(s)$ such that $V'(\theta) \equiv V(\theta)$. From which it follows

PROPOSITION 2.8   *If the polynomial $\psi[\lambda]$ (defined by (2.19)) is irreducible over $H(D)$, then Σ_0 can be identified with the algebroid Riemann surface generated by D and $\psi[\lambda]$.*

If the polynomial $\psi[\lambda]$ is not irreducible over $H(D)$, it can be factored into a number of irreducible polynomials

$$\psi[\lambda] = \psi_1[\lambda]\psi_2[\lambda] \ldots \psi_p[\lambda]$$

of degrees $N_1, N_2, \ldots, N_p$ respectively. Each polynomial $\psi_i[\lambda]$ will generate with D an algebroid Riemann surface Σ_i. Repeating the arguments of Proposition 2.8, the following proposition holds:

PROPOSITION 2.9   *If the polynomial $\psi[\lambda]$ can be factored into p irreducible* *polynomials*

$$\psi[\lambda] = \psi_1[\lambda]\psi_2[\lambda]\ldots\psi_p[\lambda]$$

then Σ_0 is the disjoint union of p components $\Sigma_1, \Sigma_2, \ldots, \Sigma_p$ such that each Σ_i can be identified with an algebroid Riemann surface generated by D and $\psi_i[\lambda]$.

The components Σ_i can now be considered in more detail; it has been shown that for each $s \in D$ there are N_i function elements of Σ_0 in Σ_i (N_i is the degree of ψ_i). It is now demonstrated that this number of function elements is the same for each component Σ_i, that is, every polynomial $\psi_i[\lambda]$ has the same degree.

Consider a loop σ describing the boundary of D

$$\sigma(t) = s_0 + \xi \exp(j2\pi t), \qquad t \in [0, 1]$$

Let $s_1 = s_0 + \xi$ be the origin of σ. Under these conditions

PROPOSITION 2.10   *Let Σ_i be one of the components of Σ_0 and let θ, θ' be arbitrary in $(z/\Sigma_i)^{-1}(s_1)$. Then there exists an integer k such that*

$$\theta = \xrightarrow[\sigma^k]{} \theta'$$

Proof   Because Σ_i is a complete analytic function in the sense of Weierstrass (Theorem 2.9), there exists a path f in D such that $\theta = \xrightarrow[f]{} \theta'$. Also since $z(\theta) - z(\theta')$, f is a closed path.

Because D is a simple region with one puncture, the fundamental group $\pi(D, s_1)$ can be identified with a free abelian group of one generator. Moreover the homotopy class containing σ can be identified with the generator of the group. Hence for some integer k, f is homotopic with σ^k, and so

$$\theta = \xrightarrow[f]{} \theta' = \xrightarrow[\sigma^k]{} \theta' \qquad\qquad \square$$

PROPOSITION 2.11   *Let c_i be a minimum contour generated in Σ_i by σ and $\psi_i[\lambda]$. Then c_i is a closed path.*

Proof   Let θ_1 be arbitrary in $(z/\Sigma_i)^{-1}(s_1)$ and m be the smallest integer such that $\theta_1 = \xrightarrow[\sigma^m]{} \theta_1$. Then m must coincide with N_i otherwise the set

$$(z/\Sigma_i)^{-1}(s_1) - \left\{\theta_1, \xrightarrow[\sigma]{} \theta_1, \ldots, \xrightarrow[\sigma^{m-1}]{} \theta_1\right\}$$

is non-empty and each θ in such a set is distinct from every $\xrightarrow[\sigma^k]{} \theta_1$, $k = 1, 2, \ldots$ (which contradicts Proposition 2.10). Now, since $m = N_i$, c_i must coincide with $\xrightarrow[\sigma^{N_i}]{} \theta_i$ as every $\theta \in (z/\Sigma_1)^{-1}(s_1)$ lies in such a path. $\square$

Let $\theta_1 \in \Sigma_0$ have centre s_1, and let m be the smallest integer for which

$$\theta_1 = \xrightarrow[\sigma^m]{} \theta_1$$

From the previous proposition, $m = N_i$ (Σ_i being the component of Σ_0 which contains θ_1). And from (2.18)

$$(\lambda - \lambda_0)^N = a(s - s_0)^M - \frac{\Delta(\lambda - \lambda_0, s - s_0)}{\alpha_N(s_0)} \tag{2.21}$$

where λ is any root of (2.14).

For sufficiently small ξ and δ we can set

$$\sup_{(s,\lambda) \in D \times U} \left| \frac{\Delta(\lambda, s)}{\alpha_N(s_0)} \right| < |a| \, \xi^M$$

Hence when s describes the circle σ, M times, the corresponding root $\lambda(s)$ (defined by analytic continuation of θ_1) describes a closed path which encircles the point λ_0, N times. Moreover this encirclement condition is independent of the point s_1 and of the function element θ_1, which defines the origin of the path described by $\lambda(s)$.

The question now arises concerning the relationship between the integers M and N (the multiplicity of the root λ_0 of the complex polynomial $\phi_{s_0}[\lambda]$) and M (the multiplicity of the zero $s = s_0$ of the analytic function $s \mapsto \phi_{\lambda_0}[s]$). The integer m is the least number of times the circle σ need be described in order to close the path described by $\lambda(s)$. Considering (2.19) it is observed that m is the smallest integer for which mM is a multiple of N. Note that if s describes σ, then $s = s_0 + \xi \exp(j2\pi t)$ and from (2.18).

$$(\lambda - \lambda_0) \simeq \eta a^{N-1} \xi^{N-1} \exp\left(j\frac{M}{N} 2\pi t \right)$$

where η is some Nth root of unity.

In conclusion the least integer m for which

$$\theta_1 = \xrightarrow[\sigma^m]{} \theta_1$$

holds is the smallest integer for which mM is a multiple of N. Moreover it has been shown that m is independent of the origin s_1 of σ and of the function element $\theta_1 \in (z/\Sigma_0)^{-1}(s_1)$ that defined the origin of the path described by λ. So m is independent of the component Σ_i which contains θ_1. Since $m = N_i$, it follows that the degrees $N_1, N_2, \ldots, N_p$ of the polynomials $\psi_1[\lambda], \psi_2[\lambda], \ldots, \psi_p[\lambda]$ all coincide with m, and because

$N_1 + N_2 + \ldots + N_p = N$

$$p = \frac{N}{m} \tag{2.22}$$

It is now clear that the components Σ_i are constructed in a similar manner to that used in the definition of minimum contour. Let s_1 be the origin of σ, and let θ_1 be arbitrary in $(z/\Sigma_0)^{-1}$. For $k = 0, 1, 2, \ldots, m-1$ the function elements $\xrightarrow[\sigma^k]{} \theta_1$ are contained in the same component of Σ_0 since they are reached through analytic continuations of θ_1 along path in D; let Σ_1 be such a component. The remaining function elements $\theta \in \Sigma_1$ can also be defined as being the result of analytic continuations of θ_1 along suitable paths in D. A function element $\theta_2 \in \Sigma_0$ whose centre is s_1 and which does not coincide with any one of $\xrightarrow[\sigma^k]{} \theta_1$, $k = 0, 1, \ldots, m-1$, cannot be reached from θ_1 by analytic continuation along a path in D. Therefore define a new component of Σ_0, say Σ_2, and the remaining elements of Σ_2 are all analytic continuations of θ_2 along paths in D. The p components of Σ_0 can be constructed in this manner. Each component will contain exactly m of the N function elements in each $(z/\Sigma_0)^{-1}(s)$, $s \in D$.

For simplicity let $z_i(\cdot)$ and $V_i(\cdot)$ represent the respective maps $z(\cdot)$ restricted to Σ_i and $V(\cdot)$ restricted to Σ_i. It has just been shown that $z_i^{-1}(s)$ has exactly m distinct function elements, therefore $s \mapsto V_i(z_i^{-1}(s))$ does not define a single valued function. It will be interesting to be able to define an analytic complex function which has the same values as the multivalued map $s \mapsto V_i(z_i^{-1}(s))$. To achieve this, consider the disc $W = \{w : 0 < |w| \le \xi^{m^{-1}}\}$ in the complex w-plane and consider the map $\rho : W \to D$ defined by

$$\rho(w) = s_0 + w^m \tag{2.23}$$

Let w_0 be the positive real mth root of ξ, then

$$\rho(w_0) = s_0 + w_0^m = s_0 + \xi = s_1$$

Consider now the closed paths C_i, $i = 1, 2, \ldots, p$, which according to Proposition 2.11 coincide with the minimum contours generated in Σ_i by the polynomials $\psi_i[\lambda]$ and by σ, and let $\theta_i \in z_i^{-1}(s_1)$ be the origin of C_i. If in the power series $\theta_i = \sum\limits_{k=0}^{\infty} a_k(s - s_1)^k$, s is replaced by $s_0 + w^m = s_0 + [(w - w_0) + w_0]^m$ and s_1 by $s_0 + w_0^m$, then a power series in w is obtained with centre w_0. Such a power series can be analytically continued along a path f in W. However, the derived power series in w is simply the power series obtained from $\xrightarrow[\rho \circ f]{} \theta_i$ on replacing s by $s_0 + [(w - w_0) + w_0]^m$ and s_1 by $s_0 + w_0^m$.

Consider the particular case when f is a closed path in W. Let γ be a circular loop describing the boundary of W

$$\gamma(t) = w_0 \exp(j2\pi t)$$

Since W is also a simple region with a single puncture, the closed path f must be homotopic with γ^k for some integer k, so

$$\xrightarrow[\rho \circ f]{} \theta_i = \xrightarrow[\rho \circ \gamma^k]{} \theta_i = \xrightarrow[(\rho \circ \gamma)^k]{} \theta_i$$

from the definitions of σ and γ it is clear that

$$\rho \circ \gamma = \sigma^m$$

and so

$$\xrightarrow[\rho \circ f]{} \theta_i = \xrightarrow[\sigma^{mk}]{} \theta_i = \theta_i$$

as

$$\xrightarrow[\sigma^m]{} \theta_i \equiv \theta_i$$

It then follows that the analytic continuation of the w-power series θ_i by an arbitrary closed path W coincides with the proper θ_i. Consequently, if w is any point of W and f any path in W with origin w_0 and extremity w, the function element $\theta = \xrightarrow[\rho \circ f]{} \theta_i$ is independent of the particular path used.

Two important conclusions can now be made: the first concerns the power series θ_i when s is replaced by $s_0 + w^m$. Because its analytic continuation for a certain point w does not depend upon the path used but only on the extremity of the path, the series must define a holomorphic function in W. The value of this function at a point $w' \in W$ is then given by the sum for $w = w'$ of

$$\theta = \sum_{k=0}^{\infty} a_k (s - \rho(w'))^k, \qquad s = s_0 + w^m$$

where $\theta = \xrightarrow[\rho \circ f]{} \theta_i$ with $0(f) = w_0$ and $e(f) = w'$, that is, the value of the function at w' coincides with $V_i(\theta)$. Formally we can then define a homomorphic function in W, $w \mapsto F_i(w)$ as

$$F_i(w) = V_i\left(\xrightarrow[\rho \circ f]{} \theta_i\right) \tag{2.24}$$

where f is any path satisfying $0(f) = w_0$ and $e(f) = w$.

The second conclusion (implicit in the first) is that a single valued function $h_i : W \to \Sigma_i$ can be defined as

$$h_i(w) = \xrightarrow[\rho \circ f]{} \theta_i \tag{2.25}$$

where, again, f is any path in W with origin w_0 and extremity w. Furthermore there is a very close relationship between W and Σ_i, expressed in:

PROPOSITION 2.12   The   map $h_i : W \to \Sigma$ defined   by   (2.25)   is   a homeomorphism.

Proof   Suppose that for w, $w' \in W$, $h_i(w) = h_i(w')$; let $\theta = h_i(w) - h_i(w')$. Since $z(\theta) = \rho(w) - \rho(w')$ (see (2.25)), then

$$s_0 + w^m = s_0 + (w')^m$$

This ensures that there exists an integer k such that $|k| < m$ and such that

$$w' = w \exp\left(j2\pi \frac{k}{m}\right)$$

Let g be the arc in W

$$g(t) = w \exp\left(j2\pi \frac{k}{m} t\right), \qquad t \in [0, 1]$$

That is, g is a circular arc with origin w and extremity w'. Since the value of $h_i(w')$ is independent of the path used, then

$$\theta = h_i(w') = \xrightarrow[\rho \circ (f \oplus g)]{} \theta_i \tag{2.26}$$

Let f and g be paths in D defined respectively as $\rho \circ f$ and $\rho \circ g$. From (2.26) it follows that

$$\theta_i = \xrightarrow[\tilde{f}]{} \theta$$

So

$$\theta_i = \xrightarrow[\tilde{f}]{} \left(\xrightarrow[\tilde{f} \oplus \tilde{g}]{} \theta_i \right) = \xrightarrow[\tilde{f} \oplus \tilde{g} \oplus \tilde{f}]{} \theta_i \tag{2.27}$$

We note that $\tilde{g}$ is a closed path with origin $\rho(w)$ which encircles the point s_0, k times,

$$\tilde{g}(t) = s_0 + g(t)^m = s_0 + w^m \exp(j2\pi kt)$$

Therefore the path $\tilde{f} \oplus \tilde{g} \oplus \tilde{f}$ is also a closed path which encircles the origin the same k times; however, the origin $\tilde{f} \oplus \tilde{g} \oplus \tilde{f}$ is the point $s_1 = s_0 + \xi$.

Alternatively from (2.27), $\tilde{f} \oplus \tilde{g} \oplus \tilde{f}$ must be homotopic with a closed path of the form $(\sigma^m)^q$ for some integer q, since they are the only paths which satisfy

$$\theta_i = \xrightarrow[(\sigma^m)^q]{} \theta_i$$

That is, $k = qm$ for some integer q. However, $|k| < m$, so $q = 0$ and $k = 0$ and therefore $w \equiv w'$.

We have shown that $w \mapsto h_i(w)$ is one to one; it is also an onto map, since given any $s \in D$, m different values of w can be found which satisfy $\rho(w) = s$.

Defining $\theta = h_i(w)$ we obtain, as above, m distinct function elements whose centre is s. These m function elements constitute the totality of all function elements in $z_i^{-1}(s)$, since there are only m function elements in $z_i^{-1}(s)$. Therefore every $\theta \in z_i^{-1}(s)$ is of the form $\theta = h_i(w)$ for some $w \in \rho^{-1}(s)$. So in conclusion $h_i : W \to \Sigma_i$ is an isomorphism.

Consider now an arbitrary parametric disc U with centre in $\theta = h_i(w)$. The map $z|_U \equiv z_i|_U$ defines a homeomorphism between U and a disc U in D with centre $z(\theta)$ (see Theorem 2.7). For a sufficiently small disc O around w, ρ defines a homeomorphism between O and $\rho(O) \subset U_0$. So $h_i|_O = (z|_U)^{-1} \circ \rho$ defines a local homeomorphism between O and $h_i(O)$. Consequently both $h_i(\cdot)$ and $h_i^{-1}(\cdot)$ are continuous, completing the proof that h_i is an homeomorphism.   □

COROLLARY 2.4   *Any two components Σ_i and Σ_j of Σ_0 are homeomorphic to each other.*

Proof   Both Σ_i and Σ_j are homeomorphic to W.   □

It is now possible to establish the main result of this section:

THEOREM 2.13: LOCAL PRINCIPLE OF THE ARGUMENT FOR SINGULAR POINTS   *In the context of the definitions of this section, let $\hat{\sigma} = \{C_i\}_{i=1}^p$ be the minimum contour generated in Σ_0 by σ. Then for suflciently small ξ*

$$\frac{1}{2\pi j} \int_{\hat{\sigma}} \frac{dV(\theta)}{V(\theta) - \lambda_0} = M$$

Proof   The integral

$$\frac{1}{2\pi j} \int_{\hat{\sigma}} \frac{dV(\theta)}{V(\theta) - \lambda_0}$$

can be evaluated as

$$\sum_{i=1}^p I_i$$

where

$$I_i \triangleq \frac{1}{2\pi j} \int_{C_i} \frac{dV(\theta)}{V(\theta) - \lambda_0}$$

2. RIEMANN SURFACES AND THE GENERALIZED PRINCIPLE 71

In I_i the integral is calculated along a closed path in Σ_i. Furthermore

$$I_i = \frac{1}{2\pi j} \int_{C_i} \frac{dV_i(\theta)}{V_i(\theta) - \lambda_0}$$

Utilizing the homeomorphism $h_i : W \to \Sigma_i$, given that the homeomorphic function $w \mapsto F_i(w)$ (see (2.24)) is defined as $F_i = V_i \circ h_i$ and that $C_i = h_i \circ \gamma$ (where $\gamma(t) = w_0 \exp(j2\pi t)$) defines the boundary of W, we obtain

$$\frac{1}{2\pi j} \int_{C_i} \frac{dV_i(\theta)}{V_i(\theta) - \lambda_0} = \frac{1}{2\pi j} \int_{\gamma} \frac{dF_i(w)}{F_i(w) - \lambda_0} \qquad (2.28)$$

The function $w \mapsto F_i(w)$ is defined and analytic in the region $W = \{w : 0 < |w| \leq \xi^{m-1}\}$. Is it possible to extend the domain of such a function to the whole disc $\bar{W} = \{w : |w| \leq \xi^{m-1}\}$?

From Proposition 2.7 every root $\lambda(s)$ of $\phi_s[\lambda] = 0$ which defines an element $\theta \in \Sigma_0$ tends to λ_0 when s tends to s_0. Therefore when w tends to the origin, $s = \rho(w)$ tends to s_0 and therefore $F_i(w)$, as a root of $\phi_s[\lambda]$, tends to λ_0. In conclusion $\lim_{w \to 0} F_i(w) = \lambda_0$ for all $i = 1, 2, \ldots, p$. Using now the Riemann extension theorem (Kendig, 1977) $w \mapsto F_i(w)$ can be extended to a holomorphic function defined in the whole disc $\bar{W} = \{w : |w| \leq \xi^{m-1}\}$ if $F_i(0)$ is defined in λ_0.

The classical Principle of the Argument (Hille, 1959) can now be utilized in evaluating the integral (2.28). Since $w \mapsto F_i(w) - \lambda_0$ is a holomorphic function in $\bar{W}$, the integral (2.28) coincides with the number of zeros in $\bar{W}$ of the function $w \mapsto F_i(w) - \lambda_0$, each zero counting as many times as its multiplicity. For sufficiently small ξ, the origin is the unique zero of $w \mapsto F_i(w) - \lambda_0$ in $\bar{W}$, we have only to determine the multiplicity of the zero.

It has been shown that m is the smallest integer for which mM is a multiple of N. Then let q be an integer satisfying $mM = qN$. From (2.21)

$$(F_i(w) - \lambda_0)^N = aw^{mM} - \frac{1}{\alpha_N(s_0)} \Delta(F_i(w) - \lambda_0, w^m)$$

So

$$|w^{-q}(F_i(w) - \lambda_0)| = \left| a - \frac{1}{\alpha_N(s_0)} w^{-mM} \Delta(F_i(w) - \lambda_0, w^m) \right|^{N-1}$$

But since $\lim_{w \to 0} w^{-mM} \Delta(F_i(w) - \lambda_0, s^m) = 0$, then $\lim_{w \to 0} |w^{-q}(F_i(w) - \lambda_0)| = |a| \neq 0$. The multiplicity of the zero $w = 0$ of the function $w \mapsto F_i(w) - \lambda_0$ is therefore q. So

$$\frac{1}{2\pi j} \int_{C_i} \frac{dV_i(\theta)}{V_i(\theta) - \lambda_0} = q, \quad \text{for} \quad i = 1, 2, \ldots, p.$$

In conclusion

$$\frac{1}{2\pi j}\int_{\hat{\sigma}}\frac{dV(\theta)}{V(\theta)-\lambda_0}=\frac{1}{2\pi j}\sum_{i=1}^{p}\int_{C_i}\frac{dV_i(\theta)}{V_i(\theta)-\lambda_0}=pq.$$

However, from (2.22) $p = N/m$ and $q \triangleq mM/N$ so $pq = M$.   □

2.7 THE GENERALIZED PRINCIPLE OF THE ARGUMENT

In this final section we establish the main result of this chapter—the Generalized Principle of the Argument—which is of crucial importance in establishing the stability of linear and nonlinear multivariable feedback systems.

We establish first a simple and local theorem for the Principle of the Argument. Let X be a simple region in the complex plane with punctures and $\phi[\lambda]$ an irreducible polynomial of degree n over $H(X)$, the set of all complex functions which are analytic in some open set containing X. Assume that X is free of all singular points of $\phi[\lambda]$ and let Σ be the algebroid Riemann surface generated by Σ and $\phi[\lambda]$. Let s_0 be a point of X and λ_0 one of the n distinct roots of the complex polynomials $\phi_{s_0}[\lambda]$. Finally let σ be a loop in X defined by

$$\sigma(t) = s_0 + \xi\exp{(j2\pi t)} \tag{2.29}$$

and let $\hat{\sigma}$ be a minimum contour generated in Σ by σ. Under these conditions we have;

THEOREM 2.14: LOCAL PRINCIPLE OF THE ARGUMENT   *For sufficiently small* ξ

$$\frac{1}{2\pi j}\int_{\hat{\sigma}}\frac{dV(\theta)}{V(\theta)-\lambda_0}=M$$

where M is the multiplicity of the zero $s = s_0$ of the complex function $s \mapsto \phi_{\lambda_0}(s)$.

Proof   By selecting ξ such that $0 < \xi \leq \min_{\theta \in z^{-1}(s_0)} R(\theta)$, the circular loop σ is contained in the region of convergence of every function element $\theta \in z^{-1}(s_0)$. Let θ_i, $i = 1, \ldots, n$ be the elements of $z^{-1}(s_0)$ and U_i, $i = 1, 2, \ldots, n$, the parametric disc with centre θ_i and radius ξ. The minimum contour $\hat{\sigma}$ generated by σ is then formed with n distinct loops $\gamma_1, \gamma_2, \ldots, \gamma_n$ and these loops are such that γ_i lies in the parametric disc U_i. So

$$\frac{1}{2\pi j}\int_{\hat{\sigma}}\frac{dV(\theta)}{V(\theta)-\lambda_0}=\frac{1}{2\pi j}\sum_{i=1}^{n}\int_{\gamma_i}\frac{dV(\theta)}{V(\theta)-\lambda_0}$$

It was shown in Section 2.5 that the function $s \mapsto F_i(s) \triangleq V\{(z|_{U_i})^{-1}(s)\}$ is well defined and holomorphic in the disc $\{s : |s - s_0| \leq \xi\}$ and coincides with the sum of the function elements θ_i; furthermore $z|_{U_i}$ defines an homeomorphism between $\{s : |s - s_0| \leq \xi\}$ and U_i. So

$$\frac{1}{2\pi j} \int_{\gamma_i} \frac{dV(\theta)}{V(\theta) - \lambda_0} = \frac{1}{2\pi j} \int_\sigma \frac{dF_i(s)}{F_i(s) - \lambda_0} \qquad (2.30)$$

Clearly since $F_i(s_0) = V(\theta_i)$ there exists a unique function $s \mapsto F_i(s)$ for which $F_i(s_0) = \lambda_0$. For simplicity assume that $s \mapsto F_1(s)$ is such a function, and hence the function $s \mapsto F_1(s) - \lambda_0$ has a zero at $s = s_0$. Moreover for sufficiently small ξ, s_0 is the unique zero of such a function in the interior of σ and every other function $s \mapsto F_i(s) - \lambda_0$, $i = 1, \ldots, n$ has no zeros in the interior of σ. Using now the classical Principle of the Argument (Hille, 1959) to evaluate (2.30).

$$\int_{\gamma_i} \frac{dF_i(s)}{F_i(s) - \lambda_0} = 0 \quad \text{for} \quad i = 2, \ldots, n$$

and that

$$\frac{1}{2\pi j} \int_{\hat{\sigma}} \frac{dV(\theta)}{V(\theta) - \lambda_0} = \frac{1}{2\pi j} \int_{\gamma_1} \frac{dF_1(s)}{F_1(s) - \lambda_0} = M^\#$$

where $M^\#$ is the multiplicity of the zero $s = s_0$ of the function $s \mapsto F_1(s) = \lambda_0$.

Now, $\phi_s[\lambda]$ can be written as

$$\phi_s[\lambda] = \alpha_0(s) + \alpha_1(s)(\lambda - \lambda_0) + \ldots + (\lambda - \lambda_0)^m \qquad (2.31)$$

with $\alpha_0(s_0) = 0$ and $\alpha_1(s_0) \neq 0$. The function $s \mapsto \alpha_0(s)$ coincides exactly with $s \mapsto \phi_{\lambda_0}(s)$. Then

$$\alpha_0(s) = (s - s_0)^M \frac{\alpha_0^{(M)}(s_0)}{M!} + 0[(s - s_0)^{M+1}]$$

Setting $a = -\alpha_0^{(M)}(s_0)[\alpha_1(s_0)M!]^{-1}$, $\phi_s[F_1(s)] = 0$ can be written as

$$F_1(s) = \lambda_0 = a(s - s_0)^M + \Delta(F_1(s) - \lambda_0, s - s_0) \qquad (2.32)$$

where $\Delta(\cdot, \cdot)$ is of the form

$$0[(s - s_0)^{M+1}] + 0(s - s_0)0(F_1(s) - \lambda_0) + 0[(F_1(s) - \lambda_0)^2]$$

Rearranging (2.32) and taking the limit as $s \to s_0$ gives

$$\lim_{s \to s_0} (s - s_0)^{-M}(F_1(s) - \lambda_0) = a \neq 0$$

So the multiplicity $M^{\#}$ of the zero $s = s_0$ of the function $s \mapsto F_1(s) - \lambda_0$ coincides with M. $\quad\square$

Only those polynomials $\phi[\lambda]$ whose coefficients are holomorphic functions in a prescribed simple region have been considered. In dynamical stability problems, polynomials with meromorphic coefficients are frequently encountered. A function $s \mapsto a(s)$ is meromorphic in a region Ω if it is holomorphic everywhere in Ω except at a finite set of points $\{s_1, s_2, \ldots, s_q\}$ (called *poles*); for each pole s_i there exists an integer m_i (called the *multiplicity* of the pole) and disc D_i with centre s_i such that $s \mapsto (s - s_i)^{m_i} a(s)$ is holomorphic and nonzero everywhere in D_i.

Therefore given a simple region Ω and an irreducible polynomial

$$\phi[\lambda] = a_0(s) + a_1(s)\lambda^n + \ldots + \lambda^n$$

with meromorphic coefficients; define a simple region with punctures, $\Omega' = \Omega - \{s_1, s_2, \ldots, s_q\}$ such that $\phi[\lambda]$ is an irreducible polynomial over $H[\Omega']$ for $\{s_1 - s_2, \ldots, s_q\}$ the collection of all poles of all coefficients $s \mapsto a_i(s)$. Consequently Ω' and $\phi[\lambda]$ can generate an algebroid Reimann surface Σ.

Consider now an arbitrary pole s_p and an arbitrary complex number λ_0, and let m_0 be the multiplicity of the pole s_p of the function $s \mapsto \phi_{\lambda_0}(s)$. Let D be a disc with centre s_p and radius $\xi > 0$ which is sufficiently small as to exclude from D every other pole or zero of $s \mapsto \phi_{\lambda_0}(s)$ and every singular point of $\phi[\lambda]$. Finally let σ be a loop in Ω' defined by

$$\sigma(t) = s_p + \xi \exp(j2\pi t)$$

and let $\hat\sigma$ be a minimum contour generated in Σ by σ. Under these conditions the following local Principle for the Argument holds for poles:

Theorem 2.15

$$\frac{1}{2\pi j} \int_{\hat\sigma} \frac{dV(\theta)}{V(\theta) - \lambda_0} = -m_0.$$

Proof   Write $\phi[\lambda]$ in D as

$$\phi[\lambda] = a_0(s) + a_1(s)(\lambda - \lambda_0) + \ldots + a_i(s)(\lambda - \lambda_0)^i + \ldots + (\lambda - \lambda_0)^n$$

with $a_0(s) = \phi_{\lambda_0}(s)$. Let m_i be the multiplicity of the pole s_p of the function $s \mapsto a_i(s)$, and let $m = \max_i m_i$. In the punctured disc $D_0 = D - \{s_p\}$ we can write

$$\phi(\lambda, s) = (s - s_p)^{-mn} \sum_{i=0}^{n} a_i(s)(s - s_p)^{m(n-i)}[(\lambda - \lambda_0)(s - s_p)^m]^i$$

Defining

$$a_i'(s) = a_i(s)(s - s_p)^{m(n-i)}$$
$$w = (\lambda - \lambda_0)(s - s_p)^m \tag{2.33}$$
$$\psi(w, s) = a_0'(s) + a_i'(s)w + \ldots + s^n,$$

we can see that every coefficient of the polynomial $\psi(w, s)$ is an analytic function in D and therefore defines with D a Riemann surface (say Σ_w).

Since $\phi(\lambda, s) = (s - s_p)^{-mn}\psi(w, s)$ and $w = (\lambda - \lambda_0)(s - s_p)^m$, every function element $\eta \in \Sigma_w$ with centre $s_0 \in D_0$ can be written as

$$\eta(s) = (\theta(s) - \lambda_0)[(s - s_0) + (s_0 - s_p)]^m \tag{2.34}$$

where θ is a function element of Σ. Then

$$z(\eta) = z(\theta)$$

and

$$V(\eta) = (V(\theta) - \lambda_0)[z(\theta) - s_p]^m$$

So

$$\frac{dV(\eta)}{V(\eta)} = \frac{dV(\theta)}{V(\theta) - \lambda_0} + m\frac{dz(\eta)}{z(\eta) - s_p} \tag{2.35}$$

Note that $\psi_0(s) = a_0'(s) = a_0(s)(s - s_p)^{mn} = a_0(s)(s - s_p)^{m_0}(s - s_0)^{mn-m_0}$. And because $a_0(s)(s - s_p)^{m_0}$ is a holomorphic non-zero function in D then $s \mapsto \psi_0(s)$ has in s_p a zero of multiplicity $mn - m_0$.

Let σ be a minimum contour generated in Σ_w by σ. Then from (2.35)

$$\frac{1}{2\pi j}\int_{\tilde{\sigma}} \frac{dV(\theta)}{V(\theta) - \lambda_0} = \frac{1}{2\pi j}\int_{\sigma} \frac{dV(\eta)}{V(\eta)} = m\frac{1}{2\pi j}\int_{\sigma} \frac{dz(\eta)}{z(\eta) - s_p}$$

The last term above can be written as

$$\frac{1}{2\pi j}\int_{\sigma} \frac{dz(\eta)}{z(\eta) - s_p} = \frac{1}{2\pi j}\int_{z(\sigma)} \frac{ds}{s - s_p}$$

and using Lemma 2.2 it follows that $z(\sigma)$ is homotopic to σ^n and therefore

$$\frac{1}{2\pi j}\int_{\sigma} \frac{dz(\eta)}{z(\eta) - s_p} = n$$

Invoking Theorems 2.13 or 2.14 (depending whether s_p is a singular point of $\psi[w]$), it follows that

$$\frac{1}{2\pi j}\int_{\sigma} \frac{dV(\eta)}{V(\eta)} = mn - m_0$$

Consequently

$$\frac{1}{2\pi j} \int_\sigma \frac{dV(\theta)}{V(\theta) - \lambda_0} = mn - m_0 - mn = -m_0 \qquad \square$$

The generalized Principle of the Argument can now be established as a consequence of Cauchy's theorem (Corollary 2.3) and the three local Principles of the Argument (Theorems 2.13, 2.14, 2.15). Let Ω be a bounded simple region of the complex plane and $\phi[\lambda]$ an irreducible polynomial of degree n whose coefficients are meromorphic in Ω. In general Ω contains both poles and singular points; as a result of Proposition 2.8 there are at most a finite collection $\{s_1, s_2, \ldots, s_q\}$ of singular points in Ω. Identically we can define the finite collection $\{z_1, z_2, \ldots, z_p\}$ of all poles of $\phi[\lambda]$ in Ω. Let $\partial\Omega$ be the boundary loop of Ω encircling Ω in the anticlockwise direction and assume that such a boundary is free of all poles or singular points.

The region

$$X = \Omega - \{s_1, \ldots, s_q\} - \{z_1, \ldots, z_p\} \qquad (2.36)$$

is now a simple region with $q + p$ punctures. X and $\phi[\lambda]$ both satisfy Hypothesis 2.1 and therefore an algebroid Riemann surface Σ can be generated by X and $\phi[\lambda]$.

Finally, consider an arbitrary complex number λ_0 distinct from any complex root of the polynomials $\phi_s[\lambda]$ when s describes $\partial\Omega$.

Under the above conditions we have:

THEOREM 2.16: GENERALIZED PRINCIPLE OF THE ARGUMENT   *Let $\partial\hat{\Omega}$ be a minimum contour generated in Σ by $\partial\Omega$, then*

$$\frac{1}{2\pi j} \int_{\partial\hat{\Omega}} \frac{dV(\theta)}{V(\theta) - \lambda_0} = N_z - N_p$$

where N_z and N_p represent respectively the number of zeros and poles in Ω of the complex function $s \mapsto \phi_{\lambda_0}(s)$, each zero or pole counting as many times as its multiplicity.

Proof   Let $w_1, w_2, \ldots, w_k$ be the zeros of $s \mapsto \phi_{\lambda_0}(s)$ in X and let $m_1, m_2, \ldots, m_k$ be their respective multiplicities. Let $n_1, n_2, \ldots, n_p$ be the multiplicity of the poles $z_1, z_2, \ldots, z_p$ of $s \mapsto \phi_{\lambda_0}(s)$ (if z_i is a pole of $\phi[\lambda]$ but not of $s \mapsto \phi_{\lambda_0}(s)$ we simply choose $n_i = 0$).

Let γ_i, $i = 1, 2, \ldots, r$, be a small circular loop in Ω with centre w_i described in the clockwise direction and with radius sufficiently small to exclude from its interior every zero (other than w_i) and every other singular point and every pole. Let σ_i, $i = 1, 2, \ldots, q$ and δ_i, $i = 1, 2, \ldots, r$

be similar loops around respectively each of the singular points and poles of $s \mapsto \phi_{\lambda_0}(s)$.

Finally consider the Riemann surface

$$\Sigma' = \Sigma - \bigcup_{i=1}^{r} z^{-1}(w_i)$$

where Σ' is the algebroid Riemann surface generated by $\phi[\lambda]$ and $X' = X - \{w_1, \ldots, w_r\}$.

The contour

$$\partial\Omega' = \{\partial\Omega, \gamma_1, \ldots, \gamma_r, \sigma_1, \ldots, \sigma_q, \delta_1, \ldots, \delta_p\} \tag{2.37}$$

is clearly homotopically trivial in X' (note that $\partial\Omega$ is described in the anticlockwise direction and every other loop is described in the clockwise direction). On utilizing Theorem 2.11, the minimum contour $\partial\hat{\Omega}'$ generated in Σ' by $\partial\Omega'$ is also homotopically trivial. Moreover the function $V'(\theta)/V(\theta) - \lambda_0$ is analytic in Σ' as all singularities of such a function correspond to zeros or poles of $s \mapsto \phi_{\lambda_0}(s)$, which by construction, are excluded from X'. Using Cauchy's theorem (Corollary 2.3)

$$\frac{1}{2\pi j} \int_{\partial\hat{\Omega}} \frac{dV(\theta)}{V(\theta) - \lambda_0} = 0 \tag{2.38}$$

The minimum contour $\partial\hat{\Omega}'$ must have the form

$$\partial\hat{\Omega}' = \{\partial\hat{\Omega}, \hat{\gamma}_1, \ldots, \hat{\gamma}_r, \hat{\sigma}_1, \ldots, \hat{\sigma}_q, \hat{\delta}_1, \ldots, \hat{\delta}_p\}$$

where $\hat{\gamma}_i$ is a minimum contour generated in Σ by γ_i, $\hat{\sigma}_i$ is generated by σ_i and $\hat{\delta}_i$ is generated by δ_i. From (2.38) we have

$$\frac{1}{2\pi j} \int_{\partial\hat{\Omega}} \frac{dV(\theta)}{V(\theta) - \lambda_0} = - \sum_{i=1}^{r} \frac{1}{2\pi j} \int_{\hat{\gamma}_i} \frac{dV(\theta)}{V(\theta) - \lambda_0} - \sum_{i=1}^{q} \frac{1}{2\pi j} \int_{\hat{\sigma}_i} \frac{dV(\theta)}{V(\theta) - \lambda_0}$$
$$- \sum_{i=1}^{p} \frac{1}{2\pi j} \int_{\hat{\delta}_i} \frac{dV(\theta)}{V(\theta) - \lambda_0} \tag{2.39}$$

Noting that γ_i is orientated in the clockwise direction, Theorem 2.14 yields

$$\frac{1}{2\pi j} \int_{\hat{\gamma}_i} \frac{dV(\theta)}{V(\theta) - \lambda_0} = -m_i \tag{2.40}$$

Consider

$$\frac{1}{2\pi j} \int_{\hat{\sigma}_i} \frac{dV(\theta)}{V(\theta) - \lambda_0}$$

if the singular point s_i is not a zero of $s \mapsto \phi_{\lambda_0}(s)$, then the integral is zero by Theorem 2.13. Assume that s_i is a zero of $s \mapsto \phi_{\lambda_0}(s)$ with multiplicity M_i. The minimum contour $\hat{\sigma}_i$ can be divided into two parts $\hat{\sigma}_i = \{\hat{\sigma}'_i, \hat{\sigma}''_i\}$ where $\hat{\sigma}'_i$ is generated by σ in the set of all function elements θ' for which $V(\theta')$ is *close* to λ_0 and when $z(\theta')$ is *close* to s_i, and similarly $\hat{\sigma}''_i$ is generated in the set of all function elements θ'' for which $z(\theta'')$ is *close* to s_i and $V(\theta'')$ is *close* to a root of $\phi_{s_i}[\lambda]$ distinct from λ_0. And so from Theorem 2.13

$$\frac{1}{2\pi j} \int_{\hat{\sigma}'} \frac{dV(\theta)}{V(\theta) - \lambda_0} = -M_i \quad \text{and} \quad \frac{1}{2\pi j} \int_{\hat{\sigma}''} \frac{dV(\theta)}{V(\theta) - \lambda_0} = 0$$

Combining the above with (2.40) gives

$$-\sum_{i=1}^{r} \frac{1}{2\pi j} \int_{\hat{\gamma}_i} \frac{dV(\theta)}{V(\theta) - \lambda_0} - \sum_{k=1}^{q} \frac{1}{2\pi j} \int_{\hat{\sigma}_k} \frac{dV(\theta)}{V(\theta) - \lambda_0} = \sum_{i=1}^{r} m_i + \sum_{k} M_k$$

where the sum $\overset{k}{\sum} M_k$ is extended to all singular points s_k which are zeros of $s \mapsto \phi_{\lambda_0}(s)$. Consequently the above becomes

$$-\sum_{i=1}^{r} \frac{1}{2\pi j} \int_{\hat{\gamma}_i} \frac{dV(\theta)}{V(\theta) - \lambda_0} - \sum_{k=1}^{q} \frac{1}{2\pi j} \int_{\hat{\sigma}_k} \frac{dV(\theta)}{V(\theta) - \lambda_0} = N_z \qquad (2.41)$$

Finally, consider

$$\frac{1}{2\pi j} \int_{\hat{\delta}_i} \frac{dV(\theta)}{V(\theta) - \lambda_0}.$$

On noting that δ_i is described in the clockwise direction, using Theorem 2.14 gives

$$\frac{1}{2\pi j} \int_{\hat{\delta}_i} \frac{dV(\theta)}{V(\theta) - \lambda_0} = -n_i$$

So

$$-\sum_{i=1}^{p} \frac{1}{2\pi j} \int_{\hat{\delta}_i} \frac{dV(\theta)}{V(\theta) - \lambda_0} = -N_p \qquad (2.42)$$

Combining (2.39), (2.41), and (2.42) we obtain

$$\frac{1}{2\pi j} \int_{\partial\hat{\Omega}} \frac{dV(\theta)}{V(\theta) - \lambda_0} = N_z - N_p \qquad (2.43)$$

$\square$

COROLLARY 2.5   *Under the conditions of Theorem 2.16, $N_z - N_p$ coincides with the number of anticlockwise encirclements of λ_0 in the λ-plane by the contour $V(\partial\hat{\Omega})$.*

Proof   Since $\theta \mapsto V(\theta)$ is analytic in Σ, every closed path in Σ is mapped conformally by $V(\cdot)$ into a closed path in the complex λ-plane. Setting $\lambda = V(\theta)$ then

$$\frac{1}{2\pi j} \int_{\partial\hat{\Omega}} \frac{dV(\theta)}{V(\theta)-\lambda_0} = \frac{1}{2\pi j} \int_{V(\partial\hat{\Omega})} \frac{d\lambda}{\lambda-\lambda_0}$$

The latter integral is simply the index function with respect to λ_0 of the contour $V(\partial\hat{\Omega})$, that is, the number of anticlockwise encirclements of λ_0 by the contour $V(\partial\hat{\Omega})$. The first integral coincides with $N_z - N_p$ as demonstrated in Theorem 2.15.   □

Remark   Although the definition of $V(\partial\hat{\Omega})$ requires the mechanism of minimum contours, its practical application is straightforward: it is only necessary to compute the root paths μ_i, $i = 1, 2, \ldots, n$, by numerically evaluating the roots of $\phi_s[\lambda]$ when s describes $\partial\Omega$ and utilizing the continuity of the roots to determine which numerical value corresponds to a particular path. These n paths are generally open, but they can be joined together by concatenation to form the contour $V(\partial\hat{\Omega})$.

Frequently the polynomial $\phi[\lambda]$ is of the form

$$\phi[\lambda] = \det(\lambda I - A)$$

where A is a $(n \times n)$ matrix whose coefficients are meromorphic complex functions in a given region Ω. Under these conditions the roots of $\phi_s[\lambda]$ are exactly the eigenvalues of $A(s)$. The paths $\mu_i (i = 1, 2, \ldots, n)$ are called *eigenvalue paths* and are numerically determined by computing for each $s \in \partial\Omega$ the eigenvalues of $A(s)$. The contour $V(\partial\hat{\Omega})$ formed by the concatenation of the eigenvalue paths is represented by $\Gamma = \{\mu_i\}_{i=1}^n$ and is called the eigenvalue contour generated by A and $\partial\Omega$. Notice that Theorem 2.16 and Corollary 2.5 were established under the assumption that the polynomial involved was irreducible over $H(\Omega)$. The polynomial

$$\phi[\lambda] = \det(\lambda I - A)$$

does not necessarily satisfy this property. However, it is always possible to factorize $\phi[\lambda]$ into a number of polynomials irreducible over $H[\Omega]$

$$\phi[\lambda] = \phi^{(1)}[\lambda] \phi^{(2)}[\lambda] \ldots \phi^{(m)}[\lambda]$$

Let Σ_k be the algebroid Riemann surface generated by $\phi^{(k)}[\lambda]$ and Ω and let $V_k : \Sigma_k \to C^1$ be the respective value function. To each Riemann surface Σ_k Theorem 2.16 can be applied from which it follows that

$$\frac{1}{2\pi j} \int_{V_k(\partial\Omega)} \frac{d\lambda}{(\lambda-\lambda_0)} = Z_k - P_k$$

where Z_k and P_k represent respectively the number of zeros and poles in

Ω of the complex function $s \mapsto \phi_{\lambda_0}^{(k)}(s)$. Thus the number of anticlockwise encirclements of the point λ_0 by the contour $V_k(\partial\Omega)$ coincides with $Z_k - P_k$. The eigenvalue contour Γ coincides with the contour $\{V_i(\partial\Omega)\}_{k=1}^m$, since a zero of $\phi_s[\lambda]$ is necessarily zero in some $\phi_s^{(k)}[\lambda]$. Therefore the index function of Γ with respect to the point λ_0 coincides with the sum of the index functions of the contours $V_k(\partial\Omega)$ with respect to the same point λ_0. Hence

$$\frac{1}{2\pi j} \int_\Gamma \frac{d\lambda}{(\lambda - \lambda_0)} = \left(\sum_{k=1}^m Z_k \right) - \left(\sum_{k=1}^m P_k \right)$$

The sums $Z = \sum_{k=1}^m Z_k$ and $P = \sum_{k=1}^m P_k$ coincide, respectively, with the number of zeros and poles of $s \mapsto \phi_{\lambda_0}(s)$ in Ω. We have now proved:

PROPOSITION 2.13   *Given a simple region Ω, a matrix A whose elements are meromorphic in Ω and a complex number λ_0 distinct from any eigenvalue of $A(s)$ when s describes $\partial\Omega$, then if $\partial\Omega$ is free of singular points, the number of zeros of the complex function $s \mapsto \det(\lambda_0 - A(s))$ in Ω coincide with the number of poles in Ω of the same function added to the number of anticlockwise encirclements of λ_0 by the eigenvalue contour Γ of $A(s)$ generated when s describes $\partial\Omega$.*

PROPOSITION 2.14   *Let $A \in H(\Omega)^{n \times n}$. The simple region Ω is free from zeros of the complex function $s \mapsto \det(\lambda_0 - A(s))$ if and only if the eigenvalue contour Γ generated when s describes $\partial\Omega$ does not contain or encircle the point λ_0.*

REFERENCES

Bers, L. (1958). "Riemann Surfaces". Courant Institute of Mathematical Science, New York.

Decarlo, R. and Saeks, R. (1977). "The encirclement condition—an approach using algebraic topology." *Int. J. Control* **26,** 179–287.

Dunford, N. and Schwartz, J. T. (1957). "Linear Operators" Part I. Interscience Publishers, New York.

Evgnafov, M. A. (1978). "Analytic Functions". Dover, New York.

Greenberg, M. H. (1967). "Lectures on Algebraic Topology". Benjamin, New York.

Hewitt, E. and Ross, K. A. (1963). "Abstract Harmonic Analysis", Vol I, Band 115. Springer Verlag, Berlin.

Hewitt, E. and Stromberg, K. (1965). "Real and Abstract Analysis". Springer Verlag, Berlin.

Hille, E. (1959). "Analytic Function Theory", Vol I, Ginn & Co, New York.

Hille, E. (1962) "Analytic Function Theory", Vol II, Ginn & Co., New York.

Hille, E. and Phillips, R. S. (1957). "Functional Analysis and Semigroups", Amer. Math. Soc. Colloquium Pub. Vol. 31.

Hilton, P. J. and Wylie, S. (1964). "Homology Theory". Cambridge University Press, Cambridge.

Kendig, K. (1977). "Elementary Algebraic Geometry". Springer Verlag, Berlin.

Kothe, F. (1969). "Topological Vector Spaces", Band 159. Springer Verlag, Berlin.

Larsen, R. (1971). "An introduction to the theory of multipliers", Band 175. Springer Verlag, Berlin.

Massey, W. S. (1967). "Algebraic Topology: An Introduction". Harcourt, Brace, World New York.

Postlethwaite, I. and MacFarlane, A. G. J. M. (1979). "A Complex Variable Approach to the Analysis of Linear Multivariable Feedback Systems", Lecture notes in Control and Information Sciences, **12,** Springer Verlag, Berlin.

Valenca, J. M. E. and Harris, C. J. (1981). "The Generalised Principle of the Argument and the Stability of Multivariable Systems", 3rd IMA Int. Conf. Control Theory, Sheffield, 1980. Academic Press, London and New York.

Chapter Three

Representation of Multipliers

3.1 INTRODUCTION

In this chapter we introduce a series of results which establishes a correspondence between the concept of a multiplier (a linear, continuous, or sequentially continuous, time-invariant operator) and the concept of transfer functions. For two important spaces, L_2 and X_2 (and their multivariable extensions, L_2^n and X_2^n) we derive a space of transfer functions which are in a one-to-one correspondence with the space of multipliers; this is essentially a representation theory for linear time-invariant operators and forms the basis of any study on the stability of feedback systems described by linear time-invariant operators. For the important spaces L_1, L_∞, X_1 and X_∞, it is not possible to develop a representation theory of the above form; we shall be able to show that every multiplier in these spaces has a transfer function which is an element of a certain space K of analytic complex functions, but we shall not prove that every element $h \in K$ is assigned to a multiplier in one of the above spaces which has h as a transfer function.

Specifically for the spaces L_1 and L_∞ we introduce another type of multiplier representation: the representation by convolution with a measure in the space $\mathcal{M}(R_+)$ of all countably additive, bounded regular complex Borel measures. We establish that there is a one-to-one correspondence between $\mathcal{M}(R_+)$ and the space $M(L_1)$ of all linear time-invariant operators of L_1 into itself, and that any element of $\mathcal{M}(R_+)$ defines a multiplier in L_∞.

Finally it is shown that the representation of multipliers in L_∞ (and X_∞) remains unsolved, since it is not possible to establish a one-to-one correspondence between $M(L_\infty)$ and a space of convolution measures or a space of transfer functions. However, there exist several weaker results (Larsen, 1971), but none is of use in stability studies of linear feedback systems.

The fundamental problem of the representation of multipliers can be stated thus: given a space of time functions E we wish to establish an explicit representation for the algebra $M(E)$ of all linear, time invariant and continuous operators of E into itself. Essentially we seek an algebra Y of complex functions such that each $A \in M(E)$ is assigned to some $h \in Y$ (the so-called transfer function of A) such that

$$\mathscr{L}(Af)(s) = h(s)(\mathscr{L}f)(s)$$

for all $f \in E$ and all s in some region of the complex plane, where $\mathscr{L}$ represents the Laplace transform operator.

3.2 REPRESENTATION OF MULTIPLIERS IN L_2 AND L_2^n

Let $M(L_2)$ represent the algebra of all multipliers in L_2 (that is, linear, continuous and time-invariant operators). Clearly $M(L_2)$ is a Banach algebra with topology induced by the topology of L_2.

Consider now the space $K(0)$ of all complex valued functions $s \mapsto h(s)$ of the complex variable s, bounded and holomorphic in the open right half plane $\{s : Re(s) > 0\}$. $K(0)$ is normed algebra under pointwise multiplication of functions and under the norm

$$\|h\| = \sup_{Re(s) > 0} |h(s)|$$

THEOREM 3.1: L_2-REPRESENTATION THEOREM   *There exists an isomorphism of rings such that to each $A \in M(L_2)$ there is assigned a transfer function $h \in K(0)$ satisfying:*

(i) $\mathscr{L}(Af)(s) = h(s)\mathscr{L}(f)(s)$

for all $f \in L_2$ and all $Re(s) > 0$

(ii) $\|A\| = \|h\|$

Proof   Let $S_{-T} : L_2 \to L_2$, $T \geq 0$, represent the operator

$$(S_{-T}f)(t) = \begin{cases} f(t+T) & \text{for} \quad t \geq 0 \\ 0 & \text{for} \quad t < 0 \end{cases}$$

Similarly let S_T represent the adjoint operator of S_{-T}. Since L_2 is reflexive, $S_T^* = (S_{-T}^*) = S_{-T}$. A linear continuous operator $A : L_2 \to L_2$ is said to be time invariant when it commutes with S_T, for all $T \geq 0$.

Given any $f \in L_2$, the Laplace transform of f is defined as the function $s \mapsto F(s)$ with domain in $Re(s) > 0$ such that

$$F(s) = \hat{f}(\phi_s), \qquad Re(s) > 0$$

where

$$\phi_s(t) = \begin{pmatrix} \exp(-st) & \forall\ t \geq 0 \\ 0 & \forall\ t < 0 \end{pmatrix}$$

and $\hat{f}(\cdot)$ is the element of L_2^* associated with $f \in L_2$. Then

$$(\mathscr{L}Af)(s) = (A\hat{f})(\phi_s) = (A^*\phi_s)(f)$$

where $A^*: L_2^* \to L_2^*$ is the adjoint of A. But since L_2 is a Hilbert space, then $L_2^* = L_2$ and hence A^* is a linear continuous operator on L_2 into itself and (Yosida, p. 195, 1971)

$$\|A^*\| = \|A\| \tag{3.1}$$

Obviously A is time invariant if and only if A^* commutes with S_{-T} for all $T \geq 0$.

Let $\psi_s \in L_2$ be defined as $A^*\phi_s$. Using the time invariance of A

$$(S_T Af)(\phi_s) = (AS_T f)(\phi_s) = \hat{\psi}_s(S_T f)$$

$$(S_T Af)(\phi_s) = (Af)(S_{-T}\phi_s)$$

For all $T \geq 0$, $S_{-T}\phi_s = \phi_s(T)\phi_s$. Hence

$$(S_T Af)(\phi_s) = \phi_s(T)\hat{\psi}_s(f)$$

Then for all $f \in L_2$, all $Re(s) > 0$ and all $T \geq 0$

$$\hat{\psi}_s(S_T f) = \phi_s(T)\hat{\psi}_s(f) \tag{3.2}$$

Consider now a sequence $\{\delta_n\}$ in $L_1 \cap L_2$ such that

(i) $\|\delta_n\|_{L_1} = 1 \qquad \forall\ n$

(ii) $\lim_n \|\delta_n \otimes f - f\|_{L_2} = 0$

where $\otimes$ represents convolution. Such a sequence is called a *weak convolution unit* and always exists (Hewitt and Stromberg, p. 400, 1965). By definition of $\{\delta_n\}$

$$\lim_n \hat{\psi}_s(\delta_n \otimes f) = \hat{\psi}_s(f) \tag{3.3}$$

Alternatively by the definition of convolution

$$\hat{\psi}_s(\delta_n \otimes f) = \hat{f}(\tilde{\phi}_n)$$

where

$$\tilde{\phi}_n(t) \triangleq \begin{cases} \hat{\psi}(S_t \delta_n) & \text{for} \quad t \geq 0 \\ 0 & \text{for} \quad t < 0 \end{cases}$$

Using (3.2), $\tilde{\phi}_n \equiv \hat{\psi}_s(\delta_n)\phi_s$, so

$$\hat{\psi}_s(\delta_n \otimes f) = \hat{f}(\tilde{\phi}_n) = \hat{\psi}_s(\delta_n)\hat{f}(\phi_s) \tag{3.4}$$

Select an $f_0 \in L_2$ such that $s \mapsto \hat{f}_0(\phi_s)$ is bounded away from zero in $Re(s) > 0$. Then

$$\hat{\psi}_s(\delta_n) = \hat{\psi}_s(\delta_n \otimes f_0)[\hat{f}_0(\phi_s)]^{-1}$$

Taking the limit in n and using (3.3)

$$\lim_n \hat{\psi}_s(\delta_n) = \hat{f}_0(\psi_s)[\hat{f}_0(\phi_s)]^{-1}$$

$$= (\mathscr{L} A f_0)(s)[(\mathscr{L} f_0)(s)]^{-1} \tag{3.5}$$

So that $\lim_n \hat{\psi}_s(\delta_n)$ is well defined for all $Re(s) > 0$. Let

$$h(s) \triangleq \lim_n \hat{\psi}_s(\delta_n) \tag{3.6}$$

Since $A f_0$ and f_0 are elements of L_2 their Laplace transform is an holomorphic function in $Re(s) > 0$ (Zamamian, 1968). Hence, from (3.5), it follows that $h(s)$ is holomorphic in $Re(s) > 0$.

From (3.4)

$$\hat{f}(\psi_s) = h(s)\hat{f}(\phi_s) \qquad \forall f \in L_2 \tag{3.7}$$

Hence, in the sense of L_2, $\psi_s \equiv h(s)\phi_s$

$$h(s)\phi_s = A^*\phi_s$$

$$|h(s)| \cdot \|\phi_s\| \le \|A^*\| \cdot \|\phi_s\|$$

Since $\|A^*\| = \|A\|$ then

$$\sup_{Re(s)>0} |h(s)| \le \|A\| \tag{3.8}$$

Therefore $s \mapsto h(s)$ is also bounded in $Re(s) > 0$ and is therefore an element of $K(0)$. Moreover $\|h\| \le \|A\|$.

Utilizing Parseval's inequality

$$\|Af\|_{L_2}^2 = \sup_{a>0} \frac{1}{2\pi} \int_{-\infty}^{\infty} |(\mathscr{L} Af)(a + j\omega)|^2 \, d\omega$$

$$= \sup_{a>0} \frac{1}{2\pi} \int_{-\infty}^{\infty} |h(a + j\omega)|^2 \, |\mathscr{L} f(a + j\omega)|^2 \, d\omega$$

$$\le \sup_{Re(s)>0} |h(s)|^2 \sup_{a>0} \frac{1}{2\pi} \int_{-\infty}^{\infty} |\mathscr{L} f(a + j\omega)|^2 \, d\omega$$

Therefore

$$\|Af\|_{L_2}^2 \le \|h\|_{K(0)}^2 \|f\|_{L_2}^2$$

and hence $\|A\| \le \|h\|_{K(0)}$. And so from (3.8)

$$\|A\| = \|h\| \tag{3.9}$$

Consider now the map $Y: M(L_2) \to K(0)$ which assigns $A \in M(L_2)$ to its Laplace transform $h \in K(0)$. From (3.4)

$$(\mathscr{L}Af)(s) = h(s)(\mathscr{L}f)(s) \tag{3.10}$$

for all $f \in L_2$ and all $Re(s) > 0$. Utilizing the linearity of the Laplace transform and equation (3.10), it follows that Y is a morphism of rings. From (3.9) this morphism is one to one; it is now only necessary to show that it is also onto to complete the proof.

Let h be arbitrary in $K(0)$, then a linear continuous operator on the Hardy-Lebesgue class $H^2(0)$ into itself is well defined as

$$(\hat{A}F)(s) = h(s)F(s) \qquad \forall\, F \in H^2(0), \quad \forall\, Re(s) > 0$$

The Laplace transform operator defines an isomorphism between L_2 and $H^2(0)$ (Yosida, p. 163, 1971), hence a linear, continuous operator $A: L_2 \to L_2$ is well defined as

$$A = \mathscr{L}^{-1}\hat{A}\mathscr{L}$$

Clearly A is time invariant and its transfer function coincides with $h(s)$. □

The isomorphism established between $M(L_2)$ and $K(0)$ transfers certain properties from one space to the other. For example $K(0)$ is a commutative algebra, hence $M(L_2)$ must also be a commutative algebra. Also since $M(L_2)$ is a Banach space, $K(0)$ is a Banach space.

The representation of multipliers in L_2 can be readily extended to L_2^n. The algebra $M(L_2^n)$ can be identified with the algebra of all $n \times n$ matrices over $M(L_2)$; that is, $M(L_2^n) \simeq M(L_2)^{n \times n}$. Since $M(L_2)$ is isomorphic with $K(0)$ (Theorem 3.1), $M(L_2)^{n \times n}$ is isomorphic with $K(0)^{n \times n}$.

THEOREM 3.2: L_2^n-REPRESENTATION THEOREM   *The ring of all multipliers in L_2^n is isomorphic with the ring of all $n \times n$ matrices over $K(0)$, in such a way that to each $A \in M(L_2^n)$ there is assigned $\hat{A} \in K(0)^{n \times n}$, called the matrix transfer function of A such that*

$$(\mathscr{L}Af)(s) = \hat{A}(s)(\mathscr{L}f)(s) \qquad \forall\, f \in L_2^n, \quad \forall\, Re(s) > 0$$

The isomorphism between $K(0)^{n \times n}$ and $M(L_2^n)$ ensures that an operator $A \in M(L_2^n)$ is invertible if and only if its matrix transfer function $\hat{A} \in K(0)^{n \times n}$ is invertible in $K(0)^{n \times n}$. Since both $M(L_2)$ and $K(0)$ are commutative rings, the result of MacLane and Birkoff (p. 304, 1967), which states that a matrix M in the space $R^{n \times n}$ of all matrices over the commutative ring R is invertible in $R^{n \times n}$ if and only if its determinant is invertible in R, can be applied to operators $A \in M(L_2^n)$. Hence $A \in M(L_2^n)$ is invertible in $M(L_2^n)$ if and only if det $\hat{A}$ is invertible in $K(0)$.

Now, since addition and multiplication in $K(0)$ are performed pointwise then

$$(\det \hat{A})(s) = \det [\hat{A}(s)]$$

An arbitrary $s \mapsto h(s)$ is invertible in $K(0)$, that is, the function $s \mapsto h(s)^{-1}$ exists in $K(0)$ if and only if $s \mapsto h(s)$ has no zeros and is bounded away from zero in $\{s : Re(s) > 0\}$. Hence $\hat{A} \in K(0)^{n \times n}$ is invertible in $K(0)^{n \times n}$ if and only if

$$\inf_{Re(s) > 0} |(\det \hat{A})(s)| > 0$$

In conclusion we have:

THEOREM 3.3   *An element $A \in M(L_2^n)$ is invertible in $M(L_2^n)$ if and only if*

$$\inf_{Re(s) > 0} |\det [\hat{A}(s)]| > 0$$

3.3 THE CONVOLUTION ALGEBRA $\mathcal{M}(R_+)$

Let R_+ represent the half real line $[0, \infty)$ equipped with the topology induced by the usual topology of R^1. Let $\bar{R}_+ = [0, \infty]$ represent the one-point compactification of R_+. The σ-algebra of all Borel sets in R_+ will be represented by B. Finally let $\mathcal{M}(R_+)$ be the space of all countably, bounded, regular complex Borel measures (Hewitt and Ross, pp. 118–127, 1963). The space $\mathcal{M}(R_+)$ is a normed space under the norm $\|\mu\| \triangleq |\mu|(R_+)$ where $|\mu|$ represents the total variation of the measure μ. One of the most important properties of $\mathcal{M}(R_+)$ is its identification with the strong dual of a space of continuous functions.

The space $C_0(R_+)$ is defined as the space of all continuous, bounded complex valued functions $t \mapsto f(t)$ such that for every $\xi > 0$ there exists a compact set B (which may depend upon f and ξ) such that

$$\sup_{t \notin B} |f(t)| < \xi$$

The space $C_0(R_+)$ is equipped with the uniform topology. Under the above conditions we have

THEOREM 3.4: RIESZ'S REPRESENTATION THEOREM   *The strong dual $C_0^*(R_+)$ of the space $C_0(R_+)$ can be identified with $\mathcal{M}(R_+)$ in such a way* *that if* $\hat{\mu} \in C_0^*(R_+)$ *is assigned to* $\mu \in \mathcal{M}(R_+)$, *then:*

$$\text{(a)} \quad \hat{\mu}(f) = \int f \, d\mu \qquad \forall f \in C_0(R_+)$$

$$\text{(b)} \quad \|\hat{\mu}\| = \sup_{\|f\|=1} |\hat{\mu}(f)| = \|\mu\| = |\mu|(R_+)$$

Proof   Hewitt and Ross (§11, 1963).   □

Given two measures μ, $\lambda \in \mathcal{M}(R_+)$ the convolution of these measures can be defined severally as:

   (i) $\mu \otimes \lambda$ is given by the element $\hat{\sigma} \in C_0^*(R_+)$ defined by

$$\hat{\sigma}(f) = \hat{\mu}(\hat{f})$$

where

$$\hat{f}(t) \triangleq \begin{cases} 0 & \text{for} \quad t < 0 \\ \hat{\lambda}(S_{-t}f) & \text{for} \quad t \geq 0 \end{cases}$$

and $\hat{\mu}$, $\hat{\lambda} \in C_0^*(R_+)$ are the functionals defined by μ and λ, f is arbitrary in $C_0(R_+)$ and $S_{-T}: C_0(R_+) \to C_0(R_+)$ is the operator defined as

$$(S_{-T}f)(t) = \begin{cases} 0 & \text{for} \quad t < 0 \\ f(t+T) & \text{for} \quad t \geq 0 \end{cases}$$

   (ii) $\mu \otimes \lambda$ is given by

$$(\mu \otimes \lambda)(E) = (\mu \times \lambda)(\hat{E})$$

where $\hat{E} \in R_+ \times R_+$ is defined as

$$\hat{E} = \{(t, \sigma) : t + \sigma \in E\}$$

and $\mu \times \lambda$ is the product of the two measures μ and λ.

$$\text{(iii)} \quad (\mu \otimes \lambda)(E) = \int_0^\infty \lambda(E_t) \, d\mu(t) = \int_0^\infty \mu(E_t) \, d\lambda(t)$$

where

$$E_t \triangleq \{\sigma \geq 0 : \sigma + t \in E\}$$

It can easily be shown (Hewitt and Ross (§19, 1963)) that the above definitions of convolution are equivalent. With multiplication defined by convolution it follows that $\mathcal{M}(R_+)$ is a commutative Banach algebra—note that $C_0^*(R_+)$ is a Banach space since $C_0(R_+)$ is a Banach space.

   Some subspaces of $\mathcal{M}(R_+)$ are particularly important; let $\mathcal{M}_a(R_+)$ represent the subspace of $\mathcal{M}(R_+)$ formed with all absolutely continuous measures; that is, every $\mu \in \mathcal{M}_a(R_+)$ vanishes on null sets. (Note: in the sequel a null set denotes any set with a Lebesgue measure of zero.) Also let $\mathcal{M}_d(R_+)$ be the subspace formed with all measures of $\mathcal{M}(R_+)$ which are concentrated on countable sets. Finally let $\mathcal{M}_s(R_+)$ represent the space of $\mathcal{M}(R_+)$ formed with all measures of $\mathcal{M}(R_+)$ concentrated on noncountable null sets. The elements of $\mathcal{M}_d(R_+)$ are called *discontinuous measures*; the elements of $\mathcal{M}_s(R_+)$ are called *continuous, singular measures*.

THEOREM 3.5   *The spaces* $\mathcal{M}_a(R_+)$, $\mathcal{M}(R_+)$ *and* $\mathcal{M}_s(R_+)$ *are closed linear subspaces of* $\mathcal{M}(R_+)$; *moreover every* $\mu \in \mathcal{M}(R_+)$ *can be uniquely written as*

$$\mu = \mu_a + \mu_d + \mu_s$$

where

$$\mu_a \in \mathcal{M}_a(R_+), \quad \mu_d \in \mathcal{M}_d(R_+) \quad and \quad \mu_s \in \mathcal{M}_s(R_+).$$

Furthermore $|\mu| = |\mu_a| + |\mu_d| + |\mu_s|$ *and in particular*

$$\|\mu\| = \|\mu_a\| + \|\mu_d\| + \|\mu_s\|$$

Proof   Hewitt and Ross (§19, 1963). □

The spaces $\mathcal{M}_a(R_+)$ and $\mathcal{M}_d(R_+)$ have special representations as Banach spaces. In particular the elements of $\mathcal{M}_a(R_+)$ obey the conditions of Theorem 1.20 which can be rewritten as:

THEOREM 3.6: RADON–NYKODYM THEOREM   *There exists an isometric isomorphism between* $\mathcal{M}_a(R_+)$ *and* $L_1(R_+)$ *such that to each* $\gamma \in \mathcal{M}_a(R_+)$ *there is assigned an* $f \in L_1(R_+)$ *which satisfies*

(a) *for any* $E \in B$

$$\gamma(E) = \int_E f(t)\, dt$$

(b) *for any* $\phi \in C_0(R_+)$

$$\hat{\gamma}(\phi) = \int_0^\infty \phi(t) f(t)\, dt$$

Moreover for each $\mu \in \mathcal{M}_a(R_+)$ *the convolution* $\mu \otimes \gamma$ *is an element of* $L_1(R_+)$ *and hence*

$$(\mu \otimes \gamma)(t) = \int_0^\infty f(t-\sigma)\, d\mu(\sigma)$$

A direct consequence of this result is that $\mathcal{M}_a(R_+)$ (and consequently $L_1(R_+)$) is an ideal of the algebra $\mathcal{M}(R_+)$.

As an example of an element of $\mathcal{M}_d(R_+)$ we can consider the measure δ_T defined for some $T \in R_+$ as

$$\delta_T(E) = \begin{cases} 1 & \text{if} \quad T \in E \\ 0 & \text{if} \quad T \notin E \end{cases} \tag{3.11}$$

THEOREM 3.7   *The measure* δ_T *defined by (3.11) lies in* $\mathcal{M}_d(R_+)$ *and corresponds to the functions* $\hat{\delta}_T(\phi) = \phi(T)$, $\forall\, \phi \in C_0(R_+)$. *Moreover any* *non-zero $\mu \in \mathcal{M}_d(\mathbf{R}_+)$ can be written uniquely as*

$$\mu = \sum_{n=0}^{\infty} \alpha_n \delta_{T_n}$$

where $\{\alpha_n\}$ is a sequence of non-zero complex numbers such that $\sum_{n=0}^{\infty} |\alpha_n| < \infty$ and $\{T_n\}$ is a sequence of distinct elements of $\mathbf{R}_+$. The variation $|\mu|$ of the measure μ is given by

$$|\mu| = \sum_{n=0}^{\infty} |\alpha_n| \, \delta_{T_n}$$

and in particular

$$\|\mu\| = \sum_{n=0}^{\infty} |\alpha_n|$$

Proof   Hewitt and Ross (§19, 1963).   □

To complete this introduction to the algebra $\mathcal{M}(\mathbf{R}_+)$ some conditions concerned with the invertibility of elements of $\mathcal{M}(\mathbf{R}_+)$ are presented.

A maximal ideal of a commutative algebra is any ideal which is not a proper subset of any other ideal other than the algebra itself. It is known (Hille and Phillips, §4.14, 1–57) that the set of all non-invertible elements in an algebra, coincides with the union of all its maximal ideals. For example, none of the elements of L_1 can be invertible on $\mathcal{M}(\mathbf{R}_+)$ since L_1 is an ideal of $\mathcal{M}(\mathbf{R}_+)$ and therefore lies in some maximal ideal. More generally it can be shown (Hewitt and Ross, 1963):

PROPOSITION 3.1   *The direct sum of the spaces $\mathcal{M}_a(\mathbf{R}_+)$ and $\mathcal{M}_s(\mathbf{R}_+)$ (represented by $\mathcal{M}_a(\mathbf{R}_+) \oplus \mathcal{M}_s(\mathbf{R}_+)$) is a closed ideal of $\mathcal{M}(\mathbf{R}_+)$.*

A multiplicative functional m in $\mathcal{M}(\mathbf{R}_+)$ is a linear continuous map

$$m : \mathcal{M}(\mathbf{R}_+) \to C^1$$

which in addition satisfies

$$m(\mu \otimes \gamma) = m(\mu) m(\gamma) \qquad \forall \, \mu, \quad \forall \, \gamma \in \mathcal{M}(\mathbf{R}_+) \tag{3.12}$$

Consider the set

$$I_m = \{\mu : m(\mu) = 0\} \tag{3.13}$$

Clearly I_m is an ideal which is also maximal and that every maximal ideal in $\mathcal{M}(\mathbf{R}_+)$ has the form (3.13). Therefore seeking the non-invertible elements of $\mathcal{M}(\mathbf{R}_+)$ is equivalent to finding the multiplicative linear functions in $\mathcal{M}(\mathbf{R}_+)$.

Consider the map $m_0 : \mu \mapsto \mu(\{O\})$, clearly m_0 is linear continuous functional. Moreover

$$m_0(\mu \otimes \gamma) = \mu \otimes \gamma(\{O\})$$
$$= \mu \times \gamma(\hat{0})$$

where

$$\hat{0} = \{(\sigma, t) \in R_1 \times R_+ : \sigma + t = O\}.$$

Then

$$\hat{0} = \{(O, O)\}$$

and

$$\mu \times \gamma(\hat{0}) = \mu \times \gamma\{(O, O)\} = \mu(\{O\})\gamma(\{O\}).$$

Hence

$$m_0(\mu \otimes \gamma) = m_0(\mu)m_0(\gamma)$$

Thus m_0 is a multiplicative linear functional, and so the set

$$I_0 = \{\mu : m_0(\mu) = 0\} \equiv \{\mu : \mu(\{O\}) = 0\}$$

is a maximal ideal. In particular every measure $\mu \in \mathcal{M}_a(R_+) \oplus \mathcal{M}_s(R_+)$ vanishes in the singleton $\{O\}$, thus it cannot be invertible. It follows that for a measure to be invertible in $\mathcal{M}(R_+)$ it must have a non-zero component concentrated at the origin. Therefore every invertible $\mu \in \mathcal{M}(R_+)$ must be of the form

$$\mu = \alpha\delta_0 + \lambda_0$$

with α a non-zero complex number and λ_0 an element of I_0, δ_0 is clearly the unit of the algebra $\mathcal{M}(R_+)$. Hence if μ^{-1} exists it must be of the form

$$\mu^{-1} = \alpha^{-1}\delta_0 + \lambda_1$$

where

$$\alpha\lambda_1 + \alpha^{-1}\lambda_0 + \lambda_0 \otimes \lambda_1 = 0$$

Some maximal ideals of special interest are directly associated with the Laplace transform. Consider the continuous linear functional

$$m_s(\mu) = \hat{\mu}(\phi_s)$$

where ϕ_s is as defined in the Proof of Theorem 3.1. The function $s \mapsto \hat{\mu}(\phi_s)$ is the Laplace transform of the measure μ; since $\phi_s \in C_0(R_+)$ for all $Re(s) > 0$ and $\|\phi_s\| = 1$, then $s \mapsto \hat{\mu}(\phi_s)$ is bounded and analytic in $Re(s) > 0$. Moreover definition (i) of convolution implies that

$$\mathcal{L}(\mu \otimes \gamma)(s) = (\mu \hat{\otimes} \gamma)(\phi_s) = \hat{\mu}(\phi_s)\hat{\gamma}(\phi_s) = (\mathcal{L}\mu)(s)(\mathcal{L}\gamma)(s)$$

Hence m_s is also a multiplicative linear functional, the corresponding maximal ideal is

$$I_s = \{\mu : \hat{\mu}(\phi_s) = 0\}$$

In conclusion, any measure whose Laplace transform has a zero in the open right half complex plane lies in some maximal ideal and therefore cannot be invertible. The converse is generally not true; however, the necessary and sufficient conditions for invertibility in terms of Laplace transforms can be established if restricted to the space $\mathcal{M}_a(R_+)\oplus\mathcal{M}_d(R_+)$.

THEOREM 3.8: HILLE AND PHILLIPS (1957)   *The space* $\mathcal{M}_a(R_+)\oplus\mathcal{M}_d(R_+)$ *is a closed regular subalgebra of* $\mathcal{M}(R_+)$. *Moreover a measure* μ *in this space is invertible if and only if*

$$\inf_{Re(s)>0} |\hat{\mu}(\phi_s)| > 0$$

3.4   REPRESENTATION OF MULTIPLIERS IN L_1 AND L_1^n

A representation theorem for operators on L_1 of the type derived in Section 3.2 for L_2 is not available; however, it is possible to establish a full representation of multipliers in L_1 in terms of a convolution algebra.

Initially we review some properties of the Laplace and Fourier transforms of function $f \in L_1$. The space L_1^* can be identified with L_∞. Since ϕ_s lies in L_∞ for all $Re(s)\geq 0$, then for any $f \in L_1$,

$$\hat{F}(s) \triangleq \int_0^\infty \phi_s(t)f(t)\,dt \tag{3.14}$$

defines a complex analytic function in $\{s : Re(s) > 0\}$ and a bounded function in $\{s : Re(s) \geq 0\}$. Moreover the Fourier transform $\omega \mapsto \hat{F}(j\omega)$ is a continuous function which satisfies

$$\lim_{|\omega|\to\infty} \hat{F}(j\omega) = 0$$

Thus $\omega \mapsto \hat{F}(j\omega)$ can be identified with an element of $C(\bar{R})$ (where $\bar{R}$ denotes the compactification of the real line). It follows (Hille, 1962) that the family of functions $\omega \mapsto \hat{F}(a+j\omega)$ converges uniformly to $\omega \mapsto \hat{F}(j\omega)$ when $a \to 0^+$. Therefore $s \mapsto \hat{F}(s)$ is bounded and holomorphic in $\{s : Re(s) > 0\}$, bounded and continuous in $\{s : Re(s) \geq 0\}$ and satisfies

$$\lim_{\rho\to\infty} \sup_{|\theta|\leq\pi/2} |\hat{F}(\rho\exp(j\theta))| = 0$$

It was shown in Section 3.3 that L_1 is an ideal of $\mathcal{M}(R_+)$, so any $\mu \in \mathcal{M}(R_+)$ defines a linear, time-invariant and bounded operator T_μ on L_1 into $L_1(T_\mu : L_1 \to L_1)$ by

$$T_\mu : f \mapsto \mu \otimes f$$

We now wish to show that every multiplier in L_1 can be defined in the same manner.

THEOREM 3.9   *Let A be arbitrary in $M(L_1)$ then:*

(a) *There exists a function $s \mapsto h(s)$ bounded and holomorphic in $Re(s) > 0$ and continuous in $Re(s) \geq 0$ such that*

$$(\mathscr{L}Af)(s) = h(s)(\mathscr{L}f)(s) \qquad \forall f \in L_1, \quad \forall Re(s) \geq 0$$

(b) *The map $A \mapsto h$ defines an injective morphism of rings*

(c) *There exists $\mu \in \mathcal{M}(\mathbf{R}_+)$ such that*
   c(i) $Af = \mu \otimes f \ \forall f \in L_1$
   c(ii) $\|A\| = \|\mu\|$
   c(iii) *The map $A \mapsto \mu$ defines an isometric isomorphism of rings*

Proof   Let $A^*: L_1^* \to L_1^*$ be the strong dual operator of A. Notice that $L_1^* = L_\infty$, hence for any $Re(s) \geq 0$

$$\psi_s = A^* \phi_s$$

is an element of L_∞.

We have $(\mathscr{L}Af)(s) = (\widehat{Af})(\phi_s) = \hat{f}(\psi_s)$ for any $f \in L_1$. Utilizing the time invariance of A and proceeding as in Theorem 3.1,

$$\phi_s(T)\hat{f}(\psi_s) = (\widehat{S_T f})(\psi_s) \tag{3.15}$$

for all $f \in L_1$ and $Re(s) \geq 0$.

The space L_1 as a convolution algebra contains an approximate convolution unit (Hewitt and Stromberg, 1965), this is a sequence $\{\delta_n\}$ in L_1 such that

$$\text{(i)} \ \|\delta_n\|_{L_1} = 1 \qquad \forall n$$

$$\text{(ii)} \ \lim_{.n} \|\delta_n \otimes f - f\|_{L_1} = 0 \qquad \forall f \in L_1$$

Consider now the complex number $(\delta_n \hat{\otimes} f)(\psi_s)$, from the definition of $\{\delta_n\}$

$$\lim_n (\delta_n \hat{\otimes} f)(\psi_s) = \hat{f}(\psi_s) \tag{3.16}$$

Alternatively from the definition of convolution

$$(\delta_n \hat{\otimes} f)(\psi_s) = \hat{f}(\psi_n)$$

where

$$\psi_n(t) = \begin{cases} (\widehat{S_t \delta_n})(\psi_s) & \text{for} \quad t \geq 0 \\ 0 & \text{for} \quad t < 0 \end{cases}$$

Using (3.15), $\psi_n(t) = \hat{\delta}_n(\psi_s)\phi_s(t)$; hence

$$(\hat{\delta}_n \otimes f)(\psi_s) = \hat{\delta}_n(\psi_s)\hat{f}(\phi_s) \tag{3.17}$$

Selecting a particular $f_0 \in L_1$ such that $s \mapsto \hat{f}_0(\phi_s)$ is bounded away from zero in $Re(s) \geq 0$ we have

$$\hat{\delta}_n(\psi_s) = (\hat{\delta} \otimes f_0)(\psi_s)[\hat{f}_0(s)]^{-1}$$

Taking the limit in n and using (3.16)

$$\lim_n \hat{\delta}_n(\psi_s) = \hat{f}_0(\psi_s)[\hat{f}_0(\phi_s)]^{-1} \qquad (3.18)$$

Therefore $\lim_n \hat{\delta}_n(\psi_s)$ exists for all $Re(s) \geq 0$, let $h(s)$ represent such a limit. Then from the previous equation it follows that $h(s)$ is holomorphic in $\{s : Re(s) > 0\}$ and continuous in $\{s : Re(s) \geq 0\}$. Furthermore from (3.17)

$$(\widehat{Af})(\phi_s) = \hat{f}(\psi_s) = h(s)\hat{f}(\phi_s) \qquad (3.19)$$

for all $f \in L_1$ and all $Re(s) \geq 0$.
    And so

$$h(s) = \lim_n (\widehat{A\delta_n})(\phi_s)$$

$$|h(s)| \leq \lim_n \|A\| \cdot \|\delta_n\|_{L_1} \cdot \|\phi_s\|_{L_\infty}$$

But since $|\phi_s\|_{L_\infty} = 1$ for all $Re(s) \geq 0$ and $\|\delta_n\|_{L_1} = 1$ for all n, thence

$$\sup_{Re(s) \geq 0} |h(s)| \leq \|A\| \qquad (3.20)$$

The proof of (a) is complete; (b) results immediately from (3.19) which shows that $A \mapsto h$ is a morphism of rings and from the uniqueness of the Laplace transform.
    To establish (c), consider the space Ψ defined as the space of all functions $\phi \in L_\infty$ of the form

$$\phi = \sum_{i=1}^n \alpha_i \phi_{s_i}$$

where α_i are complex numbers and $Re(s_i) > 0$ for all i. Thus Ψ is the space of all finite linear combinations of functions ϕ_s with $Re(s) > 0$. Notice that Ψ is a linear subspace of $C_0(R_+)$. Consider the map $\mu_n : \Psi \to C^1$ defined as

$$\mu_n(\phi) = \hat{\delta}_n(A^*\phi) = (\widehat{A\delta_n})(\phi)$$

The map $\mu_n(\cdot)$ is clearly linear and continuous; moreover

$$|\mu_n(\phi)| \leq \|A\| \cdot \|\delta_n\|_{L_1} \cdot \|\phi\|_{L_\infty}$$

$$|\mu_n(\phi)| \leq \|A\| \cdot \|\phi\|_{L_\infty}$$

For any $\phi = \sum\limits_{i=1}^{n} \alpha_i \phi_{s_i}$ in Ψ we have

$$\mu_n(\phi) = \sum_{i=1}^{n} \alpha_i \mu_n(\phi_{s_i}) = \sum_{i=1}^{n} \alpha_i \hat{\delta}_n(\psi_{s_i})$$

Hence

$$\lim_n \mu_n(\phi) = \sum_{i=1}^{n} \alpha_i h(s_i)$$

In conclusion, a linear functional can be defined as $\tilde{\mu}(\phi) = \lim\limits_n \mu_n(\phi)$ since the limit always exists.

Furthermore $|\tilde{\mu}(\phi)| \le \lim\limits_n |\mu_n(\phi)| \le \|A\| \cdot \|\phi\|_{L_\infty}$, therefore $\tilde{\mu}(\cdot)$ defines a functional in Ψ.

In conclusion: it is possible to define a linear functional $\tilde{\mu} : \Psi \to C^1$ such that

(i) $|\tilde{\mu}(\phi)| \le \|A\| \cdot \|\phi\|_{L_\infty}$ $\forall \, \phi \in \Psi$

(ii) $\tilde{\mu} : \sum\limits_{i=1}^{n} \alpha_i \phi_{s_i} \mapsto \sum\limits_{i=1}^{n} \alpha_i h(s_i)$

From the Hahn-Banach theorem it follows that a functional $\hat{\mu} \in C_0^*(R_+)$ exists such that

(i) $|\hat{\mu}(f)| \le \|A\| \cdot \|f\|_{L_\infty}$ $\forall \, f \in C_0(R_+)$

(ii) $\hat{\mu} : \sum\limits_{i=1}^{n} \alpha_i \phi_{s_i} \mapsto \sum\limits_{i=1}^{n} \alpha_i h(s_i)$ (3.21)

Now since $C_0^*(R_+)$ is identified with $\mathcal{M}(R_+)$ (Theorem 3.4) there exists a measure $\mu \in \mathcal{M}(R_+)$ which defines a functional $\hat{\mu}$. The Laplace transform of such a measure is

$$(\mathscr{L}\mu)(s) = \hat{\mu}(\phi_s) = h(s) \qquad (3.22)$$

Moreover, for any $f \in L_1$

$$\mathscr{L}(\mu \otimes f)(s) = (\mu \hat{\otimes} f)(\phi_s) = \hat{\mu}(\phi_s)\hat{f}(\phi_s) = h(s)\hat{f}(\phi_s)$$

Using (3.19)

$$\mathscr{L}(Af)(s) = (\mu \hat{\otimes} f)(\phi_s) = (\mathscr{L}\mu \otimes f)(s) = (\mathscr{L}Af)(s)$$

the uniqueness of the Laplace transform in L_1 now implies that

$$Af = \mu \otimes f \qquad \forall \, f \in L_1$$

This proves c(i). We have

$$\|Af\| \le \|\mu\| \cdot \|f\|$$

and so $\|A\| \leq \|\mu\|$. Alternatively, from (3.22) $\|\mu\| \leq A$, thus $\|\mu\| = \|A\|$, proving c(ii). This last result also establishes that the map which assigns A to μ is one to one, and as it is also onto it must be an isometric isomorphism of rings.   □

We have shown that every multiplier $A \in M(L_1)$ is represented by a transfer function $h \in K(0)$ which is in addition continuous along the imaginary axis. However, it cannot be shown that every such function defines a multiplier in L_1. Therefore a one-to-one correspondence between a space of transfer functions and the space $M(L_1)$ cannot be established in order to identify regular elements of $M(L_1)$ as those which have invertible transfer functions. Although for a sub-algebra of $M(L_1)$ it is possible to express the necessary and sufficient conditions for invertibility in terms of transfer functions (we show that $M(L_1)$ is isomorphic with $\mathcal{M}(R_+)$). Remembering from Theorem 3.8 that the space $\mathcal{M}_a(R_+) \oplus \mathcal{M}_d(R_+)$ is a regular sub-algebra of $\mathcal{M}(R_+)$ and that an element μ in such a space is invertible if and only if

$$\inf_{Re(s)>0} |\hat{\mu}(\phi_s)| > 0.$$

If we now define LA_+ (Willems, 1971) as the algebra of all linear continuous and time-invariant operators which can be expressed as the convolution with measure μ of the form

$$\mu = f_0 + \sum_{k=0}^{\infty} \alpha_k \, \delta_{T_k}$$

with $f_0 \in L_1$ and $\sum_{k=0}^{\infty} |\alpha_k| < 0$. Then from Theorem 3.8 we have

THEOREM 3.10.   *The algebra LA_+ is a regular sub-algebra of $M(L_1)$ and an element $A \in LA_+$ is invertible in $M(L_1)$ if and only if its transfer function $s \mapsto h(s)$*

$$\inf_{Re(s)>0} |h(s)| > 0$$

The multivariable extension of this result is almost immediate, if $\mathcal{M}(R_+)^{n \times n}$ represents the algebra of all $(n \times n)$ matrices over $\mathcal{M}(R_+)$ then clearly $M(L_1^n)$ is isomorphic with $\mathcal{M}(R_+)^{n \times n}$. If $LA_+^{n \times n}$ represents the sub-algebra of $M(L_1^n)$ formed with all elements which are defined by the convolution with an $(n \times n)$ matrix whose entries are elements of LA_+, then operator $A \in LA_+^{n \times n}$ is invertible in LA_+ if and only if its matrix transfer function $s \mapsto H(s)$ satisfies

$$\inf_{Re(s)>0} |\det H(s)| > 0 \qquad (3.23)$$

The algebra LA_+ can be identified directly with the commutative Banach algebra $\mathscr{A}$ of Desoer and Vidyasagar (1975), although $LA_+^{n \times n} \equiv \mathscr{A}^{n \times n}$ is not a commutative Banach algebra. For any $f \in L_p(R_+)$ $(1 \leq p \leq \infty)$ and $g \in LA_+$, it is easy to see that $f \otimes g \in L_p(R_+)$ and $\|f \otimes g\|_p \leq \|f\|_p \|g\|_{LA_+}$; in particular for $p = 2$, $\|f \oplus g\|_2 \leq \|f\|_2 \sup_\omega |\hat{g}(j\omega)|$.

3.5 REPRESENTATION OF MULTIPLIERS IN L_∞

The basic definitions and properties of the L_∞ space and its dual are given in Appendix 3.1 together with the representation theorem for operators $A : L_\infty \to L_\infty$. From the appendix we obtain the following:

THEOREM 3.11   *The convolution algebra $\mathscr{M}(R_+)$ can be identified with a sub-algebra of $M(L_\infty)$ by assigning to each*

$$\mu \in \mathscr{M}(R_+) \text{ the operator } f \mapsto \mu \otimes f$$

THEOREM 3.12   *Let A be arbitrary in $M(L_\infty)$. Then there exists a complex function $s \mapsto h(s)$ in $K(0)$ such that*

(a) $(\mathscr{L}Af)(s) = h(s)(\mathscr{L}f)(s)$ $\forall f \in L_\infty$, $\forall Re(s) > 0$

(b) $\sup_{Re(s)>0} |h(s)| \leq \|A\|$

Moreover the map which assigns A to $h \in K(0)$ is a continuous, injective morphism of rings.

Another useful result is

PROPOSITION 3.2 (Larsen, 1971)   *For an arbitrary $A \in M(L_\infty)$ there exists a unique $\mu \in \mathscr{M}(R_+)$ such that for all $f \in C_0(R_+)$*

$$Af = \mu \otimes f$$

It is important to note that Theorem 3.11 and Proposition 3.2 cannot be combined in a full representation theorem, since Proposition 3.2 states that $Af = \mu \otimes f$ for *any* $f \in C_0(R_+)$; it does not state the result for an arbitrary $f \in L_\infty$.

3.6 REPRESENTATION THEORY IN X_p-SPACES

It was shown in Section 3.2 that every multiplier in L_2 can be represented by a transfer function which is an element of $K(0)$. Unfortunately a generic $h \in K(0)$ is not necessarily defined everywhere along the imaginary axis, so it is not possible to establish a Nyquist stability criterion which can be applied to L_2 feedback systems. To establish such a criterion we introduce a family of spaces X_p derived from the more familiar L_p-spaces. The X_p spaces are examples of sequential inductive spaces whose properties are now established prior to the consideration of multipliers in X_p.

3.6.1 Sequential convergence vector spaces

The vector space E is called a *sequential convergence space* (Zemanian, 1968) if there exists a rule which identifies certain sequences, called the *convergent sequences*, and assigns to such a sequence an element of E, called the *limit*, and in addition satisfies the following axioms:

A.1 If $\{x_n\}$ and $\{y_n\}$ are convergent sequences, then for each pair of scalars α, β the sequence $\{\alpha x_n + \beta y_n\}$ is also convergent and satisfies

$$\lim_n \{\alpha x_n + \beta y_n\} = \alpha \lim_n \{x_n\} + \beta \lim_n \{y_n\}$$

A.2 The limit of any convergent sequence is unique

A.3 Every cofinal sequence of a convergent sequence is also convergent and has the same limit

A.4 The constant sequence $x_n = x$, for all n, is convergent with limit x

A.5 For any convergent sequence $\{x_n\}$ in E and any convergent sequence of scalars $\{\alpha_n\}$

$$\lim_n \{\alpha_n x_n\} = \lim_n \{\alpha_n\} \lim_n \{x_n\}$$

Any topological vector space is an example of a sequential convergence space.

Given two sequential convergence spaces E and F and an operator $T: E \to F$, T is said to be *sequentially continuous*, when for each convergent sequence $\{x_n\}$ in E the sequence $\{T(x_n)\}$ is convergent in F and satisfies $\lim_n T(x_n) = T\left(\lim_n x_n\right)$.

A subset $B \subset E$ is said to be *sequentially bounded* in E when, for each sequence $\{x_n\}$ in B and each sequence of scalars $\{\alpha_n\}$ converging to the origin, the sequence $\{\alpha_n x_n\}$ converges to the origin.

PROPOSITION 3.3 *If $T: E \to F$ is linear and sequentially continuous and $B \subset E$ is sequentially bounded, then $T(B)$ is sequentially bounded.*

Proof Let $T(x_n)$ be an arbitrary sequence in $T(B)$. If $\{\alpha_n\} \to 0$ as $n \to \infty$, then

$$\lim_n \alpha_n T(x_n) = \lim_n T(\alpha_n x_n) = T\left(\lim_n \alpha_n x_n\right) = T(0) = 0$$

due, respectively, to the linearity of T, the sequential continuity of T, the sequential boundedness of B, and finally the linearity of T. □

If E is a sequential convergence, complex vector space and $\mu : E \rightarrow C^1$ is a linear, sequentially continuous operator, then μ is called a *sequential functional* in E. The space of all distinct functionals in E is called the *sequential dual* and is represented by E'.

For any B, sequentially bounded in E, and any $\mu \in E'$, the set $\mu(B)$ is bounded in C^1 (Proposition 3.3). Hence a real, positive, finite function can be defined in E' as:

$$p_B(\mu) \triangleq \sup_{x \in B} |\mu(x)| \qquad (3.24)$$

It is trivial to show that $p_B(\cdot)$ is a finite semi-norm in E'. Given any $\mu \neq 0$, we can state that there exists some sequentially bounded set $B \subset E$ such that $p_B(\mu) \neq 0$; this derives from the fact that for any $\mu \neq 0$ there always exists some $x \in E$ such that $\mu(x) \neq 0$.

Consider now the family $\{p_B(\cdot)\}$ of all semi-norms defined as in (3.24) when B spans all sequentially bounded sets in E. From Theorem 1.4 (Köthe, 1969), this collection defines a locally convex topology in E'. The locally convex topological vector space thus generated is called the *strong sequential dual* of E and is represented by E^*.

3.6.2 Sequential inductive limit spaces

Let $\{E_a\}$, $a > 0$, be a family of topological vector spaces such that

L.1 For $b > a$, $E_a \supset E_b$

L.2 For $b > a$, the topology induced in E_b by the topology of T_a of E_a is weaker than the original topology T_b of E_b

Let X represent the vector space $\bigcup_{a>0} E_a$. The space X can be made into a sequential convergence space if the following rule of convergence is used:

L.3 A sequence $\{x_n\}$ in $\bigcup_{a>0} E_a$ converges in this space to a point x when there exists $a_0 > 0$ such that the sequence and the limit both lie in E_{a_0} and $\{x_n\}$ converges to x in the topology of E_{a_0}

It is simple to show that the rule of convergence L.3 satisfies all the axioms A.1–A.5. A space X, defined by a family of spaces which satisfy conditions L.1, L.2, equipped with the rule of convergence L.3, is called the *sequential inductive limit* of the spaces E_a.

PROPOSITION 3.4 $B \subset X$ is sequentially bounded if and only if there exists $a > 0$ such that B is a bounded subset of E_a.

Proof The propositions conditions are clearly sufficient. Conversely, assume that B is sequentially bounded and not contained in any E_a. Then a sequence $\{x_n\}$ in B can be defined such that $x_n \notin E_{a_n}$, where a_n is a sequence in R_+ converging to the origin. Let $\{\alpha_n\}$ be a sequence of non-zero positive reals converging to the origin. The definition of sequential boundedness now implies that $\{\alpha_n x_n\}$ is a convergent sequence X converging to the origin. Condition L.3 now implies that there exists some $a > 0$ such that E_a contains every element of the sequence. In particular for any $a_n < a$

$$E_{a_n} \supset E_a \supset \alpha_n x_n$$

which contradicts the hypothesis. Therefore B lies in some E_a. The rule of convergence L.3 now implies that for any sequence $\{x_n\}$ in B and any sequence $\{\alpha_n\} \to 0$, the sequence $\{\alpha_n x_n\}$ converges to the origin in E_a in the topology of E_a; thus B is bounded in E_a. $\square$

PROPOSITION 3.5 *Let E be a finitely normed space and $X = \bigcup_{a>0} F_a$ a sequential inductive limit of finitely normed spaces. If $T : E \to X$ is sequentially continuous and linear, then there exists some $a > 0$ such that $T(E) \subset F_a$.*

Proof Assume the converse of the proposition; let $a_n \to 0$ be a sequence in R_+ converging to the origin. Then, for each n there exists $x_n \in E$ such that $T(x_n) \notin F_{a_n}$. The sequence $\{x_n\}$ cannot be bounded otherwise $\{T(x_n)\}$ would have to be a sequentially bounded set (Proposition 3.3) and so lie in some F_a (Proposition 3.4) which contradicts the hypothesis. Furthermore every x_n must be non-zero as the origin is common to every F_a. The sequence $\{\|x_n\|^{-1}\}$ is therefore well defined and converges to the origin as $n \to \infty$. Let $\alpha_n = \|x_n\|^{-2} > 0$, the sequence $\{\alpha_n x_n\}$ converges to the origin as $\lim_n \|\alpha_n x_n\| = \lim_n \|x_n\|^{-1} = 0$. Hence $T(\alpha_n x_n)$ must also converge to the origin. By L.3 there exists some $a > 0$ such that F_a contains every term of the sequence. For any $a_n < a$

$$F_{a_n} \supset F_a \supset T(\alpha_n x_n) = \alpha_n T(x_n)$$

Finally as $\alpha_n \neq 0$, then $T(x_n) \in F_{a_n}$ which contradicts the hypothesis. $\square$

Let X and Y be topological spaces (respectively sequential convergence spaces) and let $L(X, Y)$ be the vector space of all linear, continuous (respectively, sequentially continuous) operators on X into Y.

THEOREM 3.13 *If E is a finitely normed space and $Y = \bigcup_{a>0} F_a$ is a*

sequentially inductive limit of finitely normed spaces, then as a vector space,
$L(E, Y)$ *can be identified with the inductive limit of the spaces* $L(E, F_a)$.

Proof For $b > a$, $F_b \supset F_a$ hence $T_b \in L(E, F_b)$ can be uniquely extended to
some $T_a \in L(E, F_a)$ by embedding $T_b(E)$ in F_a. It then follows that
$L(E, F_b) \subset L(E, F_a)$. Let $I_{ab} : L(E, F_b) \to L(E, F_a)$ be the embedding of
$L(E, F_b)$ in $L(E, F_a)$. From the definition of inductive limit (Section 1.3.3)
it is now possible to define a space $\tilde{L}$ which is the inductive limit of the
spaces $L(E, F_a)$, that is

$$\tilde{L} = \lim_{\to} I_{ab} L(E, F_b)$$

It is now only necessary to show that $L(E, Y)$ coincides with $\tilde{L}$.

Given any $T = \sum_{i=1}^{n} T_{a_i}$, $T_{a_i} \in L(E, F_{a_i})$ in $\tilde{L}$, T is clearly an element of
$L(E, Y)$. Conversely given any $T \in L(E, Y)$ there exists some $a > 0$ such
that $T(E) \subset F_a$ (Proposition 3.5), hence $T \in \tilde{L}$. □

COROLLARY 3.1   *Under the conditions of Theorem* 3.13, $L(E, Y)$ *can be
associated with the topological inductive limit of the spaces* $L(E, F_a)$,
equipped with uniform topologies.

Proof For $b > a$, the topology induced in $L(E, F_b)$ by the topology of
$L(E, F_a)$ is weaker than the original topology of $L(E, F_b)$. Utilizing
Theorem 1.7 (Köthe, 1969) it follows that $L(E, Y)$ is the topological
inductive limit of the spaces $L(E, F_a)$. □

THEOREM 3.14   *Let* $X = \bigcup_{a>0} E_a$ *be a sequential inductive limit of finitely
normed spaces and* Y *any sequential convergence space. The space*
$L(X, Y)$ *can be identified with the projective limit of the spaces* $L(E_a, Y)$.

Proof For $a > 0$, let $P_a : L(X, Y) \to L(E_a, Y)$ represent the projection

$$(P_a T)(x) \triangleq T(x), \qquad \forall x \in E_a, \qquad \forall T \in L(X, Y)$$

Identically we can define projections $P_{ba} : L(E_a, Y) \to L(E_b, Y)$ for $b > a$,
as

$$(P_{ba} T_a)(x) \triangleq T_a(x), \qquad \forall x \in E_b, \qquad \forall T_a \in L(E_a, Y)$$

The following relationships are readily verified for all $b > a > c > 0$

$$\left.\begin{array}{c} P_b \equiv P_{ba} P_a \\ P_{bc} \equiv P_{ab} P_{ac} \end{array}\right\} \tag{3.25}$$

From the definition of projective limit (Section 1.3) it is now possible to
define $\hat{L} = \lim_{\leftarrow} P_{ba} L(E_a, Y)$ of the spaces $L(E_a, Y)$. $\hat{L}$ is the subspace of

$\prod_a L(E_a, Y)$ formed by all elements $\hat{T} = \{T_a\}$ which satisfy

$$T_b = P_{ba} T_a, \qquad \forall \; b > a \qquad\qquad (3.26)$$

We wish to show that $\hat{L}$ coincides with $L(X, Y)$. Given any $T \in L(X, Y)$, T can be associated with an element $\hat{T} = \{T_a\} \in \hat{L}$ by defining $T_a = P_a T$. From (3.25) $\hat{T}$ satisfies (3.26). Conversely any $\{T_a\} \in \hat{L}$ can be associated with an element $T \in L(X, Y)$ through $T(x) \triangleq T_a(x)$ for all $x \in E_a$. The condition (3.26) makes this definition coherent for any $b > a$ and for any $x \in E_b$.

$$T(x) = T_b(x) = (P_{ba} T_a)(x) = T_a(x)$$

Hence $\hat{L} = \lim_{\leftarrow} P_{ba} L(E_a, Y) = (P_{ba} T_a)(x) = T_a(x).$ $\qquad\qquad \square$

THEOREM 3.15 *If* F *is a finitely normed space and* $X = \bigcup_{a>0} E_a$ *is a sequential inductive limit of finitely normed spaces, then:*

(i) *For any sequentially bounded set* $B \subset X$ *the function*

$$p_B(T) \triangleq \sup_{x \in B} \|T(x)\| \qquad\qquad (3.27)$$

is a finite semi-norm in $L(X, F)$.

(ii) *When* B *spans all sequentially bounded sets in* X *the family of semi-norms* $\{p_B(\cdot)\}$ *define* $L(X, F)$ *as a locally convex space.*

(iii) *The space* $L(X, F)$ *equipped with the topology defined by the family of semi-norms* $\{p_B(\cdot)\}$ *coincides with the topological projective limit of the spaces* $L(E_a, F)$, *each equipped with the uniform topology.*

Proof

(i) There exists some $a > 0$ such that B is a bounded set in E_a, in the topology of E_a (Proposition 3.4). Hence (3.27) establishes one of the semi-norms which defines the uniform topology of $L(E_a, F)$ (Yosida, IV.7, 1971).

(ii) For any non-zero $T \in L(X, F)$ there exists some $x_0 \in X$ such that $T(x_0) \neq 0$. Since a singleton is an example of a bounded set, there exists one element of the family $\{p_B(\cdot)\}$ such that $p_B(T) \neq 0$. Utilizing Theorem 1.4 (Köthe 1969), the family of semi-norms $\{p_B(\cdot)\}$ defines a locally convex topology in $L(X, F)$.

(iii) Theorem 3.14 states that $L(X, F)$ and $\lim_{\leftarrow} P_{ba} L(E_a, Y) = \hat{L}$ coincide as vector spaces. We now compare topologies. An arbitrary absolutely convex neighbourhood of the origin (n.o.) in $\hat{L}$ is of the form ((1.4), Section 1.3.3).

$$\hat{U} = \hat{L} \cap \left\{ \bigcap_{i=1}^{n} P_{a_i}^{-1} U_{a_i} \right\} \tag{3.28}$$

where U_{a_i} is an n.o. in $L(E_{a_i}, F)$.

$$U_{a_i} \triangleq \{ T_i \in L(E_{a_i}, F) : P_{B_{i,k}}(T_i) < \xi_{i,k}, \ k = 1, 2, \ldots, m_i \} \tag{3.29}$$

with $\{B_{i,k}\}$, $k = 1, 2, \ldots, m_i$, a family of bounded sets in E_{a_i} and $\{\xi_{i,k}\}$, $k = 1, 2, \ldots, m_i$, a family of non-zero positive numbers.

A general n.o. in $L(X, F)$ is

$$U = \{ T \in L(X, F) : p_{B_k}(T) < \xi_k, \ k = 1, \ldots, m \} \tag{3.30}$$

with $\{B_k\}$, $k = 1, 2, \ldots, m$, a family of sequentially bounded sets in X, and $\{\xi_k\}$, $k = 1, 2, \ldots, m$, a family of non-zero positive numbers.

Every B_k in (3.30) is a bounded set in some E_{a_k} (Proposition 3.4). Hence U can be written as

$$U = \bigcap_{k=1}^{m} \{ T \in \hat{L} : p_{B_k}(T) < \xi_k \}$$

with B_k a bounded set in E_{a_k}. Thus

$$U = \hat{L} \cap \left\{ \bigcap_{k=1}^{m} p_{a_k}^{-1} \{ T_k \in L(E_{a_k}, F) : p_{B_k}(T_k) < \xi_k \} \right\}$$

Therefore U is the set of the form of (3.28) and (3.29). Hence every absolutely convex n.o. in $L(X, F)$ is an n.o. in $\hat{L}$. Conversely any set of the form defined by (3.28) and (3.29) has the form (3.30) because every bounded set $B_{i,k}$ in E_{a_i} is a sequentially bounded set in X. Thus the two topologies coincide. ☐

The topology defined in $L(X, F)$ by the family of semi-norms $\{p_B(\cdot)\}$ is called the *strong convergence topology*.

COROLLARY 3.2   *The strong sequential dual X^* of a sequential inductive limit $X = \bigcup\limits_{a>0} E_a$ of finitely normed spaces can be identified with the topological projective limits of the strong duals E_a^* of the spaces E_a.*

$$X^* = \lim_{\leftarrow} P_{ba} E_a^*$$

Proof   Direct consequence of Theorem 3.15 with $F = C^1$. ☐

THEOREM 3.16   *Given two sequential inductive limit of finitely normed spaces, $X = \bigcup\limits_{a>0} E_a$, $Y = \bigcup\limits_{b>0} F_b$, then as a vector space $L(X, Y)$ can be* *identified with the projective limit, when* $a \to 0$ *of the spaces* $\tilde{L}_a = \bigcup_{b>0} L(E_a, F_b)$.

Proof $L(X, Y)$ is the projective limit of the spaces $L(E_a, Y)$ (Theorem 3.14). Alternatively $L(E_a, Y)$ coincides with $\tilde{L}_a$ (Theorem 3.13).   □

3.6.3   The spaces X_p

Let L_p represent the usual space of complex valued time functions $t \mapsto f(t)$ with domain R_+, such that $t \mapsto |f(t)|^p$ is integrable with respect to the Lebesgue measure.

L_p is a Banach space with topology defined by the norm

$$\|f\|_{L_p} = \int_{R_+} |f(t)|^p \, dt$$

For $1 \le p < \infty$, the strong dual L_p^* of L_p coincides with L_q where $p^{-1} + q^{-1} = 1$, and the action of $\mu \in L_p^*$ is defined as

$$\mu(f) = \int_{R_+} \mu(t)f(t) \, dt$$

The space L_∞ is also a Banach space equipped with the norm

$$\|f\|_{L_\infty} \triangleq \operatorname{ess\,sup}_{t \in R_+} |f(t)|$$

For any $a > 0$, let $L_{p,a}$ represent the set of all functions $t \mapsto f(t)$ such that $t \mapsto \exp(at)f(t)$ is an element of L_p. Let $E_a : L_{p,a} \to L_p$ be the operator which assigns $t \mapsto f(t)$ to $t \mapsto \exp(at)f(t)$; clearly E_a is an isomorphism. In $L_{p,a}$, we shall adopt the norm

$$\|f\|_{L_{p,a}} \triangleq \|E_a f\|_{L_p}$$

Under such a definition, $L_{p,a}$ and L_p are seen to be isometrically isomorphic spaces. It is straightforward to show that for any $b > a$, $L_{p,a}$ contains $L_{p,b}$ and that the topology induced in $L_{p,b}$ by the topology of $L_{p,a}$ is weaker than the original topology of $L_{p,b}$. Thus with the rule of convergence L.3, the space

$$X_p \triangleq \bigcup_{a>0} L_{p,a} \tag{3.31}$$

is a sequential inductive limit space.

THEOREM 3.17   *For* $1 \le p < \infty$, *the strong sequential dual* X_p^* *of* X_p *can be identified with the topological projective limit* $\varprojlim P_{ba} L_{q,-a}$, *where* $p^{-1} + q^{-1} = 1$.

Proof Utilizing Corollary 3.2, $X_p^* = \lim_{\leftarrow} P_{ba} L_{p,a}^*$, we therefore need to demonstrate that $L_{p,a}^* = L_{q,-a}$.

Let $\bar{\mu}$ be arbitrary in $L_{p,a}^*$, for any $f \in L_{p,a}$, $\bar{\mu}(f) = \bar{\mu}(E_{-a} E_a f)$; $E_a f$ is arbitrary in L_p when f is arbitrary in $L_{p,a}$, so $\bar{\mu} E_{-a}$ defines a functional in L_p. Let $\bar{\mu}_a \in L_p^*$ represent such a functional. We have shown that every functional in $L_{p,a}^*$ can be written as $\bar{\mu}_a E_a$, with $\bar{\mu}_a \in L_p^*$. For $q = (1 + p^{-1})^{-1}$, let $t \mapsto \mu_a(t)$ represent the functional $\bar{\mu}_a$. For any $f \in L_{p,a}$

$$\bar{\mu}(f) = \bar{\mu}_a(E_a f) = \int_{R_+} \mu_a(t) \exp{(at)} f(t) \, dt$$

Let $\mu(t) \triangleq \mu_a(t) \exp{(at)}$; $t \mapsto \mu(t)$ is an element of $L_{q,-a}$. Thus we have shown that every $\bar{\mu} \in L_{p,a}^*$ can be represented by some $\mu \in L_{q,-a}$ such that

$$\bar{\mu}(f) = \int_{R_+} \mu(t) f(t) \, dt, \qquad \forall f \in L_{p,a} \tag{3.32}$$

Topologically

$$\|\bar{\mu}\|_{L_{p,a}^*} = \sup_{\|f\|_{L_{p,a}} = 1} |\bar{\mu}(f)|$$

$$= \sup_{\|E_a f\|_{L_p} = 1} \int |\mu(t) \exp{(-at)}| \cdot |\exp{(at)} f(t)| \, dt$$

Hence

$$\|\bar{\mu}\|_{L_{p,a}^*} = \|E_{-a} \mu\|_{L_q} = \|\mu\|_{L_{q,-a}}$$

Conversely given any $\mu \in L_{q,-a}$ the integral (3.32) defines a functional in $L_{p,a}$. Thus $L_{p,a}^* = L_{q,-a}$. ☐

THEOREM 3.18   *The space* $L(X_p, X_p)$ *can be identified with* $\lim_{\leftarrow} P_{ba} \bigcup_{c > 0} L(L_{p,a} L_{p,c})$

Proof Direct consequence of Theorem 3.16. ☐

3.6.4   Multipliers in X_1, X_2, and X_∞

In the determination of graphical stability criteria the spaces X_1, X_2, and X_∞ are particularly significant.

PROPOSITION 3.6   *For* $b > a$, *the space of all linear, continuous and time-invariant operators* $A : L_{p,a} \to L_{p,b}$ *is just the singleton* $\{0\}$.

Proof Assume that there exists an operator A $(A \neq 0)$, which is linear, continuous and time-invariant operator

$$A : L_{p,a} \to L_{p,b}$$

Let $\bar{A}$ represent the operator $E_b A E_{-a}$, then $\bar{A}$ maps L_p and into L_p.

It is straightforward to show that for any $T>0$ and any $a \geq 0$

$$S_T E_a = \phi_a(T) E_a S_T$$

where

$$\phi_a(t) \triangleq \begin{cases} \exp(-at) & \text{for} \quad t \geq 0 \\ 0 & \text{for} \quad t < 0 \end{cases}$$

and

$$(S_T f)(t) = \begin{cases} f(t-T) & \text{for} \quad t \geq T \\ 0 & \text{for} \quad t < T \end{cases}$$

As A is time invariant

$$S_T \bar{A} = S_T E_b A E_{-a} = \phi_{b-a}(T) \bar{A} S_T$$

For any $f \in L_p$

$$\|S_T \bar{A} f\| = \phi_{b-a}(T) \|\bar{A} S_T f\| \leq \phi_{b-a}(T) \|\bar{A}\| \cdot \|S_T f\|$$

But for any $f \in L_p$, $\|S_T f\| = \|f\|$, then

$$\|\bar{A} f\| \leq \phi_{b-a}(T) \|\bar{A}\| \cdot \|f\| \qquad \forall f \in L_p.$$

Since $b - a > 0$, the norm $\|\bar{A} f\|$ can be made as small as desired, since T can be selected as large as necessary. Therefore $\|\bar{A} f\| = 0$ which contradicts the condition $\|A\| \neq 0$ and consequently $\|\bar{A}\| \neq 0$.

Thus the null operator is the only linear, time-invariant operator on $L_{p,a}$ into $L_{p,b}$ when $b > a$. □

Definition 3.1   For any real σ the space $K(\sigma)$ is the space of all complex valued functions $s \mapsto h(s)$ of the complex variable s, which are bounded and analytic in the half-plane $\{s : Re(s) > \sigma\}$.

Definition 3.2   The space K_σ is the space of all complex functions $s \mapsto h(s)$, analytic in $\{s : Re(s) > \sigma\}$ and such that for any $\gamma > \sigma$, $\sup_{Re(s) \geq \gamma} |h(s)|$ is finite.

Notice that K_σ is not contained in $K(\sigma)$ since there are functions $h \in K_\sigma$ for which

$$\sup_{\gamma > \sigma} \sup_{Re(s) \geq \gamma} |h(s)|$$

may not be finite.

THEOREM 3.19   *The space $M(L_{2,a}, L_{2,c})$, $c < a$ of all linear, continuous and time-invariant operators in $L_{2,a}$ into $L_{2,c}$ can be identified with the space K_{-c} in such a way that every $A \in M(L_{2,a}, L_{2,c})$ is assigned to an element $h \in K_{-c}$ such that*

$$(\mathcal{L} A f)(s) = h(s)(\mathcal{L} f)(s)$$

for all $f \in L_{2,a}$ and all $Re(s) > -c$.

Proof Consider an arbitrary $A \in M(L_{2,a}, L_{2,c})$ and introduce $\bar{A} \triangleq E_c A E_{-a}$; the operator $\bar{A}$ maps L_2 into L_2. Furthermore the time invariance of A implies

$$S_T \bar{A} = \phi_{c-a}(T) \bar{A} S_T \qquad \forall\, T \geq 0 \tag{3.33}$$

Following the proof of Theorem 3.1, introduce $\psi_s \in L_2$ defined as $\bar{A}^* \phi_s$. Then

$$(\mathscr{L} \bar{A} f)(s) = (\bar{A} f)(\phi_s) = f(\psi_s)$$

for all $f \in L_2$ and $Re(s) > 0$. Also from the proof of Theorem 3.1 we conclude that

$$(S_T f)(\psi_s) = \phi_{s+a-c}(T) f(\psi_s) \qquad \forall\, Re(s) > 0$$

Using this result and the arguments of Theorem 3.1, it follows that

$$f(\psi_s) = h_0(s) f(\phi_{s+a-c}) \tag{3.34}$$

for all $Re(s) > 0$ and for some $s \mapsto h_0(s)$ analytic in $\{s : Re(s) > 0\}$ which satisfies

$$|h_0(s)| \leq \|\bar{A}\| \left(1 + \frac{(a-c)}{Re(s)} \right)^{1/2}$$

so $s \mapsto h_0(s)$ lies in K_0.

Finally

$$(\mathscr{L} \bar{A} f)(s) = (\mathscr{L} E_c A E_{-a} f)(s) = h_0(s)(\mathscr{L} E_a E_{-a} f)(s + a - c)$$

but

$$(\mathscr{L} E_c A E_{-a} f)(s) = (\mathscr{L} A E_{-a} f)(s - c)$$

and

$$(\mathscr{L} E_a E_{-a} f)(s + a - c) = (\mathscr{L} E_{-a} f)(s + a - c - a) = (\mathscr{L} E_{-a} f)(s - c)$$

Since $E_{-a} f$ is arbitrary in $L_{2,a}$ when f is arbitrary in L_2 it follows that there exists an $h_0 \in K_0$ such that for all $g \in L_{2,a}$ and all $Re(s) > 0$

$$(\mathscr{L} A g)(s - c) = h_0(s)(\mathscr{L} g)(s - c)$$

Or

$$(LAg)(s) = h_0(s + c)(\mathscr{L} g)(s) \qquad \forall\, Re(s) > -c$$

The function $h(s) \triangleq h_0(s + c)$ is an element of K_{-c}. So that A can be assigned to a transfer function K_{-c}.

Conversely it is straightforward to show that any $h \in K_{-c}$ defines a multiplier on $L_{2,a}$ into $L_{2,c}$ through

$$Af = \mathscr{L}^{-1} \hat{h} \mathscr{L} f$$

where

$$(\hat{h}\hat{f})(s) \triangleq h(s) f(s) \qquad\qquad \square$$

THEOREM 3.20   *The space $M(X_2)$ can be identified with the projective limit $\lim_{\leftarrow} P_{ba} \bigcup_{c \leq a} K_{-c}$. Moreover any $A \in M(X_2)$ is assigned to a transfer function $s \mapsto h(s)$ analytic in some $Re(s) > -\gamma$ such that for all $f \in L_{2,a}$ and $Re(s) > -\min\{a, \gamma\}$*

$$(\mathscr{L}Af)(s) = h(s)(\mathscr{L}f)(s)$$

Proof   Direct consequence of Theorems 3.18, 3.19.   □

With minimal alterations to Theorems 3.9 and 3.12 we can establish theorems similar to Theorem 3.20 for the spaces X_1 and X_∞.

THEOREM 3.21   *Let A be arbitrary in $M(X_1)$ (respectively $M(X_\infty)$) then there exists a complex function $s \mapsto h(s)$ in $\lim_{\leftarrow} P_{ba} \bigcup_{c \leq a} K_{-c}$ and a real number $\gamma > 0$ such that for all $f \in L_{1,a}$ (respectively $L_{\infty,a}$) and all $Re(s) > -\min\{a, \gamma\}$ we have*

$$(\mathscr{L}Af)(s) = h(s)(\mathscr{L}f)(s)$$

Moreover the map which assigns A to its transfer function is an injective morphism of rings.

Let $E_a\mathscr{M}(R_+)$ represent the space of all measures μ of the form $\mu = E_a\mu_0$, with $\mu_0 \in \mathscr{M}(R_+)$, that is for any Borel set B

$$\mu(B) = \int_B \exp(at)\, d\mu_0(t).$$

With minimal alterations to Theorems 3.9 and 3.19 the following theorem can easily be derived:

THEOREM 3.22   *The space $M(X_1)$ of all multipliers on X_1 into itself is isomorphic with the projective limit when $a \to 0$ of the spaces Q_a defined by*

$$Q_a = \bigcup_{c \leq a} E_{-c}\mathscr{M}(R_+)$$

The generic element $A \in M(X_1)$ is assigned to a measure $\mu \in \lim_{\leftarrow} P_{ba}Q_a$ where $P_{ba} : Q_a \to Q_b$, $b > a$ are the appropriate projections in such a way that

$$A(f) = \mu \otimes f \qquad \forall f \in X_1.$$

3.6.5   The space of transfer functions $\mathscr{R}$

Represent by $\mathscr{R}$ the space $\lim_{\leftarrow} P_{ba} \bigcup_{c \leq a} K_{-c}$. It is important to note the difference between the frequency representation of multipliers in L_p and

X_p. We saw in Sections 3.2, 3.4 and 3.6 that multipliers in L_2, L_1 and L_∞ were associated with complex functions whose domain of analyticity excluded the imaginary axis. Therefore it is not possible to develop general Nyquist stability criteria for feedback systems represented in these spaces. Although the space $\mathscr{R}$ appears complex, its elements have an important property: they are analytic in an open region which includes the closed right half complex plane. This property is crucial to the development of Nyquist type stability criteria.

In order to analyse $\mathscr{R}$, represent by $\mathscr{R}_a$ the space $\bigcup\limits_{c \leq a} K_{-c}$. Thus $\mathscr{R} = \lim\limits_{\leftarrow} P_{ba} \mathscr{R}_a$.

If a function $s \mapsto h(s)$ lies in $\mathscr{R}_a$, then there exists a $\gamma_a \in (0, a]$ such that $s \mapsto h(s)$ is bounded and holomorphic in the half-plane $\{s: Re(s) > -\gamma_a\}$. The domain of analyticity of the function always includes the imaginary axis.

The space $\mathscr{R}$ is the projective limit of the spaces $\mathscr{R}_a$. Hence any $h \in \mathscr{R}$ can be represented by a family of functions $\{s \mapsto h_a(s)\}$ and a family of positive reals $\{\gamma_a\}$ which satisfy

(i) $a \geq \gamma_a$ for all $a > 0$

(ii) $\gamma_b \geq \gamma_a$ for $b > a$

(iii) $s \mapsto h_a(s)$ is an element of $K_{-\gamma_a}$

(iv) $h_a(s) \equiv h_b(s)$ for all $b > a$ and all $Re(s) \geq -\gamma_a$

PROPOSITION 3.6 *The space $\mathscr{R}$ coincides with the space $\bigcup\limits_{\gamma > 0} K_{-\gamma}$*

Proof Let $\bar{h}$ be an arbitrary element of $\mathscr{R}$ and let $\{h_a\}$ be the family of functions satisfying conditions (i) to (iv) above, which represent $\bar{h}$.

Let $\gamma > 0$ be chosen such that $\gamma \leq \sup\limits_{a > 0} \gamma_a$. A function $h(s)$ can be defined for any $Re(s) > -\gamma$ as

$$h(s) = h_a(s)$$

where a is such that $Re(s) \geq -\gamma_a$. The coherence and unity of this definition follows from condition (iv). Clearly $h(\cdot)$ is an element of $K_{-\gamma}$. Thus any $\bar{h} \in \mathscr{R}$ can be identified with an element of $\bigcup\limits_{\gamma < 0} K_\gamma$. Conversely, given any $h \in \bigcup\limits_{\gamma > 0} K_{-\gamma}$, let $\gamma > 0$ be such that $K_{-\gamma}$ contains $s \mapsto h(s)$. Define for any $a > 0$, a positive number γ_a as

$$\gamma_a \triangleq \min\{a, \gamma\}$$

Also define a set of functions $\{s \mapsto h_a(s)\}$ through

$$h_a(s) = h(s) \quad \text{for all} \quad Re(s) > -\gamma_a$$

Clearly the two sets $\{\gamma_a\}$ and $\{h_a\}$ satisfy conditions (i) to (iv) and therefore represent an element of $\mathcal{R}$. This demonstrates that $\bigcup\limits_{\gamma>0} K_{-\gamma}$ is contained in $\mathcal{R}$ and therefore the two spaces coincide.   □

PROPOSITION 3.7   An element $h \in \mathcal{R}$ is invertible in $\mathcal{R}$ if and only if there exists some $\gamma > 0$ such that

$$\inf_{Re(s)>-\gamma} |h(s)| > 0.$$

Proof   If the condition $\inf\limits_{Re(s)>-\gamma} |h(s)| > 0$ holds, then $h(\cdot)$ is invertible in $K_{-\gamma}$ and therefore in $\mathcal{R}$ by Proposition 3.6.

PROPOSITION 3.8   An element of $h \in \mathcal{R}$ bounded away from zero at infinity is invertible in $\mathcal{R}$ if and only if

$$\inf_{Re(s)\geq 0} |h(s)| > 0$$

Proof   The only if condition is obvious. Assume that the condition

$$\inf_{Re(s)\geq 0} |h(s)| > 0 \tag{3.35}$$

holds. Since $h(\cdot)$ is an element of $\bigcup\limits_{\gamma} K_{-\gamma}$ it is possible to find an $a > 0$ such that $s \mapsto h(s)$ is bounded and analytic in an open set containing the half plane $Re(s) \geq -a$.

Since $h(\cdot)$ is bounded away from zero at infinity, there exists a $\rho > 0$ such that

$$\inf_{|s|\geq \rho} |h(s)| > 0$$

$$Re(s) \geq -a$$

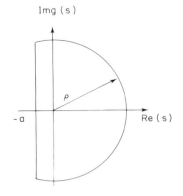

Hence all possible zeros of $h(s)$ in the half plane $Re(s) \geq -a$ exist in the compact region $D(-a;\rho) = \{s : Re(s) \geq -a, |s| \geq \rho\}$. As $s \mapsto h(s)$ is analytic in an open region containing $D(-a;\rho)$, there are at most a finite number of such zeros, let $z_1, \dots, z_n$ denote these zeros.

Because condition (3.35) is satisfied then

$$\max_{i \le n} Re(z_i) < 0$$

Select a $\gamma > 0$ such that $\gamma < -\max_{i \le n} Re(z_i)$, then

$$\inf_{Re(s) > -\gamma} |h(s)| > 0$$

Therefore using Proposition 3.7, $s \mapsto h(s)$ must be invertible in $\mathscr{R}$. $\qquad \square$

PROPOSITION 3.9 *The projective limit*

$$\varprojlim P_{ba} \bigcup_{c \le a} E_{-c} \mathscr{M}(R_+)$$

coincides with the space $\mathscr{M}(R_+)$

Proof Identical to the proof of Proposition 3.6. $\qquad \square$

3.6.6 The space X_p^n

The multivariable extension of the space X_p is the nth cartesian power of X_p, represented by X_p^n. The algebra $L(X_p^n, X_p^n)$ is clearly identified with the algebra $L(X_p, X_p)^{n \times n}$ of all $n \times n$ matrices over the ring $L(X_p, X_p)$.
In particular for $p = 2$ and for the algebra $M(X_2^n)$

$$M(X_2^n) \simeq M(X_2)^{n \times n}$$

Since $M(X_2)$ is isomorphic with $\mathscr{R}$ (Theorem 3.20), it follows that $M(X_2^n)$ and $\mathscr{R}^{n \times n}$ must be isomorphic. The ring $\mathscr{R}$ is commutative and therefore

THEOREM 3.23 *A multiplier* $A \in M(X_2^n)$ *is invertible if and only if* $\det \hat{A}$ *is invertible in* $\mathscr{R}$, *where* $\hat{A} \in \mathscr{R}^{n \times n}$ *is the matrix transfer function of* A.

REFERENCES

Hewitt, E. and Ross, K. A. (1963). "Abstract Harmonic Analysis", Vol I, Band 115. Springer Verlag, Berlin.

Hewitt, E. and Stromberg, K. (1965). "Real and Abstract Analysis", Graduate Series in Maths. Springer Verlag, Berlin.

Hille, E. (1962). "Analytical Function Theory", Vol 2, Ginn, Aylesbury.

Hille, E. and Phillips, R. S. (1957). "Functional Analysis and Semi-Groups". Amer. Math. Soc. Colloquium Pub., Vol. 31.

Köthe, G. (1969). "Topological Vector Spaces", *I*, Band 159. Springer Verlag, Berlin.

Larsen, R. (1971). "An Introduction to the Theory of Multipliers", Band 175. Springer Verlag, Berlin.

MacLane, S. and Birkhoff, G. (1967). "Algebra". Macmillan, London.

Willems, J. C. (1971). "The Analysis of Feedback Systems", MIT Research Monograph, *62*. Massachusetts Institute of Technology.

Yosida, K. (1971). "Functional Analysis". Springer Verlag, New York.

Zemanian, A. H. (1968). "Generalised Integral Transforms". Pure and Applied Mathematics, *18*, Interscience, New York.

APPENDIX 3.1   THE THEORY OF MULTIPLIERS IN L_∞

Let $w([t, \tau]) = \tau - t$ represent the usual Lebesgue measure and let $\lambda(\cdot)$ be a positive countably additive measure satisfying,

(i) $0 \le \lambda(E) \le 1$ for any Lebesgue measurable set $E \subseteq R_+$. Moreover, $\lambda(R_+) = 1$.

(ii) $\lambda(E) = 0$ if and only if $w(E) = 0$.

Let N represent the collection of all λ (null sets) and therefore the collection of all w null sets.

Given a positive valued Lebesgue measurable function $f : R_+ \to R_+$ we shall represent by $V(f)$ the set

$$V(f) = \{\alpha \ge 0 : \{t : f(t) > \alpha\} \notin N\} \tag{A.1}$$

If $V(f)$ is bounded, then the least upper bound of $V(f)$ is the essential supremum of f; otherwise $V(f)$ is unbounded and ess sup $f = \infty$.

Let B denote the family of all Borel sets in R_+. We shall represent by $L_\infty(R_+, B, N)$, or $L_\infty(R_+, B, \lambda)$ (or more simply L_∞) the space of all measurable complex valued functions $f : R_+ \to C^1$ such that ess sup $|f| < \infty$. Using the norm

$$\|f\| \triangleq \text{ess sup } |f|$$

the space L_∞ is a Banach space (Hewitt and Stromberg, 20.14, 1963). As usual we identify the two functions f and g with the same element of L_∞ when

$$\{t : f(t) - g(t) \ne 0\} \in N$$

Let b.a.(R_+, B, N) (or b.a. more simply) represent the space of all bounded additive measures $\mu(\cdot)$ in the measure space (R_+, B) with the property $\mu(E) = 0$ for every $E \in N$ and equipped with the norm,

$$\|\mu\| = |\mu|(R_+) \tag{A.2}$$

We can now state the first result concerning the dual space L^*_∞ of L_∞:

LEMMA A.1 (Yosida and Hewitt, 1952)   *The space b.a. and the dual space* L^*_∞ *of* L_∞ *are isometrically isomorphic spaces. To each* $\hat\mu \in L^*_\infty$ *there is assigned a* $\mu \in b.a.$ *such that for all* $f \in L_\infty$

$$\hat\mu(f) = \int_{R_+} f(t)\,d\mu(t) \tag{A.3}$$

This result can be considerably sharpened: consider Π to be the subspace of b.a. formed by all purely finite additive measures. That is, $\pi \in \Pi$ if and only if there exists a sequence of sets $E_1 \supseteq E_2 \supseteq \ldots \supseteq E_n \supseteq \ldots$ such that $\lim_n \mu(E_n) = 0$ for any countably additive measure μ and such that $\pi(E_n) = \pi(R_+)$ for all n. Then,

LEMMA A.2 (Dempster, 1975)   *The space* L^*_∞ *can be identified with the direct sum*

$$L_1(R_+, B, \lambda) \oplus \Pi$$

in such a way that an arbitrary $\hat\mu \in L^*_\infty$ *is uniquely represented as*

$$\hat\mu(f) = \int_{R_+} f(t)g(t)\,d\lambda(t) + \int_{R_+} f(t)\,d\pi(t) \tag{A.4}$$

for some $g \in L_1(R_+, B, \lambda)$ *and* $\pi \in \Pi$. *Moreover*

$$\|\hat\mu\| = \int_{R_+} |g(t)|\,d\lambda(t) + |\pi|\,(R_+) \tag{A.5}$$

THEOREM A.1   *Let* $t \mapsto \phi(t)$ *be a bounded function which satisfies* $\lim_{t\to\infty} |\phi(t)| = 0$, $\phi(\tau) \neq 0$ *for all* $0 \leq \tau < \infty$ *and* $\phi(t+\tau) = \phi(t)\phi(\tau)$. *Let* π *be a purely finite additive measure satisfying* $\pi(S_T E) = \phi(T)\pi(E)$ *for all* $T \geq 0$ *and* $E \in B$. *Then* $\pi = 0$.

Proof   Consider the interval $E_T = [T, \infty)$. Since $E_T = S_T R_+$, we have $\pi(E_T) = \phi(T)\pi(R_+)$. Hence $|\pi(E_T)| \leq |\phi(T)| \cdot \|\pi\|$ and $\lim_{T\to\infty} |\pi(E_T)| = \|\pi\| \lim_{T\to\infty} |\phi(T)| = 0$.

Assuming that $\|\pi\| \neq 0$, then given any $1 > \xi > 0$, there exists a $T > 0$ such that $|\pi|(E_T) < \xi\|\pi\|$. Defining $E'_T = [0, T) = R_+ - E_T$, we then have

$$\|\pi\| = |\pi|\,(E_T) + |\pi|\,(E'_T) \leq \xi\|\pi\| + |\pi|\,(E'_T).$$

Hence

$$\|\pi\| \leq (1-\xi)^{-1}\,|\pi|\,(E'_T) \tag{A.6}$$

Let μ_T be the countably additive measure defined as $\mu_T(E) = w(E'_T \cap E)$. Given any $\alpha < T$ there exists (by definition of purely finite additive measures) a set $E_\alpha \subset B$ such that

$$\text{(i)} \quad |\pi|\,(E_\alpha) = \|\pi\|$$

$$\text{(ii)} \quad \mu_T(E_\alpha) < \alpha$$

Now, let E'_α be defined as $E_\alpha \cap E'_T$; then $\mu_T(E'_\alpha) < \alpha$ and

$$\|\pi\| = |\pi|\,(E_\alpha) = |\pi|\,(E'_\alpha) + |\pi|\,(E_\alpha \cap E_T)$$
$$\leq |\pi|\,(E'_\alpha) + \xi\,\|\pi\|.$$

And so

$$\|\pi\| \leq (1-\xi)^{-1}\,|\pi|\,(E'_\alpha) \tag{A.7}$$

We can conclude that E'_α is non-empty, since it is assumed that $\|\pi\| > 0$. But since E'_α is a non-empty Borel set, there exists a nonvoid union of pairwise disjoint intervals $\bigcup_{k=1}^{\infty} I_k$, $I_k = [a_k, b_k)$ such that

$$\text{(i)} \quad \bigcup_{k=1}^{\infty} I_k \supseteq E'_\alpha$$

$$\text{(ii)} \quad \sum_{k=1}^{\infty} \mu_T(I_k) < \alpha$$

Since E'_α is contained in $[0, T)$, we can assume without loss of generality that every I_k is contained in $[0, T]$. Let us order the intervals in such a way that $a_{k+1} \geq b_k$, then the limits $\{b_k\}$ form a bounded increasing sequence. Let $b_0 \leq T$ be the limit of such a sequence. Now, given any $\delta > 0$ there exists n such that $b_0 - b_n < \delta\alpha$. Therefore $\mu_T\left(\bigcup_{k=1}^{n} I_k\right) < \alpha$ and $\mu_T[b_n, b_0] < \delta\alpha$. Considering now the finite union $\left\{\bigcup_{k=1}^{n} I_k\right\} \cup [b_n, b_0)$, we have a finite union of intervals containing E'_α $\left(\text{as } [b_n, b_0) \supseteq \bigcup_{k=n+1}^{\infty} I_k\right)$ whose $\mu_T(\cdot)$ measure is inferior to $(1+\delta)\alpha$. Since δ is arbitrary, $(1+\delta)\alpha$ can be made less than T. Therefore without loss of generality we can assume that E'_α is defined by a finite union of pairwise disjoint closed intervals $E'_\alpha = \bigcup_{k=1}^{n} I_k$, $I_k = [a_k, b_k)$; also without loss of generality we can assume that $a_{k+1} > b_k$ for all k and that $|\pi|\,(I_k) \neq 0$ for all k.

Let E''_α be the complement to $[0, T]$ of the set E'_α. Because $\alpha < T$ and $\mu_T(E'_\alpha) = w(E'_\alpha) < \alpha$, the set E''_α is necessarily non-empty. Moreover, E''_α is given by a finite union of pairwise disjoint intervals,

$$E''_\alpha = \bigcup_{k=1}^{n-1} (b_k, a_{k+1}) \cup (b_n, T] \cup [0, a_1) \tag{A.8}$$

Let $d > 0$ be defined as min $w(J)$, where J is any of the non-empty intervals in (A.8). Let us now consider an arbitrary interval $I \subseteq [0, T]$ such that $w(I) < d$. We can consider separately the cases where $I \subset E_\alpha''$ and $I \cap E_\alpha' \neq \phi$. □

Case 1: $E_\alpha'' \supset I$. $|\pi|(I) \leq |\pi|(E_\alpha'')$, since E_α'' is contained in the complement to R_+ of E_α, and since $|\pi|(E_\alpha) = \|\pi\|$, we must have $|\pi|(E_\alpha'') = 0$. Therefore $|\pi|(I) = 0$.

Case 2: $I \cap E_\alpha' \neq \phi$. In this case, $I \cap I_k$ is non-empty for some k. But since $w(I) < d$, then k is unique. Thus

$$|\pi|(I) = |\pi|(I_k \cap I) + |\pi|(E_\alpha'' \cap I)$$
$$= |\pi|(I_k \cap I) \leq |\pi|(I_k).$$

Let $I = [a, b)$, then $b - a = w(I) < d$. Let $\tau > 0$ be such that $a_{k+1} - b > \tau > b_k - a$. Such a τ exists as $a_{k+1} - b_k > d > b - a$. For any such τ, $b + \tau > a_{k+1}$ and $a + \tau > b_k$. Therefore

$$S_\tau I = [a + \tau, b + \tau) \subset (b_k, a_{k+1}) \subseteq E_\alpha''$$

by hypothesis

$$\pi(S_\tau I) = \phi(\tau)\pi(I).$$

But since $S_\tau I \subset E_\alpha''$ we have, as in Case 1, $\pi(S_\tau I) = 0$, and therefore $\pi(I) = 0$, as $\phi(\tau) \neq 0$. The above two cases demonstrate that there exists a number $d > 0$ such that every interval I contained in $[0, T]$ which satisfies $w(I) < d$ also satisfies $\pi(I) = 0$. The set E_α' can be written as a finite union of such intervals, and therefore $|\pi|(E_\alpha') = 0$. Finally from (A.7) we conclude that $\pi = 0$. □

THEOREM A.2 *If π is a purely additive finite measure, then for all $T \geq 0$ the measure $\pi_T(\cdot)$ defined as*

$$\pi_T(E) = \pi(S_T E)$$

is also purely finite additive.

Proof Let us assume that π is a real positive measure. Let $E_1 \supset E_2 \supset \ldots \supset E_n \supset \ldots$ be a sequence of sets such that $\pi(E_n) = \pi(R_+) = \|\pi\|$ for all n and $\mu(E_n) \to 0$ for a countably additive measure μ. Define $I = [0, T)$ and let $I' = [T, \infty)$ be its complement. Finally, let E_n' and E_n'' be defined respectively as $E_n \cap I$ and $E_n \cap I'$. Then

$$\|\pi\| = \pi(E_n') + \pi(E_n'')$$
$$\|\pi\| = \pi(I) + \pi(I')$$

From the above we have

$$[\pi(I) - \pi(E'_n)] + [\pi(I') - \pi(E''_n)] = 0$$

Since $E'_n \subseteq I$ and $E''_n \subseteq I$, we have $\pi(E'_n) \leq \pi(I)$ and $\pi(E''_n) \leq \pi(I')$. Both terms $\pi(I) - \pi(E'_n)$ and $\pi(I') - \pi(E''_n)$ are therefore positive. Since their sum is zero, they must both be zero. Hence

$$\pi\{[0, T)\} = \pi(E'_n)$$

$$\pi\{[T, \infty)\} = \pi(E''_n)$$

However, since E''_n is contained in $[T, \infty)$, is is possible to find a set $B_n \subseteq R_+$ such that

$$S_T B_n = E''_n$$

Therefore, $\pi_T(B_n) = \pi(S_T B_n) = \pi(E''_n) = \pi\{[T, \infty)\}$. Noting that $[T, \infty) = S_T R_+$, thus

$$\pi_T(B_n) = \pi(S_T R_+) = \pi_T(R_+) \qquad (\text{A}.9)$$

Any countably additive measure μ is defined by a L_1 function $\mu(t)$. Then

$$\mu(B_n) = \int_{B_n} \mu(t)\, dt - \int_{S_T B_n} \mu(t - T)\, dt$$

$$= \int_{E''_n} \mu(t - T)\, dt$$

Hence

$$\lim_n \mu(B_n) = \lim_n (S_T \mu)(E_n) = 0. \qquad (\text{A}.10)$$

Consequently π_T satisfies the conditions of the definition of a purely finite measure.

If π is an arbitrary complex measure, then

$$\pi = (\pi_+^{(R)} - \pi_-^{(R)}) + j(\pi_+^{(I)} - \pi_-^{(I)})$$

where $\pi_+^{(R)}$, $\pi_-^{(R)}$, $\pi_+^{(I)}$ and $\pi_-^{(I)}$ are positive measures. Then

$$\pi_T(E) = (\pi_+^{(R)}(S_T E) - \pi_-^{(R)}(S_T E)) + j(\pi_+^{(I)}(S_T E) - \pi_-^{(I)}(S_T E))$$

clearly defines a purely finite additive measure.   □

THEOREM A.3: L_∞-REPRESENTATION THEOREM *Let $A : L_\infty \to L_\infty$ be a linear, bounded time-invariant operator. Then there exists a bounded holomorphic complex function $s \mapsto h(s)$ with domain in $Re(s) > 0$ such that*

(i) $(\mathscr{L}Af)(s) = a(s)(\mathscr{L}f)(s)$,   *for all* $f \in L_\infty$ *and* $Re(s) > 0$

(ii) $\displaystyle\sup_{Re(s)>0} |h(s)| \leq \|A\|$

where $\mathscr{L}$ represents the Laplace transform operator.

Proof For any $f \in L_\infty$ and $Re(s) > 0$, the time invariance of A implies that

$$(\mathscr{L} A S_T f)(s) = (\mathscr{L} S_T A f)(s) \qquad (\text{A.11})$$

for all $T \geq 0$. Also for any $f \in L_\infty$ we have

$$(\mathscr{L} f(s) = \hat{\phi}_s(f),$$

where $\hat{\phi}_s(\cdot)$ represents the element of L_∞^* given by the L_1 function $t \mapsto \phi_s(t)$ which is defined as

$$\phi_s(t) = \begin{cases} \exp(-st) & \text{for} \quad t \geq 0 \\ 0 & \text{for} \quad t < 0 \end{cases}$$

Then

$$(\mathscr{L} A f)(s) = \hat{\phi}_s(Af) = A^* \hat{\phi}_s(f) \qquad (\text{A.12})$$

where $A^* : L_\infty^* \to L_\infty^*$ represents the dual operator of A. Let $\hat{\psi}_s \in L_\infty^*$ be defined as $A^* \hat{\phi}_s$. From (A.12) we have

$$\hat{\psi}_s(S_T f) = \hat{\phi}_s(S_T A f) = (S_{-T} \hat{\phi}_s)(Af).$$

Since

$$(S_{-T} \phi)(t) = \begin{cases} \phi_s(t+T) & \text{for} \quad t \geq 0 \\ 0 & \text{for} \quad t < 0 \end{cases}$$

we obtain $S_{-T} \hat{\phi} = \phi_s(T) \hat{\phi}_s$. Therefore

$$\hat{\psi}_s(S_T f) = \phi_s(T) \hat{\phi}_s(Af) = \phi_s(T) A^* \hat{\phi}_s(f),$$

or

$$\hat{\psi}_s(S_T f) = \phi_s(T) \hat{\psi}(f) \qquad (\text{A.13})$$

for all $f \in L_\infty$ and all $T \geq 0$. Using Lemma A.2, the element $\hat{\psi}_s \in L_\infty^*$ can be written as

$$\hat{\psi}_s = \hat{\mu}_s + \hat{\pi}_s \qquad (\text{A. 14})$$

where $\hat{\mu}_s$ is a functional defined by a countably additive measure μ_s and $\hat{\pi}_s$ is a functional defined by a purely finite additive measure π_s. From (A.13) and (A.14)

$$\hat{\mu}_s(S_T f) + \hat{\pi}_s(S_T f) = \phi_s(T) \hat{\mu}_s(f) + \phi_s(T) \hat{\pi}_s(f)$$

and we can conclude from Theorem A.2 that the measure π_s' defined by $\pi_s'(E) = \pi_s(S_T E)$ is purely finite additive. Consequently

$$\left.\begin{array}{l} \hat{\mu}_s(S_T \cdot) = \phi_s(T) \hat{\mu}_s(\cdot) \\ \hat{\pi}_s(S_T \cdot) = \phi_s(T) \hat{\pi}_s(\cdot) \end{array}\right\} \qquad (\text{A.15})$$

From Theorem A.1 we can see that $\hat{\pi}_s = 0$, and therefore $\hat{\psi}_s = \hat{\mu}_s$ is defined by an element of L_1: let $t \mapsto \psi_s$ be such an element.

Let $\{\delta_n\}$ be a sequence of elements $L_1 \cap L_\infty$ which satisfy

(i) $\|\delta_n\|_{L_1} = 1 \qquad \forall\, n$

(ii) $\lim_n \|\delta_n^* f - f\|_{L_\infty} = 0 \quad \forall\, f \in L$

Such a sequence is called an approximate convolution unit (Hewitt and Stromberg, 1965).

For any $f \in L_\infty$ the number $\hat{\psi}_s(f)$ can be written as $\hat{f}(\psi_s)$, where $\hat{f}(\cdot)$ is the element of L_1^* defined by f, as $\hat{\psi}$ is defined by an element of L_1. Now, consider the complex numbers $\hat{\psi}_s(\delta_n^* f) = (\widehat{\delta_n^* f})(\psi_s)$. From condition (ii) above,

$$\lim_n (\widehat{\delta_n^* f})(\psi_s) = \hat{f}(\psi_s)$$

Alternatively, by definition of convolution

$$(\widehat{\delta_n^* f})(\psi_s) = \hat{f}(\psi_s^{(n)})$$

where

$$\psi_s^{(n)}(t) = \begin{cases} S_t \hat{\delta}_n(\psi_s) & \text{for } t \geq 0 \\ 0 & \text{for } t > 0 \end{cases}$$

Using (A.13)

$$\psi_s^{(n)}(t) = \phi_s(t) \hat{\delta}_n(\psi_s),$$

therefore

$$(\widehat{\delta_n^* f})(\psi_s) = \hat{\delta}_n(\psi_s) \hat{f}(\phi_s) \tag{A. 16}$$

The function $s \mapsto \hat{f}(\phi_s)$ represents the Laplace transform of $f(\cdot)$. Choose f such that $s \mapsto \hat{f}(\phi_s)$ is bounded away from zero in $Re(s) > 0$, then

$$\hat{\delta}_n(\psi_s) = (\widehat{\delta_n^* f})(\psi_s)\{\hat{f}(\phi_s)\}^{-1}$$

On taking limits, we see that $\lim_n \hat{\delta}_m(\psi_s)$ exists such that

$$\lim_n \hat{\delta}_n(\psi_s) = \hat{f}(\psi_s)\{\hat{f}(\phi_s)\}^{-1} \tag{A.17}$$

Let $s \mapsto h(s)$ be defined as $\lim_n \hat{\delta}_n(\psi_s)$. From (A.16) it is clear that

$$\hat{\psi}_s(f) = h(s)\phi_s(f) \tag{A.18}$$

for all $Re(s) > 0$ and all $f \in L_\infty$. Equivalently

$$(\mathscr{L}Af)(s) = h(s)(\mathscr{L}f)(s) \tag{A.19}$$

From (A.17), $s \to h(s)$ is holomorphic in $Re(s) > 0$ as $s \mapsto (\mathscr{L}Af)(s)$ and $s \mapsto (\mathscr{L}f)(s)$ are both holomorphic functions; moreover, from (A.18)

$$\hat{f}(\psi_s - h(s)\phi_s) = 0$$

for all $f \in L_1^*$. Consequently, in the sense of L_1

$$h(s)\phi_s = \psi_s = A^*\phi_s$$

and so

$$|a(s)| \cdot \|\phi_s\|_{L_1} \le \|A^*\| \cdot \|\phi_s\|_{L_1}$$

But since $\|A^*\| = \|A\|$ (Yosida, p. 195)

$$\sup_{Re(s)>0} |h(s)| \le \|A\| \tag{A.20}$$

In conclusion, $s \mapsto h(s)$ is bounded and holomorphic in $Re(s) > 0$, bounded by $\|A\|$ and satisfies

$$(\mathscr{L}Af)(s) = h(s)(\mathscr{L}f)(s)$$

for all $f \in L_\infty$ and all $Re(s) > 0$. $\qquad\square$

Define $K(0)$ as the space of all complex functions $s \mapsto h(s)$ bounded and holomorphic in $Re(s) > 0$ equipped with the norm

$$\|h\| = \sup_{Re(s)>0} |h(s)|$$

Under pointwise sum and multiplication of functions, $K(0)$ is clearly a normed algebra.

The space $M(L_\infty)$ of all multipliers in L_∞ is also a normed algebra when we define multiplication as composition of operators. Theorem A.3 then establishes a relationship between a subspace of $K(0)$ and $M(L_\infty)$ and we can formally state:

THEOREM A.4   *The map $\theta : M(L_\infty) \to K(0)$ which assigns a multiplier $A \in L_\infty$ to its transfer function $s \mapsto h(s)$ is continuous and is an injective morphism of rings.*

Proof   An immediate consequence of the relationship

$$\|a\|_{K(0)} = \sup_{Re(s)>0} |h(s)| \le \|A\|_{M(L_\infty)}$$

is that θ is continuous. In addition, as a result of (A.19) and of the uniqueness of the Laplace transform in L_∞, θ is a morphism of rings, that is

$$\theta(A + A') = \theta(A) + \theta(A') \quad \text{and} \quad \theta(A \circ A') = \theta(A) \cdot \theta(A')$$

Finally, θ is an injective map derived similarly from the uniqueness of the Laplace transform. $\qquad\square$

Convolution, invertibility and multipliers in L_∞

Let $\mathcal{M}(R_+)$ represent the convolution algebra of all countably additive, bounded, regular, complex Borel measures (Hewitt and Ross, 1963). Each $\mu \in \mathcal{M}(R_+)$ defines a linear time-invariant continuous operator $A : L_\infty \to L_\infty$ through $Af = \mu * f$. Moreover, we have $\|A\| \leq |\mu|(R_+)$. Finally, the uniqueness of the Laplace transform shows that two distinct elements $\mu, \mu' \in \mathcal{M}(R_+)$ define two distinct multipliers. We can therefore conclude that $\mathcal{M}(R_+)$ can be identified with a subclass of the space $M(L_\infty)$ of all multipliers in L_∞.

Let $\mathcal{M}_a(R_+)$ and $\mathcal{M}_d(R_+)$ represent the sub-algebras of $\mathcal{M}(R_+)$ formed respectively with all measures absolutely continuous with respect to the Lebesgue measure and all measures concentrated on countable sets. The direct sum $\mathcal{M}_a(R_+) \oplus \mathcal{M}_d(R_+)$ is a regular sub-algebra of $\mathcal{M}(R_+)$ (Hewitt and Ross, 1963); moreover we have the following important result in feedback stability theory (Hille and Phillips, 1957).

THEOREM A.5   *An element* $\mu \in \mathcal{M}_a(R_+) \oplus \mathcal{M}_d(R_+)$ *is invertible in this space if and only if*

$$\inf_{Re(s)>0} |\hat{\mu}(s)| > 0$$

where $s \mapsto \hat{\mu}(s)$ *represents the Laplace transform of the measure* μ.

REFERENCES

Dempster, M. A. H. (1975). "Abstract Optimization and Its Applications", Lectures School of Mathematic Science. Melbourne University, Melbourne.

Desoer, C. A. and Vidyasagar, M. (1975). "Feedback Systems: Input–Output Properties". Academic Press, New York and London.

Harris, C. J. and Valenca, J. M. E. (1980). "Extended Space Theory in the Study of System Operators". RMCS Tech. Report, E. & E.E. Dept.

Hewitt, E. and Ross, K. A. (1963). "Abstract Harmonic Analysis", Vol. I, Band 115. Springer Verlag, Berlin.

Hewitt, E. and Stromberg, K. (1965). "Real and Abstract Analysis", Graduate Series in Mathematics. Springer Verlag, Berlin.

Valenca, J. M. E. and Harris, C. J. (1980) "Nyquist criterion for input/output stability of multivariable systems." *Int. J. Control* **31,** 917–935.

Yosida, K. and Hewitt, K. (1952). "Finitely additive measures." *Trans. Amer. Math. Soc.* **72,** 46–66.

Hille, E. and Phillips, R. S. (1957). "Functional Analysis and Semi-Groups". Amer. Math. Soc.

Chapter Four

Linear Input–Output Stability Theory

4.1 INTRODUCTION

In this chapter we combine the Principle of the Argument of Chapter 2 and the Representation Theory of Chapter 3 to obtain graphical criteria of the Nyquist type which are applicable in determining the stability of linear multivariable distributed feedback systems.

The generalization of the Nyquist stability criterion for multivariable feedback systems derived from sets of differential equations has been proposed by MacFarlane and Postlethwaite (1977, 1978, 1979); their study of the Principle of the Argument is based upon the concept of algebraic functions defined on Riemann surfaces. A more fruitful approach was initiated by DeCarlo and Saeks (1977), who based their study on covering map theorems. This approach, to the best of our knowledge, has not been pursued elsewhere, but it has convinced us of the potential value of a topological study of Riemann surfaces and the consequent Principles of the Argument of Chapter 2. Although none of the above criteria can accommodate distributed or infinite dimensional systems, Callier and Desoer (1973, 1976) and Desoer and Wang (1980) introduced criteria for the stability of systems represented by a class of transfer functions which included some distributed systems.

In the following, the necessary and sufficient conditions for input–output stability of linear multivariable feedback systems are developed. It follows that the definitions of a system and of stability must be based entirely on input–output properties. The only dynamical systems representation admissible *a priori* comes from the properties of the input–output maps which define the system, and so the existence of any other representation (including the representation by transfer functions) must be deduced from these properties. Based on these arguments a series of transfer function type representations for various input–output maps was developed in Chapter 3. Only for dynamical systems defined on the L_2

121

and X_2 spaces was it possible to establish a full representation, that is, a space of transfer functions which are isomorphic with the space of input–output maps can be defined explicitly. For general L_2 and X_2 feedback systems it is therefore possible to state necessary and sufficient conditions for closed loop stability in terms of the open loop transfer function.

The lack of a full Representation theorem for systems defined upon the L_1, L_∞ and X_∞ spaces makes it impossible to state, in similar terms to L_2 and X_2 systems, necessary and sufficient conditions for closed loop stability. However, departing from the above philosophy of input–output systems, we can impose restrictions on the explicit representation of these systems and obtain for these restricted systems some necessary and sufficient conditions for input–output stability. To achieve this end, systems defined on L_1 and L_∞ are restricted to those explicitly represented by an element of the algebra LA_+ (which coincides with the algebra $\mathscr{A}(0)$ of Callier and Desoer (1978)), and similarly systems defined on X_1 and X_∞ are restricted to those represented by an element of the algebra LA_- (equivalent to $\mathscr{A}_-(0)$ of Callier and Desoer (1978)). For a feedback system whose open loop transfer function is included in these restricted classes, a result of Hille and Phillips (1957) enables us to obtain necessary and sufficient conditions for the existence of the feedback system in the algebra LA_+ or LA_-; this result does not by itself establish necessary and sufficient conditions for input–output stability. Trying to identify LA_+ (respectively LA_-) stability with input–output stability is equivalent to stating the regularity of the sub-algebra LA_+ (respectively LA_-) in $M(L_1)$ and $M(L_\infty)$ (respectively $M(X_1)$ and $M(X_\infty)$). In Chapter 3 it was shown that $M(L_1)$ and $M(X_1)$ are respectively isomorphic to $\mathscr{M}(R_+)$ and $\mathscr{M}_-(R_+)$; since LA_+ and LA_- are respectively regular sub-algebras of $\mathscr{M}(R_+)$ and $\mathscr{M}_-(R_+)$, we see that through the representation theorems the equivalence between LA_+ and LA_- stability and input–output stability can be established.

In the study of linear feedback systems defined on L_∞ and X_∞ a different approach is adopted, by which the sufficient conditions of input–output stability provided by a result of Hille and Phillips (1957) are combined with the necessary conditions provided by the representation theorems of Chapter 3 for these spaces.

Throughout this chapter we note that the various representation theorems of Chapter 3 for the above spaces are essential to the establishment of the equivalence between LA_+ or LA_- stability and input–output stability.

The stability criteria of this chapter will assume that the open loop system is stable. This limitation may at first seem strange, because the generalized Principle of Argument established in Chapter 2 considers systems described by matrix transfer functions with meromorphic coefficients and therefore systems with open loop unstable poles can easily be considered. The reason for imposing this apparently severe limitation on open loop dynamic behaviour lies in our inability to establish a representation for unstable input–output systems. It is not possible to provide the necessary and sufficient conditions for the stability of open loop unstable systems based on transfer function concepts when the structure or existence of a transfer function for unstable input–output systems remains unknown.

It is possible to extend the Nyquist criterion to unstable systems simply by adding unstable poles to the usual stable transfer functions and considering the appropriate number of encirclements of the critical point through the generalized Principle of the Argument, but this is a mathematically unsatisfactory solution. Although the theory of extended spaces (see Chapter 5) has allowed a rigorous mathematical treatment of general input/output systems whose response is unbounded in finite time, these studies have unfortunately not been linked with the theory of linear systems and in particular with the existence of transfer functions. Future developments in the problem of determining the stability of open loop unstable systems will probably provide this link.

In Section 4.2 we introduce several analytical L_p- and X_p-stability criteria $(p = 1, 2, \ldots, \infty)$; the X_p-space and the associated X_p-stability theory is developed to overcome the difficulties associated with the behaviour along the imaginary axis of a transfer function representing a general L_p-system. In Section 4.3 we consider a graphical stability criteria for a restricted class of L_2 systems. Finally in Section 4.4 we introduce general Nyquist type multivariable stability criteria for X_p-systems and for a restricted class of L_p-systems.

4.2   GENERAL ANALYTIC FORMULATION OF STABILITY

Consider a linear multivariable time-invariant dynamical system modelled by

$$y = Gu \qquad (4.1)$$

where u lies in some space E of C^n-valued time functions and G is an operator that maps E into itself. Some restrictions must be placed on E and G so that the model (4.1) accurately describes physical systems that exhibit stability:

(i) The elements of E must be in some manner bounded, since the output of a stable physical system cannot be unbounded. The spaces L_p and X_p (or their multivariable versions) are good candidates for the space E. G must therefore be a bounded operator in one of these spaces.

(ii) The outputs of a stable physical system must exhibit a degree of insensitivity, or robustness, to small variations in both the inputs to the system and system parameters. Such a constraint has two implications. First there must be a mechanism in E which allows the degree of proximity between two distinct elements of E to be determined; this implies that E must be a topological space on a sequential convergence space (see Chapter 3). Secondly the operator G must be continuous or sequentially continuous.

These considerations justify the following definition of stability:

Definition 4.1   Let E be one of the spaces L_p, L_p^n, X_p or X_p^n. The system $y = Gu$, is said to be E-stable when G is a continuous bounded operator on E into itself (when $E = L_p$ or L_p^n) or when G is a sequentially continuous, sequentially bounded operator on E into itself (when $E = X_p$ or X_p^n) for $u \in E$.

Consider now the structured feedback system represented by the functional equation

$$y = G(u - y) \qquad G \in M(E), \qquad u \in E \qquad (4.2)$$

with u arbitrary in E and G a linear time-invariant bounded operator on E into itself.

The fundamental problem of stability theory lies in deducing the conditions for the stability of the feedback system (4.2) in terms of the properties of the open loop map G. To solve this problem some generic results are established first:

LEMMA 4.1   *The feedback system* $y = G(u - y)$, $G \in M(E)$, $u \in E$ *is E-stable if and only if the operator* $(I + G)$ *is invertible in the algebra* $M(E)$ *of all multipliers on E into itself.*

Proof   The "if" condition of the lemma is obvious. To prove the "only if" condition assume that (4.2) is a stable system according to Definition 4.1. By this definition, for any $u \in E$ there exists a unique solution $y \in E$ to the Equation (4.2). A map $\hat{G} : E \to E$ is now well defined by assigning u to the solution of (4.2); $y = \hat{G}u$. Since $u = (I + G)y$, $\hat{G} \equiv (I + G)^{-1}$. The operator $(I + G)$ is then invertible in the algebra of all operators of E into itself. Moreover $(I + G)^{-1}$ is clearly linear and time invariant. Using the bounded inverse theorem (Bachman and Narici, pp. 265, 271) and the fact that $(I+G)^{-1}$ must be an onto map, it follows that $(I+G)^{-1}$ is also bounded. Thus $(I+G)^{-1}$ is an element of the algebra $M(E)$.   □

Lemma (4.1) is equivalent to determining the stability of the feedback system (4.2). An immediate consequence of this lemma and Theorem 3.3 for $E = L_2^n$ is:

THEOREM 4.1: L_2^n-STABILITY   *The feedback system represented by the functional equation*

$$y = G(u - y) \qquad G \in M(L_2^n), \qquad u \in L_2^n$$

is L_2^n-stable if and only if $\inf\limits_{Re(s)>0} |det\,(I + \hat{G}(s))| > 0$, where $\hat{G} \in K(0)^{n \times n}$ is the matrix transfer function of G.

Equally, as a direct consequence of Lemma 4.1, Theorem 3.22 and Proposition 3.7, a similar result for X_2-stability can be given:

THEOREM 4.2: X_2^n-STABILITY   *The feedback system represented by the functional equation*

$$y = G(u - y) \qquad G \in M(X_2^n), \qquad u \in X_2^n$$

is X_2^n-stable if and only if there exists some $\gamma > 0$ such that

$$\inf\limits_{Re(s)>-\gamma} |det\,(I + \hat{G}(s))| > 0$$

where $\hat{G} \in \mathcal{R}^{n \times n}$ is the matrix transfer function of G.

Consider now analytic stability conditions in L_1 and L_∞ systems.

LEMMA 4.2   *A multiplier $G \in M(L_1)$ (respectively $M(L_\infty)$) is invertible in $M(L_1)$ (respectively $M(L_\infty)$) only if its transfer function $s \mapsto h(s)$ satisfies*

$$\inf\limits_{Re(s)>0} |h(s)| > 0$$

Proof   Assume that G is invertible in $M(L_1)$ (respectively $M(L_\infty)$). Using Theorem 3.9 (respectively Theorem 3.12) the inverse operator G^{-1} has a transfer function $s \mapsto \bar{h}(s)$ bounded and analytic in $Re(s) > 0$, which by definition of a transfer function must coincide with $s \mapsto h^{-1}(s)$. It therefore follows that $\inf\limits_{Re(s)>0} |h(s)| > 0$; otherwise $s \mapsto \bar{h}(s)$ could not be bounded and analytic.   □

Figure 4.1 illustrates the relationships between the spaces involved in the stability of L_2, L_1 and L_∞ systems. Note that the space LA_+ (Willems, 1971) coincides with the space $A(0)$ of Callier and Desoer (1978), and for this space, Theorem 3.10 specifies the necessary and sufficient conditions

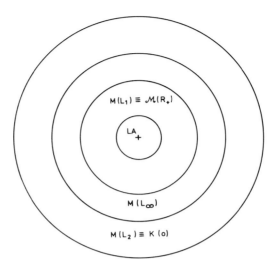

FIG. 4.1   Relationship between stability spaces

for invertibility of the open loop operator in terms of its frequency description. Note also that $LA_+ \equiv A(0)$, defined as $\mathcal{M}_a(R_+) \oplus \mathcal{M}_d(R_+)$ is a regular subalgebra of $\mathcal{M}(R_+) \equiv M(L_1)$.

LEMMA 4.3   *A multiplier $G \in M(L_1)$ which lies in the subalgebra LA_+ is invertible in $M(L_1)$ if and only if $\inf_{Re(s)>0} |h(s)| > 0$, where $s \to h(s)$ is the transfer function of G.*

Proof   Direct consequence of Theorem 3.10.   □

LEMMA 4.4   *A multiplier $G \in M(L_\infty)$ which lies in the subalgebra LA_+ is invertible in $M(L_\infty)$ if and only if the transfer function $s \mapsto h(s)$ satisfies $\inf_{Re(s)>0} |h(s)| > 0$.*

Proof G is invertible in LA_+ if and only if $\inf_{Re(s)>0} |h(s)| > 0$ (Theorem 3.8), thus the condition $\inf_{Re(s)>0} |h(s)| > 0$ is sufficient to guarantee invertibility in $M(L_\infty)$. The "only if" part of the lemma was established in Lemma 4.2.   □

Lemmas 4.2 to 4.4 are now utilized to establish some analytic stability criteria for L_1 and L_∞ systems.

THEOREM 4.3   *The feedback system represented by the functional equation $y = G(u - y)$ with $G \in M(L_1^n)$ (respectively $G \in M(L_\infty^n)$ and $u \in L_1^n$ (respec-*

tively $u \in L_\infty^n$) *is* L_1-*stable* (*respectively* L_∞-*stable*) *only if* $\inf\limits_{Re(s)>0} |\det(I+ \hat{G}(s))| > 0$ *where* $\hat{G} \in K(0)^{n \times n}$ *is the matrix transfer function of G.*

Proof Since $M(L_1^n) \equiv M(L_1)^{n \times n}$ (respectively $M(L_\infty^n) \equiv M(L_\infty)^{n \times n}$) the operator $(I + G)$ is invertible in $M(L_1^n)$ (respectively $M(L_\infty^n)$) if and only if its determinant is invertible in $M(L_1)$ (respectively $M(L_\infty)$). Using Lemma 4.2, $\det(I + G)$ is invertible in the space of multipliers only if $\inf\limits_{Re(s)>0} |\det(I + \hat{G}(s))| > 0$. □

Note that the above theorem is only a necessary condition for L_1 and L_∞-stability, but by restricting the operator G to the sub-algebra $LA_+^{n \times n}$ we have the following necessary and sufficient conditions for L_1^n and L_∞^n stability:

THEOREM 4.4 *If G is an element of* $M(L_1^n)$ (*respectively* $M(L_\infty^n)$) *contained in the sub-algebra* $LA_+^{n \times n}$, *then the functional equation* $y = G(u - y)$ *with* $u \in L_1^n$ (*respectively* L_∞^n) *is* L_1^n-*stable* (*respectively* L_∞^n-*stable*) *if and only if* $\inf\limits_{Re(s)>0} |\det(I + \hat{G}(s))| > 0$

Proof Using Lemma 4.1, the system $y = G(u - y)$ is stable if and only if $(I + G)$ is invertible in the algebra of multipliers $M(L_1^n)$ (respectively $M(L_\infty^n)$). The operator $(I + G)$ is invertible in the algebra of multipliers if and only if its determinant is invertible in $M(L_1)$ (respectively $M(L_\infty)$). Since the operator G lies in $LA_+^{n \times n}$ by definition, $\det(I + G)$ is an element of LA_+. Now, utilizing Lemma 4.3 (respectively Lemma 4.4), it follows that the feedback system is stable if and only if $\inf\limits_{Re(s)>0} |\det(I + \hat{G}(s))| > 0$. □

To complete this section, the stability conditions for feedback systems defined on X_1 and X_∞ spaces are considered in detail:

LEMMA 4.5 *A multiplier* $G \in M(X_1)$ (*respectively* $M(X_\infty)$) *is invertible in* $M(X_1)$ (*respectively* $M(X_\infty)$) *only if there exists some* $\gamma > 0$ *such that* $\inf\limits_{Re(s)>-\gamma} |h(s)| > 0$, *where* $h \in \mathcal{R}$ *is the transfer function of the operator G.*

Proof If G is invertible, its inverse G^{-1} has a transfer function (see Theorem 3.21) $s \mapsto \tilde{h}(s)$, which is an element of $\mathcal{R}$, and by definition of a transfer function must coincide with $s \mapsto h^{-1}(s)$ in the intersection of the domains of both functions. Finally, from Proposition 3.7, a scalar $\gamma > 0$ must exist such that $\inf\limits_{Re(s)>-\gamma} |h(s)| > 0$. □

Theorem 3.22 and Proposition 3.9 showed that the space $M(X_1)$ can be identified with the algebra of measures

$$\mathcal{M}_-(R_+) = \bigcup_{\gamma>0} E_{-\gamma}\mathcal{M}(R_+)$$

where $E_{-\gamma}\mathcal{M}(R_+)$ represents the space of all measures μ of the form $\mu = E_{-\gamma}\,\mu_0$ with $\mu \in \mathcal{M}(R_+)$ (see Section 3.6.4). In the study of feedback systems defined on L_1 a sub-algebra LA_+ of $\mathcal{M}(R_+)$ was selected for which it is possible to state necessary and sufficient conditions for invertibility. Similarly for the study of X_1-feedback systems we introduce the sub-algebra LA_- of $M(X_1)$ defined by

$$LA_- = \bigcup_{\gamma>0} E_{-\gamma}\{\mathcal{M}_a(R_+) \oplus \mathcal{M}_d(R_+)\} \tag{4.3}$$

We recognize in LA_- the space $A_-(0)$ of Callier and Desoer (1978).

LEMMA 4.6 LA_- *is a regular sub-algebra of* $\mathcal{M}_-(R_+)$ *and* $\mu \in LA_-$ *is invertible in* LA_- *if and only if there exists some* $a>0$ *for which* $\inf_{Re(s)>-a}|\hat{\mu}(s)|>0$, *where* $\hat{\mu}$ *represents the Laplace transform of* μ.

Proof   Consider an arbitrary $\mu \in LA_-$ invertible in $\mathcal{M}(R_+)$; then there exists some $a>0$ and some $\gamma_1 \in LA_+$ such that $\mu \in E_{-a}\,\gamma_1$. Identically there exists some $0<b\leq a$ and some $\hat{\gamma}_0 \in \mathcal{M}(R_+)$ such that $\mu^{-1} = E_{-b}\,\hat{\gamma}_0$. Defining $\gamma_0 = E_{-(a-b)}\gamma_1$ we see that γ_0 lies in $E_{-(a-b)}LA_+ \subset LA_+$. So μ and μ^{-1} can be written as

$$\mu = E_{-b}\gamma_0, \qquad \gamma_0 \in LA_+$$
$$\mu^{-1} = E_{-b}\hat{\gamma}_0, \qquad \hat{\gamma}_0 \in \mathcal{M}(R_+)$$

We have $\mu \otimes \mu^{-1} = \delta$, so

$$(\mathcal{L}\mu)(s)\,.\,(\mathcal{L}\mu^{-1})(s) = 1 \qquad \forall\, Re(s)>-b$$
$$(\mathcal{L}\gamma_0)(s+b)\,.\,(\mathcal{L}\hat{\gamma}_0)(s+b) = 1 \qquad \forall\, Re(s)>-b$$
$$(\mathcal{L}\gamma_0)(s)\,.\,(\mathcal{L}\hat{\gamma}_0)(s) = 1 \qquad \forall\, Re(s)>0$$

The unicity of the Laplace transform in $\mathcal{M}(R_+)$ implies that in the sense of $\mathcal{M}(R_+)$, $\hat{\gamma}_0 = \gamma_0^{-1}$. Since $\gamma_0 \in LA_+$ and LA_+ is a regular sub-algebra of $\mathcal{M}(R_+)$ we must have $\hat{\gamma}_0 \in LA_+$; hence $\mu^{-1} = E_{-b}\hat{\gamma}_0$ lies in $E_{-b}\,LA_+$ and therefore in LA_-. This proves that LA_- is a regular subalgebra of $\mathcal{M}_-(R_+)$.

Moreover, as γ_0 is invertible in LA_-, we must have by Theorem 3.8

$$\inf_{Re(s)>0}|(\mathcal{L}\gamma_0)(s)|>0$$

and thus

$$\inf_{Re(s)>-b}|\hat{\mu}(s)|>0 \qquad\qquad \square$$

THEOREM 4.5 *The feedback system represented by the functional equation* $y = G(u-y)$, $u \in X_1^n$ *(respectively* X_∞^n*) with* $G \in M(X_1^n)$ *(respectively* $G \in M(X_\infty^n)$*) is* X_1^n*-stable (respectively* X_∞^n*-stable) only if there exists some* $a > 0$ *such that*

$$\inf_{Re(s)>-a} |\det (I + \hat{G}(s))| > 0$$

where $\hat{G} \in \mathscr{R}^{n \times n}$ *is the transfer function of operator G.*

Proof Is a direct consequence of Lemmas 4.1 and 4.5. Note that like Theorem 4.3, the above X_1^n (X_∞^n)-stability theorem provides only necessary conditions. However, by restricting the feedforward operator G to the sub-algebra $LA^{n \times n}$ we have the following necessary and sufficient conditions for X_1^n (X_∞^n) stability. □

THEOREM 4.6: $X_1^n(X_\infty^n)$ STABILITY *If G is an element of $M(X_1^n)$ (respectively $M(X_\infty^n)$) contained in the sub-algebra $LA_-^{n \times n}$, then the functional equation*

$$y = G(u-y) \qquad u \in X_1^n \text{ (respectively } X_\infty^n)$$

represents an X_1^n-stable (respectively X_∞^n-stable) feedback system if and only if there exists some $a > 0$ such that

$$\inf_{Re(s)>-a} |\det (I + \hat{G}(s))| > 0$$

where $\hat{G} \in \mathscr{R}^{n \times n}$ is the matrix transfer function of G.

Proof The "only if" part was proved in Theorem 4.5; the "if" part results from Lemmas 4.1 4.6. □

4.3 SOME GRAPHICAL STABILITY CRITERIA FOR L_2-SYSTEMS

The problems associated with graphical L_2-stability criteria considered in this section are independent of number of inputs and outputs, and therefore it is assumed the feedback system

$$y = G(u-y) \qquad G \in M(L_2^n), \qquad u \in L_2^n \tag{4.4}$$

is single input–single output and that the open loop system is represented by the transfer function $s \mapsto h(s) = \hat{G}(s)$. In Section 4.2 it was shown that this feedback system is L_2-stable if and only if

$$\inf_{Re(s)>0} |\det (I + \hat{G}(s))| = \inf_{Re(s)>0} |(1 + h(s))| > 0$$

Therefore the stability of system (4.4) consists of finding the zeros of the complex function $s \mapsto (1 + h(s))$ in the closed right half plane $Re(s) \geq 0$. The problem of determining these zeros can be divided into three subproblems:

(i) Finding the zeros of $(1 + h(s))$ in the open right half plane $\{s : Re(s) > 0\}$.

(ii) Finding the points on the imaginary axis where $(1 + h(s))$ has an infinium of zero. These are points of the form $s = j\omega$ such that for any $\xi > 0$,

$$\inf_{\substack{|s - j\omega| < \xi \\ Re(s) > 0}} |(1 + h(s))| = 0$$

(iii) Finding the zeros of $(1 + h(s))$ at infinity.

For practical implementation these zeros can be determined by a Nyquist type stability criterion. Such a criterion can only solve subproblems (i) and (ii) and therefore can only provide necessary and sufficient conditions for closed loop stability when $(1 + h(s))$ has no zeros at infinity. It is therefore assumed that there exists some method of establishing the existence of zeros of $(1 + h(s))$ at infinity. Usually only functions $h(s)$ which are such that $(1 + h(s))$ is bounded away from zero at infinity are considered.

For arbitrary a, ρ define

$$D(a; \rho) \triangleq \{s : Re(s) > a, |s| \leq \rho\} \tag{4.5}$$

Assuming that $s \mapsto h(s)$ is bounded away from zero at infinity, then there exists some $\rho > 0$ such that all possible zeros of $(1 + h(s))$ in the closed right half plane are in $D(0; \rho)$. The classical Principle of the Argument (see Section 2.7) is conventionally used to determine the number of zeros of a function $s \mapsto F(s)$ in a compact simple region such as $D(0; \rho)$. However, this approach can only detect these zeros if the domain of analyticity of the function contains that region. Notice that in our case the region $D(0; \rho)$ contains points of the imaginary axis and the function $s \mapsto h(s)$ is not necessarily analytic on the imaginary axis.

It is well known (Hille, 1962) that an element $h \in K(0)$ can be extended to the imaginary axis in the complex plane through a function $\omega \mapsto h(j\omega)$ defined *almost everywhere* as

$$h(j\omega) = \lim_{\sigma \to 0^+} h(\sigma + j\omega)$$

The question now arises: is it possible by considering the behaviour of $s \mapsto h(s)$ on the boundary of $D(0; \rho)$ to determine the number of zeros of

$(1 + h(s))$ in $D(0; \rho)$? Along the imaginary axis $\omega \mapsto h(j\omega)$ is defined (only) almost everywhere, and therefore its locus does not necessarily define an arc. Even when $\omega \mapsto h(j\omega)$ is defined everywhere, the answer to the above question for a general $h \in K(0)$ would still be no, as seen in the following example:

Let $h(s) = \alpha \exp(-1/s)$, with $\alpha > 1$. Clearly $h(\cdot)$ lies in $K(0)$ and therefore defines a multiplier in L_2 with itself. The function $\omega \mapsto h(j\omega)$ is defined everywhere as

$$h(j\omega) = \lim_{\sigma \to 0^+} h(\sigma + j\omega) = \begin{cases} 0 & \text{if} \quad \omega = 0 \\ \alpha \exp\left(-\dfrac{1}{j\omega}\right) & \text{if} \quad \omega \neq 0 \end{cases}$$

If the Principle of the Argument were applicable the number of zeros of $(1 + h(s))$ in $D(0; \rho)$ could be determined by the number of encirclements of the -1 point by the locus of $h(s)$ when s describes the boundary $\partial D(0; \rho)$ of $D(0; \rho)$. The first difficulty arises when it is noted that although $(1 + h(j\omega)) \neq 0$ everywhere, the function $s \mapsto (1 + h(s))$ has a zero at the origin. Indeed, using the concept of a zero it can easily be shown that for any $\xi > 0$.

$$\inf_{\substack{|s| < \xi \\ Re(s) > 0}} |(1 + h(s))| = 0$$

A second difficulty is that $\omega \mapsto h(j\omega)$ is not continuous so it cannot define an arc through its locus.

Another question now arises: is there any arc which encircles the -1 point the same number of times as there are zeros of $(1 + h(s))$ in $D(0; \rho)$? This question is equivalent to another: is there any function $s \mapsto \tilde{h}(s)$ continuous and with finite total variation on $\partial D(0; \rho)$, whose locus, when s describes $\partial D(0; \rho)$, encircles the -1 point the same number of times as there are zeros of $s \mapsto (1 + h(s))$ in $D(0; \rho)$?

For the above example the totality of the zeros of $s \mapsto (1 + h(s))$ in $Re(s) > 0$ are the points

$$s_n = \frac{1}{(ln\alpha + j(2n+1)\pi)} \quad \text{for} \quad n = 0, \pm 1, \pm 2, \ldots$$

Notice that the number of such points are infinite. The locus of any $s \mapsto \tilde{h}(s)$ in the circumstances of the above questions would have to encircle the -1 point an infinite number of times without containing this point. This property is incompatible with the required continuity and finite total variation of $s \mapsto \tilde{h}(s)$ in $\partial D(0; \rho)$. Hence no arc under the conditions of the above questions can exist in $D(0; \rho)$.

In utilizing the Principle of the Argument (Section 2.7) to detect the zeros of $(1 + h(s))$ in $D(0; \rho)$ the class of functions to which the Principle of the Argument is applicable must be restricted in such a way that every $h(\cdot)$ in that class satisfies at least the following properties:

(P.1)   The domain of $h(s)$ must be extended to every point on the imaginary axis.

(P.2)   When s describes $\partial D(0; \rho)$ the function $s \mapsto h(s)$ must be continuous with finite total variation.

(P.3)   The total variation of zeros of $h(s)$ in $\partial D(0; \rho)$ must be finite.

(P.4)   The integral

$$\frac{1}{2\pi j} \oint_{\partial D(0;\rho)} \frac{dh(s)}{h(s)}$$

must be defined and coincide with the number of zeros of $h(s)$ in $D(0; \rho)$.

Definition 4.2   The space $K_a(0)$ is the space of all $h \in K(0)$ for which the function $\omega \mapsto \lim_{\sigma \to 0^+} h(\sigma + j\omega)$ defined everywhere is absolutely continuous in any compact interval of the imaginary axis and has finite total variation on the whole axis.

It follows from Hewitt and Stromberg (1963) that for every $h \in K_a(0)$, the function $\omega \mapsto h(j\omega) = \lim_{\sigma \to 0^+} h(\sigma + j\omega)$ is continuous differentiable almost everywhere and its total variation is given by

$$\int_{-\infty}^{\infty} \left| \frac{d}{d\omega} h(j\omega) \right| d\omega$$

And so $\omega \mapsto (d/d\omega) h(j\omega)$ defines an element of $L_1(-\infty, \infty)$.

PROPOSITION 4.1   *Given an $h \in K_a(0)$ there exists a number $h(\infty)$ such that $h(s)$ tends uniformly to $h(\infty)$ when $|s| \to \infty$ and $\lim_{\omega \to \pm\infty} h(j\omega) = h(\infty)$.*

Proof   Since $\omega \mapsto h(j\omega)$ is absolutely continuous in any compact interval

$$h(j\omega) = h(j\omega_0) + \int_{\omega_0}^{\omega} H(\lambda) \, d\lambda$$

where $H(\omega) = (d/d\omega) h(j\omega)$ (Hewitt and Stromberg, 1965). Also, since $H(\cdot) \in L_1(-\infty, \infty)$, $\lim_{\omega \to \infty} \int_0^{\omega} H(s) \, ds$ is well defined. Let $h(\infty) = h(j\omega_0) + \int_{\omega_0}^{\infty} H(\lambda) \, d\lambda$. Using Theorems 18.3.5 and 18.3.6 of Hille (1962), it follows that $h(\infty) = \lim_{|s| \to \infty} h(s)$ uniformly in the sector $|\arg(s)| \le \pi/2$.   □

A consequence of the above result is that the function $\omega \mapsto h(j\omega)$ can be extended to a function uniformly continuous and absolutely continuous on the compact interval $[-\infty, \infty]$. Furthermore from Hille (1962):

PROPOSITION 4.2   For any $h \in K_a(0)$ the function $\omega \mapsto h(\sigma + j\omega)$ converges uniformly in the compact interval $[-\infty, \infty]$ to $\omega \mapsto h(j\omega)$ as $\sigma \to 0^+$.

Also for the sub-algebra $K_a(0)$ of $K(0)$ the following two important propositions can be established:

PROPOSITION 4.3   Any $h \in K_a(0)$ can be extended to a function $s \mapsto \tilde{h}(s)$ bounded and analytic in $Re(s) > 0$ and continuous in the compactification of the closed right half plane $\{s : Re(s) \geq 0, |s| \leq \infty\}$.

Proof   Define

$$\tilde{h}(s) = \begin{cases} h(s) & \text{for all} \quad Re(s) > 0, |s| < \infty \\ h(\infty) & \text{for} \quad |s| = \infty \\ h(j\omega) & \text{for} \quad s = j\omega \end{cases}$$

The continuity of $\tilde{h}(\cdot)$ results immediately from Propositions 4.1 and 4.2.

□

Since the function $\omega \mapsto h(j\omega)$ is continuous in $[-\infty, +\infty]$ and absolutely continuous in the same interval it defines an arc through its locus. But since $h(j\infty) = h(-j\infty)$ then the arc is closed; let γ_0 represent this loop. Identically let γ_a, $a > 0$ be the loop described by $\omega \mapsto h(a + j\omega)$ when ω describes $[-\infty, +\infty]$.

PROPOSITION 4.4   Let $h \in K_a(0)$ be such that $\omega \mapsto h(j\omega)$ has no zeros. Under the above definitions for γ_a and γ_0, there exists some $\xi > 0$ such that for all $a \leq \xi$ the loops γ_0 and γ_a are homotopic in the punctured plane $C^1 - \{0\}$.

Proof   The fact that $\omega \mapsto h(j\omega)$ is free of zeros and continuous in $[-\infty, \infty]$; Proposition 4.2 implies that there exists an $\xi > 0$ such that

$$\inf_{0 \leq Re(s) \leq \xi} |h(s)| > 0$$

Let $H_a : [0, 1] \times [-\infty, +\infty] \to C^1$ be defined for any $a \leq \xi$ as

$$H_a(t, \omega) = h(at + j\omega) \quad \text{for} \quad t \in [0, 1], \omega \in [-\infty, +\infty]$$

Since $a \leq \xi$ the range of $H_a(\cdot, \cdot)$ is contained in $C^1 - \{0\}$; moreover Proposition 4.3 implies that $H_a(\cdot, \cdot)$ is continuous. We also have

$$H_a(t, \pm\infty) = h(\infty) \qquad \forall \ t \in [0, 1],$$

$\omega \mapsto H_a(0, \omega) \equiv \omega \mapsto h(j\omega)$ and $\omega \mapsto H_a(1, \omega) \equiv \omega \mapsto h(a + j\omega)$. Therefore by the definition of homotopy (see Section 2.1.2), γ_0 and γ_a are homotopic loops.   □

THEOREM 4.7   Let $h \in K_a(0)$ be such that $\omega \mapsto h(j\omega)$ is free of all zeros in the interval $[-\infty, +\infty]$. Then the zeros of $s \mapsto h(s)$ in the compact right half s-plane are finite in number and coincide with the number of clockwise encirclements of the origin by the loop described by $h(j\omega)$ when ω describes $[-\infty, +\infty]$.

Proof From Proposition 4.4, there exists some $\xi > 0$ such that $\inf_{0 \le Re(s) \le \xi} |h(s)| > 0$. Since $h(s)$ converges uniformly when $|s| \to \infty$ to $h(\infty) \ne 0$ then there exists a $\rho > 0$ such that $\inf_{|s| \ge \rho} |h(s)| > 0$. Then all possible zeros of $s \mapsto h(s)$ in the compact right half s-plane are interior points of the simple region

$$D(\xi; \rho) = \{s : Re(s) \ge \xi, |s| \le \rho\}$$

But since $s \mapsto h(s)$ is analytic in an open set which contains $D(\xi; 0)$ these zeros are at most finite in number. Equally the classical Principle of the Argument (Section 2.7) can be utilized to obtain

$$Z = \frac{1}{2\pi j} \oint_{\partial D(\xi; \rho)} \frac{dh(s)}{h(s)}$$

where Z is the number of zeros of $s \mapsto h(s)$ in $D(\xi; \rho)$. In particular

$$
\begin{aligned}
Z &= \lim_{\rho \to \infty} \frac{1}{2\pi j} \oint_{\partial D(\xi; \rho)} \frac{dh(s)}{h(s)} \, ds \\
&= -\frac{1}{2\pi j} \int_{\xi - j\infty}^{\xi + j\infty} \frac{h'(s)}{h(s)} \, ds + \lim_{\rho \to \infty} \frac{1}{2\pi j} \int_{\Gamma_\rho} \frac{h'(s)}{h(s)} \, ds
\end{aligned}
$$

where Γ_ρ is the arc of the circle $\{s : Re(s) \ge \xi, |s| = \rho\}$.
  The integral

$$\frac{1}{2\pi j} \int_{\Gamma_\rho} \frac{h'(s)}{h(s)} \, ds = \frac{1}{2\pi j} \int_{h(\Gamma_\rho)} \frac{dZ}{Z}$$

represents the index function with respect to the origin of $h(\Gamma_\rho)$. When $\rho \to \infty$, $h(\Gamma_\rho)$ tends to a single point $h(\infty) \ne 0$, therefore the index function tends to zero. Thus

$$-Z = \frac{1}{2\pi j} \int_{\xi - j\infty}^{\xi + j\infty} \frac{dh(s)}{h(s)}$$

This integral is the index function with respect to the origin of the loop γ_ξ. Proposition 4.4 demonstrated that γ_ξ is homotopic to γ_0 in $C^1 - \{0\}$, and so Z coincides with the number of clockwise encirclements of the origin by the locus of $\omega \mapsto h(j\omega)$ when ω describes $[-\infty, +\infty]$.   □

As a direct consequence of Theorems 4.1 and 4.7 we are able to state the following Nyquist stability criterion for transfer functions $h \in K_a(0)$.

THEOREM 4.8: NYQUIST STABILITY CRITERION FOR $K_a(0)$ SYSTEMS   *The feedback system defined by the functional equation*

$$y = G(u - y), \, u \in L_2$$

with $G \in M(L_2)$ represented by a transfer function $h \in K_a(0)$ is L_2-stable if and only if the locus described by $h(j\omega)$ when ω describes $[-\infty, +\infty]$ does not contain nor encircle the -1 point.

4.4 GRAPHICAL STABILITY CRITERIA FOR MULTIVARIABLE SYSTEMS

In this section graphical stability criteria of the Nyquist type applicable to open loop stable multivariable distributed feedback systems are introduced. These criteria are based on the results of Section 4.2 and on the generalized Principle of the Argument and its consequences (see Theorem 2.16 and Propositions 2.14 and 2.15).

Given the linear feedback system

$$y = G(u - y) \tag{4.6}$$

the analysis of L_2, L_1 or L_∞ closed loop systems is based upon the determination of the zeros of the complex function $\Delta(s) = \det(I + \hat{G}(s))$ in the compact right half s-plane (see Theorems 4.1, 4.3 and 4.4). The analysis of X_2, X_1 and X_∞ closed loop systems is based upon the existence of some $a > 0$ such that $\Delta(s)$ has no zeros in $Re(s) > -a$ (see Theorems 4.2, 4.5 and 4.6). Thus in using the generalized Principle of the Argument to determine these zeros it is important to note two conditions which limit the class of dynamical systems to which this result can be applied:

(i) The Principle of the Argument determines zeros of a function in a simple region, hence it cannot be used to determine the zeros of $\Delta(s)$ at infinity.

(ii) The Principle of the Argument requires the function $\Delta(s)$ to be analytic or meromorphic in an open set containing the simple region to which it is applied. Consequently it cannot be used in a general L_p-stability criterion, since the transfer functions involved are not necessarily analytic on the imaginary axis.

The transfer function associated with a multiplier in X_2, X_1 or X_∞ is an element of $\mathcal{R}$ and is therefore always analytic in some open set which contains the right half s-plane. A problem still remains: the analytic stability criterion of Theorems 4.2, 4.5 and 4.6 searches for an $a > 0$ such that $\Delta(s) = \det(I + \hat{G}(s))$ has no zeros in $Re(s) > -a$, therefore a precise simple region to which the Principle of the Argument could be applied is not defined. This difficulty is associated with the fact that Nyquist-type criteria normally use the behaviour of transfer functions along the imaginary axis. However, this difficulty can be resolved, keeping compatibility with the usual Nyquist type criteria, if the condition that $s \mapsto \Delta(s)$ is bounded away from zero at infinity is imposed. Under these conditions, Proposition 3.8 which states that an element of $\mathcal{R}$ bounded away from zero at infinity is invertible in $\mathcal{R}$ if and only if $\inf_{Re(s) \geq 0} |h(s)| > 0$, can be utilized. This condition also solves the difficulty associated with the determination of zeros at infinity. We can then define a simple region

$$\Omega = \{s : Re(s) \geq 0, |s| \leq \rho\} \tag{4.7}$$

contained in the domain of analyticity of the transfer function such that the stability of feedback systems can be assessed by the presence or absence of zeros of $\Delta(s)$ in Ω.

In conclusion, the Principle of the Argument can be used to establish X_p-stability criteria (but not a general L_p-stability criterion) if the condition that $s \mapsto \det(I + \hat{G}(s))$ is bounded away from zero at infinity is imposed.

Another condition that this condition helps to resolve is the possibility of the existence of an infinite number of branch points along the imaginary axis (see also Desoer and Wang, 1980). The generalized Principle of the Argument requires that the boundary of the simple region to which it is applied must be free of branch points; these branch points are the zeros of the polynomial $\phi[\lambda] = \det(\lambda - \hat{G}(s))$. Because we are dealing with simple regions Ω of the form (4.7) and the discriminant $D(s)$ (see Equation (2.13)) is an analytical function in an open set containing Ω, there are at most a finite number of such points in Ω and in particular in the region of the imaginary axis which lies in the simple region Ω. Thus along the imaginary axis a finite number of indentations can be constructed (as is usually done with Nyquist D loops) which frees the boundary $\partial\Omega$ of Ω of all branch points. It might be thought that the difficulties associated with an infinite number of branch points on the imaginary axis will persist if the case of an eigenvalue contour Γ generated by describing the whole imaginary axis is considered; this happens when $\lim_{|s| \to \infty} \hat{G}(s)$ exists uniformly. Note that the contour Γ is the limit when

$\rho \to \infty$ of the eigenvalue contour Γ_ρ generated when s describes the boundary loop $\partial \Omega_\rho$ of the region $\{s: |s| \leq \rho, \ Re(s) \geq 0\}$. The Principle of the Argument is not applied to Γ but to Γ_ρ, which is legitimately constructed since the number of possible branch points in $\partial \Omega_\rho$ is at most finite. The index function of Γ with respect to the -1 point is just a convenient method of determining the limit when $\rho \to \infty$ of the index function of the contours Γ_ρ, and this limit must exist since $\Delta(s)$ is bounded away from zero at infinity.

In the sequel consider a Nyquist D region of the form

$$\Omega_\rho = \{s: Re(s) \geq 0, |s| \leq \rho\} \tag{4.8}$$

indented in the usual manner along the imaginary axis so as to avoid all branch points and zeros of $\Delta(s)$ which may lie on the imaginary axis. The anti-clockwise orientated boundary loop of Ω_ρ is represented by $\partial \Omega_\rho$.

It is also assumed that transfer functions $s \mapsto \hat{G}(s)$ in $\mathscr{R}^{n \times n}$ satisfy at least one of the following conditions:

c(i) There exists a $\rho > 0$ such that $\inf\limits_{|s| \geq \rho} |\det (I + \hat{G}(s))| > 0$.

c(ii) There exists in disjoint circles $D_1, D_2, \ldots, D_m$, $m \leq n$, none of which contains the -1 point, and there exists a $\rho > 0$ such that for any $|s| \geq \rho$, every eigenvalue of $\hat{G}(s)$ is contained in one of the circles D_i.

c(iii) The matrix transfer function $\hat{G}(s)$ tends to a constant matrix $\hat{G}(\infty)$ uniformly as $|s| \to \infty$.

Condition c(i) is just a restatement of the requirement that $s \mapsto \det (I + \hat{G}(s))$ must be bounded away from zero at infinity; condition c(iii) contains condition c(ii), which in turn contains condition c(i).

The multivariable Nyquist stability criteria for X_2^n, X_1^n and X_∞^n systems can now be given.

THEOREM 4.9   *The feedback system*

$$y = G(u - y), \qquad G \in M(X_2^n), \qquad u \in X_2^n \tag{4.9}$$

is X_2^n-stable if and only if:

(i) *When G satisfies condition c(i), the eigenvalue contour Γ_ρ generated when s describes $\partial \Omega_\rho$ does not encircle or contain the -1 point, and none of the possible branch points on the imaginary axis corresponds to eigenvalues with value -1; or*

(ii) *When G satisfies condition c(ii), any contour formed by the concatenation of the eigenvalue paths generated when s describes the region of the imaginary axis $-\rho \leq \omega \leq \rho$ and closed by arcs contained in the* circles $D_1, D_2, \ldots, D_m$ *do not contain or encircle the* -1 *point, and in addition none of the possible branch points on the imaginary axis corresponds to an eigenvalue of* -1; *or*

(iii) *When G satisfies condition* c(iii), *the eigenvalue contour* Γ *generated when s describes the whole imaginary axis do not encircle or contain the* -1 *point, and none of the possible branch points on the imaginary axis corresponds to an eigenvalue of* -1.

Proof   In any of the conditions c(i)–c(iii), $\Delta(s) = \det(I + \hat{G}(s))$ is bounded away from zero at infinity. Thus, using Theorem 4.2 and Proposition 3.8, the feedback system (4.9) if and only if $\Delta(s)$ has no zeros in the simple region Ω_ρ. Proposition 2.15 can now be used to determine these zeros: if the eigenvalue contour Γ_ρ, generated when s describes $\partial \Omega_\rho$, does not contain or intersect the -1 point, then there are no zeros of $\Delta(s)$ in the indented region Ω_ρ. All possible zeros in the closed right half s-plane are therefore branch points. However, by hypothesis, none of these points corresponds to an eigenvalue of -1, so none can be a zero of $\Delta(s)$; this establishes part (i) of Theorem 4.9. Parts (ii) and (iii) of the theorem differ only from part (i) in the manner in which the encirclements of the -1 point by Γ_ρ are counted.

In part (ii) only the section of Γ_ρ which corresponds to s describing the region of $\partial \Omega_\rho$ on the imaginary axis and its indentations is used. The remainder of Γ_ρ is contained, by hypothesis, in the circles $D_1, D_2, \ldots, D_m$. Therefore the conditions of part (ii) of the theorem are satisfied if and only if the conditions in part (i) are satisfied; this establishes part (ii).

In part (iii), consider the distinct eigenvalues $\lambda_1, \lambda_2, \ldots, \lambda_m$ of $G(\infty)$, the theorem hypothesis guarantees that they are all distinct from -1. Since $\hat{G}(s)$ converges uniformly to $\hat{G}(\infty)$ when $|s| \to \infty$, it is possible to find a $\rho > 0$ and circles $D_1, D_2, \ldots, D_m$ with centres $\lambda_1, \lambda_2, \ldots, \lambda_m$ which do not contain the -1 point, such that $|s| \geq \rho$ implies that all eigenvalues of $\hat{G}(s)$ (including the eigenvalues which correspond to possibly infinite branch points on the imaginary axis) are contained in the union of the circles. Then, in this case, condition (iii) of the theorem is equivalent to conditions (ii); this completes the proof.   □

THEOREM 4.10   *The feedback system*

$$y = G(u - y),$$

with $u \in X_1^n$ *(respectively* $u \in X_\infty^n$*) and G represented by an element of* $LA_-^{n \times n}$, *is* X_1^n-*stable (respectively* X_∞^n-*stable) if and only if:*

(i) *When G satisfies condition* c(i), *the eigenvalue contour* Γ_ρ *generated* *when s describes $\partial\Omega_\rho$ does not encircle or contain the -1 point and none of the possible branch points on the imaginary axis corresponds to an eigenvalue of -1; or*

(ii) *When G satisfies condition c(ii), any contour formed by the concatenation of the eigenvalue paths of G generated when s describes the region of $\partial\Omega_\rho$ on the imaginary axis, and closed by arcs contained in the union of the circles $D_1, D_2, \ldots, D_m$, does not contain or encircle the -1 point, and in addition none of the possible branch points on the imaginary axis corresponds to an eigenvalue of -1.*

Proof Identical to the proof of Theorem 4.9 but utilizing Theorem 4.6 instead.   □

THEOREM 4.11   *The feedback system*

$$y = G(u - y)$$

with $G \in M(X_1^n)$ (respectively $G \in M(X_\infty^n)$) is X_1^n-stable (respectively X_∞^n-stable) only if the conditions of Theorem 4.10 are satisfied for $u \in X_1^n$ (respectively $u \in X_\infty^n$).

Proof Identical to Theorem 4.9 but utilizing Theorem 4.5 instead.   □

We now consider graphical stability criteria for L_2^n, L_1^n and L_∞^n feedback systems. Following the discussion made at the beginning of this section and in Section 4.3, we can only consider systems which are represented by transfer functions in $K_a(0)^{n \times n}$.

THEOREM 4.12   *The feedback system*

$$y = G(u - y), \qquad u \in L_2^n$$

with $G \in M(L_2^n)$ represented by an element of $K_a(0)^{n \times n}$ is L_2^n-stable if and only if the eigenvalue contour generated when s describes the compact imaginary axis does not contain or encircle the -1 point.

Proof Direct consequence of Theorems 4.7 and 4.1 (see also Valenca and Harris, 1980).   □

THEOREM 4.13   *The feedback system*

$$y = G(u - y)$$

with $u \in L_1^n$ (respectively $u \in L_\infty^n$) and $G \in LA_+^{n \times n}$ such that $\hat{G}(s)$ converges uniformly as $|s| \to \infty$ to a constant matrix, is L_1^n-stable (respectively L_∞^n-stable) if and only if the eigenvalue contour generated when s describes the compact imaginary axis does not encircle or contain the -1 point.

Proof Under the conditions of this theorem, there exists a $\rho > 0$ such that $\inf\limits_{|s|\geq\rho} |\det (I + \hat{G}(s))| > 0$. Moreover since $\Delta(s) = \det (I + \hat{G}(s))$ is an element of LA_+, $s \mapsto \Delta(s)$ is bounded and analytic in the interior of the region $\Omega_\rho = \{s: |s| \leq \rho,\ Re(s) \geq 0\}$ and continuous in the whole region. Moreover the properties of the Laplace transform of the elements of LA_+ show that $s \mapsto \Delta(s)$ must have total variation in the region of the imaginary axis $-\rho \leq \omega \leq \rho$. Using the arguments of Proposition 4.4 and Theorem 4.7, the zeros of $\Delta(s)$ in the closed right half s-plane are finite in number and can be calculated as the index function with respect to the origin of the loop described by $\Delta(s)$ when s describes $\partial\Omega_\rho$. Since $\hat{G}(s)$ tends to a constant matrix as $|s| \to \infty$, this loop coincides with the index function of the loop described by $\Delta(s)$ when s describes the imaginary axis. Finally, utilizing the fact that $s \mapsto \Delta(s)$ has no zeros in $Re(s) \geq 0$ if and only if the eigenvalue contour Γ does not encircle or contain the -1 point (Valenca and Harris, 1980), we complete the proof.   □

4.5 NOTES

Rosenbrock (1969, 1974), in investigating the stability of linear multivariable feedback systems, attempted a reduction of the stability problem to a series of simultaneous scalar problems whereby classical frequency domain design techniques could be utilized. In this Inverse Nyquist Array (INA) technique the aim was to diminish loop interaction by achieving diagonal dominance of the rational matrix transfer function of the open loop system by elementary matrix operations through a cascade compensator. This approach was employed by other workers whose similar aim was to reduce a multivariable feedback control problem to a series of single loop problems by iteration algorithms such as the sequential return difference approach of Mayne (1973).

A more fundamental and general approach to the stability of multivariable feedback systems is through a generalization of the scalar control design techniques of poles, zeros, root-loci, and Nyquist and Bode diagrams. An initial attempt to generalize the Nyquist criterion to multivariable systems was made by Bohn and Kasvard (1963); however, complex variables based proofs of the Nyquist criterion followed with increasing generality by Barman and Katzenelson (1974), Postlethwaite and MacFarlane (1979), Desoer and Wang (1980), and Valenca and Harris (1980). In parallel with these recent generalizations of the Nyquist stability criterion complementary generalizations of root loci or characteristic frequency loci techniques based upon algebraic function theory were developed by Postlethwaite (1977), MacFarlane *et al.* (1977) and Postlethwaite and MacFarlane (1979).

These natural and fundamental approaches to the multivariable feedback problem have been accompanied by an increasing collection of specifically multivariable systems approaches such as the dyadic method of Owens (1978), matrix transfer factorization of Sain (1975), frequency domain compensation, decoupling and pole placement of Wolovich (1974), and the related state space approach of Davison (1976) which highlights the importance of system insensitivity or robustness to parameter variations. An outstanding source of original and historically important frequency domain control design methods for multivariable systems is MacFarlane (1979).

REFERENCES

Bachman, G. and Narici, L. (1966). "Functional Analysis". Academic Press, New York and London.

Barman, J. F. and Katzenelson, N. (1974). "A generalized Nyquist type stability criterion for multivariable feedback systems." *Int. J. Control* **20**, 593–622.

Bohn, E. V. and Kasvand, T. (1963). "Use of matrix transformations and system eigenvalues in the design of linear multivariable control systems." *Proc. IEE* **110**, 989–997.

Callier, F. M. and Desoer, C. A. (1973). "Necessary and sufficient conditions for stability of n-input n-output convolution feedback systems with a finite number of unstable poles." *IEEE Trans.* **AC-18**, 295–298.

Callier, F. M. and Desoer, C. A. (1976). "Open loop unstable convolution feed-back systems, with dynamic feedback." *Automatica* **12**, 507–518.

Callier, F. M. and Desoer, C. A. (1978). "An algebra of transfer functions for distributed linear time invariant systems". *IEEE Trans. Circuit and Systems* **25**, 651–662.

Davison, E. J. (1976). "The robust decentralized control of a general servomechanism problem". *IEEE Trans.* **AC-21**, 14–24.

DeCarlo, R. and Saeks, R. (1977). "The Encirclement condition: an approach using Algebraic Topology". *Int. J. Control* **26**, 279–287.

Desoer, C. A. and Wang, V. T. (1980). "On the generalized Nyquist stability criterion". *IEEE Trans.* **AC-25**, 187–196.

Hille, E. (1962). "Analytic Function Theory" Vol 2. Ginn & Co, Aylesbury.

Hille, E. and Phillips, R. S. (1957). "Functional analysis and semi-groups." *Amer. Math. Soc. Colloquium Pub.* **31**.

Hewitt, E. and Stromberg, K. (1965). "Real and Abstract Analysis", Graduate Series in Mathematics. Springer Verlag, Berlin.

MacFarlane, A. G. J. (1979). "Frequency Response Methods in Control Systems". IEEE Press, J. Wiley, New York.

MacFarlane, A. G. J., Kouvaritakis, B., and Edmunds, J. M. (1977). "Complex variable methods for multivariable feedback systems analysis and design", Alternatives for Linear Multivariable Control. National Eng. Consortium, Chicago, USA, 189–228.

MacFarlane, A. G. J. and Postlethwaite, I. (1977). "Characteristic frequency functions and characteristic gain functions." *Int. J. Control* **26**, 265–278.

MacFarlane, A. G. J. and Postlethwaite, I. (1977). "The generalized Nyquist stability criterion and multivariable root loci." *Int. J. Control* **25**, 81–127.

MacFarlane, A. G. J. and Postlethwaite, I. (1978). "Extended Principle of the Argument." *Int. J. Control* **27,** 49–55.

Mayne, D. Q. (1973). "The design of linear multivariable systems." *Automatica* **9,** 201–207.

Owens, D. H. (1978). "Feedback and Multivariable systems". Peter Peregrinus, London.

Postlethwaite, I. (1977). "The asymptotic behaviour, the angles of departure and the angles of approach of the characteristic frequency loci." *Int. J. Control* **25,** 677–695.

Postlethwaite, I. and MacFarlane, A. G. J. (1979). "A Complex Variable Approach to the Analysis of Linear Multivariable Feedback Systems", Lecture Notes in Control and Information Sciences, **12,** Springer Verlag, Berlin.

Rosenbrock, H. H. (1969). "Design of multivariable control systems using the inverse Nyquist array." *Proc. IEE.* **116,** 1929–1936.

Rosenbrock, H. H. (1974). "Computer Aided Control System Design." Academic Press, London and New York.

Sain, M. K. (1975). "A free modular algorithm for minimal design of linear multivariable systems." Proc. 6th IFAC World Congress, part 1B, 9.1.1–9.1.7.

Sandberg, I. W. (1966). "On generalizations and extensions of the Popov criterion". *IEEE Trans.* **CT-13,** (1), 117–118.

Valenca, J. M. E. and Harris, C. J. (1980) "Nyquist criterion for input/output stability of multivariable systems." *Int. J. Control* **31,** 917–935.

Willems, J. C. (1971) "The Analysis of Feedback Systems", Research Monograph 62. MIT Press, Cambridge, Mass.

Wolovich, W. A. (1974). "Linear Multivariable Systems". Springer, New York.

Zames, G. (1966). "On the input–output stability of time varying nonlinear feedback systems". Parts I and II. *IEEE Trans.* **AC-11,** 228–238, 456–476.

Chapter Five

Extended Space Theory in the Study of System Operators

5.1 INTRODUCTION

The concept of input–output stability is based on the existence of an operator representing the system which maps a Banach space of inputs into a Banach space of outputs. In Chapter 3 a representation theory for stable operators was developed; however, for control system studies in considering the stability of feedback systems the open loop operator is frequently unstable or at least oscillatory. Function spaces that grow without bound are not contained in Banach spaces, and some mathematical description of unstable operators is necessary if feedback stability is to be interpreted from open loop system descriptions. This is achieved by establishing the stability problem in an *extended space* which contains well-behaved as well as asymptotically unbounded functions or those which oscillate; essentially these extended spaces are developed as an extension of an associated normed linear space (say, L_p) and which contain the unextended space (say, L_p) as subsets. The generalized extended space therefore contains all functions which are integrable or summable over *finite* intervals which yet may diverge asymptotically or oscillate.

In this chapter we consider in detail extended spaces and operators in extended spaces, not only because of their importance in determining conditions for the stability of feedback systems but also because of their significance in general mathematical systems theory. In Section 5.2 a close relationship between extended spaces and locally convex spaces equipped with a projective limit type of topology is established. In particular, for practical frequency domain stability criteria, the extended L_{2e} space (whose topology is given by a system of positive semi-norms) can be identified with the projective limit of $L_2[0, T]$; in addition the extended space L_{2e} is shown to be complete. Supporting material for this section can be found in Section 1.3. The relationship between a unique fixed

143

point of an operator and the concept of generalized causality is developed in Section 5.3, and it is shown that strong causality effectively requires the presence of an infinitesimal delay in the operator. To ensure the existence and uniqueness of solution to mathematical models of dynamical systems, it is shown in Section 5.4 that it is necessary to invoke a continuity condition (such as Lipschitz continuity) on the system operators. One of the most powerful mechanisms for developing frequency domain stability is that of passivity; in Section 5.5, passivity (or positivity for causal operators) and the concepts of extended Hilbert spaces are developed and related to the invertibility of operators and well-posedness of feedback systems. It is demonstrated that incremental passivity for operators in feedback systems ensures not only the boundedness of solution but also its uniqueness, existence and continuous dependence as well as the invertibility of the return difference operator. The passivity theorem is shown to be quite stringent in its operator requirements for closed loop stability; however, by introducing a multiplier into the feedback loop it is shown in Section 5.6 that a variety of transformed dynamical systems are input–output equivalent. Additionally the factorization of such multipliers into causal and non-causal components allows a L_2-stability condition to be expressed in terms of the composition of the multiplier and the loop operators. This technique is used effectively in Chapter 7 to generate the multivariable Popov and off-axis circle stability criteria. Finally, the concept of conicity or equivalently sectoricity, which is closely related to passivity notions, for causal operators is introduced in Section 5.7 as a prelude to developing circle-type stability criteria for non-linear multivariable feedback systems in Chapters 6 and 7.

5.2   FUNDAMENTAL RESULTS

Consider a linear space E equipped with a system of finite semi-norms $SN = \{p_a(\cdot)\}$ satisfying:

  sn(i) $p_a(x) \leq p_b(x)$ whenever $b > a$ for all $x \in E$
  sn(ii) For each non-zero $x \in E$ there exists at least one $a \in \Gamma$ such that

$$p_a(x) \neq 0.$$

where a is in a given totally ordered set Γ.

  Condition sn(ii) is sufficient to guarantee that the system of semi-norms defines a topology, M_d, in E (Chapter 1, Theorem 1.4), and with such a topology, $E[M_d]$ is a locally convex space.

Example 5.1   Consider the set of all measurable functions $f(t)$ which are square integrable in any bounded interval $[0, T]$, i.e.

$$\int_0^T f(t)^2 \, dt < \infty \qquad \forall \, T > 0$$

If our totally ordered set Γ is the positive real axis $R_+ = [0, \infty)$, for any $T > 0$ a semi-norm can be defined by

$$P_T(f) = \left\{ \int_0^T f(t)^2 \, dt \right\}^{1/2} \tag{5.1}$$

It is obvious that this system of semi-norms satisfy both conditions $sn(i)$ and $sn(ii)$.

Every semi-norm $p_a(\cdot)$ can define a relationship of equivalence $\mathscr{R}_a$ in E by

$$x = y(\bmod \mathscr{R}_a) \quad \text{if} \quad p_a(x - y) = 0 \tag{5.2}$$

If N_a is the null space of $p_a(\cdot)$, given by

$$N_a = \{ x \in E : p_a(x) = 0 \} \tag{5.3}$$

then clearly N_a is a linear closed subset of E and the quotient space E/N_a is a normed locally convex space (Theorem 1.6). Using E_a to represent the quotient space E/N_a and A_a to represent the canonical mapping from E into E_a, then $\|A_a x\| = p_a(x)$ and $\|\bar{x}\| = p_a(x)$ for an arbitrary x in the equivalence class $\bar{x}$. Using Theorem 1.11 it is now possible to define linear continuous onto maps $A_{ab} : E_b \to E_a$, $b > a$ as

$$A_{ab} = A_a A_b^{(-1)}$$

With such maps the space $E[M_d]$ is topologically isomorphic with the topological projective limit $\varprojlim A_{ab}(E_b)$ with E_b equipped with the norm topology. As we shall see, due to this isomorphism, the space $E[M_d]$ inherits some of the properties of the quotient space E_a.

Consider the subspace E_0 of E formed with all $x \in E$ for which the net $\{p_a(x)\}$ is bounded; because the net is non-decreasing it must have a limit. Define a positive function in E_0

$$p(x) = \lim_a p_a(x)$$

which clearly satisfies $p(x) \geq p_a(x)$, $\forall \, a \in \Gamma$. The space $E[M_d]$ is said to be the *extended version* of E_0.

PROPOSITION 5.1   The space E_0 is a normed locally convex space equipped with the norm $\|x\| = p(x) = \lim_a p_a(x)$. Moreover, the norm topology of E_0 is stronger than the topology induced in E_0 by the topology of E.

Proof E_0 is obviously linear and $p(\cdot)$ a semi-norm. Moreover, if $x \in E_0$ is such that $p(x) = 0$, then $p_a(x) = 0$, for all $a \in \Gamma$, which implies that $x = 0$; thus $\|x\| = p(x)$ defines a finite norm. The norm topology of E_0 is stronger than the induced topology as $p(x) \geq p_a(x)$ for all $a \in \Gamma$.   □

Example 5.2: Extended L_p spaces, L_{pe}   Consider the Banach spaces $L_p[0, T]$, $(1 \leq p \leq \infty)$ consisting of all L_p functions (see Section 1.5) with support contained in $[0, T]$. Also consider the space of all measurable functions $f: R_+ \to R$ for which $P_T f \in L_p[0, T]$ for any $T \geq 0$ (the truncation operator P_T is defined in Example 1.10); this space is represented by L_{pe}. The space L_{pe} is clearly linear and contains L_p. Moreover since $\{\|P_T f\|\}$ is not necessarily a bounded net, the space L_{pe} is not finitely normed.

The positive functions

$$p_T(f) \triangleq \|P_T f\|_p$$

define a family of semi-norms which clearly satisfy conditions $sn(i)$ and $sn(ii)$ of this section. Thus L_{pe} can be equipped with a topology defined by these semi-norms. The subspace of L_{pe} formed by all $f \in L_{pe}$ for which $\{p_T(f)\}$ is a bounded net coincides precisely with L_p; thus L_{pe} is the extended version of L_p.

Consider now Theorem 1.10; replacing in this theorem F by L_{pe}, E_a by $L_p[0, T]$ and P_a by P_T, and noticing that

$$L_{pe} \equiv \bigcap_{T \geq 0} P_T^{(-1)} L_p[0, T]$$

by definition of L_{pe}, then we can say that L_{pe} can be identified with the topological projective limit of the spaces $L_p[0, T]$.

$$L_{pe} \simeq \lim_{\leftarrow} P_T P_T^{(-1)} L_p[0, T]$$

From the same result we conclude that L_{pe} can be identified with the topological projective limit of the spaces L_{pe}/N_T, where N_T is the null space of $p_T(\cdot)$, this is not surprising due to the isomorphism between L_{pe}/N_T and $L_p[0, T]$ which can easily be established by following the arguments of Example 1.10.

Of particular importance in the sequel is the case when $p = 2$ and the resultant stability criterion can be interpreted in the frequency domain (see Chapter 6).

One of the most important properties that $E[M_d]$ can inherit from the spaces E_a is completeness.

PROPOSITION 5.2   *If every E_a is complete then $E[M_d]$ is also complete.*

Proof   Kothe (1969), Section 19.10.   □

The above proposition and the completeness of every $L_p[0, T]$ space gives:

COROLLARY 5.1   *The extended space L_{pe} is complete.*

5.3 OPERATORS IN EXTENDED SPACES

In the study of feedback systems through input-output operators we are primarily interested in the mapping of operators from the extended space $E[M_d]$ into itself. In the sequel we will assume that Γ is the half line $R_+ = [0, \infty)$.

Definition 5.1   Consider a system of operators $\{G_a\}$, where G_a maps E_a into itself such that for all $b > a$

$$G_a A_{ab} = A_{ab} G_b \tag{5.4}$$

for $A_{ab} : E_b \to E_a$ as defined in Proposition 5.2. Such a system is said to satisfy the *generalized causality condition*. If in addition for each $\xi > 0$ there exists a $\delta > 0$ such that for all $a \in \Gamma$ and for all $x \in E_a$ there exists $b > a + \delta$ such that for all $y, z \in A_{ab}^{(-1)} x$

$$\|G_b y - G_b z\|_{E_b} \leq \xi \|y - z\|_{E_b} \tag{5.5}$$

then the system of operators is said to satisfy the *strong generalized causality condition*.

PROPOSITION 5.3   *If $\{G_a\}$ is a system of operators satisfying the generalized causality condition, then a unique operator G mapping $E[M_d]$ into itself can be defined such that*

$$A_a G x = G_a A_a x \quad \text{for all} \quad x \in E \quad \text{and} \quad a \in \Gamma$$

Proof   Let $\underset{\sim}{E}$ denote the topological cartesian product $\prod_a E_a$ and let $\tilde{E}$ denote the projective limit of the spaces E_a, which (as we saw in Section 5.2) can be identified with E. For any $x \in E$ let (x_a) be the corresponding vector in $\tilde{E}$. A vector can be defined in $\underset{\sim}{E}$ through

$$y_a \triangleq G_a x_a$$

The generalized causality condition now implies, that for any $b > a$,

$$A_{ab} y_b = A_{ab} G_b x_b = G_a A_{ab} x_b = G_a x_a = y_a$$

Thus $\tilde{y}$ is an element of $\tilde{E}$ and, consequently, of E. An operator $G : E \to E$ can now be defined as $G : (x_a) \mapsto (G_a x_a)$; thus by definition,

$$A_a G x = G_a x_a = G_a A_a x$$

In this study we consider only operators which satisfy the generalized causality condition. In the extended space L_{2e}, the generalized causality condition is equivalent to the classical definition of causality [J. C. Willems, 1969, 1971] or non-anticipatory operator G, which satisfies

$$P_T G = P_T G P_T, \qquad (5.6)$$

and the operators $\{P_T G\}$ form the system of operators $\{G_a\}$ of Proposition 5.3. We note that the truncation operator P_T is a continuous linear operator on G and its operator norm is at most 1 (that is P_T is the resolution of identity on L_{2e}).

PROPOSITION 5.4   *Let operators* $G, F : L_{2e} \to L_{2e}$ *be causal: if the*

   (i) *Domain of* $G \triangleq D(G) = D(F)$, *then* $G + F$ *is causal.*

   (ii) *Range of* $G \triangleq R(G) \subset D(F)$, *then* GF *is causal.*

Proof   (i) Let $x, y \in D(G)$ and $P_T x = P_T y$,   then $P_T G x = P_T G y$ and $P_T F x = P_T F y$.   So   that $P_T G x + P_T F x = P_T G y + P_T F y \Rightarrow P_T (G + F) x = P_T (G + F) y$ hence $G + F$ is causal.

   (ii) Now,   since $Gx, Gy \in R(G) \subset D(F)$ then $P_T F(Gx) = (P_T FG)x = P_T F(Gy) = (P_T FG)y$, hence FG is causal.   □

An equivalent definition to the above is the mapping $G : L_{2e} \to L_{2e}$ is said to be causal if for all $T \geq 0$ and all $u_1, u_2 \in L_{2e}$ with $P_T u_1 = P_T u_2$, the equality $P_T G u_1 = P_T G u_2$ holds. The operator G is said to be *anti-causal* if the operator $(I - P_T)G$ commutes with $(I - P_T)$ on L_{2e}. It is clear that a memoryless operator is one which is both causal *and* anti-causal, that is, G is an instantaneous non-anticipatory operator. The concept of causality allows us to make a general definition of a dynamical system as one which has a causal or non-anticipatory mapping $G : U \to Y$, that is, future inputs do not effect past outputs.

Example 5.3   Consider the mapping $G : L_2(-\infty, \infty) \to L_2(-\infty, \infty)$ defined by the convolution integral

$$(Gu)(t) = \int_{-\infty}^{\infty} g(t - \tau) u(\tau) \, d\tau$$

for $g \in L_1(-\infty, \infty)$, $u \in L_2(-\infty, \infty)$. The mapping G is causal if and only if $g(t) = 0$ for $t < 0$.

The proof of the following proposition is obvious from the above definitions:

PROPOSITION 5.5   *If* $\{G_a\}$ *is a system of operators satisfying the generalized* *causality condition and $G : E \to E$ is defined by this system, then*

   (i) *G is continuous if every G_a is continuous.*

  (ii) *G is onto if and only if every G_a is onto.*

 (iii) *G is one-to-one if every G_a is one-to-one.*

 (iv) *Two operators G and H are distinct if and only if for some $a \in \Gamma$, $G_a \neq H_a$.*

A more important result relates the fixed points of G with the fixed points of $\{G_a\}$:

PROPOSITION 5.6   *If G is defined by the system of operators $\{G_a\}$ satisfying the generalized causality condition then $x \in E$ is a fixed point of G if and only if $A_a x$ is a fixed point of G_a for every $a \in \Gamma$.*

Proof   If $x = (x_a)$ is a fixed point of g, then $x_a = G_a x_a$ and x_a is a fixed point of G_a. Conversely if every x_a is a fixed point of G_a, then $x = (x_a) = (G_a x_a) = Gx$ and $\underline{x}$ is a fixed point of G.   □

PROPOSITION 5.7   *If G is defined by a system of operators $\{G_a\}$ satisfying the strong generalized causality condition, if every E_a is complete, and if for some $\underline{c}$, G_c has a fixed point x_c, then G has a fixed point $x \in E$ which satisfies $A_c x = x_c$. Furthermore, if x_c is the unique fixed point of G_c in E_c, then x is the unique fixed point of G in E.*

Proof   For every $a < c$ $G_a A_{ac} x_c = A_{ac} G_c x_c = A_{ac} x_c$; therefore x_a as defined by $A_{ac} x_c$ is a fixed point of G_a. We now seek possible fixed points of G_b for $b > c$. Using Proposition 5.6, if a fixed point $x \in E$ of G exists and satisfies $A_c x = x_c$, then $A_b x$ is a fixed point of G_b and is contained in $A_{cb}^{-1} x_c$. Furthermore, if x_c is a unique fixed point of G_c in E_c, then all possible fixed points $\bar{x} \in E$ of G satisfy

$$A_b \bar{x} \in A_{cb}^{-1} x_c$$

Therefore every possible fixed point of G_b must lie in $A_{cb}^{-1} x_c$. Since A_{cb} is linear and continuous, the space $A_{cb}^{-1} x_c$ is a closed linear subspace of E_b, and since E_b is complete, the space $A_{cb}^{-1} x_c$ is also complete.

    Let y be arbitrary in $A_{cb}^{-1} x_c$, then

$$A_{cb}(G_b y) = G_c(A_{cb} y) = G_c x_c = x_c$$

Therefore $G_b y \in A_{cb}^{-1} x_c$, and so G_b maps $A_{cb}^{-1} x_c$ into itself.

    Consider now some real number $0 < \xi < 1$ and the strong causality condition; then there exists a $\delta > 0$ and a $b > c + \delta$ such that

$$\|G_b y - G_b z\| \leq \xi \|y - x\|$$

for all $y, z \in A_{cb}^{-1}x_c$. Therefore G_b is a contraction mapping the complete space $A_{cb}^{-1}x_c$ into itself, and by the contraction mapping theorem, Theorem 1.19 (Section 1.4), a unique fixed point x_b of G_b exists in $A_{cb}^{-1}x_c$. Moreover, if x_c is the unique fixed point of G_c in E_c, then x_b is the unique fixed point of G_b in E_b, as $A_{cb}^{-1}x_c$ contains all possible fixed points of G_b. Replacing c by b and repeating the above argument we can now show that for all $a < b$, $x_a = A_{ab}x_b$ is a fixed point of G_a in E_a; moreover x_a is unique if x_c is unique, otherwise there would be more than one fixed point of G_b. Finally, repeating the above arguments we can find a fixed point of T_{b_2}, $b_2 > b + \delta > c + 2\delta$ (note that δ is only a function of ξ and not of c or x_c). And so by induction we can define a sequence $\{b_n\}$ in Γ, with $b_0 = c$, $b_1 = b$ such that

$$b_{n+1} > b_n + \delta$$

and such that a fixed point $x_{b_n} \in E_{b_n}$ of G_{b_n} exists satisfying $A_{cb_n}x_{b_n} = x_c$. Moreover, if x_c is unique, x_{b_n} is also unique. But since $\{b_n\}$ is an unbounded sequence, it is possible to define uniformly an $x \in E$ such that $A_{b_n}x = x_{b_n}$, $n = 1, 2, \ldots$, and $A_c x = x_c$. The point x is a fixed point of G in E. Finally, if x_c is unique, x is also unique, as every x_{b_n} is unique. $\square$

Example 5.4   In the extended space L_{2e} the strong causality condition can be expressed as: if $P_t x = P_t y$, then for any $\xi > 0$ there exists a $dt > 0$ such that

$$\|P_{t+dt}(Gx - Gy)\| \leq \xi \|P_{t+dt}(x - y)\|$$

So that the strong causality condition effectively requires the presence of an infinitesimal delay in the operator G.

PROPOSITION 5.8   *If $\{G_a\}$ is a system of linear continuous maps satisfying the generalized causality condition and G is the operator defined by such a system, then:*

(i) $\sigma(G_a) \subset \sigma(G_b)$ $\forall\, a < b$

(ii) $\sigma(G) = \bigcup_a \sigma(G_a)$

where $\sigma(\cdot)$ represents the spectrum of an operator.

Proof   For any $y \in E_b$, there exists a unique solution, $x \in E_b$ of the equation $\lambda x = G_b x + y$, for λ arbitrary in the resolvent set of G_b. Projecting this equation E_a, with $a < b$

$$\lambda A_{ab}x = A_{ab}G_b x + A_{ab}y = G_a(A_{ab}x) + A_{ab}y$$

Since y is arbitrary in E_b, $A_{ab}y$ is arbitrary in E_a, and therefore λ also belongs to the resolvent set of G_a. Hence $\rho(G_b) \subset \rho(G_a)$ and taking complements gives $\sigma(G_a) \subset \sigma(G_b)$. Identically it can be proven that for any $a \in \Gamma$,

$$\sigma(G_a) \subset \sigma(G) \quad \text{and} \quad \bigcup_a \sigma(G_a) \subset \sigma(G) \tag{5.7}$$

Conversely suppose that λ is an arbitrary point in the intersection $\bigcap_a \rho(G_a)$. Then for an arbitrary $y = (y_a) \in \tilde{E}$, the equation

$$\lambda x = G_a x + y_a \tag{5.8}$$

has a unique solution for each $a \in \Gamma$. Let $x^{(a)}$ be such a solution then,

$$\lambda A_{ab} x^{(b)} = A_{ab} G_b x^{(b)} + A_{ab} y_b = G_a(A_{ab} x^{(b)}) + y_a$$

Since the solution of (5.8) is unique, we have

$$x^{(a)} = A_{ab} x^{(b)} \qquad \forall \, a < b,$$

and consequently the vector $(x^{(a)}) \in \tilde{E}$, and λ belongs to the resolvent set of G. Hence $\bigcap_a \rho(G_a) \subset \rho(G)$, and taking complements gives $\sigma(G) \subset \bigcap_a \sigma(G_a)$; taken with the above results, (5.8), condition (ii) of Proposition (5.4) follows. ☐

Example 5.5 Suppose that G is a causal mapping of L_{2e} into itself; then the operators G_T defined by

$$G_T = P_T G$$

are maps of $L_2[0, T]$ into itself and the system of operators $\{G_T\}$ satisfies the generalized causality condition. Moreover from Proposition 5.8 we conclude

PROPOSITION 5.9 *If G is a causal operator of L_{2e} into itself defined by the system of operators $\{G_T\}$, and $(c - G)^{-1}$ exists as an operator from L_{2e} into itself, then*

   (i) *For all $T \geq 0$, $(c - G_T)^{-1}$ exists as an operator from $L_2[0, T]$ into itself.*
   (ii) *$(c - G)^{-1}$ is causal.*
   (iii) *$P_T(c - G)^{-1} = (c - G_T)^{-1}$, i.e. $(c - G)^{-1}$ is defined by the system of operators $\{(c - G_T)^{-1}\}$.*

5.4 WELL POSEDNESS AND FEEDBACK SYSTEMS

To ensure the existence and uniqueness of solution to mathematical models of dynamical systems it is usual to invoke some continuity condition upon system operators. Although linear extended spaces are not normed, it is possible to define the concepts of continuity and boundedness. For simplicity we consider L_p^n spaces in the sequel.

If G is a causal mapping of the extended space L_{pe}^n into itself, then G is said to be *locally Lipschitz continuous* on L_{pe}^n if $P_T G P_T = P_T G = G_T$ is Lipschitz continuous on L_p^n for all $T \geq 0$, i.e.

$$\sup_{\substack{x, y \in L_p^n \\ P_T x \neq P_T y}} \left\{ \frac{\|P_T (Gx - Gy)\|}{\|P_T (x - y)\|} \right\} < \infty, \qquad \forall\, T \geq 0$$

Furthermore if the operator G is unbiased (i.e. $G(0) = 0$) and for all $T \geq 0$ $P_T G P_T$ is bounded on L_p^n, then the operator G is said to be *locally bounded*. Since G_T is Lipschitz continuous for each $T \geq 0$, then the Lipschitz norm (or gain) $\|G_T\| \geq \|G_{T'}\|$ whenever $T > T'$. That is, $\|G_T\| = \|P_T G P_T\|$ is a monotone non-decreasing function of T. If the non-decreasing sequence of real numbers $\{\|G_T\|\}$ is bounded, then a limit exists such that

$$\|G\| = \lim_{T \to \infty} \|G_T\| \tag{5.9}$$

In addition if G is a causal unbiased operator on L_p^n, (or L_{pe}^n) and is Lipschitz continuous, then its Lipschitz gains or norms on L_{pe}^n and L_p^n are equivalent.

Consider the feedback system

$$y = F(u - Gy), \qquad u \in L_{pe}^m \tag{5.10}$$

which has solution

$$y = (I + FG)^{-1} Fu \tag{5.11}$$

provided that the operator $(I + FG)^{-1}$ exists. Assume the following conditions on the system operators: (i) the feedforward operator F is causal, $F: L_{pe}^m \to L_{pe}^n$, unbiased and locally Lipschitz continuous on L_{pe}^m; (ii) the feedback operator G is causal, $G: L_{pe}^n \to L_{pe}^m$ and locally Lipschitz continuous on L_{pe}^n. In addition, either G or F is strongly causal (see example 5.4); this is equivalent to the generalized causality condition defined through the projective limit of normed spaces.

Definition 5.2 The feedback system model $y = F(u - Gy)$ is said to be physically *well posed* if the system feedback error $e = u - Gy$ and output solutions y are unique and Lipschitz continuous upon the inputs, and are causally dependent on finite intervals.

As we shall see, the above definition is essentially satisfied if the operator $(I + FG)$ is invertible on $L_{pe}^m \times L_{pe}^n$ and the inverse $(I + FG)^{-1}$ is causal and Lipschitz continuous on $L_{pe}^m \times L_{pe}^n$. The condition that F or G is strongly causal is motivated by the fact that all physical systems exhibit some form of delay in the system loop. The above conditions ensure that the feedback system (5.10) is a suitable approximation to a physical system. To see this, the map

$$A(y) = F(u - Gy), \qquad A : L_{pe}^m \to L_{pe}^n \tag{5.12}$$

is strongly causal, since F or G is strongly causal. If $\delta > 0$ is the delay element present in operator $A(\cdot)$, then for all $T < \delta$, the null function $y(t) = 0$ is a fixed point of $P_T A$ in $L_p^n[0, T]$. Since the space $L_p^n[0, T]$ is complete, we can use Proposition 5.7 to establish that there exists a fixed point $y \in L_{pe}^n$ of $A(\cdot)$. Also since the null function is the unique fixed point of $P_T A$ in $L_p^n[0, T]$ for $T < \delta$, then the proof of Proposition 5.7 shows that y is a unique fixed point of $A(\cdot)$.

In conclusion the conditions (i) and (ii) imposed upon the system operator, F, G, are sufficient to guarantee that the feedback system (5.10) has a unique solution in L_{pe}^n.

5.5 PASSIVITY IN FEEDBACK SYSTEMS

A special Banach space, the so-called Hilbert space, which possesses the additional structure of an inner product enables us to generate positive definite quadratic functions that can be associated with the energy of physical systems. The Hilbert space approach is also the basis of the orthogonal projection theorem which has played such an important role in control and estimation (Luenberger, 1969) and in the stability of ordinary differential equations via Lyapunov's direct method (Curtain and Pritchard, 1977). In the following we introduce the concepts of extended Hilbert spaces, passivity, positivity and their interrelationships with previous concepts such as the invertibility of operators $(I + FG)$ and well-posedness of feedback systems (see Section 5.4).

Definition 5.3: *Inner Products*   An inner product $\langle \cdot, \cdot \rangle$ that maps the linear space HS over the complex or real field F ($\langle \cdot, \cdot \rangle : HS \times HS \to F$) is such that

$$\text{(i) } \langle \alpha x + \beta y, z \rangle = \alpha \langle x, z \rangle + \beta \langle y, z \rangle$$

$$\text{(ii) } \langle x, y \rangle = \langle y, x \rangle^* \tag{5.13}$$

$$\text{(iii) } \langle x, x \rangle > 0 \Leftrightarrow x \neq 0$$

for all $\alpha, \beta \in F$; $x, y \in HS$.

Utilizing the inner product, the function $\|x\| = \langle x, x \rangle^{1/2}$ is a norm on HS

and the normed linear space $(HS, \|\cdot\|)$ if complete is a *Hilbert space*. This norm and the inner product have the following properties:

(i) $\langle y, y \rangle = 0 \Rightarrow y = 0$

(ii) $|\langle x, y \rangle| \leq \|x\| \cdot \|y\|$ (Schwartz inequality)   (5.14)

(iii) $\|x + y\|^2 + \|x - y\|^2 = 2(\|x\|^2 + \|y\|^2)$ (parallelogram law)

for all $x, y \in H$.

The *adjoint* G^* of a bounded operator G on a Hilbert space is defined by

$$\langle Gx, y \rangle = \langle x, G^*y \rangle \qquad \forall\, x, y \in H.$$

Example 5.6   Consider the space $HS = L_2[[0, T], R^n]$ of n-vector valued functions $x : [0, T] \times R^n \to R^n$, with the inner product

$$\langle x, y \rangle = \int_0^T x'(t)y(t)\, dt,$$

this space is a Hilbert space. If $G(t, \tau)$ is an $(n \times n)$ continuous valued matrix on $[0, T] \times [0, T]$, then the adjoint of the operator $Gx : HS \to HS$,

$$(Gx)(t) = \int_0^t G(t, \tau)x(\tau)\, d\tau$$

is

$$(G^*y)(t) = \int_t^T G'(\tau, t)y(\tau)\, d\tau.$$

In addition, the operator G is said to be *self-adjoint* on the Hilbert space HS if $G^* = G$; an obvious self-adjoint operator is the truncation operator P_T.

Definition 5.4: *Positivity*   A self-adjoint operator G $(G \in (HS, \|\cdot\|))$ is *positive* if

$$\langle Gx, x \rangle \geq 0 \qquad \text{for all} \quad x \in HS \qquad (5.15)$$

and *strictly positive* if

$$\langle Gx, x \rangle \geq \beta \|x\|^2 \quad \text{for} \quad \beta > 0.$$

Self-adjoint and positive operators occur frequently in control theory and have the following properties:

(i) If $G \in (HS, \|\cdot\|)$ is self-adjoint and $x \in H$, then $\|G\| = \sup_{\|x\|=1} |\langle Gx, x \rangle|$.

Also for any $G \in (HS, \|\cdot\|)$ GG^* is clearly self-adjoint and $\|GG^*\| = \|G\|^2 = \sup_{\|x\|=1} \langle Gx, Gx \rangle$

(ii) There exist constants α, β such that

$$\alpha \|x\|^2 \leq \langle Gx, x \rangle \leq \beta \|x\|^2 \quad \text{for all} \quad x \in HS,$$

If G is a positive operator, then $\alpha \geq 0$, but if G is strictly positive, then $\alpha > 0$ and G has a bounded linear inverse G^{-1} such that

$$\beta^{-1} \|x\|^2 \leq \langle G^{-1}x, x \rangle \leq \alpha^{-1} \|x\|^2 \quad \text{for all} \quad x \in HS,$$

also G has a unique strictly positive square root $G^{1/2}$.

Note that if the operator G can be decomposed such that $G = N^*N$, then G is self-adjoint and $\langle Gx, x \rangle = \|Nx\|^2$ so that G is also a positive operator. If in addition $N^*N = NN^*$, then $\|Nx\| = \|N^*x\|$ and the bounded linear operator N on the Hilbert space HS is said to be *normal*. Self-adjoint operators are generalizations of real symmetrical matrices, and positive operators are generalizations of positive definite matrices.

THEOREM 5.2   *Let $G : HS \rightarrow HS$ be a linear operator such that*

$$\inf_{\substack{\|x\|=1 \\ x \in HS}} \langle Gx, x \rangle = \gamma > 0,$$

then G is bounded, one to one, and onto, and the inverse G^{-1} is bounded with $\|G^{-1}\| \leq \gamma^{-1}$.

Proof   The proof in Phillips (1959) requires the assumption that G is bounded; we can see that this is unnecessary because if G is bounded, then for each $x \in HS$ with $\|x\| = 1$, $|\langle Gx, x \rangle| \leq \|Gx\| . \|x\| \leq \|G\|$, that is, $-\|G\| \leq \langle Gx, x \rangle \leq \|G\|$ and so if

$$\inf_{\substack{\|x\|=1 \\ x \in HS}} \langle Gx, x \rangle > -\infty$$

which of course includes the condition of the theorem. Conversely if $\inf \langle Gx, x \rangle > -\infty$, then for $\lambda > 0$ sufficiently large

$$\inf_{\substack{\|x\|=1 \\ x \in HS}} \langle (\lambda I + G)x, x \rangle < 0$$

Then by the above theorem $(\lambda I + G)$ is bounded and consequently G is bounded.   □

COROLLARY 5.2   *Let $G : HS \rightarrow HS$ be a linear operator; then G is bounded if*

$$\inf_{\substack{\|x\|=1 \\ x \in HS}} \langle Gx, x \rangle > -\infty$$

If $\{P_T : T \in R\}$ is the resolution of identity on $L_2[0, T]$, then a continuous operator $G : L_2[0, \tau] \rightarrow L_2[0, \tau]$ is such that

$$\langle Gx - Gy, P_T(x-y) \rangle \geq \gamma \|P_T(x-y)\|^2$$

for all $x, y \in L_2[0, \tau]$ and $T \in R$. If $\gamma > 0$, then Theorem 5.2 and the above condition are sufficient to establish that the operator G^{-1} is causal.

All of the above well-known results have been stated for bounded linear operators mapping a Hilbert space into a Hilbert space, that is, for causal operators on normed linear spaces with an inner product norm. To deal with non-causal or anticipative operators we now introduce the *extended Hilbert space*, HS_e, which is the space of all $x \in F$ such that for all $T \in R_+$, $x_T = P_T x$ has finite norm $\|x_T\| = \langle x_T, x_T \rangle < \infty$.

The scalar products $\langle \cdot, \cdot \rangle$ in HS_e have the following properties:

(i) From Schwartz inequality (5.14)

$$\langle x_T, y_T \rangle = \langle x_T, y \rangle = \langle x, y_T \rangle = \langle x, y \rangle_T < \infty \qquad \forall\ x, y \in HS_e \text{ and } T \in R$$
(5.16)

(ii) $\|x_T\|$ is monotonically increasing with T and

$$\lim_{T \to \infty} \|x_T\| = \|x\| \qquad \forall\ x \in HS_e$$
(5.17)

Having introduced the concept of positive operators on Hilbert spaces, we now introduce the notion of *passivity* for operators on HS_e (Sandberg, 1964; Zames, 1966):

Definition 5.5
   (i) An operator $G : HS_e \rightarrow HS_e$ is said to be *passive* if and only if $\langle Gx, x \rangle_T \geq \alpha$, for some *constant* α and for all $x \in HS_e$, $T \in R$. In addition G is said to be *strictly passive* if and only if $\langle Gx, x \rangle_T \geq \beta \|x_T\|^2 + \alpha$, for $\beta > 0$ and for all $x \in HS_e$, $T \in R$.
   (ii) An operator $G : HS_e \rightarrow HS_e$ is *incrementally passive* if and only if $\langle Gx - Gy, x - y \rangle_T \geq 0$, for all $x, y \in HS_e$, $T \in R$. In addition G is *strictly incrementally passive* if and only if there exists a $\delta > 0$ such that

$$\langle Gx - Gy, x - y \rangle_T \geq \delta \|x - y\|_T^2 \qquad \forall\ s, y \in HS_e, \quad T \in R.$$

The concept of passivity has been used to establish the boundedness or stability of open loop unstable feedback systems of the form (5.10); however, no assumptions concerning the existence, uniqueness and continuity of solutions can be made except in the case of incremental passivity. (This is directly analogous to the small gain and incremental gain theorems. See Chapter 6.)

Note that if the operator $G : HS_e \rightarrow HS_e$ is linear then G is passive if and only if it is incrementally passive, and G is strictly passive if and only if it is strictly incrementally passive (for G linear β may be taken as zero).

Let $G \in Y^{n \times n}$, the space of all linear time-invariant and bounded operators of L_2^n into itself, and define the convolution operator

$$(Gu)(t) = \int_0^t G(t - \tau)u(\tau) \, d\tau \qquad \forall \, u \in L_{2e}^n[0, T]$$

Since G is causal, then $(Gu) : L_{2e}^n \rightarrow L_{2e}^n$ and

$$\langle u, Gu \rangle_T = \langle u_T, Gu_T \rangle$$

LEMMA 5.1   *The operator (G) is passive if and only if $\{\hat{G}(j\omega) + \hat{G}(j\omega)^*\}$ is positive definite for all $\omega \in R$, and (G) is strictly passive if and only if for some $\delta > 0$ the least eigenvalue of $\{\hat{G}(j\omega) + \hat{G}(j\omega)^*\}$ is $\geq \delta$ for all $\omega \geq 0$.*

Proof   Now, $\langle Gu, u \rangle = \langle u, Gu \rangle^* = \langle u, Gu \rangle \, \forall \, u \in L_2^n$ since the functions are real valued. Therefore

$$\langle Gu, u \rangle = \tfrac{1}{2}[\langle u, Gu \rangle + \langle Gu, u \rangle]$$

$$= \frac{1}{2} \int_{-\infty}^{\infty} [(G \otimes u)(t)^T u(t) + u(t)^T (G \otimes u(t)] \, dt$$

$$= \frac{1}{4\pi} \int_{-\infty}^{\infty} \hat{u}(j\omega)^* [\hat{G}(j\omega)^* + \hat{G}(j\omega)] \hat{u}(j\omega) \, d\omega$$

where Parseval's theorem has been used.

But $\hat{G}(j\omega) + \hat{G}(j\omega)^*$ is Hermitian, and so

$$\hat{u}(j\omega)^* [\hat{G}(j\omega) + \hat{G}(j\omega)^*] \hat{u}(j\omega) = \lambda[\hat{G}(j\omega) + \hat{G}(j\omega)^*] \hat{u}(j\omega)^* \hat{u}(j\omega)$$

And so

$$\langle Gu, u \rangle \geq \tfrac{1}{2} \inf_{\omega \in R_+} \lambda[\hat{G}(j\omega) + \hat{G}(j\omega)^*] \|u\|^2 \qquad\qquad \square$$

Example 5.7   Consider the feedback system

$$y = NG(u - y), \qquad u \in L_2^n$$

where G is an operator of L_2^n onto L_2^n such that

$$(Gx)(t) = \int_{-\infty}^{\infty} G(t - \tau)x(\tau) \, d\tau$$

with $G(t)$ an $n \times n$ matrix on R whose elements are on

$$L_2^n[0, \infty) \cap L_1(0, \infty)$$

and $N: R^n \to R^n$ is a continuous function which is such that

$$N(0) = 0, \quad \|N(x)\| < \alpha \|x\|, \quad \forall \, x \in R^n, \quad \alpha > 0$$

and

$$\gamma_N = \inf_{\substack{x_1, x_2 \in L_2^n \\ x_1 \neq x_2}} \left\{ \frac{\langle N(x_1) - N(x_2), x_1 - x_2 \rangle}{\|x_1 - x_2\|^2} \right\} > -\infty$$

We note that if the non-linear operator N is incrementally passive (incrementally strictly passive), then this implies that $\gamma_N \geq 0$ ($\gamma_N > 0$).

Let

$$k = \tfrac{1}{2} \inf_{\substack{\|x\|=1 \\ x \in R^n}} x^T (\hat{G}(j\omega) + \hat{G}(j\omega)^*) x$$

Clearly $k \geq 0$ if $[\hat{G}(j\omega) + \hat{G}(j\omega)^*]$ is positive semi-definite (and then by Lemma 5.1 operator G is passive).

Similarly let

$$\lambda = \sup_{\omega \in R} \Lambda[\hat{G}(j\omega)]$$

where $\Lambda[A]$ is the square root of the largest eigenvalue of A^*A. And so

$$\|G\| \geq \lambda.$$

It now follows that

$$\gamma_G + \gamma_N \|B\|^2 \geq k + \gamma_N \lambda^2 > 0$$

If $\gamma_G > 0$, then operator G is invertible. And since

$$(I + NG) = (G^{-1} + N)G \quad \text{then} \quad (I + NG)^{-1} = G^{-1}(G^{-1} + N)^{-1}.$$

But since

$$\gamma_{G^{-1}+N} \geq \gamma_N + \gamma_G \|G\|^{-2} \geq k + \gamma_N \lambda^{-2} > 0$$

it follows that the operator $(I + NG)$ is invertible and Lipschitz continuous. Under these conditions if the operators N, G are causal, then $(1 + NG)^{-1}$ is also causal and the feedback system $y = NG(u - y)$ has a unique solution $y = (I + NG)^{-1} NGu \in L_2^n$ and the mapping $u \mapsto y$ is Lipschitz. (*Note:* we have not required that N be Lipschitz.)

If instead, the operators N, G are only defined on L_{2e}^n, then the condition $k + \gamma_N \lambda^2 > 0$ is sufficient to establish that for any $u \in L_{2e}^n$ there exists a unique $y \in L_{2e}^n$ that satisfies the feedback equation.

The notions of passivity and positivity are connected through causal and non-causal operators. Suppose that $G: HS \to HS$ is a causal operator, then for any $u \in HS_e$ and $T \in R$, $u_T \in HS$.

$$\langle u, Gu \rangle_T = \langle u_T, (Gu)_T \rangle = \langle u_T, (Gu_T)_T \rangle = \langle u_T, Gu_T \rangle \qquad (5.18)$$

By (strict) passivity

$$\langle u, Gu \rangle_T = \beta \|u_T\|^2 + \alpha, \quad \beta > 0 \quad (\beta \geq 0) \tag{5.19}$$

But if addition $u \in HS$, then let $T \to \infty$ in (5.19) and noting that

$$\lim_{T \to \infty} \|x_T\| = \|x\|$$

(5.19) becomes

$$\langle u, Gu \rangle \geq \beta \|u\|^2 + \alpha, \quad \beta > 0 \quad (\beta \geq 0) \tag{5.20}$$

which is the condition for (*strict*) *positivity*. This demonstrates that for causal operators $G : HS \to HS$, G is (strictly) positive if and only if G is (strictly) passive; in other words positivity and passivity are equivalent for causal operators. If it is not difficult to show that if $G : HS \to HS$ is linear and its adjoint G^* is causal then G is anticausal (or anticipative).

THEOREM 5.3 *Consider the feedback system* $y = F(u - Gy)$, *where* $F : HS_e \to HS_e$, $G : HS_e \to HS_e$. *Assume that for* $u \in HS$, *then there exists a solution* $y \in HS_e$. *Suppose that*

$$\text{(i)} \quad \|Fx\|_T \leq \alpha \|x\|_T + \beta_1 \tag{5.21}$$

$$\text{(ii)} \quad \langle x, Fx \rangle_T \geq \gamma \|x\|_T^2 + \beta_2 \tag{5.22}$$

$$\text{(iii)} \quad \langle Gx, x \rangle_T \leq \delta \|Gx\|_T^2 + \beta_3 \tag{5.23}$$

Under these conditions, if $(\delta + \gamma) > 0$, *then* $u \in H$, y, $u - Gy = e$, $Fe, \in HS$, *the map* $u \mapsto Fe$ *is passive, and for* $\beta_1 = \beta_2 = \beta_3 = 0$ *then the maps* $u \mapsto e$, $u \mapsto y$, $u \mapsto Fe, \in L_2^n$.

Proof Now,

$$\langle u - Gy, F(u - Gy) \rangle_T = \langle u, F(u - Gy) \rangle_T \tag{5.24}$$

Substituting (5.21–23) into the above gives

$$\gamma \|u - Gy\|_T^2 + \delta \|Gy\|_T^2 \leq \alpha \|u\|_T \|u - Gy\|_T + \beta_1 \|u\|_T - \beta_3 - \beta_2 \tag{5.25}$$

But since

$$\|u - Gy\|_T^2 \geq \|u\|_T^2 + \|Gy\|_T^2 - 2 \|u\| \cdot \|Gy\|$$

then

$$(\gamma + \delta) \|Gy\|_T^2 \leq 2 \|Gy\|_T \left\{ \|u\|_T \left(\gamma + \frac{\alpha}{2} \right) \right\} + \beta_1 \|u\|_T - \gamma \|u\|_T^2 - \beta_2 - \beta_3$$

$$\leq 2 \|Gy\|_T \left\{ \|u\|_T \left(\gamma + \frac{\alpha}{2} \right) \right\} + |\gamma| \cdot \|u\|_T^2 + \beta_1 \|u\|_T - \beta_2 - \beta_3$$

or

$$\|Gy\|_T^2 \leq 2 \|Gy\|_T \, a(T) + b(T) \tag{5.26}$$

where

$$a(T) = (\gamma + \delta)^{-1} \|u_T\| \left(\gamma + \frac{\alpha}{2}\right), \qquad b(T) = (\gamma + \delta)^{-1}(|\gamma| \cdot \|u_T\|^2$$
$$+ \beta_1 \|u_T\| - \beta_2 - \beta_3),$$

are monotonically increasing with T if $(\gamma + \delta) > 0$ and both tend to finite constants a, b as $T \to \infty$, since $u \in HS$. Hence for all $T \in R$,

$$\|Gy\|_T \le a(T) + |a(T)^2 + b(T)^2|^{1/2}$$
$$\le a + (a^2 + b^2)^{1/2}, \tag{5.27}$$

Therefore $Gy \in HS$, $u - Gy \in HS$, and by (5.26) $F(u - Gy) = y \in HS$.
    Now

$$\langle u, Fe \rangle_T = \langle e, Fe \rangle_T + \langle Gy, y \rangle_T$$
$$\ge \gamma \|e\|_T^2 + \beta_2 + \delta \|Gy\|_T^2 + \beta_2,$$

But $Gy = u - e$ and $\|Gy\|_T^2 \le \|u\|_T^2 + \|e\|_T^2$. Therefore

$$\langle u, Fe \rangle_T \ge (\gamma + \delta) \|e\|_T^2 + \beta_2 + \beta_3 \ge \beta_2 + \beta_3$$

and the mapping $u \mapsto Fe$ is passive.
    For $\beta_1 = \beta_2 + \beta_3 = 0$ the coefficients $a(T)$, $b(T)$ in (5.26) are homogeneous polynomials in $\|u\|$ of order one and two respectively, so that $\|Gy\| \le \lambda \max (\|u\|)$ and thence for $u \in L_2^n$, $e = u - Gy \in L_2^n$. Finally the finite gain condition (5.21) gives $\|Fe\|_T \le \alpha \|e\|_T$, hence $y = F(e) \in L_2^n$. We note that when $\delta = 0$, the above theorem holds if F is strictly passive with finite gain and G is passive.   □

Suppose now that the operators F and G are respectively strictly incrementally passive and incrementally passive, i.e.

$$\langle Fx - Fz, x - z \rangle_T \ge \gamma_1 \|x - z\|_T^2, \qquad 0 < \gamma_1 < \infty \tag{5.28}$$

$$\langle Gx - Gz, x - z \rangle_T \ge 0, \tag{5.29}$$

for all $x, z \in HS_e$, $T \in R$. Also the operators F and G are unbiased $(F(0) = 0, G(0) = 0)$ and F has finite incremental gain such that

$$\|Fx - Fz\|_T \le \alpha_1 \|x - z\|_T \tag{5.30}$$

for all $x, z \in HS_e$, $T \in R$. The above finite gain condition on F implies that the operator F is causal, and the map $F: HS_e \to HS_e$ is uniformly Lipschitz continuous in $P_T HS_e$ with Lipschitz constant α_1.
    Setting $z = 0$ in (5.28–30) and $\beta_1 = \beta_2 = \beta_3 = 0$, $\gamma = \gamma_1$, and $\alpha = \alpha_1$ in (5.21–23), we conclude from Theorem 5.3 that $e, y \in HS$; utilizing (5.25) in the proof of Theorem 5.3 for pairs of inputs (u_1, u_2) and associated

feedback errors (e_1, e_2), Equations (5.28–30) gives

$$\gamma_1 \|e_1 - e_2\|^2 \le \alpha_1 \|u_1 - u_2\|_T \|e_1 - e_2\|_T \qquad (5.31)$$

This implies that if $u_1 = u_2$, then $e_1 = e_2$, $y_1 = y_2$ and the solution y to the feedback system is unique. Clearly from (5.31) since $\gamma_1, \alpha_1 > 0$ then

$$\|e_1 - e_2\| \le a(T)$$

where $a(T) = \gamma_1^{-1}\alpha_1 \|u_1 - u_2\| < \infty$ increases monotonically with T. Therefore as $u_1 \to u_2$, $\|u_1 - u_2\| \to 0$ and $\|e_1 - e_2\| \to 0$, so that mapping $u \mapsto e$ is uniformly continuous on HS.

We have briefly shown that incremental passivity conditions on the operators F, G ensure not only boundedness of solution but also its uniqueness, existence and continuous dependence. But since the solution to $y = F(u - Gy)$ is $y = (I + FG)^{-1}Fu$, then the above incremental passivity conditions and finite gain (or equivalently the mapping $P_T F : P_T HS_e \to P_T HS_e$ is continuous) condition upon operators G and F are also sufficient for the invertibility of the operator $(I + FG)$.

In the special case when the operator $(I + FG)$ is a linear causal map from HS_e to itself, then if $(I + FG)$ is strictly passive, the mapping $(I + FG)^{-1} : HS_e \to HS_e$ is causal and strictly passive. Also, from Section 5.4, the feedback system $y = F(u - Gy)$ is well posed.

5.6 THE THEORY OF MULTIPLIERS†

Lemma 5.1 establishes the passivity condition for a convolution operator $Gu : L_2 \to L_2$, $u \in L_2$ as $Re\{\hat{G}(j\omega)\} \ge 0$ for all ω or equivalently $\arg\{\hat{G}(j\omega)\} \in (-\pi/2, \pi/2)$. For those feedback systems (see Theorem 5.3) whose loop operators do not satisfy the stringent passivity condition the loop transformation Theorem 6.1 can be employed by introducing a multiplier $\hat{Q}(s)$ (Willems, 1971) such that $Q \otimes G$ is passive or $\arg\{\hat{Q}(s)\hat{G}(s)\} \in (-\pi/2, \pi/2)$. A well-known example of a multiplier in stability theory is the Popov stability criterion $Re[(1 + qj\omega)\hat{G}(j\omega)] \ge 0$ for all ω, whereby the multiplier $\hat{Q}(s) = 1 + qs$ has been used. A variety of stability criteria with simple graphical interpretations for non-linear feedback systems can be derived if the multiplier can be factorized into the product of a causal and an anticausal component.

Let B be a Banach algebra with identity I, let $P_+ : B \to B$ be a linear projection on B (that is $P_+ P_+ = P_+$). Define, $P_- \triangleq I - P_+$, assume that $\|P_+\|, \|P_-\| \le 1$, and let B_+, B_- be sub-algebras of B.

† Multipliers here refer to loop operators and should not be confused with multipliers used in the representation theory of Chapter 3.

Let $\{\tilde{Q}^k\}$, $\{\tilde{Q}_+^k\}$ and $\{\tilde{Q}_-^k\}$ be sequences in B, B_+ and B_- respectively and define the associated power series

$$\tilde{Q} = I + \sum_{k=1}^{\infty} \tilde{Q}^k r^k, \tag{5.32}$$

$$\tilde{Q}_+ = I + \sum_{k=1}^{\infty} \tilde{Q}_+^k r^k, \tag{5.33}$$

$$\tilde{Q}_- = I + \sum_{k=1}^{\infty} \tilde{Q}_-^k r^k, \tag{5.34}$$

which converge for some $r_0 \geq |r|$ ($r \in C^1, r_0 \in R_+$). Assuming that these series are related by $\tilde{Q} = \tilde{Q}_+ \tilde{Q}_-$, substituting these series and equating equal powers of r gives

$$\tilde{Q}_1^1 = \tilde{Q}_+^1 + \tilde{Q}_-^1$$

and so

$$\tilde{Q}_+^1 = P_+ \tilde{Q}^1, \qquad \tilde{Q}_-^1 = P_- \tilde{Q}^1$$

and

$$\tilde{Q}^n = \tilde{Q}_+^n + \tilde{Q}_-^n + \sum_{k=1}^{n-1} \tilde{Q}_+^k \tilde{Q}_-^{n-k}, \qquad n = 2, 3, \dots \tag{5.35}$$

So

$$\tilde{Q}_+^n = P_+ \left(\tilde{Q}^n - \sum_{k=1}^{n-1} \tilde{Q}_+^k \tilde{Q}_-^{n-k} \right) \tag{5.36}$$

$$\tilde{Q}_-^n = P_- \left(\tilde{Q}^n - \sum_{k=1}^{n-1} \tilde{Q}_+^k \tilde{Q}_-^{n-k} \right) \tag{5.37}$$

for $n = 2, 3, \dots$. Thus the $\tilde{Q}_+^k$, $\tilde{Q}_-^k$ are successively uniquely determined by the $\tilde{Q}^k$'s.

Consider now the equations, for $|r| \leq 1$ and some $Z \in B$ such that $\|Z\| < 1$

$$\tilde{Q}_+ \triangleq N_+(\tilde{Q}_+) = I + r P_+(Z \tilde{Q}_+) \tag{5.38}$$

$$\tilde{Q}_- \triangleq N_-(\tilde{Q}_-) = I + r P_-(\tilde{Q}_- Z) \tag{5.39}$$

For any $\tilde{Q}, \tilde{Q}' \in B$, the above definitions give

$$\|r P_+(Z(\tilde{Q}_+ - \tilde{Q}'_+))\| \leq r \|Z\| . \|\tilde{Q}_+ - \tilde{Q}'_+\|$$

$$\|r P_-(\tilde{Q}_- - \tilde{Q}'_-)\| \leq r \|Z\| . \|\tilde{Q}_- - \tilde{Q}'_-\|$$

and since $r \|Z\| < 1$, then from the above inequalities the contraction mapping Theorem 1.19 shows that (5.38) and (5.39) have unique solutions $\tilde{Q}_+, \tilde{Q}_- \in B$ for all $|r| \leq 1$; moreover by the functional iteration method the convergent series (5.33), (5.34) give the solutions $\tilde{Q}_+ \in B_- \oplus I$, $\tilde{Q}_- \in B_- \oplus I$.

From (5.38) and (5.39)

$$(I - rZ)\tilde{Q}_+ = I - rP_-(Z\tilde{Q}_+) \tag{5.40}$$

$$\tilde{Q}_-(I - rZ) = I - rP_+(\tilde{Q}_-Z) \tag{5.41}$$

Therefore

$$\|rP_-(Z\tilde{Q}_+)\| \le |r| . \|Z\| . \|\tilde{Q}_+\| \le \frac{|r| . \|Z\|}{1 - |r| . \|Z\|},$$

the same upper bound holds for $\|rP_+(\tilde{Q}_-Z)\|$. And so $I - rP_-(Z\tilde{Q}_+)$, $I - rP_+(\tilde{Q}_-Z)$, and $(I - rZ) \in B$ are all invertible in B for $|r| < \frac{1}{2}\|Z\|^{-1}$. Furthermore these inverses are representable by unique, convergent power series of the form (5.32), (5.33) in the sphere of radius $\frac{1}{2}\|Z\|^{-1}$. Consequently (5.40) and (5.41) yield

$$(I - rZ)^{-1} = \tilde{Q}_+(I - rP_-(Z\tilde{Q}_+))^{-1}$$
$$= (I - rP_+(\tilde{Q}_-Z))^{-1}\tilde{Q}_-$$

From which

$$\tilde{Q}_+ = (I - rP_+(\tilde{Q}_-Z))^{-1}$$
$$\tilde{Q}_- = (I - rP_-(Z\tilde{Q}_+))^{-1}$$
$$(I - rZ)^{-1} = \tilde{Q}_+\tilde{Q}_-$$

But since $(I - rZ)^{-1}$, $\tilde{Q}_+$, $\tilde{Q}_-$ are each representable by a convergent power series for $|r| < \|Z\|^{-1}$ we can set $r = 1$ and so

$$I - Z = (\tilde{Q}_+\tilde{Q}_-)^{-1} \triangleq Q_-Q_+ = Q.$$

We have now established the multiplier factorization theorem:

THEOREM 5.4   Let $Q \in B$. If there exists a $Z \in B$ such that $\|Z\| < 1$ and $Q = I - Z$ then

(i) $Q = I - Z = Q_-Q_+$ with $Q_-, Q_+ \in B$ where Q_-, Q_+ are invertible in B

(ii) $Q_-, (Q_-)^{-1} \in I \oplus B_-$

   $Q_+, (Q_+)^{-1} \in I \oplus B_+$

where $O \oplus B_+$ denotes the subspace of all elements in B of the form $\alpha I + Q$, $\alpha \in R$, $Q \in B_+$ etc.

We note that the Banach algebra need not be commutative; this is particularly significant for the multivariable case. Consider the Banach algebra $B = LA_+^{n \times n}$ (see Section 3.4) which represents the sub-algebra of

$M(L_1^n)$ formed with all elements which are defined by the convolution with an $(n \times n)$ matrix whose entries are elements of LA_+. If $(LA_+^{n \times n})_+$ consists of all causal impulse responses in $LA_+^{n \times n}$ and $(LA_+^{n \times n})_-$ consists of all anticausal impulse responses in $LA_+^{n \times n}$, it is not difficult to establish the corollary to Theorem 5.4:

COROLLARY 5.4   *Let $Q \in LA_+^{n \times n}$. If there exists a $Z \in LA_+^{n \times n}$ such that $\|Z\|_{LA_+} < 1$ and $Q = I - Z$, then there exists Q_-, $Q_+ \in LA_+^{n \times n}$ that admit the factorization $Q = Q_- Q_+$ where Q_-, Q_+ are invertible in $LA_+^{n \times n}$ and Q_-, $Q_-^{-1} \in (LA_+^{n \times n})_-$, Q_+, $Q_+^{-1} \in (LA_+^{n \times n})_+$.*

Consider the special case of a Banach algebra of the class of all linear continuous maps from the Hilbert space HS into itself. Consider the feedback system

$$y = Fe, \qquad e = u - Gy \qquad\qquad (5.42)$$

where $u \in HS$, $e \in HS_e$ and F, G are causal maps from HS to HS. We now establish the important result that the three feedback systems in Fig. 5.1 are input–output equivalent and L_2-stability for one system implies L_2-stability of the others.

Assume that a non-causal map $Q : HS \to HS$ is factored such that $Q = Q_- Q_+$; $Q_- Q_+ : HS \to HS$ where Q^{-1}, Q_+^{-1}, Q_-^{-1} are well defined

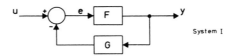

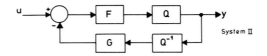

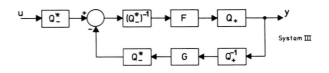

FIG. 5.1   Input–output equivalence through multipliers

mappings of HS into HS each with finite gain (that is $\gamma(\theta^{-1})<\infty$ etc), Q_- is linear and hence Q_-^* and $(Q_-^*)^{-1}$ are well defined.

Let x and $z \in HS$ and such that $x = Q_-^* z$; from the properties of the multiplier $\|x\| \le \gamma(Q_-^*)\|z\|$ and $\|z\| \le \gamma[(Q_-^*)^{-1}]\|x\|$. Consider some operator $H: HS \to HS$, then

$$\langle z/QHz\rangle = \langle z/Q_-Q_+Hz\rangle = \langle Q_-^* z/Q_+Hz\rangle$$
$$= \langle x/Q_+H(Q_-^*)^{-1}x\rangle$$

That is the strict positivity condition on operator QH

$$\langle z/QHz\rangle \ge \alpha_1 \|z\|^2 \qquad \forall\, z \in HS, \quad \alpha_1 \ge 0$$

is equivalent to

$$\langle x/Q_+H(Q_-^*)^{-1}x\rangle \ge \alpha_2 \|x\|^2, \qquad \forall\, x \in HS, \quad \alpha_2 \ge 0 \tag{5.43}$$

By similar reasoning the positivity condition

$$\langle z/HQ^{-1}z\rangle \ge 0 \qquad \forall\, z \in HS$$

on operator HQ is equivalent to

$$\langle x/Q_-^* HQ_+^{-1}x\rangle \ge 0 \qquad \forall\, x \in HS \tag{5.44}$$

Given that the feedback system operators $F, G: HS \to HS$ are causal, then by definition, QF and GQ are non-causal and the loop operators of system III (Fig. 5.1), $Q_+F(Q_-^*)^{-1}$ and $Q_-^*GQ_+^{-1}$ are causal and by inequalities (5.43) and (5.44) respectively strictly positive and positive. The passivity Theorem 5.3 can be utilized to establish L_2-stability since

$$\gamma[Q_+F(Q_-^*)^{-1}] \le \gamma[Q_-Q_+F(Q_-^*)^{-1}Q_-^*]\gamma(Q_-^{-1})\gamma[(Q_-^*)^{-1}]$$
$$\le \gamma[Q_-^{-1}]\gamma[QF]\gamma[(Q_-^*)^{-1}]<\infty$$

provided that $\gamma[QF]<\infty$.

THEOREM 5.5 *The feedback system* $y = F(u - Gy)$, $F, G: HS \to HS$ *and causal,* $u \in HS$, *is L_2-stable if a non-causal operator* $Q = Q_-Q_+: HS \to HS$ *exists such that*

(i) $Q_+, Q_+^{-1}, Q_-^*, (Q_-^*)^{-1}$ *are causal operators.*
(ii) QF *is strictly positive and* $\gamma[QF]<\infty$
(iii) GQ^{-1} *is positive*

5.7 SECTORICITY

We now introduce the concept of conicity or equivalently sectoricity for causal unbiased operators $G: L_2^n \to L_2^n$

Definition 5.6   (i) G is said to be *inside* (respectively *outside*) the sector $S\{a, b\}$ for scalars $a, b \in R$, $b \geq a$ if and only if

$$\langle (G - aI)x_T, (G - bI)x_T \rangle \leq 0$$

(respectively, ≥ 0)

holds for all $t \geq 0$ and $x \in L_2^n$. Or equivalently (ii) G is said to be *interior* (respectively, *exterior*) conic with parameters c and r if and only if

$$\|(G - cI)x_T\| \leq r \|x_T\|$$

(respectively, $\leq r \|x_T\|$)

holds for all $t \geq 0$, $x \in L_2^n$ and $c = \frac{1}{2}(a + b)$, $r = \frac{1}{2}(b - a)$.

The equivalent definitions of conic relations and sectoricity degenerate into the Definition 5.4 of positive operators if $a = 0$ and $b \to \infty$.

A natural extension of the above definitions to multivariable sectors is possible if diagonal matrices $A = \text{diag}(a_i)$, $B = \text{diag}(b_i)$; $a_i, b_i \in R$, $b_i \geq a_i$ for $i = 1, 2, \ldots, n$, are introduced:

Definition 5.7   (i) G is said to be *inside* (respectively, *outside*) the sector $S\{A, B\}$ if and only if

$$\langle (Gx - Ax)_T, (Gx - Bx)_T \rangle \leq 0$$

(respectively, ≤ 0)

or equivalently (ii) G is said to be *interior* (respectively, *exterior*) conic if and only if

$$\|(Gx - \tfrac{1}{2}(A + B)x)_T\| \leq \|\tfrac{1}{2}(B - A)x_T\|$$

(respectively, $\geq \|\tfrac{1}{2}(B - A)x_T\|$)

holds for all $x \in L_2^n$ and $T \geq 0$.

Definition 5.8 G is said to be *inside* (respectively *outside*) the complex scalar sector $S\{a, b\}$ for $a, b \in C^1$, $a - a^* = b - b^*$ $Re(a) \leq Re(b)$ if and only if

$$\langle (\hat{G}(j\omega) - aI)x, (\hat{G}(j\omega) - bI)x \rangle \leq 0$$

(respectively, ≥ 0)

for all $x \in L_2^n$ and $\omega \in R_+$.

Definitions 5.6 and 5.7 encompass non-linear operators, whereas Definition 5.8 is purely a linear definition. These definitions can easily be extended to frequency-dependent sectors:

Definition 5.6a G is said to be inside the *frequency-dependent* sector $S\{a(j\omega), b(j\omega)\}$,   for $a(j\omega), b(j\omega) \in C^1$, $a(j\omega) - a(j\omega)^* = b(j\omega) - b(j\omega)^*$,

$Re(a(j\omega)) \le Re(b(j\omega))$, $\forall\, \omega$ if and only if

$$\langle(\hat{G}(j\omega) - a(j\omega)I)x, (\hat{G}(j\omega) - b(j\omega))Ix\rangle \le 0 \qquad \forall\, x \in L_2^n \text{ and } \omega \in R.$$

Definition 5.7a G is said to be inside the *frequency-dependent* sector $S\{A(j\omega), B(j\omega)\}$, for $A(j\omega) = \text{diag}\{a_i(j\omega)\}$, $B(j\omega) = \text{diag}\{b_i(j\omega)\}$; $a_i(j\omega)$, $b_i(j\omega) \in C^1$, $a_i(j\omega) - a_i(j\omega)^* = b_i(j\omega) - b_i(j\omega)^*$; $Re(a_i(j\omega)) \le Re(b_i(j\omega))$ $\forall\, \omega \in R$, $i = 1, 2, \ldots, n$, if and only if

$$\langle(\hat{G}(j\omega) - \hat{A}(j\omega))x, (\hat{G}(j\omega) - \hat{B}(j\omega))x\rangle \le 0 \qquad \forall\, x \in L_2^n, \quad \omega \in R.$$

These frequency-dependent sector definitions can be equivalently restated in terms of the Euclidean norm, and definitions for outside sectors can be obtained by reversing the inequality sign and simultaneously ensuring that the Nyquist plot of $\hat{G}(s)$ does not encircle the point $(c, 0)$ for $c = \frac{1}{2}(a(j\omega) + b(j\omega))$, $\forall\, \omega \in R$.

LEMMA 5.2   If G_1 is inside the sector $S\{a_1, b_1\}$ and G_2 is inside sector $S\{a_2, b_2\}$ for $b_1, b_2 > 0$, then

(i) αG_1 is inside $S\{\alpha a_1, \alpha b_1\}$.

(ii) $(G_1 + G_2)$ is inside $S\{a_1 + a_1, b_1 + b_2\}$

(iiiA) If $a_1 > 0$ then G_1^{-1} is inside $S\{b_1^{-1}, a_1^{-1}\}$

(iiiB) If $a_1 < 0$, then G_1^{-1} is outside $S\{a_1^{-1}, b_1^{-1}\}$.

Proof

(i) $\langle(\alpha G_1 x)_T - \alpha a_1 x_T, (\alpha G_1 x)_T - \alpha b_1 x_T\rangle$

$$= \alpha^2\langle(G_1 x)_T - a_1 x_T (G_1 x)_T - b_1 x_T\rangle \le 0 \quad (5.45)$$

for any α. An important special case is when $\alpha = -1$, then $-G_1$ is inside $S\{-a_1, -b_1\}$ if G_1 is inside $S\{a_1, b_1\}$.

(ii) Now, by the triangle inequality and Definition 5.6 for G_1 and G_2

$$\|[(G_1 + G_2)x]_T - \tfrac{1}{2}(b_1 + b_2 + a_1 + a_2)x_T\|$$

$$\le \|(G_1 x_T) - \tfrac{1}{2}(a_1 + b_1)x_T\| + \|(G_2 x)_T - \tfrac{1}{2}(a_2 + b_2)x_T\|$$

$$\le \tfrac{1}{2}(b_1 - a_1)\|x_T\| + \tfrac{1}{2}(b_2 - a_2)\|x_T\|$$

$$= \tfrac{1}{2}(b_1 + b_2 - a_1 - a_2)\|x_T\| \quad (5.46)$$

(iii) Suppose that $y = G_1^{-1}x$ and $x = G_1 y$, $a_1 \ne 0$ and $b_1 > 0$. Then

$$\langle(G_1^{-1}x)_T - b_1^{-1}x_T, (G_1^{-1}x)_T - a_1^{-1}x_T\rangle = \langle y_T - b_1^{-1}(G_1 y)_T, y_y - a_1^{-1}(G_1 y)_T\rangle$$

$$= (a_1 b_1)^{-1}\langle(G_1 y)_T - a_1 y_T, (G_1 u)_T - b_1 y_T\rangle \quad (5.47)$$

The sign of the above inner product depends upon $a_1 \gtrless 0$, and so part (iii) of Lemma 5.2 follows.   □

Note that throughout Lemma 5.2 the words inside and outside are fully interchangable, since by Definition 5.6 only a sign change is necessary.

The following lemma enables inside and outside sectors to be manipulated in a mixed manner.

LEMMA 5.3   *If operator G_1 is outside the sector $S\{c_1 - r_1, c_1 + r_1\}$ and G_2 is inside the sector $S\{c_2 - r_2, c_2 + r_2\}$, $r_1 > r_2$; then $(G_1 + G_2)$ is outside the sector $S\{c_1 - r_1 + c_2 + r_2, c_1 + r_1 + c_2 - r_2\}$.*

Proof   Now, G_1 satisfies the inequality

$$\|(G_1 - c_1 I)x\| \ge r_1 \|x\|, \qquad \forall x \in L_2^n$$

and G_2 satisfies the inequality

$$-\|(G_2 - c_2 I)x\| \ge r_2 \|x\|, \qquad \forall x \in L_2^n$$

which taken together imply that

$$\|(G_1 - c_1 I)x\| - \|(G_2 - c_2 I)x\| \ge (r_1 - r_2) \|x\|, \qquad \forall x \in L_2^n$$

and from the triangle inequality

$$\|\{G_1 + G_2 - (c_1 + c_2 I\}x\| \ge (r_1 - r_2) \|x\|, \qquad \forall x \in L_2^n \qquad (5.48)$$
$$\square$$

A similar result can be readily established for frequency-dependent sectors by employing a generalization of Lemma 1 of Zames (1966).

LEMMA 5.4   *Suppose that operators $G_1, G_2 \in LA_+^{n \times n}$ have transfer function matrices $\hat{G}_1(j\omega), \hat{G}_2(j\omega)$. If*

(i) $\|(\hat{G}_1(j\omega) - c_1(j\omega)I)x(j\omega)\| \ge \|r_1(j\omega)x(j\omega)\|$, $\omega \in R$, $\forall x(j\omega)$ and the Nyquist plot of $\hat{G}_1(j\omega)$ does not encircle $(c_1, 0)$, and

(ii) $\|(\hat{G}_2(j\omega) - c_2(j\omega)I)x(j\omega)\| \le \|r_2(j\omega)x(j\omega)\|$, $\omega \in R$, $\forall x(j\omega)$; then $\|(\hat{G}_1(j\omega) + \hat{G}_2(j\omega) - (c_1 + c_2))x(j\omega)\| \ge \|(r_1(j\omega) - r_2(j\omega))x(j\omega)\|$ and $(G_1 + G_2)$ is outside the sector $S\{c_1 - r_1 + c_2 + r_2, c_1 + r_1 + c_2 - r_2\}$ for $r_2(j\omega) > r_1(j\omega)$, $\omega \in R$, and for all $x(j\omega)$.

Conditions (i) and (ii) above are respectively equivalent to: G_2 is outside sector $S\{c_1 - r_1, c_1 + r_1\}$ and G_2 is inside sector $S\{c_2 - r_2, c_2 + r_2\}$.

A somewhat simpler result for convolution operators can be obtained for symmetric frequency-independent sectors:

LEMMA 5.5   *Let $G \triangleq g \otimes u$; $u \in L_2^n$, $g = \{g_{ij}\} \in LA_+^{n \times n}$, $g_{ij} \in LA_+$. Also let*

$$p_{ij} \triangleq \sum_{k=1}^{n} \hat{g}_{ki}^*(j\omega) g_{ij}(j\omega)$$

Then if either of the following two conditions are satisfied, G is inside the *sector $S\{-r, r\}$:*

(i) *Condition* A:

$$\sup_{\omega \in R_+} \left\{ |p_{ii}| + \sum_{j=1}^{n} |p_{ij}| \right\} \leq r^2; \qquad i = 1, 2, \ldots, n$$

(ii) *Condition* B:

$$\sup_{\omega \in R_+} \left\{ |p_{ii}| + \sum_{j=1}^{n} |p_{ji}| \right\} \leq r^2; \qquad i = 1, 2, \ldots, n$$

Proof G is inside the sector $S\{-r, r\}$ if and only if

$$\|Gx\| \leq r \|x\|, \qquad \forall\, x \in L_2^n$$

A sufficient condition for the above can be written in terms of the induced norm as

$$\|\!|\!| G |\!|\!| \triangleq \sup_{\forall\, x \in L_2^n} \frac{\|Gx\|}{\|x\|} \leq r$$

But by Parseval's theorem $\|\!|\!| \hat{G} |\!|\!| = \|\!|\!| G |\!|\!|$, and so a sufficient condition for G to be inside $S\{-r, r\}$ is

$$\|\!|\!| \hat{G}(j\omega) |\!|\!| \leq r \tag{5.49}$$

However, it is well known (Desoer and Vidyasagar, 1975) that the induced L_2^n norm

$$\|\!|\!| G(j\omega) |\!|\!| = \max_i \lambda_i (\hat{G}^*(j\omega)\hat{G}(j\omega)\}^{1/2}, \qquad \omega \in R_+$$

and so Condition (5.49) can be rewritten as

$$\max_{i,\omega \in R_+} \lambda_i (\hat{G}^*(j\omega)\hat{G}(j\omega)) \leq r^2 \tag{5.50}$$

The lemma is now established by identifying the matrix $\hat{G}^*(j\omega)\hat{G}(j\omega)$ with $P = \{p_{ij}\}$ and applying Gershgorin's theorem for the column and row conditions. $\qquad\square$

In order to establish input-output stability as well as the existence and uniqueness of solutions to feedback systems it is necessary to introduce incremental sectors.

Definition 5.9 G is said to be *incrementally inside* (respectively, *incrementally outside*) the sector $S\{a, b\}$, if $b \geq a$ and

$$\langle (Gx - Gy)_T - a(x - y)_T, (Tx - Gy)_T - b(x - y)_T \rangle \leq 0$$

$$(\text{respectively,} \quad \geq 0)$$

for all $x, y \in L_2^n$ and $T \geq 0$.

Consider for example operator $G : L_{2e} \rightarrow L_{2e}$, where G is incrementally inside $S\{a, b\}$. Then G satisfies the Lipschitz condition $b(x - y) \geq G(x) - G(y) \geq a(x - y)$. So that operator G not only lies in a sector in the plane, its slope has upper and lower bounds.

5.8   NOTES

The concept of extended spaces was first suggested by Sandberg (1964, 1965) and Zames (1966), who used it to develop input–output stability criteria for time varying scalar non-linear feedback systems. Treatment of extended spaces and causality can be found in many texts on control and network theory (Desoer and Vidyasagar, 1975; Dolezal, 1979; Mees, 1981). The supporting mathematics for Section 5.2 on topological projective limits and generalized extended spaces can be found in Section 1.3; the origins of this material can be found in Kothe (1969) and Valenca (1978). An extensive treatment of the concept of causality and well-posedness of feedback systems can be found in the excellent text of Willems (1971) and in Willems (1969); the generalization to strong generalized causality can be found in Valenca (1978). The various passivity theorems have been developed by many research workers, including Sandberg (1964), Zames (1966), Cho and Narendra (1968) and Harris and Husband (1981). The associated concept of multipliers can be found in O'Shea (1966), Narendra and Taylor (1973), Willems (1971), and Desoer and Vidyasagar (1975). The development of sectoricity and conicity was originally due to Zames (1966) and extended to frequency-dependent multivariable sectors by Husband and Kouvaritakis (1981).

REFERENCES

Cho, Y. and Narendra, K. S. (1968). "An off-axis circle criterion for the stability of feedback systems with a monotonic nonlinearity." *IEEE Trans* **AC-13**(4), 413–416.

Curtain, R. F. and Pritchard, A. J. (1977). "Functional Analysis in Modern Applied Mathematics". Academic Press, London and New York.

Desoer, C. A. and Vidyasagar, M. (1975). "Feedback Systems: Input–Output Properties". Academic Press, London and New York.

Dolezal, V. (1979). "Monotone Operators and Applications in Control and Network Theory". Elsevier, Amsterdam.

Harris, C. J. and Husband, R. K. (1981). "An off-axis multivariable circle stability criterion", *Proc. IEE* **128**, 5, 215–218.

Husband, R. K. and Kouvaritakis, B. (1981). "The use of sectors in the derivation of stability criteria for nonlinear systems". *OUEL Rept* No 1359/81, Oxford University.

Kothe, G. (1969). "Topological Vector Spaces", Band 159. Springer Verlag, Berlin.

Luenberger, D. G. (1969). "Optimization by Vector Space Methods". Wiley, New York.

Mees, A. I. (1981). "Dynamics of Feedback Systems". Wiley, Chichester.

Narendra, R. S. and Taylor, J. H. (1973). "Frequency Domain Criteria for Absolute Stability". Academic Press, New York and London.

Phillips, R. S. (1959). "Dissipative operators and hyperbolic systems of partial differential equations." *Trans. Amer. Math. Soc.* **90,** 193–254,

Sandberg, I. W. (1964). "On the L_2 boundedness of solutions of nonlinear functional equations." *Bell Syst. Tech. J.* **43,** 1581–1599.

Sandberg, I. W. (1965). "Some results on the theory of physical systems governed by nonlinear functional equations." *Bell Syst. Tech. J.* **44,** 439–453.

Valenca, J. M. E. (1978). "Stability of Multivariable Systems", D Phil Thesis. Oxford University.

Willems, J. C. (1969). "Stability, instability, invertibility and causality." *SIAM J. Control* **7,** 645–671.

Willems, J. C. (1971). "The Analysis of Feedback Systems", Research Monograph 62. MIT Press, Cambridge, Mass.

Zames, G. (1966). "On the input–output stability of time varying nonlinear feedback systems. Part I: Conditions derived using concepts of loop gain conicity and positivity." *IEEE Trans* **AC-11,** (No. 2), 228–238.

Zames, G. (1966). "On the input–output stability of time varying nonlinear feedback systems. Part II: Conditions involving circles in the frequency plane and sector nonlinearities." *IEEE Trans* **AC-11,** (No. 3), 465–475.

Chapter Six

Stability of Nonlinear Multivariable Systems— Circle Criteria

6.1 INTRODUCTION

In order to specify a dynamical system mathematically a suitable space of input and output functions needs to be defined. Frequently it is necessary to represent either dynamical systems which are open loop unstable or function spaces which grow without bound with increasing time. Such functions are clearly not contained in Banach spaces, which are usually used to model dynamical systems (such as L_p-spaces), but by establishing the problem in extended spaces (see Chapter 5) which contain both well-behaved as well as asymptotically unbounded functions, rigorous system analysis can be made on finite time intervals.

Consider a finite interval $I \subset R = (-\infty, \infty)$ and a normed space V with norm $\|\cdot\|$. Let Z be a linear function space mapping I into V, that is, $Z: I \to V$. For each $T \in I$, let P_T be the truncation operator (or projection operator) such that

$$f_T(t) = (P_T f)(t) = \begin{cases} f(t) & \text{for} \quad t \le T \\ 0 & \text{for} \quad t > 0 \end{cases}$$

$T > 0$ and $f \in Z$.

By introducing a norm $\|\cdot\|$ on Z, we define a normed linear subspace E of the linear space Z.

Definition 6.1 E is the space of all functions $f \in Z$ such that

  (i) $\|f\| < \infty$
 (ii) $P_T f \in E$ for all $T \in I$
(iii) The mapping $T \mapsto \|P_T f\|$ is for every $f \in E$ an increasing bounded function of T such that $\|f\| = \lim_{T \to \infty} \|P_T f\|$.

For example the spaces which consist of all measurable functions

$g(t): I \to R$ such that

$$\int_0^T |g(t)|^p \, dt < \infty \qquad \forall \, T \in I, \, p \in [1, \infty)$$

satisfy conditions (i)–(iii) of Definition 6.1.

Definition 6.2   The *extension* of the normed linear space E is the *extended space* E_e, which is the space of all $f \in Z$ such that

(i) $P_T f \in E$ for all $T > 0$

(ii) If the $\lim_{T \to \infty} \|P_T f\|$ exists, then it coincides with $\|f\|$

We note that the above definition of the extended version E_e of E equipped with a family of semi-norms is consistent with the theory of locally convex spaces with a projective limit type of topology covered in Section 5.2.

A mathematical model of an input–output system can be derived through a relationship G on E_e or a set of pairs (u, y) of functions in E_e, where $u \in E_e$ we denote as the *input* and $y \in E_e$ as the *output*, that is, $G: u \to y$. However, this definition allows the possibility of multivalued relationships in which an input (or output) is paired with several outputs. If G is restricted to a single valued mapping with domain $(G) = E_e$, then G is an operator that maps E_e into itself.

Consider an input–output system G with input signals $u(t)$ and output signals $y(t)$ (which may belong to different spaces) related by

$$y = G(u) \qquad (6.1)$$

These functions are assumed to be sufficiently well behaved for their norms to exist, and functions which differ only on sets of measure zero are assumed as equivalent. All such systems will be assumed to causal or non-anticipative, that is

$$y_T = (G(u_T))_T \qquad \forall \, T \in I \qquad (6.2)$$

Definition 6.3   An operator $G: E_e \to E_e$ is said to be *input–output stable* if there are non-negative constants δ, γ such that

$$\|(G(u))_T\| \le \gamma \|u_T\| + \delta, \qquad T \in I \qquad (6.3)$$

for $u_T \in E$.

In the sequel we concentrate on mappings on L_p^n spaces for m-input-n-output dynamical systems, that is, $G: L_{pe}^m \to L_{pe}^n$; so that the above definition of input–output stability specializes to:

Definition 6.4   The mapping G is L_p-*stable* if

(i) $G(u) \in L_p^n$ for $u \in L_p^m$, and

(ii) there exist non-negative constants γ, δ such that

$$\|G(u)\|_p \le \gamma \|u\|_p + \delta, \quad \text{for} \quad u \in L_p^m \tag{6.4}$$

Effectively this definition of input–output stability requires that the system is L_p-stable if, whenever the input belongs to the unextended space L_p^m, the resulting output $y = G(u)$ belongs to L_p^n and the norm of the output is less than γ times the norm of the input plus a bias δ. The gain of the operator G, assuming that G is unbiased $(G(0) = 0)$, is given by

$$\gamma(G) = \inf_\gamma \left[\gamma \in R_+ : \|G(u_T)\|_p \le \gamma \|u_T\|_p + \delta, \forall u, \forall T \right] \tag{6.5}$$

Clearly, condition (ii) of Definition 6.4 can be alternatively written as $\gamma(G) < \infty$. Frequently the bias δ is taken as zero for physical operators G and the gain of G is then given by

$$\gamma(G) = \sup_{\substack{u \in L_{pe}^n \\ T \in I}} \frac{\|(G(u))_T\|_p}{\|u_T\|_p} \tag{6.6}$$

That is the supremum is taken over all possible input–output pairs and over all truncations. These gains are not distinguished from function norms, and truncated functions are used in the definition, since they are not known *a priori* to be finite. If $p = \infty$, the above concept of L_∞-stability is called *bounded* input–output stability, that is, a bounded input produces a bounded output. The above definition of L_p-stability is further weakened by some authors (Valenca and Harris, 1979) by dropping the requirement of part (ii) in Definition 6.4.

Our prime concern is in determining the stability of feedback systems with m-inputs and n-outputs defined by dynamical relationships of the form

$$y = G(u, y), \quad u \in L_{pe}^m, \tag{6.7}$$

If $G(u, y) : L_{pe}^m \times L_{pe}^n \to L_{pe}^n$ with $G(0) = 0$ is strongly causal with a delay element δ greater than zero, then Proposition 5.7 shows that there exists a fixed point $y \in L_{pe}^n$ of $G(u, y)$. And since $y = 0$ is the unique fixed point of $P_T G$ in $L_p^n[0, T]$ for $T < \delta$, then the proofs of Propositions 5.3, 5.7 show that for each $u \in L_p^m$ there exists a unique solution $y \in L_{pe}^n$ of (6.7). The operator $G(u, y)$ is too general for detailed study or for the derivation of practical stability criteria. A more tractable and representative feedback system can be obtained by decomposing the operator $G(u, y)$ such that

$$y = F(u - Gy), \quad u \in L_{pe}^m \tag{6.8}$$

which, if F is a linear operator, has solution

$$y = (I + FG)^{-1} Fu \tag{6.9}$$

provided that the operator $(I + FG)^{-1}$ exists.

The feedback system (6.8) is well posed or equivalently a suitable approximation to a physical system with solutions y, $e = u - Gy$, which are unique and Lipschitz continuous (see Section 5.4) if

(i) the feedforward operator $F : L_{pe}^m \to L_{pe}^n$ is causal, unbiased, and Lipschitz continuous on L_{pe}^m

(ii) the feedback operator $G : L_{pe}^n \to L_{pe}^m$ is causal and locally Lipschitz continuous on L_{pe}^n

(iii) either F or G is strongly causal

(iv) the operator $(I + FG)$ is invertible on $L_{pe}^m \times L_{pe}^n$ and the inverse is causal and Lipschitz continuous on $L_{pe}^m \times L_{pe}^n$. These rather severe restrictions on operators F and G can be dropped in the determination of feedback stability. However, the question of existence uniqueness and continuity of solution cannot be ascertained without some constraints upon operators F and G.

The feedback system (6.8) can be further structured by factorizing it in such a way that all nonlinearities are represented by a memoryless operator N and the memory of the system is contained in a linear time-invariant operator H, such that

$$y = F(u - HN(y)) \tag{6.10}$$

where $N : L_2^n \to L_2^n$ is a Lipschitz continuous map with $N(0) = 0$. Although the nonlinearities are contained in the feedback loop, other system configurations can be transformed into representation (6.10). For example if

$$y = N(F(u - Hy)), \tag{6.11}$$

so that the nonlinearity is contained in the feedforward path. On defining $x = F(u - Hy)$ then $y = N(x)$ and

$$x = F(u - HN(x)) \tag{6.12}$$

This is identical in structure to (6.10), so if $x \in L_p^n$, then $y = N(x) \in L_p^n$ and the feedback system (6.11) is L_p^n-stable if and only if system (6.12) is L_p^n-stable.

The feedback system (6.10) can be interpreted as a condition for the existence of a unique fixed point in L_p^n of the operator $G(u, y)$. The contraction mapping theorem can provide sufficient conditions for the existence of such a unique point. If $G(\cdot)$ is a contraction, that is

$$\|G\| = \sup_{x \neq y} \frac{\|Gx - Gy\|}{\|x - y\|} < 1 \tag{6.13}$$

then $G(\cdot)$ has a unique fixed point in L_p^n. The Lipschitz norm of $G(\cdot)$ can be bounded by

$$\|G\| \leq \sup_{x \neq y} \frac{\|FHN(x) - FHN(y)\|}{\|x - y\|} \tag{6.14}$$

Then the contraction condition becomes

$$\|G\| \leq \|FH\| . \|N\| < 1 \tag{6.15}$$

so that the feedback system (6.10) is L_p^n-stable if $F: L_p^m \to L_p^n$ and $\|FH\| . \|N\| < 1$. In this case the feedback system $y = Su$ is bounded in its gain by

$$\|S\| \leq \frac{\|F\|}{1 - \|FH\| . \|N\|} \tag{6.16}$$

A frequency domain interpretation of the loop gain condition (6.15) can be made if $p = 2$, since if operator FH is a stable linear time-invariant L_2^n-map into itself, it is representable by a matrix transfer function $\widehat{FH}(s) \in K(0)^{n \times n}$ (see Section 3.2 and the L_2-Representation Theorem 3.2), where $K(0)^{n \times n}$ is the space of all bounded and holomorphic complex functions with domain $\{s : Re(s) > 0\}$. And by Parseval's theorem for $u \in L_2^n$, $\widehat{FH}(s) \in K(0)^{n \times n}$

$$\|FHu\|_2^2 = (2\pi)^{-1} \int_{-\infty}^{\infty} u^*(j\omega) \widehat{FH}^*(j\omega) \widehat{FH}(j\omega) u(j\omega) \, d\omega$$

For each $\omega \in R$, the matrix $\widehat{FH}^*(j\omega) \widehat{FH}(j\omega)$ is positive definite, therefore if $\Lambda[\widehat{FH}(j\omega)]$ is the maximum eigenvalue of this matrix then

$$\|FH\|_2 = \sup_{\omega \in R} \Lambda^{1/2}[\widehat{FH}(j\omega)] \tag{6.17}$$

So that the feedback system (6.10) is L_2^n-stable if $F: L_2^m \to L_2^n$ and

$$\sup_{\omega \in R} \Lambda^{1/2}[\widehat{FH}(j\omega)] . \|N\| < 1 \tag{6.18}$$

This stability criterion is not particularly useful because

(i) it requires the open-loop system to be stable

(ii) it has no simple graphical interpretation (unless $\widehat{FH}(j\omega)$ is a normal matrix)

(iii) it effectively requires that the open-loop gain be small at all frequencies, which is inconsistent with closed-loop dynamic performance.

In the following we develop L_p-stability criteria that have a simple graphical interpretation and which incorporate open-loop unstable operators.

In the remainder of this section we establish the loop transformation theorem which effectively eliminates the above stringent loop gain requirement.

Consider the general feedback system

$$y = F(u - HN(y))$$

where F and H are linear operators that map E_e^n into itself, and $N : E_e^n \rightarrow E_e^n$ is a memoryless nonlinear map. Let $u \in E_e^n$ and define an arbitrary operator $N_0 : E_e^n \rightarrow E_e^n$ such that the above feedback system can be transformed into

$$(I + FHN_0)y = Fu - FH(N - N_0)(y)$$

or

$$y = (I + FHN_0)^{-1}Fu - (I + FHN_0)^{-1}FH(N - N_0)(y) \qquad (6.19)$$

provided that $(I + FHN_0)^{-1} : E_e^n \rightarrow E_e^n$.

THEOREM 6.1: LOOP TRANSFORMATION THEOREM *Let linear operators F, H, N_0, $(I + FHN_0)^{-1}$ map E_e^n into E_e^n, then $y \in E_e^n$ is a solution to $y = F(u - HN(y))$ if and only if it is a solution to (6.19) for $u \in E_e^n$.*

The loop gain condition (6.15) can now be rewritten as

$$\|(I + FHN_0)^{-1}FH\| \cdot \|N - N_0\| < 1 \qquad (6.20)$$

Clearly by approximating N as closely as possible by a linear time-invariant matrix gain $N_0 \in R^{n \times n}$ the stringent open-loop gain (6.15) has been dramatically reduced. Note that if we set $G = (I + FHN_0)^{-1}FH$ then

$$G^{-1} = (FH)^{-1} + N_0^{-1} \qquad (6.21)$$

which is of particular significance in deriving graphical stability criteria when $E_e^n = L_{2e}^n$ and FH is representable by a matrix transfer function. The loop transformation theorem holds when the operator N is nonlinear and when the space E_e^n is replaced by E^n.

6.2 SMALL GAIN THEOREMS

There are essentially three small gain theorems that establish the input–output stability of nonlinear feedback systems. The strictest assumes that a Lipschitz condition is known for the nonlinearity and makes strong predictions concerning stability and the existence and uniqueness of solution. The second or intermediate gain theorem assumes only uniform continuity and bounded total gain of the nonlinearity and establishes intermediate results concerning stability and existence of solution but makes no prediction on uniqueness or continuity. The third small gain theorem (the subject of this section) is the least conservative as well as most general; it drops the uniform continuity condition and predicts boundedness of solution—if they are known to exist.

6.2.1 Boundedness small gain theorem

The boundedness small gain theorem is a very general theorem which gives sufficient conditions for bounded input–output stability. The important questions of existence, uniqueness and continuity of solution are divorced from the stability question and are usually assumed *a priori*.

Consider the feedback system

$$y = F(u - Ny), \qquad u \in E_e \tag{6.22}$$

Let operators $F, H : E_e \to E_e$, and system error $e = u - Ny \in E_e$. Then from (6.22)

$$u = e + Ny$$
$$y = Fe \tag{6.23}$$

Suppose that the operators F, G are such that

$$\|(Fe)_T\| \le \gamma_F \|(e)_T\| + \beta_F \tag{6.24}$$
$$\|(Ny)_T\| \le \gamma_N \|(y)_T\| + \beta_N \tag{6.25}$$

For all $T \in I$, $e \in E_e$, $y \in E_e$; $\gamma_F, \gamma_N \ge 0$ and constants β_F, β_N. Note that it has been assumed *a priori* that $e \in E_e$ and u is defined according to the system equations (6.23). This reversal of the usual definition of feedback system signal dependences is made to avoid the question of uniqueness and existence of solution to (6.22). The constants β_i and gains γ_i are given by

$$\inf_{\gamma_i, \beta_i} \{\gamma_i \|e\| + \beta_i\}$$

for each i. The constants β_i are included in the problem formulation so that the following small gain theorem applies to nonlinearities with discontinuities and hysteresis.

Now

$$y = Fe \Rightarrow \|y_T\| = \|(Fe)_T\| \le \gamma_F \|e_T\| + \beta_F \tag{6.26}$$

And

$$e = u - Ny \Rightarrow \|e_T\| \le \|u_T\| + \|(Ny)_T\| \le \|u_T\| + \gamma_N \|y_T\| + \beta_N \quad (6.27)$$

Combining (6.26) and (6.27) yields

$$\|e_T\| \le (1 - \gamma_F\gamma_N)^{-1}(\|u_T\| + \gamma_N\beta_F + \beta_N) \quad (6.28)$$

and

$$\|y_T\| \le \gamma_F(1 - \gamma_F\gamma_N)^{-1}(\|u_T\| + \gamma_N\beta_F + \beta_N) + \beta_F \quad (6.29)$$

provided that $\gamma_F\gamma_N < 1$ for all $T \in I$.

The gain product $\gamma_F\gamma_N$ and term $\gamma_N\beta_F + \beta_N$ can be replaced in inequalities (6.28), (6.29) by γ_{FN} and β_{FN} respectively if the bound

$$\|(FN)_T\| \le \gamma_{FN} \|e_T\| + \beta_{FN}, \qquad \forall\, T \in I$$

is utilized. This substitution of individual operator gains by the loop gain γ_{FN} follows from the inequality

$$\gamma_{FN} \le \gamma_F\gamma_N \quad (6.30)$$

THEOREM 6.2: BOUNDED INPUT-OUTPUT STABILITY   *If the feedback system* $y = F(u - N(y))$ *has system operators that satisfy inequalities (6.24) and (6.25) for all* $T \in I$ *and* $\|u\| < \infty$ *then the system is bounded input-output stable if the loop gain* $\gamma_F\gamma_N$ *is less than unity, and the norms of system error and output satisfy*

$$\|e\| \le (1 - \gamma_F\gamma_N)^{-1}(\|u\| + \gamma_N\beta_F + \beta_N)$$
$$\|y\| \le \gamma_F \|e\| + \beta_F$$

This theorem holds for continuous time or discrete time systems as well as multivariable and infinite dimensional dynamic systems; indeed the operators F, N can be generalized multivalued relations which include hysteresis and saturation effects.

An alternative and more useful bounded input–output stability results on utilization of the loop transformation Theorem 6.1. The feedback system (6.22) can be transformed into

$$y = (I + FN_0)^{-1}Fu - (I + FN_0)^{-1}F(N - N_0)(y) \quad (6.31)$$

provided that the inverse operator $(I + FN_0)^{-1}$ exists in F_e for arbitrary operator $N_0: E_e \to E_e$. Now, setting

$$G = (I + FN_0)^{-1}F \quad (6.32)$$

as a closed-loop "transfer function", then

$$y = Gu - G(N - N_0)(y)$$

Supposing that the arbitrary operator N_0 is such that

$$\|(N - N_0) y_T\| \leq \gamma_{N'} \|y_T\| + \beta_{N'} \tag{6.33}$$

for all $T \in I$, $y \in E_e$, and real constants γ, β, thence the bound for y is given by

$$\|y\| \leq (\|G\| \cdot \|u\| + \beta_{N'})(1 - \|G\| \cdot \gamma_{N'})^{-1} \tag{6.34}$$

Clearly the condition

$$\gamma_{N'} \|G\| = \gamma_{N'} \|(I + FN_0)^{-1} F\| < 1 \tag{6.35}$$

is sufficient for bounded input–output stability provided that $(I + FN_0)^{-1} \in E$.

Example 6.1   Consider the spaces $E = L_p^n$, $p \in [1, \infty]$ for the feedback system (6.22) with $u \in L_p^n$. F is a linear time-invariant operator and is represented by the convolution

$$(Fe)(t) = F \otimes e = \int_0^t F(t - \tau) e(t) \, dt \tag{6.36}$$

We note that the norm on the convolution operator is bounded by

$$\|F \otimes e\|_p \leq \|F\|_1 \cdot \|e\|_p \tag{6.37}$$

And in particular when $p = 2$

$$\|F \otimes e\|_2 \leq \sup_{\omega \in R} |\hat{F}(j\omega)| \cdot \|e\|_2, \tag{6.38}$$

where $\hat{F}(s)$ is the Laplace transform matrix of operator F, which we assume for simplicity to be analytic in $Re(s) \geq 0$.

The subsystem N is a memoryless, but not necessarily time-invariant, operator from $R^{n \times n}$ into itself and satisfies the bound condition (6.33). Under these conditions we have

THEOREM   6.3   *The feedback system* $y = F(u - N(y))$ *is* L_p^n-*stable* ($u \in L_p^n \Rightarrow e$, $y \in L_p^n$) *for* $p = [1, \infty]$ *if*

$$\gamma_{N'} \|(I + FN_0)^{-1} F\|_p < 1$$

for $N_0 \in R^{n \times n}$ *and*

$$\inf_{Re(s) > 0} |\det (I + \hat{F}(s) N_0)| > 0$$

The last condition follows from the Nyquist condition (see Sections 3.2, 4.2) and ensures that the closed-loop operator $(I + FN_0)^{-1} F$ is stable.

The various nonlinear multivariable stability results derived in this chapter are of little practical value unless they can be interpreted graphically in a similar manner to the Nyquist criterion for linear multivariable systems. The merit of such an approach is that it can easily be integrated with the vast numbers of computer-aided design methods that have been established (Rosenbrock, 1974) for the control system design of linear multivariable systems. To obtain a frequency domain interpretation of Theorem 6.3, we set $p=2$ and consider those $F: L_{2e}^n \to L_{2e}^n$ which are linear time-invariant operators characterized by a matrix transfer function $\hat{F}(s)$ such that each element $\hat{f}_{ij}(s)$ is a meromorphic function in $Re(s)>0$ and satisfies the condition $\lim_{|s|\to\infty} \hat{f}_{ij}(s)=0$. Under these conditions Theorem 6.3 established that if $u \in L_2^n$ then e, $y \in L_2^n$ if

$$\inf_{Re(s)>0} |\det(I+N_0\hat{F}(s))|>0 \quad \text{for} \quad N_0 \in R^{n\times n}$$

and

$$\gamma_{N'}\|(I+FN_0)^{-1}F\|_2 = \gamma_{N'}\sup_{\omega\in R}\Lambda^{\frac{1}{2}}[(I+\hat{F}(j\omega)N_0)^{-1}\hat{F}(j\omega)]<1 \quad (6.39)$$

for all $\gamma_{N'} \in R$. Where $\Lambda[Z]$ denotes the largest eigenvalue of Z^*Z.

These conditions establish the conditions for boundedness of solutions y, e to the feedback system $y = F(u - N(y))$ and assume a priori that such solutions exist. Questions concerning existence, uniqueness, and continuity of solution can only be established if the operator N is Lipschitz continuous.

A graphical interpretation of the above L_2^n stability result can only be made if the operator $\hat{G} = (I+\hat{F}N_0)^{-1}\hat{F}$ is normal, since this means that at each frequency ω the eigenspaces of the matrix transfer function $\hat{G}(j\omega)$ form a mutually orthogonal set spanning the whole space C^n. And the norm for a normal operator $G: L_2^n \to L_2^n$ is given by

$$\|G\|_2 = \sup_{\omega\in R} \max_{\lambda\in\sigma[\hat{G}(j\omega)]} |\lambda|$$

where $\sigma[\hat{G}]$ represents the set of eigenvalues of G. Otherwise the above stability criterion has to be numerically evaluated via the norm

$$\|G\|_2 = \sup_{\omega\in R}\Lambda^{\frac{1}{2}}[\hat{G}(j\omega)]$$

Suppose that the nonlinearity N is such that

$$\alpha(z^Tz) \le z^T(Nz)(t) \le \beta(z^Tz), \forall t \in R_+, \forall z \in R^n$$

where α and β are scalars. If we select $N_0 = \frac{1}{2}(\alpha+\beta)I$, the norm condition

$$\|(N-N_0(z_T)\| \le \gamma_{N'}\|(z_T)\|, \forall T \in R_+, \forall z \in R^n \quad (6.40)$$

is minimized by the gain $\gamma_{N'} = \frac{1}{2}(\beta - \alpha)$. Then if the linear operator $F : L_{2e}^n \to L_{2e}^n$ is normal, the condition (6.39) simplifies to

$$\frac{1}{2}(\beta - \alpha)\sup_{\omega \in R} \max_{\lambda \in \sigma[\hat{F}(j\omega)]} \left| \frac{\lambda}{(1 + c\lambda)} \right| < 1 \qquad (6.41)$$

where $c = \frac{1}{2}(\alpha + \beta)$.

The n-eigenvalues $\lambda_i(j\omega)$ $(i = 1, 2, \ldots, n)$ can be defined such that they take on the values of the eigenvalues of $\hat{F}(j\omega)$ at each ω; in terms of these eigenvalues the condition (6.41) can be rewritten as

$$|c + \lambda_i(\omega)^{-1}| > \frac{1}{2}(\beta - \alpha) \qquad (6.42)$$

for $i = 1, 2, \ldots, n$ and for all $\omega \in R$. That is, to satisfy stability condition (6.42) every loci $\lambda_i(\omega)^{-1}$ must be *exterior* to the circle $C[-\beta, -\alpha]$ in the complex plane with centre at $-c = -\frac{1}{2}(\alpha + \beta)$ and radius $\frac{1}{2}(c - \alpha) = \frac{1}{4}(\beta - \alpha)$, (Fig. 6.1). Since $\lambda_i(\omega)^{-1}$ takes on the values of the eigenvalues of $|\hat{F}(j\omega)|^{-1}$ for each ω, there is a close connection between this criterion and the Inverse Nyquist Array (Rosenbrock, 1974).

An alternative graphical interpretation of inequalities (6.41), (6.42) can be obtained by transforming the inequalities through the conformal mapping $\omega = z^{-1}$. Under such a mapping a circle $C[a, b]$ becomes a circle $C[a^{-1}, b^{-1}]$, provided that both a and b are non-zero. Moreover, if the open interval (a, b) does not include the origin, then the interior of $C[a, b]$ is transformed into the *interior* of the circle $C[a^{-1}, b^{-1}]$; if, however, $b > 0 > a$, the interior of $C[a, b]$ is mapped into the *exterior* of $C[a^{-1}, b^{-1}]$. In making the transform $\omega = z^{-1}$ the position of the origin relative to the limits (α, β) of the nonlinearity is clearly crucial. Thence if α and β have the same sign and are non-zero, conditions (6.41), (6.42)

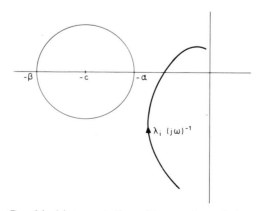

FIG. 6.1   Graphical interpretation of inverse boundedness theorem

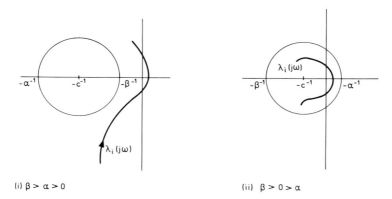

(i) $\beta > \alpha > 0$ (ii) $\beta > 0 > \alpha$

FIG. 6.2   Graphical interpretation of boundedness theorem

are satisfied if the Nyquist plots of $\lambda_i(\omega)$ are exterior to the circle $C[-\alpha^{-1}, -\beta^{-1}]$ (Fig. 6.2(i)). But when $\beta > 0 > \alpha$, condition (6.42) is satisfied when the plots of $\lambda_i(\omega)$ are *interior* to the circle $C[-\beta^{-1}, -\alpha^{-1}]$ (Fig. 6.2(ii)). The special cases of $\alpha = 0$ and $\beta = 0$ can be obtained from the above by taking the limits $\alpha \to 0$, $\beta \to 0$, respectively.

Theorem 6.3 required that, in addition to conditions (6.41) or (6.42) being satisfied by the above circle criterion, the following are simultaneously satisfied:

$$\inf |\det (I + \hat{F}(s)N_0)| > 0$$

or

$$(I + \hat{F}N_0)^{-1}\hat{F} \in K(0)^{n \times n} \tag{6.43}$$

In the following, two separate cases of the forward transfer function matrix are considered: an open-loop stable plant, and where $\hat{F}$ has poles with positive real part.

Consider first the feedback system $y = F(u - N(y))$ with $\hat{F}(s)$ open loop stable: linear condition (6.43) is satisfied if and only if the linear feedback system

$$y = F(u - N_0 y), \; u \in L_2^n \tag{6.44}$$

is stable. The Nyquist encirclement theorem ensures that system (6.44) is L_2^n-stable if and only if the plots of the eigenvalues of $\hat{F}(j\omega)$ do not encircle the point $-c^{-1} = -2(\alpha + \beta)^{-1}$.

Consider now the second case when $\hat{F}(s)$ has p-poles in the right half s-plane. Then from the Nyquist encirclement theorem $(I + \hat{F}N_0)^{-1}\hat{F} \in K(0)^{n \times n}$ when the total number of clockwise encirclements of $-c^{-1}$ by the eigenloci, $\lambda_i(\omega)$, of $\hat{F}(j\omega)$ is $(n \times p)$. We are now able to state the small gain circle theorem:

THEOREM 6.4   *Consider the feedback system* $y = F(u - N(y))$ *for* $u \in L_n^2$, $F: L_{2e}^n \to L_{2e}^n$ *a normal operator with matrix transfer function* $\hat{F}(s)$ *and* N *a nonlinear operator such that*

$$\alpha(z^T z) \leq z^T(Nz)(t) \leq \beta(z^T z)$$

for all $t \in R_+$ *and* $z \in R^n$, α *and* β *scalars. Then* y, $e = u - N(y) \in L_2^n$ *if*
   (a) $\hat{F}$ *is a stable normal operator and the eigenloci* $\lambda_i(\omega)$ *of* $\hat{F}(j\omega)$ (i) *do not encircle or intersect the circle* $C[-\beta^{-1}, -\alpha^{-1}]$ *for* α, β *of the same sign and non-zero or* (ii) *if* $\beta > 0 > \alpha$, *the plots* $\lambda_i(\omega)$ *lie inside the circle* $C[-\beta^{-1}, -\alpha^{-1}]$ *or* (iii) *if* $\beta > \alpha = 0$, *the eigenloci* $\lambda_i(\omega)$ *lie to the right of the abscissa* $-\beta^{-1}$, *that is*

$$Re(\lambda_i(\omega)) > -\beta^{-1}, \qquad \forall \omega \in R, i = 1, 2, \ldots, n$$

or

   (b) $\hat{F}$ *is a normal operator with p-right half poles, and the eigenloci of* $\hat{F}(j\omega)$ *do not intersect the circle* $C[-\beta^{-1}, -\alpha^{-1}]$ *but encircle it* $(n \times p)$ *times in the clockwise direction for* α, β *of the same sign and non-zero.*

Note
   (i) In the above case (b) for $\beta > 0 > \alpha$ it is not possible to satisfy conditions (6.42) and (6.43) simultaneously, since the point $-c^{-1}$ is exterior to the circle $C[-\beta^{-1}, -\alpha^{-1}]$.
   (ii) When $\beta \to \alpha > 0$, the nonlinearity $N(y) \to \alpha Iy$ and the critical circle $C[-\beta^{-1}, -\alpha^{-1}]$ converges to the critical point $(-\alpha^{-1}, 0)$ in the complex plane and the above theorem becomes a multivariable Nyquist stability criterion.
   (iii) The restriction that $\hat{F}(s)$ should be a normal operator is quite severe, but by using the loop transformation Theorem 6.1 to approximate $\hat{F}(s)$ by a normal operator, a modified circle criterion can be readily derived.

6.3   INTERMEDIATE SMALL GAIN THEOREM

The small gain Theorem 6.2 predicts boundedness of solution to feedback systems if the solutions are already known to exist, by utilizing the boundedness of system operators. This sector-based theorem holds under very weak system assumptions and is of a very general nature, but it is not easily implemented for practical use. If we now make the additional requirement that the nonlinearity in the loop be uniformly continuous with bounded norm, we can utilize the Brouwer and Schauder-Tikhonov fixed point theorems 1.16 and 1.17 to establish existence as well as boundedness of solution, although uniqueness and continuity of solution cannot be predicted without the further assumption that the system operators be Lipschitz continuous. The question of existence of solution is crucial in ensuring that the system model equations are well posed, since a physical system must have a response to some stimulus.

The main results in this section on the boundedness and existence of solution to feedback systems depend upon fixed point theorems for compact operators. In the following we utilize the fixed point theorems for compact operators to generate bounded response theorems for dynamic feedback systems.

Fixed point theorems in linear vector spaces are essential in establishing the existence and uniqueness of solution under certain structural conditions to nonlinear differential or integral equations that represent dynamical systems.

Let X be a normed vector space and define a space E on X by

$$E = \{x : R_+ \to X / \|x\|_E < \infty\}$$

where the norm $\|.\|_E$ is given.

If M is a subset of E such that every continuous mapping of M onto itself has at least one fixed point, then M has the fixed point property. The conditions necessary for $M \subset E$ to have the fixed point property are contained in the Schauder-Tikhonov fixed point theorem 1.17, which shows that for any mapping $F : E \to E$, with $FM \subset M$ and *compact*, F has a fixed point in M. We note that there is no requirement that the vector space E be a Banach space. All that is required for F to have a fixed point is that the operator F is continuous and FM is compact. A general property of compact sets is that a compact subset of M of a normed space E is closed and bounded; the converse of this result is only true when the space E is finite dimensional.

A compactness criterion is given in the following:

THEOREM 6.5   *Let X and Y be normed spaces and $F : X \to Y$ a linear operator. Then F is compact if and only if it maps every bounded sequence $\{x_n\} \in X$ onto a sequence $\{Fx_n\} \in Y$ which has a convergent subsequence.*

Proof   (Dunford and Schwartz, Part 1, 1957).   □

In the special case of finite dimensional vector spaces the above simplifies to:

THEOREM 6.6   *The operator F is compact if dim $(X) < \infty$ or if F is bounded and dim $(F(x)) < \infty$*

An important operator $F: E \to E$ in systems theory is the convolution operator

$$(Fx)(t) = f \otimes x$$
$$= \int_0^t f(t - \tau)x(\tau) \, d\tau, \qquad t \in [0, T] \tag{6.45}$$

where for each t, $f(t)$ is a compact linear operator on X and $\int_0^t |f(t)|^2 \, dt < \infty$. We note from Theorem 6.6 that F is automatically compact if $\dim(E) < \infty$. Suppose that a bounded continuous operator $N: E \to E$ exists such that $\|Nx\| \leq \gamma \|x\|$ for all $x \in E$, then the operator $Z = F \otimes N$ is compact on the extended space E_e, when E is either the $L_p = \{x: R_+ \to R / \|x\|_p = \{\int_0^\infty |x(t)|^p\}^{1/p} \, dt < \infty\}$ for $p = [1, \infty)$ or the periodic function space $PF_\tau = \{x: R \to R / x(t + \tau) = x(t), \quad \forall t \in R, \quad \text{and} \quad \|x\| = [\int_0^\tau |x(t)|^2 \, dt]^{1/2} < \infty\}$. The proof of this last statement for these important spaces follows from application of Theorem 6.5 (see also Dunford and Schwartz, pp. 516–518, part I, 1957). Note that using the topology introduced in Chapter 5 for extended spaces, a set M is compact in $L_{p,e}$ if and only if for all $T \geq 0$, the set $P_T(M)$ is compact in $L_p[0, T]$.

Consider now the n-input–output feedback system

$$y = F(u - N(y)), \ u \in E \tag{6.46}$$

where F is a linear operator on E and $N: E_e \to E_e$ is a bounded nonlinear continuous operator. The above system can be rewritten via the loop transformation Theorem 6.1 as

$$y = (I + \phi N_0)^{-1} Fu - (I + \phi N_0)^{-1}\phi(N - N_0)(y) - (I + \phi N_0)^{-1}(F - \phi)N(y) \tag{6.47}$$

where N_0 is an arbitrary time invariant operator on $R^{n \times n}$ and $\phi: E \to E$ is a linear operator which is such that $(I + \phi N_0)^{-1}\phi \triangleq G$ is a bounded linear map on E. Clearly if $G: E \to E$, then $(I + \phi N_0)^{-1} = (I - GN_0)$ is also a bounded linear map on E, and system (6.47) can be rewritten as

$$y = (I - GN_0)Fu - (I - GN_0)(F - \phi)N(y) - G(N - N_0)(y) \tag{6.48}$$

Suppose now that the operator N_0 is selected such that

$$\|(N - N_0)y_T\| \leq \gamma_N \|y_T\| + \beta_N, \ \gamma_N > 0, \ \beta_N \geq 0 \tag{6.49}$$

and define

$$K(\phi) = (\|y_T\|)^{-1} \|(1 - GN_0)(F - \phi)N(y_T)\| \tag{6.50}$$

as a measure of the error of approximation of operator F by ϕ. Then on taking norms of transformed feedback system (6.48) and applying the above definition, a solution $y \in E$ exists to (6.46) and every solution $y \in E_e$ satisfies

$$\|y_T\| \leq \frac{\|(1 - GN_0)Fu_T\| + \beta_N}{(1 - K(\phi) - \gamma_N \|G\|)}, \qquad \forall \, T \in I \qquad (6.51)$$

provided that

$$\gamma_N \cdot \|G\| \cdot (1 - K(\phi))^{-1} = \gamma_N \cdot \|(I + \phi N_0)^{-1}\phi\| (1 - K(\phi))^{-1} < 1 \qquad (6.52)$$

Obviously if $F = \phi$ then $K(\phi) = 0$ and the above loop gain condition simplifies to

$$\gamma_N \|(I + FN_0)^{-1}F\| < 1 \qquad (6.53)$$

but there is now much less flexibility in weakening the loop gain requirement (6.53) through the loss of choice in operator ϕ. In addition, if $F : E_e \to E_e$, it may no longer be possible to ensure that $(I + FN_0)^{-1} F$ is a linear operator on E.

Suppose now that a solution $y^* \in E$ to (6.48) is such that $y^* = My^*$ where the operator M is given by

$$My = (I - GN_0)Fu - [(I - GN_0)(F - \phi)N + G(N - N_0)](y) \qquad (6.54)$$

is well defined and continuous on E through the assumptions made on operators F, N, N_0 and ϕ. Clearly every fixed point y^* is contained in the ball

$$B = \{y : \|y\| \leq (1 - K(\phi) - \gamma_N \|G\|)^{-1}(\|(I - GN_0)Fu\| + \beta_N)\} \qquad (6.55)$$

So for any $My \in B$ or $MB \subset B$ and MB compact, then by the Schauder fixed point theorem 1.17, M has a fixed point in B.

THEOREM 6.7: BOUNDED RESPONSE THEOREM   *Let E_e be a space on which the composition of a linear convolution operator and a bounded continuous operator is compact. Let $G = (I + \phi N_0)^{-1}\phi$ be a bounded linear map on E for $N_0 \in R^{n \times n}$ and $\phi : E \to E$. Let N be a continuous nonlinear operator on E_e such that*

$$\|(N - N_0)y_T\| \leq \gamma_N \|y_T\| + \beta_N, \qquad \forall \, y \in E, \, \gamma_N > 0, \, \beta_N \geq 0$$

Then every solution $y^* \in E$ to $y = F(u - N(y))$ for $u \in E$ exists and every solution $y \in E_e$ satisfies

$$\|y\| \leq (1 - K(\phi) - \gamma_N \|G\|)^{-1}(\|(I - GN_0)Fu\| + \beta_N)$$

provided that $(1 - K(\phi))^{-1}\gamma_N \|G\| < 1$.

In practice we select operator N_0 such that $\|(N - N_0)\|$ is minimized (effectively minimizing γ_N) and simultaneously ensure that $(I + \phi N_0)^{-1}$ exists in E. This guarantees the minimum gain condition (6.49) with the least stringent requirement on loop gain (6.52) for stability. Also $K(\phi)$ is minimized by approximating the operator F by ϕ as closely as possible, while ensuring that $G : E \rightarrow E$. This is trivial in the scalar case since we can always set $F = \phi$, but for multivariable systems we select in the following ϕ to be a normal operator (although F is rarely normal in practical systems) so that Theorem 6.7 has a simple graphical interpretation.

COROLLARY 6.7 *Suppose that $E = L_p^n$ and $u \in L_p^n$ ($p = [1, \infty)$), F is a linear time-invariant operator defined by the convolution $F \otimes e$ such that $F \in L_1^{n \times n}$ with Laplace transform matrix $\hat{F}(s)$, and that $N : R^{n \times n} \rightarrow R^{n \times n}$ is a time-varying memoryless nonlinear operator that satisfies $\|(N - N_0)y_T\| \leq \gamma_N \|y_T\|$. Then the feedback system $y = F(u - N(y))$ is L_p^n-stable if there exist operators $N_0 \in R^{n \times n}$, ϕ such that*

$$\gamma_N (1 - K(\phi))^{-1} \|(I + \phi N_0)^{-1} \phi\| < 1$$
$$\inf_{Re(s) > 0} |\det (I + \hat{\phi}(s)N_0)| > 0$$

and

$$K(\phi) \|y\| = \|(I - GN_0)(F - \phi)N(y)\| \qquad (K(\phi) < 1)$$

for $\hat{G} = (I + \hat{\phi}N_0)^{-1}\hat{\phi}$ analytic in $Re(s) \geq 0$

A graphical interpretation of this boundedness and existence result for feedback systems can be readily seen if $E = L_2^n$ and the nonlinear operator is bounded such that

$$\alpha(z^T z) \leq z^T (N(z))(t) \leq \beta(z^T z)$$

for all $t \in R_+$, $z \in R^n$ and $\beta > \alpha$ scalars. For the above limits on the nonlinearity the optimum choice for N_0 is $\frac{1}{2}(\alpha + \beta)I$, and the norm on $(N - N_0)$ is minimized by $\gamma_N = \frac{1}{2}(\beta - \alpha)$. The necessary loop gain condition for stability of (6.46) can be written as

$$\sup_{\omega \in R} \max_{\lambda \in [\hat{\phi}(j\omega)]} \frac{1}{2} \left| \frac{\lambda}{(1 + c(\phi)\lambda)} \right| (\beta(\phi) - \alpha(\phi)) < 1 \qquad (6.56)$$

where

$$c(\phi) = \frac{1}{2}(\alpha(\phi) + \beta(\phi))$$

and

$$\alpha(\phi) = \frac{1}{2}(\alpha + \beta) - \frac{1}{2}(\beta - \alpha)(1 - K(\phi))^{-1}$$
$$\beta(\phi) = \frac{1}{2}(\alpha + \beta) + \frac{1}{2}(\beta - \alpha)(1 - K(\phi))^{-1}$$

We note that condition (6.56) is identical to (6.41) for the small gain theorem and therefore has the same graphical interpretations, except that now $\hat{\phi}(j\omega)$ replaces $\hat{F}(j\omega)$ and $\alpha(\phi)$, $\beta(\phi)$ replace α and β respectively. And so that condition (6.56) is satisfied if every loci $\lambda_i^{-1}(\omega)$ ($\lambda_i(\omega)$ are the eigenvalues of $\hat{\phi}(j\omega)$) is exterior to the circle $C[-\beta(\phi), -\alpha(\phi)]$ in the complex plane. Equally the conformal mapping $\omega = z^{-1}$ can be used such that condition (6.56) is satisfied when the eigenloci $\lambda_i(\omega)$ are exterior to the circle $C[-\alpha(\phi)^{-1}, -\beta(\phi)^{-1}]$ if $\alpha(\phi)$ and $\beta(\phi)$ are of the same sign.

The closed-loop approximation gain condition (6.56) is insufficient to ensure L_2^n-stability for the feedback system (6.46), since in addition $K(\phi) < 1$ and $(I + \phi N_0)^{-1}F$ and $(I + \phi N_0)^{-1}\phi$ must both exist in $K(0)^{n \times n}$. Clearly if the linear forward operator F is stable, then the normal operator ϕ is selected from the class of stable linear operators such that $K(\phi) < 1$, and in addition $(I + \phi N_0)^{-1} \in K(0)^{n \times n}$ if and only if the linear feedback system

$$y = \phi(u - N_0 y) \tag{6.57}$$

is L_2^n-stable. The Nyquist encirclement theorem ensures that (6.57) is stable if the eigenloci of $\hat{\phi}(j\omega)$ do not encircle the point $-c(\phi)^{-1} = -(\tfrac{1}{2}(\alpha(\phi) + \beta(\phi)))^{-1}$.

If, however, $\hat{F}(s)$ has p-poles in the right half s-plane and admits the decomposition $\hat{F}(s) = \hat{F}_0(s) d(s)^{-1}$, where $d(s)$ is a monic polynomial in s with all its zeros in the right half s-plane. Then the approximation operator $\hat{\phi}(s)$ is selected such that $\hat{\phi}(s) = \hat{\phi}_0(s) d(s)^{-1}$ where $\hat{\phi}_0(s)$ is a normal matrix operator of analytic functions in the right half s-plane. So $(I + \phi N_0)^{-1}\phi \in K(0)^{n \times n}$ and $(I + \phi N_0)^{-1}F \in K(0)^{n \times n}$ when the total number of encirclements of the point $-c(\phi)^{-1}$ by the eigenloci of $\hat{\phi}(j\omega)$ is $(n \times p)$. It is not difficult to see that we have not only satisfied all the conditions of the small gain Theorem 6.3 but also established an existence condition for the solutions to (6.46) for a non-normal open-loop linear operator F which is compact.

THEOREM 6.8   *Consider the feedback system* $y = F(u - N(y))$; *for* $u \in L_2^n$, $F: L_{2e}^n \to L_{2e}^n$ *is a compact operator with matrix transfer function* $\hat{F}(s)$ *and feedback nonlinear operator* $N(y)$ *which is bounded and continuous such that*

$$\alpha(z^T z) \le z^T (Nz)(t) \le \beta(z^T z), \qquad \forall t \in R_+, z \in R^n$$

and α *and* β *are scalars. Solutions to this feedback system exist such that* $y \in L_2^n$, $e = u - N(y) \in L_2^n$ *if*

   (a) $\hat{F}(s)$ *is a stable open-loop operator, and the eigenloci* $\lambda_i(j\omega)$ *of the normal approximation* $\hat{\phi}(j\omega)$ *to* $\hat{F}(j\omega)$ (i) *do not encircle or intersect the circle* $C[-\beta^{-1}(\phi), -\alpha^{-1}(\phi)]$ *for* $\alpha(\phi)$, $\beta(\phi)$ *the same sign and*

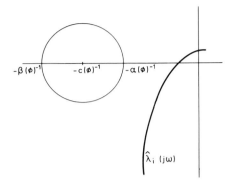

(i) $\beta(\phi) \geq \alpha(\phi) > 0$

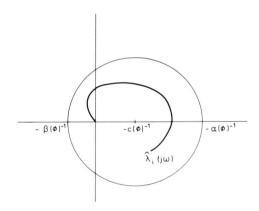

(ii) $\beta(\phi) > 0 > \alpha(\phi)$

FIG. 6.3   Circle criterion for non-normal operators

non-zero, (ii) if $\beta(\phi) > 0 > \alpha(\phi)$ the plots $\lambda_i(j\omega)$ lie inside the circle $C[-\beta^{-1}(\phi), -\alpha^{-1}(\phi)]$ or (iii) if $\beta(\phi) > \alpha(\phi) = 0$, the plots of $\lambda_i(j\omega)$ lie to the right of the abscissa $-\beta(\phi)^{-1}$ for $i = 1, 2, \ldots, n$ and for all $\omega \in R$

or

    (b) *$\hat{F}(s)$ has p-right half poles and admits the decomposition $\hat{F}(s) = \hat{F}_0(s)\, d(s)^{-1}$ where $d(s)$ is a monic polynomial with all zeros in $Re(s) > 0$, and the Nyquist plots of $\lambda(\hat{\phi}(j\omega))$ do not intersect the circle $C[-\beta^{-1}(\phi), -\alpha^{-1}(\phi)]$ but encircle it $(n \times p)$ times in the clockwise direction for $\alpha(\phi), \beta(\phi)$ of the same sign* *where*

$$\alpha(\phi) = \tfrac{1}{2}(\alpha + \beta) - \tfrac{1}{2}(\beta - \alpha)(1 - K(\phi))^{-1}$$
$$\beta(\phi) = \tfrac{1}{2}(\alpha + \beta) + \tfrac{1}{2}(\beta - \alpha)(1 - K(\phi))^{-1}$$

provided that

$$K(\phi) = \|(I - GN_0)(F - \phi)N\| < 1$$

for $G = (I + \phi N_0)^{-1}\phi$ *and* $N_0 = \tfrac{1}{2}(\alpha + \beta)I$.

This theorem is crucially dependent on the error of approximation $K(\phi)$ between the compact linear operator F and its normal representation ϕ being less than unity. The choice for ϕ depends upon the structure of F. For example, (i) if F is diagonally dominant, then select $\phi = \text{diag}(F)$; (ii) if F is nearly self adjoint, then select $\phi = \tfrac{1}{2}(F + F^*)$; identically if $F \approx -F^*$, then select $\phi = \tfrac{1}{2}(F - F^*)$; (iii) if F is block diagonal, then each block can be approximated by a normal operator in the above theorem. For further discussion on the choice of ϕ see Section 7.3.

6.4 THE INCREMENTAL GAIN THEOREM

The incremental gain theorem has its origins in the contraction mapping theorem and ensures existence, uniqueness, boundedness, and continuity of solution to nonlinear feedback systems. The fact that the spaces on which the operators and inputs are defined are complete normed linear vector spaces (that is Banach spaces) is exploited in the following to establish the existence, uniqueness and continuity of solution as well as stability.

Definition 6.5   Consider two Banach spaces B and D with respective norms $\|.\|_B, \|.\|_D$. The map $G : B \to D$ is said to be *Lipschitz continuous* if a scalar $\hat{\gamma}_G > 0$ exists such that

$$\|G(x_T) - G(y_T)\|_D \le \hat{\gamma}_G \|x_T - y_T\|_B \qquad (6.58)$$

for all $x, y \in B$ and $T \in I$.

Obviously a Lipschitz continuous operator is also a continuous mapping. The infimum of all γ satisfying (6.58) is called the Lipschitz norm of the operator G, or more simply the incremental norm of G. That is

$$\|G\|_I = \inf_{\hat{\gamma}_G} \{\hat{\gamma}_G > 0 : \|G(x) - G(y)\|_D \le \hat{\gamma}_G \|x - y\|_B, \forall x, y \in B\}$$

or

$$\|G\|_I = \sup_{x \ne y} \frac{\|G(x) - G(y)\|_D}{\|x - y\|_B}$$

If $G(0) = 0$ and if G is Lipschitz continuous, then

$$\|G\|_I \geq \|G\|_B = \sup_{x \neq 0} \frac{\|G(x)\|_D}{\|x\|_B}$$

Definition 6.6   Let G be a Lipschitz continuous operator from a Banach space B into itself. Then if $\|G\|_I < 1$, the mapping $G : B \to B$ is called a *contraction*.

The Banach fixed point theorem 1.19, showed that if B is a Banach space and G a contraction in B, then G has a *unique* fixed point in B.

Consider some Banach space B and define Lipschitz continuous operators G, F that map B into itself; assume that G is invertible and its inverse G^{-1} is Lipschitz on B and that $\|G^{-1}\|_I \|F\|_I < 1$.

THEOREM 6.9   *Under these conditions, the operator $M = F + G$ is invertible in B, M^{-1} is Lipschitz continuous on B, and*

$$\|M^{-1}\|_I \leq (\|G^{-1}\|_I - \|F\|_I)^{-1}$$

Proof   Clearly $M = (I + FG^{-1})G$, since G^{-1} is invertible. Under the conditions of the theorem the operator $N = (I + FG^{-1})$ is invertible, consequently $H = I + F$ is invertible by definition.

Define $x_i = (I + FG^{-1})^{-1} z_i$ for $z_i \in B$, then

$$z_i = (I + FG^{-1}) x_i \quad \text{or} \quad x_i = FG^{-1} x_i + z_i$$

and hence by taking norms

$$\|x_1 - x_2\| = \|N^{-1} z_1 - N^{-1} z_2\| \leq (1 - \|F\|_I \|G^{-1}\|_I)^{-1} \|z_1 - z_2\|.$$

Hence N^{-1} is Lipschitz on B and so by definition of M, $M^{-1} = G^{-1} N^{-1}$ is Lipschitz, also $\|N^{-1}\|_I \leq (I - \|F\|_I \|G^{-1}\|_I)^{-1}$. $\square$

If we take the special case of $G = I$, the identity operator we have the obvious corollary which is useful in studying feedback systems.

COROLLARY 6.9   *Let $F : B \to B$ be Lipschitz on B with $\|F\|_I < 1$, then the operator $H = I + F$ is invertible and its inverse is Lipschitz on B with $\|H^{-1}\|_I \leq (1 - \|F\|_I)^{-1}$.*

Suppose that we make further restrictions on the operator G such that its a Lipschitz operator mapping a Hilbert space HS onto itself and it is incrementally passive, that is

$$\langle Gx - Gy, x - y \rangle \geq \delta \|x - y\|^2 \; \forall \, x, y \in HS, \, \delta > 0$$

THEOREM 6.10   *Under these conditions the operator $G : HS \to HS$ is invertible, G^{-1} is Lipschitz on HS with $\|G^{-1}\|_I \leq \delta^{-1}$, and for all $x, y \in HS$*

$$\langle G^{-1}x - G^{-1}y, x - y \rangle \geq \delta \|G\|_I^{-2} \|x - y\|^2$$

Proof Utilizing the definition of incremental passivity, the Schwartz inequality shows that the operator G is invertible by the fixed point theorem. For some x, $y \in HS$, putting $x = G^{-1}\eta$, $y = G^{-1}\xi$ we have η, $\xi \in HS$ and so

$$\|G\eta - G\xi\| \leq \|G\|_I \|\eta - \xi\|$$

equally

$$\|G^{-1}x - G^{-1}y\| \geq \|G\|_I^{-1} \|x - y\|$$

Using this result in the incremental passivity condition we have

$$\langle G^{-1}x - G^{-1}y, x - y \rangle \geq \delta \|G^{-1}x - G^{-1}y\|^2$$
$$\geq \delta \|G\|_I^{-2} \|x - y\|^2 \qquad \square$$

Consider now the feedback system

$$y = Fe, \qquad e = u - Gy \qquad (6.59)$$

where $u \in B_e$; F, $G : B_e \to B_e$ and for each $T \in I$, $P_T B_e$ is a Banach space. Suppose that the operators F, G are Lipschitz continuous on B_e with respective incremental gains $\hat{\gamma}_F$, $\hat{\gamma}_G$. For this feedback system to be well posed, the operators F, G are required to be causal and at least one must be strongly causal. The strong causality requirement on F or G is motivated by the fact that all physical systems exhibit some form of delay in the system dynamics.

Clearly for some $T \in I$

$$y_T = \{F(u - Gy)\}_T \triangleq M(y_T)$$

The incremental norm conditions on F and G applied to operator $M(y)$ for y_T, $y_{T'} \in B_e$ for all $T \in I$ give

$$\|\{F(u_{T'} - (Gy')_T)\} - \{F(u_T - (Gy)_T)\}\| \leq \hat{\gamma}_F \|(Gy'_T)_T - (Gy_T)_T\|$$
$$\leq \hat{\gamma}_F \hat{\gamma}_G \|y_{T'} - y_T\|$$

Hence operator M is a contraction of $P_T B_e$ if $\hat{\gamma}_F \hat{\gamma}_G < 1$ and y_T is a uniquely defined element on $P_T B_e$.

Now, utilizing the well-known triangle inequality of norms and the incremental gain condition on the causal operator G for the system error $e = u - Gy$, we get for any $T \in I$, u', $u \in B_e$

$$\|e_{T'} - e_T\| \leq \|u_{T'} - u_T\| + \hat{\gamma}_G \|y_{T'} - y_T\| \qquad (6.60)$$

But $y_T = (Fe_T)_T$ implies that

$$\|y_{T'} - y_T\| \leq \hat{\gamma}_F \|e_{T'} - e_T\| \qquad (6.61)$$

Therefore (6.60) becomes on rearrangement

$$\|e_{T'} - e_T\| \leq (1 - \hat{\gamma}_F \hat{\gamma}_G)^{-1} \|u_{T'} - u_T\| \qquad (6.62)$$

provided that $\hat{\gamma}_F\hat{\gamma}_G < 1$. And hence from (6.61)

$$\|y_{T'} - y_T\| \leq \hat{\gamma}_F(1 - \hat{\gamma}_F\hat{\gamma}_G)^{-1} \|u_{T'} - u_T\| \tag{6.63}$$

We are now able to state:

THEOREM 6.11: INCREMENTAL GAIN THEOREM   *Assume that the space $P_T B_e$ is a Banach space for each $T \in I$. Let F, G be causal operators on B_e with associated incremental gains $\hat{\gamma}_F$, $\hat{\gamma}_G$ respectively. Then if $\hat{\gamma}_F\hat{\gamma}_G < 1$, there exists for the feedback system*

$$y = F(u - Gy), \; u \in B_e$$

unique solutions y, $e = u - Gy \in B_e$, and the map $u \mapsto e$ is uniformly continuous on B_e and B. In addition if $u \in B$, then e, $y \in B$.

Note that if the operators F, G are linear, then the small gain and incremental gain theorems are identical if $\beta_G = \beta_F = 0$.

The loop gain conditions (6.62), (6.63) can be further strengthened by application of the loop transformation theorem to both operators F and G. That is, following the approach introduced in the intermediate gain theorem 6.7, approximate the linear operator F by an operator $\phi \in B$ and the memoryless operator G by $G_0 \in R^{n \times n}$. Therefore (6.59) transforms to

$$y = (I - DG_0)Fu - (I - DG_0)(F - \phi)G(y) - D(G - G_0)(y)$$
$$\triangleq M(y)$$

provided that $D = (I + \phi G_0)^{-1}\phi$ is a bounded linear map on B. If the Lipschitz continuous operator $M(y): B \to B$ is a contraction on the Banach space B, then there exists a unique solution $y \in B$ which is a fixed point of $M(y)$. That is

$$\|(I - DG_0)(F - \phi)\| \cdot \|G\| + \|D(G - G_0)\| < 1 \tag{6.64}$$

and operators $(I + \phi G_0)^{-1}F$, $(I + \phi G_0)^{-1}\phi : B \to B$. If we define the error of approximation of F by ϕ as

$$K(\phi) = \|(I + \phi G_0)^{-1}(F - \phi)\| \cdot \|G\| \tag{6.65}$$

then the sufficient loop gain condition (6.64) for stability can be written as

$$\hat{\gamma}_{G-G_0}(1 - K(\phi))^{-1}\|D\| < 1 \tag{6.66}$$

if $K(\phi) < 1$.

Example 6.2   Consider the Banach spaces $B = L_p^n$, $p = [1, \infty]$ for the feedback system (6.59) with $u \in L_p^n$, F a causal linear time-invariant convolution operator described by matrix transfer function $\hat{F}(s)$, and G a memoryless nonlinear operator that satisfies

$$\|(G - G_0)x' - (G - G_0)x\| \le \hat{\gamma}_G \|x' - x\|, \qquad \forall x \in R^n,$$

where $G_0 \in R^{n \times n}$. Then, similarly to the small gain theorem, application of the loop transformation theorem shows that the feedback system (6.59) is L_p^n-stable for $p = [1, \infty]$ if

$$\|(I + FG_0)^{-1}F\|_1 \hat{\gamma}_G < 1$$

and

$$\inf_{Re(s) > 0} |\det (I + G_0 \hat{F}(s))| > 0$$

In addition, for each $u \in L_p^n$, each solution $e, y \in L_p^n$ is unique and depends continuously upon u.

We have now established for the space $B = L_p^n$ three gain theorems which provide sufficient conditions for input–output L_p-stability with varying conclusions concerning the existence, uniqueness, and continuity of solution, each dependent on the structural assumptions imposed upon loop operators. In all cases it was necessary to compute the norms $\|F\|_p$ and/or $\|(I + FG_0)^{-1}F\|_p$ to ascertain stability. For $p = 2$ we have shown that

$$\|F\|_2 = \sup_{\omega \in R} \Lambda^{1/2}[\hat{F}(j\omega)]$$

where $\Lambda[\hat{F}]$ is the largest eigenvalue of $\hat{F}(j\omega) \hat{F}(j\omega)^*$; otherwise only the lower bound

$$\|F\|_p \ge \sup_{\omega \in R} |\hat{F}(j\omega)|$$

is available for the norm $\|F\|_p$ in terms of the frequency response of the convolution operator F. It is therefore not surprising that the majority of graphically interpreted stability criterion are for L_2 spaces.

Example 6.3   Consider the space $B = L_2^n$ and a linear convolution operator $F : L_2^n \to L_2^n$ which is normal (that is commutes with its complex conjugate), then

$$\|F\|_2 = \sup_{\omega \in R} \max_{\lambda \in \sigma[\hat{F}(j\omega)]} |\lambda| \tag{6.67}$$

where $\sigma[A]$ represents the set of eigenvalues of some matrix A. Suppose now that the operator G in the feedback system (6.59) is such that $G : R^n \to R^n$ and satisfies

$$\alpha(y' - y) \le G(y') - G(y) \le (\beta - \xi)(y' - y)$$

for y, $y' \in L_2^n$, α and β scalars and ξ some arbitrarily small positive constant. By setting $F = \phi$, $K(\phi) = 0$ in (6.65) and the gain condition (6.66) is minimized by selecting

$$G_0 = \tfrac{1}{2}(\alpha + \beta)I$$

in which case

$$\hat{\gamma}_{G-G_0} = \tfrac{1}{2}(\beta - \alpha)$$

and the incremental gain condition (6.67) (which is sufficient for L_2^n-stability of the feedback system (6.59)) simplifies to

$$\tfrac{1}{2}(\beta - \alpha) \, \|(I + \tfrac{1}{2}(\alpha + \beta)F)^{-1}F\|_2 < 1$$

The above norm condition is readily evaluated through (6.67), since the operator $(I + \tfrac{1}{2}(\alpha + \beta)F)^{-1}F$ is also a normal operator.

For a graphical interpretation of the incremental gain theorem, consider the following structured feedback system

$$y = F(u - GN(y)) \quad \text{for} \quad u \in L_2^n \tag{6.68}$$

where N is a nonlinear memoryless Lipschitz continuous map of L_2^n into itself such that there exist numbers α_i, β_i satisfying

$$\alpha_i(y_i - y_i') \leq N(y)_i - N(y')_i \leq \beta_i(y_i - y_i') \tag{6.69}$$

for all $y, y' \in L_2^n$ and $i = 1, 2, \ldots, n$. G is a linear time-invariant operator of L_2^n into itself and as such is representable by a matrix transfer function $\hat{G}(s) \in K(0)^{n \times n}$. F is a linear time-invariant mapping of L_{2e}^n into L_{2e}^n, characterized by a matrix transfer function $\hat{F}(s)$ such that each element $\hat{f}_{ij}(s)$ is a meromorphic function in the half-plane $Re(s) > 0$ and satisfies the condition $\lim_{|s| \to \infty} \hat{f}_{ij}(s) = 0$.

By approximating the linear operator FG by a normal operator ϕ and the nonlinear operator N by some $N_0 \in R^{n \times n}$ and by applying the loop transformation theorem to (6.68)

$$y = -(I + \phi N_0)^{-1}(FG - \phi)N(y) - (I + \phi N_0)^{-1}\phi(N - N_0)(y)$$
$$+ (I + \phi N_0)^{-1}Fu \tag{6.70}$$

Applying the contraction mapping theorem to (6.70) shows that for $u \in L_2^n$, the solution $y \in L_2^n$ is unique and continuously dependent upon t if the linear operators $(I + \phi N_0)^{-1}\phi$, $(I + \phi N_0)^{-1}(FG - \phi)$ and $(I + \phi N_0)^{-1}F$ are all elements of $K(0)^{n \times n}$ (that is, they are L_2^n stable operators) and

$$(1 - K(\phi))^{-1} \, \|(I + \phi N_0)^{-1}\phi(N - N_0)\| < 1 \tag{6.71}$$

Where $K(\phi) = \|(I + \phi N_0)^{-1}(FG - \phi)\| \cdot \|N\|$ is the error of approximation of FG by ϕ and must be less than unity for (6.71) to hold. The effective loop gain condition (6.71) can be minimized by appropriate selection of N_0 as diag (c_i). And so

$$\|N - N_0\| \leq \max_i \{|\alpha_i - c_i|, |\beta_i - c_i|\}$$

By selecting $c_i = \frac{1}{2}(\alpha_i + \beta_i)$ $(i = 1, 2, \ldots, n)$, the norm $\|N - N_0\|$ is minimized to $\max_i \frac{1}{2}(\beta_i - \alpha_i)$. When $\alpha_i = \alpha$ and $\beta_i = \beta$ for all i, we have the same optimum choices of $N_0 = \frac{1}{2}(\alpha + \beta)I$, and $\|N - N_0\| = \frac{1}{2}(\beta - \alpha)$ as in the small gain and intermediate gain theorems.

Suppose that the scalars $\alpha \leq \min_i \alpha_i$, $\beta \geq \max_i \beta_i$, then the stability condition (6.71) can be rewritten as

$$\sup_{\omega \in R} \max_{\lambda \in \sigma[\hat{\phi}(j\omega)]} \frac{1}{2} \left| \frac{\lambda}{(1 + c\lambda)} \right| (\beta - \alpha) < 1 - K(\phi) \tag{6.72}$$

This has the same graphical interpretation as inequality (6.56) for the intermediate gain theorem, and by similar reasoning we are able to state:

THEOREM 6.12 *Consider the feedback system* $y = F(u - GN(y))$, *where* $N : L_2^n \to L_2^n$ *is Lipschitz continuous such that*

$$\alpha_i(y_i - y_i') \leq N(y)_i - N(y')_i \leq \beta_i(y_i - y_i')$$

for all y, $y' \in L_2^n$ *and* $i = 1, 2, \ldots, n$. $G : L_2^n \to L_2^n$ *is linear time invariant operator with matrix transfer function* $\hat{G}(s) \in K(0)^{n \times n}$, *and* $F : L_{2e}^n \to L_{2e}^n$ *is a linear time-invariant operator with matrix transfer function* $\hat{F}(s) = \{\hat{f}_{ij}(s)\}$ *which is meromorphic in* $Re(s) > 0$ *with* $\lim_{|s| \to \infty} \hat{f}_{ij}(s) = 0$.

Then the solution $y \in L_2^n$ *is unique and continuously dependent upon t if* $u \in L_2^n$ *and there exists a normal operator* ϕ *that approximates FG such that*

(a) $\hat{F}(s)$ *is stable and* (i) *if* $\beta(\phi)$ *and* $\alpha(\phi)$ *are non-zero and have the same sign, the eigenloci* $\lambda_i(\omega)$ *of* $\hat{\phi}(j\omega)$ *do not encircle or intersect the circle* $C[-\beta(\phi)^{-1}, -\alpha(\phi)^{-1}]$, *or* (ii) *if* $\beta(\phi) > 0 > \alpha(\phi)$, *the plots of* $\lambda_i(\omega)$ *lie inside the circle* $C[-\beta(\phi)^{-1}, -\alpha(\phi)^{-1}]$.

or

(b) $\hat{F}(s)$ *has p-poles in* $Re(s) > 0$, *and* $\beta(\phi)$ *and* $\alpha(\phi)$ *have the same sign and are non-zero, the eigenloci* $\lambda_i(\omega)$ *of* $\hat{\phi}(j\omega)$ *do not intersect the circle* $C[-\beta(\phi)^{-1}, -\alpha(\phi)^{-1}]$ *and encircle this circle in the clockwise direction* $(n \times p)$ *times where*

$$\alpha(\phi) = \frac{1}{2}(\alpha + \beta) - \frac{1}{2}(\alpha - \beta)(1 - K(\phi))^{-1}$$
$$\beta(\phi) = \frac{1}{2}(\alpha + \beta) + \frac{1}{2}(\alpha - \beta)(1 - K(\phi))^{-1}$$

$$\alpha = \min_i \alpha_i, \quad \beta = \max_i \beta_i, \quad K(\phi) = \|(I + \phi N_0)^{-1}(FG - \phi)\| . \|N\| \quad and$$
$$N_0 = \tfrac{1}{2}(\alpha + \beta)I.$$

An obvious practical restriction of this Nyquist type result is that it requires the computation of the eigenvalues of the normal operator $\hat{\phi}(j\omega)$. However, when $\hat{\phi}(j\omega)$ is diagonal, take $N_0 = \mathrm{diag}\,(c_i)$, $c_i = \tfrac{1}{2}(\alpha_i + \beta_i)$ and condition (6.71) can be written as

$$\sup_{\omega \in R} \max_i \frac{1}{2} \left| \frac{\hat{\phi}_{ii}(j\omega)}{1 + c_i \hat{\phi}_{ii}(j\omega)} \right| (\beta_i(\phi) - \alpha_i(\phi)) < 1 \qquad (6.73)$$

where

$$\alpha_i(\phi) = c_i - \frac{1}{2} \frac{(\beta_i - \alpha_i)}{(1 - K(\phi))}$$

$$\beta_i(\phi) = c_i + \frac{1}{2} \frac{(\beta_i - \alpha_i)}{(1 - K(\phi))}$$

and

$$\phi = \mathrm{diag}\,(\phi_{ii})$$

This is satisfied if the Nyquist plots of $\hat{\phi}_{ii}(j\omega)^{-1}$ are exterior to the circle $C[-\beta_i(\phi), -\alpha_i(\phi)]$ and hence generates an alternative graphical stability interpretation of Theorem 6.12 directly in terms of the elements of $\hat{\phi}(j\omega)$.

An alternative approach which directly uses the elements $\hat{\phi}_{ij}(j\omega)$ of $\hat{\phi}(j\omega)$ and avoids the requirement that ϕ be diagonal is based upon Gershgorin's theorem. It is well known that the union of the Gershgorin circles with centres $\rho_{ii}(j\omega)$ and radius

$$r_i(\omega) = \sum_{k \neq i}^{n} |\rho_{ik}(j\omega)| \quad or \quad \sum_{k \neq i}^{n} |\rho_{ki}(j\omega)|$$

or

$$\sum_{k \neq i}^{n} \tfrac{1}{2}(|\rho_{ik}(j\omega)| + |\rho_{ki}(j\omega)|)$$

contains the ith eigenvalue of the matrix $\Gamma(j\omega) = \{\rho_{kr}(j\omega)\}$ for $i = 1, 2, \ldots, n$. So if $\hat{\phi}_{ij}(j\omega)$ are the generic elements of the matrix transfer function $\hat{\phi}(j\omega)$, then the sufficient conditions for L_2^n stability of the feedback system (6.68) have the following alternative graphical interpretation: if the envelopes of all circles with centres $\hat{\phi}_{ii}(j\omega)$ and radii $r_i(\omega)$ do not encircle or intersect the circle $C[-\beta(\phi)^{-1}, -\alpha(\phi)^{-1}]$ for $\beta(\phi) \geq \alpha(\phi) > 0$ or lie inside $C[-\beta(\phi)^{-1}, -\alpha(\phi)^{-1}]$ if $\beta(\phi) > 0 > \alpha(\phi)$ for $\hat{F}(s)$ stable. If, however, $\hat{F}(s)$ has p-right-half poles, then the feedback system (6.68) is stable if $\beta(\phi) > \alpha(\phi) > 0$ and the Gershgorin circles $\hat{\phi}(j\omega)$ do not intersect the circle $C[-\beta(\phi)^{-1}, -\alpha(\phi)^{-1}]$ but encircle it in the clockwise direction $(n \times p)$ times (see Fig. 6.4).

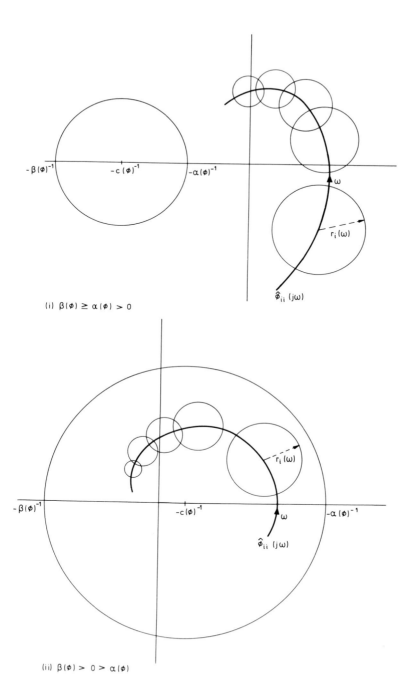

(i) $\beta(\phi) \geq \alpha(\phi) > 0$

(ii) $\beta(\phi) > 0 > \alpha(\phi)$

FIG. 6.4 L_2^n-stability criterion for non-normal operators using Gershgorin's theorem. (i) $\beta(\phi) \geq \alpha(\phi) > 0$ (ii) $\beta(\phi) > 0 > \alpha(\phi)$

199

Returning to the stability condition (6.73) for the case when $\hat{\phi}(j\omega) =$ diag $\{\phi_{ii}(j\omega)\}$ and $N_0 = $ diag $\{c_i\}$, $c_i = \frac{1}{2}(\alpha_i + \beta_i)$, this sufficient stability condition can be rewritten as

$$\sup_{\omega \in R} \max_i \left| \frac{c_i \hat{\phi}_{ii}(\omega)}{(1 + c_i \hat{\phi}_{ii}(\omega))} \right| \frac{R_i}{|c_i|} < 1 \qquad (6.74)$$

where $R_i = \frac{1}{2}(\beta_i - \alpha_i)(1 - K(\phi))^{-1}$. If now the Nyquist plots of $\hat{\phi}_{ii}(j\omega)$ are replaced by plots of $c_i \hat{\phi}_{ii}(j\omega)$, then the critical circle for the plot of $c_i \hat{\phi}_{ii}(\omega)$ is $C[-c_i\beta_i^{-1}, -c_i\alpha_i^{-1}]$. This latter circle is called an M-stability circle with M-value of

$$M_i = c_i R_i^{-1} = \frac{(\alpha_i + \beta_i)}{(\beta_i - \alpha_i)}(1 - K(\phi))^{-1}$$

From the plot of $c_i \hat{\phi}_{ii}(j\omega)$, a value of $M_p(c_i\phi_{ii})$ can be determined that corresponds to a maximum value of M (Fig. 6.5), and so the stability inequality (6.74) can be rewritten as

$$\max_i M_p(c_i\phi_{ii})M_i^{-1} < 1 \qquad (6.75)$$

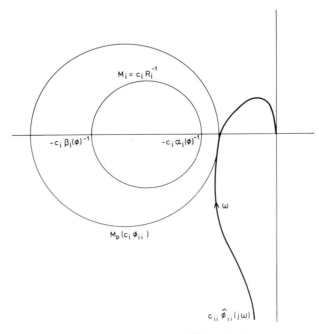

FIG. 6.5 M circle stability criterion

which is the familiar M-circle stability criteria. The parameter

$$\theta = \left(1 - \max_i M_p(c_i\phi_{ii})M_i^{-1}\right)^{-1}$$

can be considered as the effective gain margin of the feedback system (6.68).

The effect of plant or output disturbances η upon the feedback system

$$y = F(u - GN(y)) + \eta \qquad (6.76)$$

by setting $u \equiv 0$, since now $\|y\|$ is a measure of the sensitivity of the feedback system to disturbances. By application of the loop transformation theorem to (6.76) with $u = 0$, $N_0 = \text{diag } c_i$, $\phi = \text{diag } \phi_{ii}$

$$y = (I + \phi N_0)^{-1}\eta - [(I + \phi N_0)^{-1}(FG - \phi)N + (I + \phi N_0)^{-1}\phi(N - N_0)(y)]$$

provided that

$$\|(I + \phi N_0)^{-1}(FG - \phi)\| \cdot \|N\| + \|(I + \phi N_0)^{-1}\phi(N - N_0)\| < 1$$

the contraction mapping theorem gives

$$\|y\| < \frac{\|(I + \phi N_0)^{-1}\eta\| (1 - K(\phi))^{-1}}{1 - (1 - K(\phi))^{-1}\|(I + \phi N_0)^{-1}\phi(N - N_0)\|}$$

$$= \theta(1 - K(\phi))^{-1} \|(I + \phi N_0)^{-1}\eta\| \qquad (6.77)$$

If the disturbance n-vector $\eta = \{\eta_i\}$ has independent elements with known power spectral density then

$$\|y\| < \theta(1 - K(\phi))^{-1}\left\{\sum_{i=1}^{n} \frac{1}{2\pi} \int_{-\infty}^{\infty} \frac{|\hat{\eta}_i(j\omega)|^2}{|1 + c_i\hat{\phi}_{ii}(j\omega)|^2} d\omega\right\}^{1/2} \qquad (6.78)$$

Clearly for disturbance rejection or minimum system sensitivity, it is desirable that the Nyquist plots $c_i\hat{\phi}_{ii}(j\omega)$ are set as far as possible from $(-1, 0)$. For practical evaluation it is necessary to know those η_i which are important and the bandwidth of significant frequencies.

In the control system design the linear operator FG usually contains some free design elements. A possible design strategy might be: (i) consider the initial FG from the class of operators that ensure a well-posed system with approximation normal operator ϕ_0 equal to, say, $\text{diag }(FG)$; (ii) compute $K(\phi_0)$ and then test closed-loop stability via the circle criterion; (iii) from the graphical stability criterion design for a new ϕ_1 and larger gain margin θ; (iv) for this new value of ϕ_1 change the free elements of FG to an operator closer to ϕ_1 and repeat process iteratively until $\|y\| < \xi$, some prescribed error criterion.

It has been assumed throughout that the plant dynamics are known exactly. This is rarely the case in practical systems, and feedback is incorporated not just to improve stability but also to reduce system sensitivity either to parametric variability or to external disturbances. The design objective in this case is to evaluate a compensator in the feedback loop which guaranteed that output performance specifications are satisfied over the range of plant uncertainty or set of disturbances.

Consider the feedback system

$$y = F(u - GN(y)), \qquad u \in L_p^n$$

By considering the feedback signal $z = GN(y)$ to the *comparator* this dynamical system can be equally expressed as

$$z = FGN(u - z) \tag{6.79}$$

Assume that F, G, N are continuous operators from L_{pe}^n to L_{pe}^n.

The operators, F, G, and N are assumed to be Lipschitz continuous and operator $F_\lambda = [f_{ij}(\lambda)]$, with parameter vector λ, known only to belong to a set Λ; the problem is to select feedback operators GN (or G and N separately) so that the system response is contained within the set of desired responses Z (assumed known *a priori*) irrespective of the values of $\lambda \in \Lambda$.

Provided that $(I + FGN)^{-1} : L_{pe}^n \to L_{pe}^n$, then (6.79) can be rewritten as

$$z = (I + F_\lambda GN)^{-1} F_\lambda GN u$$
$$\equiv T_\lambda u, \, u \in L_p^n \tag{6.80}$$

Since Z is known *a priori* the closed loop operator T_λ can be defined to belong to a desired set $V(\lambda, z)$ of stable operators dependent upon the parameter set Λ and Z.

Set $P = GN$ and

$$L_\lambda = F_\lambda P = F_\lambda F_0^{-1} F_0 P = F_\lambda F_0^{-1} L_0$$

where F_0 is arbitrary and invertible. The problem is now given some $F_0 \in F_\lambda$ find $P = GN = L_0 F_0^{-1}$ that satisfies (6.80) for any $z \in Z$. Define $Q_\lambda = F_0^{-1} F_\lambda$ then

$$T_\lambda = (I + Q_\lambda L_0)^{-1} Q_\lambda L_0$$
$$= (I - (L_0^{-1} + Q_\lambda)^{-1} L_0^{-1}) \tag{6.81}$$

Given some initial L_0^0, (6.81) gives T_0^0, we now select L_0^i such that $\lim_i T_0^i = T_0 \subset V$, and hence the required L_0 can be established. Equation (6.81) can be written as an iterative equation

$$T_0^n = [I - ((L_0^{n-1})^{-1} + Q_\lambda)^{-1} (L_0^n)^{-1}][I + (L_0^{n-1})^{-1}] T_0^0$$
$$= (I - A^{n-1} (L_0^n)^{-1}) B^{n-1} T_0^0 \quad \text{for} \quad n = 1, 2, \ldots \tag{6.82}$$

where $A^{n-1} = [(L_0^{n-1})^{-1} + Q_\lambda]^{-1}$ and $B^{n-1} = I + (L_0^{n-1})^{-1}$ with $L_0^{-1} = 0$. The convergence of this algorithm can be proven in two cases.

(i) V is a compact set. By assumption $(I + F_\lambda GN)^{-1}$ exists and F_λ, G, N, $(I + F_\lambda GN)^{-1}$ are operators mapping $L_{pe}^n \to L_{pe}^n$ for all $\lambda \in \Lambda$, then $T_\lambda : L_{pe}^n \to L_{pe}^n$ for all $\lambda \in \Lambda$. The algorithm requires that $\{T_\lambda^n\} \subset V$, but V is compact so the sequence $\{T_\lambda^n\}$ is also compact. Therefore by the Arzela-Ascoli theorem $\{T_\lambda^n\}$ is a convergent sequence. The limit T_0 generates the transmission operator L_0, which in turn provides the compensator solution $GN = L_0 F_0^{-1}$.

(ii) V is a bounded set. Select L_0^n such that the sequence $\{T_\lambda^n\}$ is monotone in the following sense: let $\{V_i\}$ be a sequence of closed spheres in the space L_{pe}^n such that $V \supset V_1 \supset V_2 \ldots \supset V_n \ldots$ and $T_\lambda^{n+1} \notin V_n$ and $T_\lambda^{n+1} \in V_{n+1}$ with $T_\lambda' \in S$. Then by the nested sphere theorem, the sequence $\{T_\lambda^n\}$ converges to T_0.

It has been assumed throughout that the operator T_λ is L_p^n-stable. This can be tested for $p = 2$ via the previous circle criterion for a given N. The above proofs also hold for time-varying operators, provided they are continuous with respect to the time argument.

6.5 AN M-MATRIX STABILITY CRITERION

For feedback systems with a particular algebraic structure the following graphical stability criterion based upon the properties of M-matrices may succeed when previous criteria prove unsuccessful.

Consider an arbitrary n vector $x = \{x_i\} \in L_2^n$ with norm

$$\|x\|_1 = \max_i \{\|x_i\|_{L_2}\} = \max_i \left\{ \int_{-\infty}^{\infty} x_i^2(t)\, dt \right\}^{1/2}$$

In the previous graphical L_2^n-stability studies the norm

$$\|x\|_2 = \left\{ \sum_{i=1}^{n} \|x_i\|_{L_2}^2 \right\}^{1/2}$$

has been used. But since $\|x\|_1 \le \|x\|_2 \le n^{1/2} \|x\|_1$, then the above two norms are equivalent and define the same topology in L_2^n and L_2^n-stability by one norm implies L_2^n-stability by the other.

For any $x \in L_2^n$, let $\tilde{x} \in R_+^n$ be the vector whose ith element is $\|x_i\|_{L_2}$. Similarly for $x \in L_{2e}^n$, $\tilde{x}_T \in R_+^n$ denotes the vector whose ith element is $\|P_T x_i\|_{L_2}$, for P_T a truncation operator.

Let $B(L_2^n, L_2^n)$ represent the space of all Lipschitz continuous operators $F : L_2^n \to L_2^n$ satisfying the unbiased condition $F(0) = 0$; the Lipschitz norm on this space is a norm in the usual sense. Let $B_c(L_2^n, L_2^n) \subset B(L_2^n, L_2^n)$ be the space formed with all causal operators F whose entries are elements of $B_c(L_2, L_2)$. For a Lipschitz continuous operator $F: L_2^n \to L_2^n$, represented by a matrix $\{f_{ij}\}$ of causal Lipschitz continuous mappings $f_{ij}: L_2 \to L_2$, let $\tilde{F} = \{\|f_{ij}\|_1\} \in R_+^{n \times n}$. Similarly if $F: L_{2e}^n \to L_{2e}^n$ is a causal mapping such that for $T \geq 0$, $P_T F: L_2^n[0, T] \to L_2^n[0, T]$ is a Lipschitz continuous operator then $\tilde{F}_T = \{\|P_T f_{ij}\|_1\} \in R_+^{n \times n}$, and for any $T' > T$, $\tilde{F}_{T'} \geq \tilde{F}_T$ and $\lim_{T \to \infty} \tilde{F}_T \leq \tilde{F}$.

Consider now the feedback system

$$y = -Fy + u \qquad (6.83)$$

with $F \in B_c(L_2^n, L_2^n)$. If F is well posed for each $u \in L_{2e}^n$, then there exists a unique solution $y \in L_{2e}^n$ to the feedback system (6.83). Moreover, since F is causal

$$P_T y_i = \sum_{j=1}^{n} (P_T f_{ij})(P_T y_j) + P_T u_i, \qquad \forall T \geq 0$$

for $i = 1, 2, \ldots, n$. Taking $\|.\|_1$ norms of the above gives

$$\tilde{y}_T \leq \tilde{F}_T \tilde{y}_T + \tilde{u}_T \qquad (6.84)$$

If the spectral radius $r_\sigma(F) = \sup_{\lambda \in \sigma(F)} |\lambda|$ of the operator F is such that $r_\sigma(F) < 1$, then because $\tilde{F} > \tilde{F}_T$, $r_\sigma(\tilde{F}_T) < r_\sigma(\tilde{F}) < 1$ and so $(I - \tilde{F}_T)^{-1} \in R_+^{n \times n}$, and inequality (6.84) becomes

$$\tilde{y}_T \leq (I - \tilde{F}_T)^{-1} \tilde{u}_T$$

But $(I - \tilde{F}_T)^{-1} \leq (I - \tilde{F})^{-1}$, since $r_\sigma(\tilde{F}_T) < r_\sigma(\tilde{F}) < 1$ and $\tilde{F}_T$, $\tilde{F} \in R_+^{n \times n}$. So if $u \in L_2^n$ then

$$\tilde{y}_T \leq (I - \tilde{F})^{-1} \tilde{u}, \qquad \forall T \geq 0$$

and $y \in L_2^n$. We have now established the fundamental L_2^n-stability result:

THEOREM 6.13   *Given that the feedback system $y = -Fy + u$ with $F \in B_c(L_2^n, L_2^n)$ is well posed and $u \in L_2^n$, then if $r_\sigma(\tilde{F}) < 1$ there exists a unique solution $y \in L_2^n$.*

The condition $r_\sigma(F) < 1$ is equivalent to the condition on the matrix $M = \{m_{ij}\} = (I - F) \in R^{n \times n}$, that each $m_{ij} \leq 0$ for $i \neq j$ and $M^{-1} \in R_+^{n \times n}$ or equivalently every principle minor of M is positive non-zero (that is, M is an M-matrix—a generalization of the Minkowski matrix).

Again consider the structured feedback system

$$y = F(u - GN(y)), \, u \in L_2^n \qquad (6.85)$$

where N is a memoryless Lipschitz continuous map of L_2^n into itself such that there are numbers α_i, β_i $(i = 1, 2, \ldots, n)$ which satisfy

$$\alpha_i(y_i - y_i') \leq N(y)_i - N(y')_i \leq \beta_i(y_i - y_i')$$

for all y, $y' \in L_2^n$; $G : L_2^n \to L_2^n$ is a linear time-invariant operator represented by a matrix transfer function $\hat{G}(s) \in K(0)^{n \times n}$, $F : L_{2e}^n \to L_{2e}^n$ is a linear time-invariant operator with matrix transfer function $\hat{F}(s)$ such that each $\hat{f}(s)_{ij}$ are meromorphic functions in $Re(s) > 0$ and $\lim_{|s| \to \infty} \hat{f}(s)_{ij} = 0$.

For some arbitrary matrix $N_0 \in R^{n \times n}$, the loop transformation theorem 6.1 allows the feedback system (6.85) to be written as

$$y = (I + \phi N_0)^{-1} Fu - (I + \phi N_0)^{-1}(FG - \phi)N(y) - (I + \phi N_0)^{-1}\phi(N - N_0)(y) \tag{6.86}$$

provided that $(I + \phi N_0)^{-1}F$, $(I + \phi N_0)^{-1}\phi \in K(0)^{n \times n}$. In this case the variable

$$v = (I + \phi N_0)^{-1} \qquad Fu \in L_2^n$$

if $u \in L_2^n$. So (6.86) can be rewritten as

$$y = v - VN(y) - UN_1(y) \tag{6.87}$$

where $V = (I + \phi N_0)^{-1}(FG - \phi)$, $U = (I + \phi N_0)^{-1}\phi$ and $N_1(y) = N(y) - N_0 y$.

Consider first the situation $\alpha_i \geq \alpha$, and $\beta \geq \beta_i$ for all i and FG a normal operator such that $\phi = FG$ and hence $V = 0$. In this case $N_0 = \frac{1}{2}(\alpha + \beta)I$, and utilizing the $\|.\|_1$ norm equation, (6.87) becomes

$$\tilde{y} \leq \tilde{v} + \widetilde{UN}_1 \tilde{y} \tag{6.88}$$

$\widetilde{UN}_1$ is bounded by

$$[\widetilde{UN}_1]_{ij} \leq \|U_{ij}\| \frac{(\beta - \alpha)}{2}$$

$$= \sup_{\omega \in R} |\hat{U}_{ij}(j\omega)| \frac{(\beta - \alpha)}{2} \triangleq Q_{ij} \tag{6.89}$$

where $\hat{U}(j\omega) = (I + \frac{1}{2}(\alpha + \beta) \widehat{FG}(j\omega))^{-1}\widehat{FG}(j\omega)$. Clearly each Q_{ij} is positive and $Q = \{Q_{ij}\} \in R_+^{n \times n}$. Hence

$$\tilde{y}(I - Q) \leq \tilde{v}$$

and by Theorem 6.13, provided that $r_\sigma(Q) < 1$ and $v \in L_2^n$, the solution y to (6.85) is unique and $y \in L_2^n$. Under these conditions:

THEOREM 6.14   *The feedback system $y = F(u - GN(y))$ is L_2^n-stable with a* unique solution $y \in L_2^n$, if $u \in L_2^n$, FG is a normal operator, $U = (I + \frac{1}{2}(\alpha + \beta)FG)^{-1}FG \in K(0)^{n \times n}$ and $r_\sigma(Q) < 1$ (or equivalently $(I - Q)$ is an M-matrix) where

$$Q = \{Q_{ij}\} = \left\{ \sup_{\omega \in R} \frac{1}{2} |\hat{U}_{ij}(j\omega)| (\beta - \alpha) \right\}$$

The requirement that FG is a normal operator is clearly restrictive for practical considerations; suppose now that the normal approximation operator is set equal to diag (FG) and $N_0 = $ diag (c_i) where $c_i = \frac{1}{2}(\alpha_i + \beta_i)$, minimizes the norm $\|N - N_0\|$. In this case

$$\|UN_1(y)\|_{ij} \le \frac{1}{2} \|U_{ij}\| (\beta_i - \alpha_i) \tilde{y}_i \triangleq P_{ij} \tilde{y}_j$$

where $P_{ii} = \sup_{\omega \in R} \frac{1}{2} |\hat{L}_{ii}(j\omega)| (|1 + c_i \hat{L}_{ii}(j\omega)|)^{-1}(\beta_i - \alpha_i)$ for $i = j$ and $P_{ij} = 0$ for $i \ne j$, i, $j = 1, 2, \ldots, n$, and $L_{ij} \triangleq \{FG\}_{ij}$. And so for the choice $\phi = $ diag (FG)

$$\widetilde{UN}_1(y) \le P\tilde{y} \tag{6.90}$$

where $P = $ diag $(P_{ii}) \in R_+^{n \times n}$.
   Similarly

$$\|VN(y)\|_{ij} \le \|V_{ij}\| \max_i \{|\beta_i|, |\alpha_i|\} \tilde{y}_j$$

$$\triangleq Q_{ij} \tilde{y}_j$$

where $Q_{ij} \triangleq \sup_{\omega \in R} |\hat{L}_{ij}(j\omega)| \cdot (|1 + c_i \hat{L}_{ii}(j\omega)|)^{-1} \max \{|\beta_i|, |\alpha_i|\}$ for $i \ne j$, i, $j = 1, 2, \ldots, n$, and $Q_{ii} = 0$ for all $i = j$. Clearly

$$\widetilde{VN}(y) \le Q\tilde{y} \tag{6.91}$$

where $Q = \{Q_{ij}\} \in R^{n \times n}$.
   Taking $\|.\|_1$ norms of (6.87) and utilizing inequalities (6.90) and (6.91) gives

$$\tilde{y}(I - Q - P) \le \tilde{V} \tag{6.92}$$

Suppose that $r_\sigma(Q + P) < 1$. Then $(I - Q - P)$ is an M-matrix and therefore $(I - Q - P) \in R_+^{n \times n}$ and inequality (6.92) can be rewritten as

$$\tilde{y} \le (I - Q - P)^{-1} \tilde{V} \tag{6.93}$$

and by Theorem (6.13) $\tilde{y} \in L_2^n$ if $\tilde{v} \in L_2^n$. Under the above conditions:

THEOREM 6.15   *The feedback system $y = F(u - GN(y))$ is L_2^n-stable with a unique solution $y \in L_2^n$ if $(I + \phi N_0)^{-1}\phi \in K(0)^{n \times n}$, $\phi = $ diag (FG) and $N_0 = $ diag $(\frac{1}{2}(\alpha_i + \beta_i))$ and $r_\sigma(S) < 1$ or equivalently $(I - S)$ is an M-matrix where $s_{ii} = P_{ii}$ for $i = j$ and $s_{ij} = Q_{ij}$ for $i \ne j$.*

The above stability result has a simple graphical interpretation if Gershgorin's theorem is invoked. The feedback system $y = F(u - GN(y))$ is L_2^n stable if the envelope of Gershgorin circles of radii

$$(\beta_i - \alpha_i)^{-1} \max\{|\beta_i|, |\alpha_i|\} \sum_{\substack{j=1 \\ j \neq 1}}^{n} |\widehat{FG}(j\omega)|_{ij}$$

centred on the Nyquist plot of $\{FG(j\omega)\}_{ii}$ do not encircle or intersect the circle $C[-\beta_i, -\alpha_i]$, for $i = 1, 2, \ldots, n$.

A necessary condition for the establishment of the M-matrix theorem 6.13 was that $(I + \phi N_0)^{-1}\phi \in K(0)^{n \times n}$; if the operator $\phi = \text{diag}(FG)$ is stable, then this condition is equivalent to requiring the L_2^n-stability of the linear system

$$y = \phi(u - N_0 y)$$

But since $N_0 = \text{diag}(c_i)$, the condition

$$(I + \phi N_0)^{-1}\phi \in K(0)^{n \times n} \tag{6.94}$$

is satisfied if the Nyquist plot of $\{\widehat{FG}(j\omega)\}_{ii}^{-1}$ does not encircle the point $-c_i$. But since the point $-c_i$ is contained within the circle $C[-\beta_i, -\alpha_i]$, condition (6.94) is automatically satisfied by the above M-matrix graphical interpretation via Gershgorin's theorem.

Suppose now that F contains p poles in the right half s-plane and admits the representation $\hat{F}(s) = \hat{F}_0(s)\hat{d}^{-1}(s)$ where $\hat{d}(s)$ is a monic polynomial with p zero in the right-half s-plane and $\hat{F}_0(s)$ is a matrix transfer function which is analytic in the right-half s-plane. Under these conditions the multivariable Nyquist theorem enables us to state that condition (6.94) is satisfied if the Nyquist plot of $\{\widehat{FG}(j\omega)\}_{ii}^{-1}$ encircles the circle $C[-\beta_i, -\alpha_i]$ $(n \times p)$ times.

6.6 SYSTEM DIAGONALIZATION AND DESIGN

The use of input–output or frequency domain methods in the analysis and design of linear feedback systems represented by matrix transfer functions of rational polynomials in s is now well established (Harris and Owens, 1979; McFarlane, 1979). These apparently distinct linear multivariable design techniques have been essentially based upon the mechanism of generating a series of pseudo-scalar design problems. Although these approaches to multivariable design have a fundamentally different basis, a theoretical unit does exist through the use of permissible input–output transformations. The question now arises of whether such linear multivariable design methods be applied to the design of controllers or compensators for nonlinear multivariable feedback systems of the form

$$y = F(u - GN(y)), \qquad u \in L_2^n \tag{6.95}$$

where F, $G: L_2^n \to L_2^n$ are linear time-invariant operators with matrix transfer functions $\hat{F}(s)$, $\hat{G}(s) \in K(0)^{n \times n}$ and $N: L_2^n \to L_2^n$ is Lipschitz continuous such that

$$\alpha_i(y_i - y_i') \le N(y)_i - N(y')_i \le \beta_i(y_i - y_i') \tag{6.96}$$

Furthermore we assume that the open-loop transfer function $\hat{F}(s)$ can be decomposed as $\hat{F}(s) = \hat{F}_1(s)\hat{K}(s)$ where $\hat{K}(s) \in K(0)^{n \times n}$ is the forward system controller or compensator that is to be designed in order to achieve closed loop stability and adequate system dynamic behaviour. All of the graphical stability criteria introduced in this chapter are readily implemented if the loop transfer function is diagonally dominant; in addition essentially scalar control or compensation design methods are appropriate. We therefore seek transformation methods that achieve diagonal dominance over the operating bandwidth of the system (6.95).

Introduce the transformation $\hat{F}_1(s) \mapsto \hat{F}_2(s)$ where $\hat{F}_1(s) = P_1\hat{F}_2(s)P_2$; for P_1 and P_2 square non-singular matrices such that $\hat{F}_2(s) = P_2^{-1}\hat{F}_1(s)P_1^{-1}$. Such transformations are introduced to achieve a form of diagonal dominance and compensation of $\hat{F}_1(s)$ while not introducing any new dynamics (other than desired control performance) into the feedback system. Special cases of this transformation are:

(i) Precompensation

The transformation pair (I_n, K^{-1}) where $K \in R^{n \times n}$ can be regarded as the map $\hat{F}_1(s) \mapsto \hat{F}_2(s)K$ and describes the methods of constant precompensation whereby the high frequency eigenvectors of the characteristic loci (Kouvaritakis, 1979) and the approximate commutative control (MacFarlane and Kouvaritakis, 1977) are realigned and the pseudo-diagonalization of $\hat{F}(s)$ associated with the Inverse Nyquist Array of Rosenbrock (1974).

Essentially the problem of precompensation is to find a $K \in R^{n \times n}$ such that at some frequency of interest $s = j\omega_1$

$$\hat{F}(j\omega_1) = \{f_{ij}(j\omega)\} \triangleq \hat{F}_1(j\omega_1)K \tag{6.97}$$

is diagonally dominant. We note that the ith column of $\hat{F}$ is determined by the ith column of K, and we can consider the independent choice of the n columns of K when attempting to satisfy

$$|f_{ii}| \geq \sum_{\substack{j=1 \\ j \neq i}}^{n} |f_{ji}| \left(\geq \sum_{\substack{j=1 \\ j \neq i}}^{n} |f_{ij}| \right) \tag{6.98}$$

for column (row) dominance for $i = 1, 2, \ldots, n$. Clearly we require

$$1 > \frac{\displaystyle\sum_{\substack{j=1 \\ j \neq i}}^{n} |f_{ji}|}{|f_{ii}|} \triangleq J_i^c(s) \quad \text{or} \quad 1 > \frac{\displaystyle\sum_{\substack{j=1 \\ j \neq i}}^{n} |f_{ij}|}{|f_{ii}|} = J_i^r(s)$$

for all i and s for diagonal dominance. Consequently the diagonal dominance of a complex matrix is essentially a min–max problem, that is, we seek the solution of

$$\min_{K} \max_{\omega \in \Delta\omega_b} J_i(j\omega)$$

where $\Delta\omega_b$ is the frequency bandwidth of interest.

One way of achieving diagonal dominance is via a *permutation* matrix $K_2 \in R^{n \times n}$ in which we seek to permute the row (column) of $\hat{F}_1(s)$ to obtain the best overall column (row) dominance of the resultant transfer function matrix. Each row permutation affects two column dominance (similarly for permutation upon row dominance), so what is required is the least possible maximum dominance measure via an appropriate permutation matrix. This method determines the dominance of the permuted matrix transfer function column by column (row by row) by solving

$$\min_{K_2} \max_{i} \left\{ \sum_{\substack{j=1 \\ j \neq i}}^{n} \{\hat{F}_1(s)K_2\}_{ij} \right\}, \qquad i = 1, 2, \ldots, n$$

In its simplest form K_2 is a matrix in which each row and column contains only a single entry of unity, all other entries being zero. The effect of permutation matrix K_2 is to renumber all inputs, essentially deciding on the optimum pairing of inputs and outputs of the compensated matrix transfer function to achieve dominance. Practical numerical algorithms for implementing various diagonal dominance schemes can be found in Bryant and Yeung (1981).

(ii) Pre- and post-compensation

Here it is usual for $P_1, P_2 \in R^{n \times n}$, although Rosenbrock (1974) has introduced a complex matrix $K(s) \in K(0)^{n \times n}$ in cascade with an elementary permutation matrix $K \in R^{n \times n}$ such that

$$K(s) = \prod_{r=1}^{n} K^{(r)}(s), \qquad K^{(r)}(s) = \begin{bmatrix} 1 & 0 & \cdots & & & 0 \\ 0 & 1 & & & & \cdot \\ \cdot & & 0 \cdots 1\alpha_{ij}^{(r)}(s)\, 0 \cdots 0 \\ \cdot & & & & & \cdot \\ \cdot & & & & & \cdot \\ 0 & & & & & 1 \end{bmatrix}$$

and $\det K(s) = 1$. That is, $K^{(r)}(s)$ is a unit diagonal matrix with the addition of a single entry $\alpha_{ij}^{(r)}(s) \in K(0)(i \neq j)$ which is a rational function. The matrix $K(s)$ has the effect of adding to column j of $\hat{F}_1(s)K$ a multiple of $\alpha_{ij}^{(r)}(s)$ of column i. This approach is particularly appropriate to the Inverse Nyquist Array design method.

(iii) Permissible matrices P_1, P_2

In their most general form $P_1, P_2 \in C^{n \times n}$ which must also be restricted to the class of non-singular realizable matrices for practical implementation. This complex pair (P_1, P_2) are restricted to the class of permissible matrices defined by

$$P_1 = (a_1, \ldots, a_n), \qquad P_2 = \begin{pmatrix} b_1^T \\ \vdots \\ \vdots \\ b_n^T \end{pmatrix}; \quad a_i, b_i \in C^n$$

where the columns (rows) of P_1, P_2 are real or exist in complex conjugate pairs and $b_j^* = b_{l(j)}$ whenever $a_j^* = a_{l(j)}$ for $1 \leq j \leq n$. (The map $j \mapsto l(j)$ is an isomorphic map of integers $(1, \ldots, n)$ onto itself by the structure of P_1 and so $l(l(j)) = j$ for $1 \leq j \leq n$).

It is straightforward to show for a permissible pair (P_1, P_2) that the matrix product $P_1 P_2$ is real and nonsingular and that the pairs (P_1, P_1^{-1}), (P_2^{-1}, P_2) and (P_2^{-1}, P_1^{-1}) are also permissible.

The power of permissible matrices in achieving diagonal dominance over a frequency interval is illustrated in the following theorem due to Owens (1981):

THEOREM 6.16   If $\det \hat{F}_1(j\omega_1) \neq 0$ and $\hat{F}_1(j\omega_1)\,\hat{F}_1(j\omega_1)^{-1}$ has a complete set of eigenvectors, then there exists a permissible pair (P_1, P_2) such that $\{\hat{F}_2(s) = P_2^{-1}\hat{F}_1(s)P_1^{-1}\}_{s=j\omega_1}$ is diagonal and diagonally dominant in an open frequency interval that contains ω_1.

The system (6.95) can be rewritten by utilizing the loop transformation theorem as

$$y = -(I + \phi N_0)^{-1}(FG - \phi)N(y) - (I + \phi N_0)^{-1}\phi(N - N_0)(y)$$
$$+ (I + \phi N_0)^{-1}Fu; \qquad \phi \in K(0)^{n \times n}, N_0 \in R^{n \times n}$$

Earlier stability studies (e.g. Theorem 6.8) indicated that closed-loop stability depended upon the linear operator $(I + \phi N_0)^{-1}\phi$ and hence the eigenvalue plots of $\hat{\phi}(j\omega)$ around some critical circle in the complex plane. Where ϕ is a normal approximation to FG and N_0 is selected such that $\|(N - N_0)(y)\|$ is minimized. It is straightforward to show that

$$(I + \phi N_0)^{-1}\phi = P_2^{-1}(I + \phi_1 N_0')^{-1}\phi_1 P_1^{-1}$$

and that $\det(I + \phi N_0) = \det(I + \phi_1' N_0')$ where $\phi' = P_2^{-1}\phi P_1^{-1}$, and $N_0' = P_2^{-1}N_0 P_1^{-1}$. These identities indicate that the permissible transformation (P_1, P_2) on $\hat{F}(s)$ is also a similarity transformation on the closed loop stability question.

For finite dimensional systems F_1' and K have rational polynomials as elements and for physical realizability these polynomials must have real coefficients. These realizability requirements hold for the permissible pair (P_1, P_2) if and only if

$$\{\hat{F}_2'^*(s)\}_{jk} \equiv \{\hat{F}_2'(s^*)\}_{l(j)l(k)}, \qquad \forall j, k \tag{6.99}$$
$$\{\hat{K}_1^*(s)\}_{jk} \equiv \{\hat{K}_1(s^*)\}_{l(j)l(k)}, \qquad \forall j, k \tag{6.100}$$

We note that the set of all transfer function matrices satisfying (6.99), (6.100) are closed under multiplication and inversion.

For approximate commutative control $(P_1, P_2) = (V_1^{-1}, W_1^{-1})$ so that $K(s) = W_1 \operatorname{diag}\{k_j(s)\}V_1$ and $\hat{K}_1(s) = P_2^{-1}KP_1^{-1} = \operatorname{diag}\{k_j(s)\}$ for $j = 1, 2, \ldots, n$. Where W_1 (respectively V_1) is a real approximation to the eigenvector (inverse eigenvector) of $\{\hat{F}_1'(s)\}_{s=j\omega_1}$.

The method of dyadic expansions (Harris and Owens, 1979) utilizes complex permissible transformations such that $\hat{F}_1'(s)$ is diagonal at some desired frequency ω_1 and diagonally dominant over a bandwidth that includes $s = j\omega_1$, and $\hat{K}_1(s) = \operatorname{diag}\{k_j(s)\}$.

To achieve adequate closed-loop control a controller transfer matrix $K_c(s)$ is usually placed in cascade with the diagonalization matrix K. $K_c(s)$ is selected as a non-singular diagonal matrix with all its singularities in $Re(s) < 0$ and so that each entry provides the appropriate independent loop control. Additionally the gain of each controller is adjusted to overcome the problem that dominance methods are not usually scale invariant and some preadjustment of each loop is necessary before control.

6.7 NOTES

The functional analysis approach in determining input–output stability is intuitively more appealing and general than the Lyapunov approach (Willems, 1970; La Salle and Lefeschetz, 1961; Venkatesh, 1977). It also serves to provide a unified approach to several different kinds of stability and yet provides solutions to problems that could have not been provided by any other means.

We have seen in Sections 6.1, 6.2 that the definition of input–output stability depends on the type of norm used and that different norms give rise to non-equivalent definitions. Moreover it is clear *a priori* that any of them will be equivalent to stability in the sense of Lyapunov with respect to a given state space representation of the system (Araki, 1978). It has, however, been shown by Willems (1969) that under fairly weak assumptions a certain type of input–output stability does ensure the existence of Lyapunov functions. In addition Willems has established the equivalence of L_2-stability and global asymptotic stability of state space representation for finite dimensional systems.

The study of input–output stability of nonlinear feedback systems was originated (Zames, 1966; Sandberg, 1964) as an alternative to Lyapunov's direct method. In this early work the now-classical circle stability criterion for nonlinear single input–single output systems was established (Holtzman, 1970; Narendra and Taylor, 1973). Sandberg (1964–1966) introduced the concept of extended spaces (see Chapter 5 for a detailed study) to establish the stability conditions for multivariable systems defined on the spaces L_2^n, L_p^n, and L_∞^n; unfortunately these conditions did not have a simple graphical interpretation. The first multivariable circle criterion was established by Falb *et al.* (1969) whereby the system

$$y = FN(e), \qquad e = y - u$$

with $N(\cdot) = \mathrm{diag}\{N_i(\cdot)\}$ is L_2^n-stable if all $N_i(e_i)$ are contained within the sector $S\{\alpha, \beta\}$, the linear element of the feedback system is normal for all frequencies and the eigenloci of $\hat{F}(s)$ do not encircle or intersect the on axis circle $C[-\alpha^{-1}, -\beta^{-1}]$. In 1973 Rosenbrock and Cook extended these results to the more general class of nonlinearities, $N_i(e_i) \in S\{\alpha_i, \beta_i\}$. However, Rosenbrock and Cook's results were dependent upon various types of diagonal dominance of the linear operator, so that a Gershgorin circle envelope centred along the Nyquist plots of diag $(\hat{F}(s))$ could be utilized rather than the computationally difficult eigenvalues in determining stability. These results were extended by Araki (1976), using more general sector conditions instead of the concept of positivity; further extension of these methods to include compact operators and slope restricted nonlinearities have been made by Mees (1976) and Cook (1976).

Mees and Rapp (1978) and Valenca and Harris (1979) independently extended the earlier work of Falb *et al.* (1969) for multivariable feedback systems to account for non-normal linear operators and more general types of nonlinearities; in these methods the linear operator is approximated by a normal operator such that the critical circle diameter in the Nyquist plane is dependent upon the norm of the error of approximation.

Similar results to those of Rosenbrock (1973) and Cook (1973) for multivariable feedback systems consisting of a linear composite operator and a diagonal operator can be obtained using M-matrices (Araki, 1976, Harris and Valenca, 1981) (See also Section 6.5.)

REFERENCES

Araki, M. (1976). "Input–output stability of composite feedback systems." *IEEE Trans* **AC-21**(3), 254–259.

Araki, M. (1978). "Stability of large scale nonlinear *systems*—quadratic order theory of composite systems method using M-matrices," *IEEE Trans* **AC-23,** 129–142.

Bryant, G. F. and Yeung, L. F. (1981). "Dominance optimisation in multivariable design." IEE Conf: "Control and its Applications", Pub. No. 194, 28–32.

Cook, P. A. (1973). "Modified multivariable circle theorems." *In* "Recent Mathematical Developments in Control" (Ed. D. J. Bell), 367–372, Academic Press, London and New York.

Cook, P. A. (1976). "Stability of systems containing slope restricted non-linearities." *In* "Recent Theoretical Developments in Control" (Ed. M. J. Gregson), 161–174. Academic Press, London and New York.

Cook, P. A. (1976). "Conditions for the absence of limit cycles." *IEEE Trans.* **AC-21**(4), 339–345.

Dunford, N. and Schwartz, J. T. (1957). "Linear Operators", Part I. Interscience, New York.

Falb, P. L., Freedman, M. I. and Zames, G. (1969). "Input/output stability – a general viewpoint". Proc. 4th IFAC Congress, Warsaw, **41,** 3–15.

Harris, C. J. and Owens, D. H. (1979). "Multivariable control systems." IEE Control and Science Record (*Proc IEE* **126**).

Harris, C. J. and Valenca, J. M. E. (1981). "A circle stability criterion for large scale systems." IEE Conf: "Control and its Applications", Pub. No. 194, 272–275.

Holtzman, J. M. (1970). "Nonlinear System Theory—a Functional Analysis Approach". Prentice Hall, Englewood Cliffs, New Jersey.

Kouvaritakis, B. (1979). "Theory and practice of the characteristic locus design method." *Proc. IEE* **126,** 542–548.

LaSalle, J. P. and Lefeschetz, S. (1961). "Stability by Lyapunov's direct method with applications". Academic Press, London and New York.

MacFarlane, A. G. J. (1979). "Frequency Response Methods in Control Systems". IEE Press, Wiley, New York.

Mees, A. I. (1976). "On using the circle criterion to predict existence of solutions". *In* "Recent Theoretical Developments in Control" (Ed. M. J. Gregson), 175–192. Academic Press, London and New York.

Mees, A. I. and Rapp, P. E. (1978). "Stability criteria for multiloop nonlinear feedback systems." 4th IFAC Symp. Multivariable Tech. Sys., Fredricton, Canada, 183–188. Pergamon Press, Oxford.

Narendra, K. S. and Taylor, J. H. (1973). "Frequency domain criteria for absolute stability". Academic Press, New York and London.

Owens, D. H. (1981). "Some unifying concepts in multivariable feedback design". *Int. J. Control* **33**, 701–711.

Rosenbrock, H. H. (1973). "Multivariable circle theorems", In "Recent Mathematical Developments in Control" (Ed. D. J. Bell), 345–365. Academic Press, New York and London.

Rosenbrock, H. H. (1974): "Computer-Aided Control System Design". Academic Press, London and New York.

Sandberg, I. W. (1964): "A frequency domain condition for the stability of feedback systems containing a single time varying nonlinearity." *Bell System. Tech. J.* **43**, 1601–1608.

Sandberg, I. W. (1964). "On the L_2 boundedness of solutions of nonlinear functional equations." *Bell Syst. Tech. J.* **43**, 1581–1599.

Sandberg, I. W. (1965). "Some results on the theory of physical systems governed by nonlinear functional equations." *Bell Syst. Tech. J.* **44**, 439–453.

Valenca, J. M. E. and Harris, C. J. (1979). "Stability criteria for nonlinear multivariable systems." *Proc IEE* **126**, 623–627.

Venkatesh, Y. V. (1977): "Energy methods in time varying systems stability and instability analyses", LNI Physics No. 68. Springer Verlag, Berlin.

Willems, J. C. (1969). "Stability, instability, invertibility and causality." *SIAM J. Control* **7**, 645–671.

Willems, J. L. (1970). "Stability Theory of Dynamical Systems." Nelson, London.

Zames, G. (1966). "On the input–output stability of time varying nonlinear feedback systems. Part I: Conditions derived using concepts of loop gain conicity and positivity". *IEEE Trans.* **AC11**(2), 228–238.

Zames, G. (1966). "On the input–output stability of time varying nonlinear feedback systems. Part II: Conditions involving circles in the frequency plane and sector nonlinearities". *IEEE Trans.* **AC11**(3), 465–475.

Chapter Seven

Stability of Nonlinear Multivariable Systems– Passivity Results

7.1 PASSIVITY STABILITY THEOREMS

The loop transformation theorem (6.1) results in a reduction in the stringent loop gain condition for closed-loop stability associated with the three small gain theorems of Chapter 6 (or equivalently, results in a shift in the conicity of the feedback and feedforward operators). This transformation technique can also result in a feedback system with passive operators so that the passivity theorem can be applied directly to determine closed loop stability. A second and significant transformation associated with the passivity theorem is the introduction of multipliers in cascade with the system loop operators (see Section 5.6). Usually the loop transformation theorem is used to ensure that the feedback operator is passive through a conicity transformation, and then a compensating multiplier is introduced to produce a passive operator in the feedforward operator without affecting the passivity of the feedback operator.

The three small gain theorems required a normed linear vector space structure; however, the passivity theorem (5.3) requires in addition an inner product space (which if complete is a Hilbert space HS). The passivity theorem showed that the feedback system $y = F(u - N(y))$ is stable for operators $N, F: HS_e \rightarrow HS_e$, if the operator F is strictly passive with finite gain and N is passive. If in addition the operators F and N are both unbiased and are respectively *strictly* incrementally passive and incrementally passive, then the solutions $e, y \in HS$ are unique and uniformly continuous on HS for $e = u - N(y)$.

Consider the class of feedback systems

$$y = F(u - N(y)), \qquad u \in L_2^n \qquad (7.1)$$

with $F: L_2^n \rightarrow L_2^n$ a linear time-invariant operator such that $Fu \triangleq F \otimes u$ for $F \in LA_-^{n \times n}$. Also the nonlinearity N is assumed to be both causal and

215

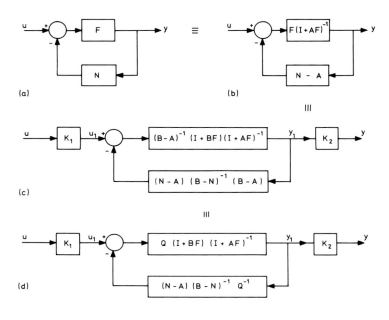

where $A = \alpha I$, $B = \beta I$, $K_2 = (B - N)^{-1} Q^{-1}$

and $K_1 = (I + AF)(I + BF)^{-1}(B - A)F(I + AF)^{-1}$

FIG. 7.1   Equivalent systems through loop transformations

anticausal, unbiased and incrementally sector bound by the inequality:

$$\langle N(x-y)-(\alpha+\xi)(x-y), N(x-y)-(\beta-\xi)(x-y)\rangle_T \le 0 \qquad (7.2)$$

for all $x, y \in L_{2e}^n$, $T \in R$ and α, β, ξ constant scalars such that $\xi > 0$, $\beta > \alpha$.
   Introduce the multiplier

$$Qu = Q \otimes u, \qquad \forall u \in L_2^n, \qquad Q \in LA_-^{n \times n} \qquad (7.3)$$

where

$$\hat{Q}(s) \triangleq \hat{\theta}(s)I, \qquad \hat{\theta}(s) = \prod_{k=0}^{r}(s+a_k)(s+b_k)^{-1}$$

and

$$b_k > a_k > 0 \quad \text{for all } k$$

The multiplier $\hat{\theta}(s)$ is defined such that its poles and zeros alternate along
the negative real axis and $|\arg \hat{\theta}(j\omega)| \le \pi/2$ and as such its inverse $\hat{\theta}^{-1}(s)$

(and $\hat{Q}^{-1}(s)$) exists. By repeated operation of the loop transformation theorem (6.1), and introduction of the multiplier Q, the feedback system (7.1) of Fig. 7.1(a) is equivalent to Fig. 7.1(d) (see Section 5.6 for system equivalence), and so from the passivity theorem (5.3) we have:

THEOREM 7.1: PASSIVITY THEOREM (MULTIPLIER)   *The feedback system* $y = F(u - N(y))$, $u \in L_2^n$ *is* L_2^n-*stable if*

$$\text{s(i)} \quad Q(I + BF)(I + AF)^{-1} \text{ is strictly passive}$$

$$\text{s(ii)} \quad F(I + AF)^{-1} \text{ and } (I + BF)^{-1} : L_2^n \to L_2^n$$

where $F \in LA_-^{n \times n}$ *is a convolution operator and* $N : R^n \to R^n$ *is a memory-less Lipschitz continuous nonlinearity with sector bounds given by* (7.2).

Proof   The passivity theorem demonstrates that the input–output system $u_1 \mapsto y_1$ of Fig. 7.1 is L_2^n stable if conditions s(i) and s(ii) hold and the feedback operator

$$\text{s(iii)} \quad (N - A)(B - N)^{-1}Q^{-1} \text{ is passive}$$

We now show that condition s(iii) is automatically satisfied by virtue of the sector constraint on $N(y)$ and by the existence of the inverse Q^{-1} in L_2^n.

Let $\psi \triangleq (N - A)(B - N)^{-1}$, by the sector inequality N and $(N - A)$ are incrementally inside the sectors $S\{\alpha + \xi, \beta - \xi\}$ and $S\{\xi, \beta - \alpha - \xi\}$ respectively. This implies that $(B - N)$ and $(B - N)^{-1}$ are strictly increasing inside the respective sectors $S\{\xi, \beta - \alpha - \xi\}$ and $S\{(\beta - \alpha - \xi)^{-1}, \xi^{-1}\}$. So ψ is incrementally inside the positive sector $S\{\xi(\beta - \alpha - \xi)^{-1}, \xi^{-1}(\beta - \alpha - \xi)\}$, or ψ is strictly incrementally passive.

An equivalent condition to condition s(iii) is

$$\langle \psi Q^{-1} x', x' \rangle \geq 0$$

or

$$\langle \psi x, Qx \rangle \geq 0, \qquad \forall x, x' \in L_2^n \tag{7.4}$$

Now, $\hat{Q}(s)$ can be expanded in partial fractions as

$$\hat{Q}(s) = \sum_{i=1}^{r} (\hat{g}_i(s) + k_0)I$$

where $\hat{g}_i(s) = k_i s(s + b_i)^{-1}$, $k_i > 0$ and $k_0 \geq 0$. Therefore

$$\langle \psi x, Qx \rangle = \langle k_0 x, \psi x \rangle + \sum_{i=1}^{r} \langle \psi x, k_i x \rangle$$

Clearly $\langle k_0 x, \psi x \rangle$ is positive, and it only remains to show that terms

$\langle \psi x, k_i x \rangle$ are positive. Let $x = \dot{z} + b_i z$ for all $(\dot{z} + b_i z) \in L_2$. Then

$$\langle \psi x, k_i x \rangle = \langle \psi(\dot{z} + b_i z), k_i x \rangle$$

$$= \frac{k_i}{b_i} \langle \psi(\dot{z} + b_i z), b_i \dot{z} \rangle$$

But for strictly increasing ψ, $\langle \psi(y), x \rangle = 0$ implies that $\langle \psi(y + \dot{x}), x \rangle \geq 0$. Therefore $\langle \psi x, k_i x \rangle \geq 0$ if $\langle \psi(b_i z), b_i \dot{z} \rangle \geq 0$ which is guaranteed by a theorem due to Zames and Falb (1968).

Having shown that $(B - N)^{-1}$ is strictly increasing inside the sector $S\{(\beta - \alpha - \xi)^{-1}, \xi^{-1}\}$ and $Q^{-1} \in L_2^n$, if $y_1 \in L_2^n$, then also $y = (B - N)^{-1} Q^{-1} y_1 \in L_2^n$.

Finally condition s(ii) of the theorem and the positivity of $(B - A)$ ensure that the operator $K_1 : L_2^n \to L_2^n$, and if $u \in L_2^n$ then also $u_1 \in L_2^n$. □

If we drop the restriction on the multiplier and set $Q = I$, Theorem 7.1 simplifies to the well-known results of Rosenbrock (1973) and Cook (1973) whereby the feedback system (7.1) is L_2^n stable if the operator $(I + BF)(I + AF)^{-1}$ exists on L_2^n and is positive real. Although this result is somewhat simpler, it is far more conservative than the passivity result in determining stability via the nonlinearity sector constraints.

An interesting connection between the passivity and the incremental small gain theorem can be demonstrated through the identity

$$Y = (I + BF)(I + AF)^{-1}$$
$$= (I + Z)(I - Z)^{-1} \tag{7.5}$$

It is not difficult to see that

$$Z = \tfrac{1}{2}(B - A)[\tfrac{1}{2}[B + A] + F^{-1}]^{-1}$$

Assuming that Y is finite and unity is not an eigenvalue of Z, then $(I - Z)$ is nonsingular and Z is finite.

As $Y + Y^*$ is positive definite from the passivity theorem, then

$$x^*(Y + Y^*)x > 0, \quad \cdot \ \forall x \in C^n \neq 0 \tag{7.6}$$

Setting $y = (I - Z)^{-1}x$, it follows that

$$x^*(Y + Y^*)x = y^*((I - Z^*)(I + Z) + (I + Z^*)(I - Z))y$$
$$= 2y^*[I - Z^*Z]y$$
$$= 2(\|y\|^2 - \|Zy\|^2)$$
$$\geq 2\|y\|^2 (I - \|Z\|^2) > 0 \quad \text{if} \quad y \neq 0$$

Hence $\|Z\| < 1$, which implies that unity cannot be an eigenvalue of Z, and $(I - Z)$ is nonsingular with Z finite. Recalling the definitions of operators

A, B, then $\frac{1}{2}(B-A)=\frac{1}{2}(\beta-\alpha)I$, and $\frac{1}{2}(B-A)=\frac{1}{2}(\alpha+\beta)I$, and so the above stability condition $\|Z\|<1$ is equivalent to

$$\frac{1}{2}(\beta-\alpha)\|(I+\frac{1}{2}(\alpha+\beta)F)^{-1}F\|<1, \qquad (7.7)$$

which is the incremental small gain theorem condition for L_2^n-stability. We note that the converse of the above result holds, that is, if $\|Z\|<1$, then $Y=(I+Z)(I-Z)^{-1}$ is finite and $(Y+Y^*)$ is positive definite.

The norm condition $\|Z\|<1$ can be seen as essential in establishing the various stability results. The question now arises: can we establish that $\|Z\|<1$ by considering only the diagonal elements of the matrix transfer function $\hat{Z}(s)$ or its inverse $\tilde{Z}(s)$?

Suppose that the complex matrix $\tilde{Z}(s)=\{\tilde{z}_{ij}(s)\}$ is weighted mean dominant, that is

$$|\tilde{z}_{ii}(s)|-\sum_{\substack{j=1\\j\neq i}}^{n}\lambda_j\lambda_i^{-1}\frac{1}{2}[|\tilde{z}_{ij}(s)|+|\tilde{z}_{ji}(s)|]>1 \qquad (7.8)$$

for $\lambda_i>0$ and $i=1,2,\ldots,n$.

Define the Hermitian matrix

$$X=\frac{1}{2}(\Phi^*\tilde{Z}+\tilde{Z}^*\Phi)$$

where $\Phi\triangleq\text{diag}\{\tilde{z}_{ii}\,|\tilde{z}_{ii}|^{-1}\}$ is a unitary matrix, so that the diagonal elements of X are real, and by (7.8)

$$x_{ii}-\sum_{\substack{j=1\\j\neq i}}^{n}\lambda_j\lambda_i^{-1}|x_{ij}|>1, \qquad i=1,2,\ldots,n$$

And so by Gershgorin's theorem the eigenvalues of X are greater than unity, therefore

$$\inf_{y\neq 0}\frac{y^*Xy}{\|y\|^2}>1$$

but since

$$\|\tilde{Z}y\|\cdot\|y\|=\|\tilde{Z}y\|\cdot\|\Phi y\|\geq y^*Xy$$

then

$$\inf_{y\neq 0}\frac{\|\tilde{Z}y\|}{\|y\|}=\|\hat{Z}\|^{-1}\geq\inf_{y\neq 0}\frac{y^*Xy}{\|y\|^2}>1$$

so

$$\|\hat{Z}\|<1$$

In conclusion any complex matrix $\tilde{Z}(s)$ that satisfies the dominance condition (7.8) has an inverse $\hat{Z}(s)$ with spectral norm less than unity.

Now for the feedback system (7.1) a complex matrix $\hat{Z}(s)$ exists such that

$$\hat{Z}(s) = \tfrac{1}{2}(B - A)[I + \tfrac{1}{2}(B + A)\hat{F}(s)^{-1}]^{-1}$$

where $B = \beta I$, $A = \alpha I$, hence

THEOREM 7.2 (Rosenbrock and Cook (1973)) *Given the feedback system* $y = F(u - N(y))$, $u \in L_2^n$ *with* $F \in LA_-^{n \times n}$ *characterized by a matrix transfer function* $\hat{F}(s)$ *and* $N : R^n \to R^n$ *a sector bound nonlinearity that satisfies*

$$\alpha(y' - y) \le N(y') - N(y) \le (\beta - \xi)(y' - y)$$

for $y, y' \in L_2^n$, $\xi > 0$ *and* α, β *scalars. It is* ${}^c L_2^n$-*stability if*

$$|\tfrac{1}{2}(\beta - \alpha) + \tilde{f}_{ii}(s)| - \sum_{\substack{j=1 \\ j \ne i}}^{n} \tfrac{1}{2}\{|\tilde{f}_{ij}(s)| + |\tilde{f}_{ji}(s)|\} > \tfrac{1}{2}(\beta + \alpha) \qquad (7.9)$$

for $i = 1, 2, \ldots, n$, *and each* $s \in \Gamma'$, *provided that each* $\tilde{F}(s)$ *exists for all* s *on the contour* $\Gamma(r' \ge r)$.

Note The contour Γ consists of the imaginary axis from $s = -ir$ to $s = +ir$ together with a semicircle of radius r, the contour Γ is indented into the left half s-plane to avoid imaginary poles of $\hat{f}_{ii}(s)$, and r is large enough to include in Γ all right half poles of $\hat{f}_{ii}(s)(i = 1, 2, \ldots, n)$.

Now if F is a causal linear time-invariant stable operator $F \in LA_-^{n \times n}$ with matrix transfer function $\hat{F}(s)$ and the nonlinearity $N : R^n \to R^n$ satisfies the incremental sector condition (7.2) for $\xi > 0$ and $\beta \ge \alpha$, then the concepts of passivity and positivity are equivalent (see Sections 5.5 and 5.7) and stability criteria based upon sectoricity arguments can be derived for the feedback system

$$y = F(u - N(y)), \qquad u \in L_2^n \qquad (7.10)$$

Apply the loop transformation theorem 6.1 to this system with feedback/feedforward operator $A = \tfrac{1}{2}(\alpha + \beta)I$. In this case, $N - A = N - \tfrac{1}{2}(\alpha + \beta)I$, $(I + AF)^{-1}F = (F^{-1} + A)^{-1} = (F^{-1} + \tfrac{1}{2}(\alpha + \beta)I)^{-1}$, (Fig. 7.1(b)). From Definition 5.9 and Inequality (7.2), N is inside the sector $S\{\alpha + \dfrac{\xi}{2}, \beta - \dfrac{\xi}{2}\}$ for $\beta \ge \alpha$ and $\xi > 0$, and so from the summation property of sectors (Lemma 5.2), $N - \tfrac{1}{2}(\alpha + \beta)I$ is inside the sector $S\{\tfrac{1}{2}(\alpha + \xi - \beta), \tfrac{1}{2}(\beta - \alpha - \xi)\}$. Or from Definition 5.6, in terms of Euclidean norms

$$\|(Nx - \tfrac{1}{2}(\alpha + \beta)Ix)\| \le \tfrac{1}{2}(\beta - \alpha - \xi)\|x\|, \quad \text{for} \quad x \in L_2^n \qquad (7.11)$$

However, the induced norm is defined by

$$\|\!|\!| G \|\!|\!| \triangleq \sup_{\forall x \in L_2^n} \frac{\|Gx\|}{\|x\|}$$

Therefore the condition that $(N - \frac{1}{2}(\alpha + \beta)I)$ is inside $S\{\frac{1}{2}(\alpha + \xi - \beta),$ $\frac{1}{2}(\beta - \alpha - \xi)$ can be rewritten as

$$\||(N - \tfrac{1}{2}(\alpha + \beta)I)\|| \leq \tfrac{1}{2}(\beta - \alpha - \xi) \tag{7.12}$$

by taking sums over all $x \in L_2^n$ in Inequality (7.11)

Suppose now that the linear operator F is outside the sector $S\{-\alpha^{-1}, -\beta^{-1}\}$ for $\beta \geq \alpha > 0$, so that F^{-1} is outside $S\{-\alpha, -\beta\}$. From the summation properties of sectors (Lemma 5.2), the transformed linear operator $(F^{-1} + \frac{1}{2}(\alpha + \beta)I)$ is outside $S\{-\frac{1}{2}(\beta - \alpha), \frac{1}{2}(\beta - \alpha)\}$ or equivalently $(F^{-1} + \frac{1}{2}(\alpha + \beta))^{-1}$ is *inside* the sector $S\{-2(\beta - \alpha)^{-1}, 2(\beta - \alpha)^{-1}\}$. As for the nonlinear operator $(N - \frac{1}{2}(\alpha + \beta)I)$, the induced norm equivalent condition for sectoricity can be employed,

$$\||(F^{-1} + \tfrac{1}{2}(\alpha + \beta)I)^{-1}\|| \leq 2(\beta - \alpha)^{-1} \tag{7.13}$$

for $(F^{-1} + \frac{1}{2}(\alpha + \beta)I)^{-1}$ inside $S\{-2(\beta - \alpha)^{-1}, 2(\beta - \alpha)^{-1}\}$.

Now, multiplying inequalities (7.12), (7.13) gives

$$\||(I + FN_0)^{-1}F\|| \cdot \||(N - N_0)\|| < \frac{(\beta - \alpha - \xi)}{(\beta - \alpha)} < 1$$

for $N_0 = \frac{1}{2}(\alpha + \beta)$ and $\xi > 0$. Which by the small gain theorem 6.2, is a sufficient condition for L_2^n input–output stability of the feedback system (7.10).

THEOREM 7.3 *Given the feedback system* $y = F(u - N(y))$, $u \in L_2^n$ *with* $F \in LA_-^{n \times n}$ *characterized by matrix transfer function* $\hat{F}(s)$. *Then if*

(i) $N : R^n \to R^n$ *is inside the sector* $S\left\{\alpha + \dfrac{\xi}{2}, \beta - \dfrac{\xi}{2}\right\}$ *for* $\xi > 0$

(ii) $\beta \geq \alpha > 0$; F *is outside the sector* $S\{-\alpha^{-1}, -\beta^{-1}\}$,

or for $\beta > 0 > \alpha$; F *is inside the sector* $S\{-\beta^{-1}, -\alpha^{-1}\}$ *the feedback system is* L_2^n *input–output stable.*

The proof for $0 > \alpha$ follows identically that for $\alpha > 0$, except that inside sector conditions are utilized. This theorem was originally derived by Zames (1966).

To generate graphical interpretations of the passivity theorem we assume that the linear time-invariant operators F, Q are causal so that the concepts of passivity and positivity are equivalent.

THEOREM 7.4: POSITIVITY STABILITY THEOREM *The feedback system* $y = F(u - N(y))$ *is* L_2^n*-stable if the following conditions are satisfied*

$$\text{s(i)} \quad (I - AB^{-1})[\{BN^{-1} - I + B(F - \Phi)\}^{-1} - AB^{-1}]Q^{-1}$$

Table 7.1

Proof of theorem 7.4   Consider the following set of loop transformations to the feedback system (7.1):

Operation (Referred to the forward operator)	Input compensation	Forward operator	Output compensation	Feedback operator
	—	F	—	N
$+B^{-1}$, feedforward	$(F+B^{-1})^{-1}F$	$F+B^{-1}$	$(I-B^{-1}N)^{-1}$	$N(I-B^{-1}N)^{-1}$
$+F-\Phi$, negative feedforward	$(\Phi+B^{-1})^{-1}(G+B^{-1})$	$+B^{-1}$	$I+(F-\Phi)(N^{-1}-B^{-1})^{-1-1}$	$(N^{-1}-B^{-1})^{-1}I+(F-B(N^{-1}-B^{-1})^{-1-1}$
$(A^{-1}-B^{-1})^{-1}$, negative feedback	—	$(\Phi+B^{-1})(\Phi+A^{-1})$ $(A^{-1}-B^{-1})$	—	$N^{-1}-B^{-1}+F-\Phi^{-1}-(A^{-1}-B^{-1})^{-1}$
Extracting constants	$A^{-1}-B^{-1}$	$(\Phi+B^{-1})(\Phi+A^{-1})^{-1}$	—	$(A^{-1}-B^{-1})(N^{-1}-B^{-1}+F-\Phi)^{-1}-I$
Rearranging and further extraction	A	$(I+B\Phi)(I+A\Phi)^{-1}$	B^{-1}	$(I-AB^{-1})N^{-1}-B^{-1}+F-\Phi^{-1}-AB^{-1}$
Introducing a Multiplier Q		$Q(I+B\Phi)(I+A\Phi)^{-1}$	Q^{-1}	$[(I-AB^{-1})N^{-1}-B^{-1}+F-\Phi^{-1}-AB^{-1}]Q^{-1}$

is positive

$\qquad$ s(ii) $Q(I + B\Phi)(I + A\Phi)^{-1}$ *is strictly positive*

$\qquad$ s(iii) $(\Phi + B^{-1})^{-1} : L_2^n \to L_2^n$.

Where matrices A and $B \in R^{n \times n}$ and Φ is an arbitrary linear time-invariant operator which satisfies the conditions: (a) Φ has an impulse response, Φ in LA_{-}^{n+n} and (b) $\hat{\Phi}(j\omega)$ is normal for all frequencies ω.

Proof For proof of Theorem 7.4, see Table 7.1 opposite. $\qquad\square$

Theorem 7.4 is now verified by applying the passivity theorem for positive operators to the above transformed feedback and feedforward elements, and noting that the input and output compensators are operators on L_2^n by virtue of the conditions of the theorem. In the proof of this theorem the approximation or bounding matrices A, B are only required to be elements of $R^{n \times n}$.

7.2   OFF-AXIS CIRCLE CRITERIA

7.2.1   The linear operator $\hat{F}(j\omega)$ is normal

If the linear portion of the feedback system is normal, that is, $\hat{F}(j\omega)$ commutes with its complex conjugate $\hat{F}(j\omega)^*$ for all ω, then Theorem 7.4 has a simple off-axis graphical interpretation by selecting $\Phi \equiv F$. The conditions of Theorem 7.4 then reduce to:

$\qquad$ s'(i) $Q^{-1}(N - A)(B - N)^{-1}$ is positive

$\qquad$ s'(ii) $(I + BF)(I + AF)^{-1}Q$ is strictly positive

$\qquad$ s'(iii) $(F + B^{-1})^{-1} : L_2^n \to L_2^n$

(reversing the position of the multiplier).

By selecting $A = \alpha I$ and $B = \beta I$ we have:

THEOREM 7.5: OFF-AXIS CIRCLE CRITERION FOR NORMAL OPERATORS
(i) $\alpha > 0$

The feedback system $y = F(u - N(y))$, $u \in L_2^n$ is L_2^n-stable if the eigenloci of $\hat{F}(j\omega)$, $\omega \geq 0$ do not encircle or intersect the critical off-axis circle passing through the points $(-\alpha^{-1} - \gamma, 0)$ and $(-\beta^{-1} + \gamma, 0)$ in the complex plane for some $\gamma > 0$ (Fig. 7.2(i)).
(ii) $\alpha < 0$

The feedback system $y = F(u - N(y))$, $u \in L_2^n$ is L_2^n-stable if the eigenloci of $\hat{F}(j\omega)$, $\omega \geq 0$ lie entirely inside a critical off-axis circle passing through the points $(-\beta^{-1} + \gamma, 0)$ and $(-\alpha^{-1} - \gamma, 0)$ for some $\gamma > 0$ (Fig. 7.2(ii)).

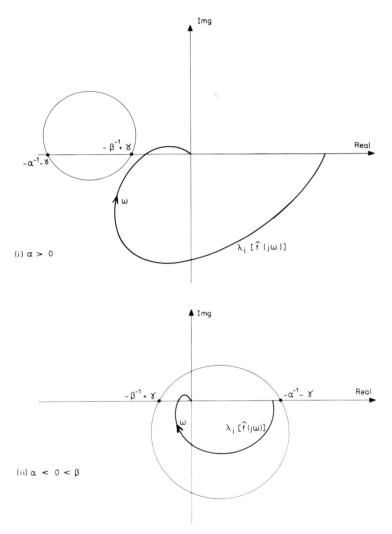

FIG. 7.2   Off-axis circle criterion for normal operators

Proof   Case (i) $\alpha > 0$. Let $N' = (N - A)(B - N)^{-1}$. Then it follows by standard sector arguments that N' is incrementally inside the sector $S\{0, (\beta - \alpha - \xi)\xi^{-1}\}$.

To establish condition s'(i) it is sufficient to show that

$$\langle Q^{-1} N' x, x \rangle \geq 0 \qquad \forall x \in L_2^n$$

If $(N')^{-1}Q$ is inside a positive sector, it follows that $Q^{-1}N'$ is also inside a positive sector. Therefore to establish s'(i) it suffices to show that

$$\langle (N')^{-1}Qx, x \rangle \geq 0 \qquad \forall x \in L_2^n \tag{7.14}$$

Now, $(N')^{-1}$ is incrementally inside the sector $S\{\xi(\beta - \alpha - \xi)^{-1}, \infty\}$, that is, an incrementally positive operator. By a simple vector generalization of Zames theorem (1966, pp. 475–476) it follows that $(N')^{-1}Q$ is positive, hence condition s'(i) is satisfied by the above choice of operators $A = \alpha I$, $B = \beta I$, and $\alpha, \beta > 0$.

To establish Theorem 7.5, it only remains to show that the graphical conditions of the theorem ensure that conditions s'(ii) and s'(iii) are satisfied.

It has been shown (Valenca, 1978) that since $\hat{F}(j\omega)$ is normal, $(F + B^{-1})^{-1}: L_2^n \to L_2^n$ if and only if the eigenloci of $\hat{F}(j\omega)$ do not encircle the point $-\beta^{-1}$ for $B = \beta I$.

$Q(I + B\Phi)(I + A\Phi)^{-1}$ can be identified with F, provided condition s(iii) is satisfied. As $\hat{\Phi}(j\omega)$ is a normal operator, a unitary matrix exists at each frequency to decompose $\hat{\Phi}(j\omega)$ into diagonal form. It can also be shown that the same similarity transformation decomposes $\hat{F}(j\omega) + \hat{F}(j\omega)^*$ into diagonal form. Hence from Lemma 5.1 condition s'(ii) is satisfied if and only if

$$\operatorname*{Re}_{\omega \geq 0} \theta(j\omega) \left\{ \frac{1 + \beta \lambda_i \{\hat{\Phi}(j\omega)\}}{1 + \alpha \lambda_i \{\hat{\Phi}(j\omega)\}} \right\} \geq \delta > 0 \qquad i = 1, 2, \ldots, n \tag{7.15}$$

which can be recognised as a multivariable version, of Cho and Narendra's (1968) off-axis circle result for scalar feedback systems.

Proof Case (ii) $\alpha < 0$. This proof follows identically to Case (i) except for reversal of the inequality sign in the inner products.   □

Example 7.1 As a numerical example consider the feedback system (7.1) with linear portion given by

$$\hat{F}(s) = \frac{1}{s(s+1)^2(s+6)} \begin{bmatrix} (s+2) & -2 \\ -2 & (s+5) \end{bmatrix}$$

The eigenvalues of $\hat{F}(s)$ are given by $\hat{\lambda}_1(s) = (s(s+6)(s+1))^{-1}$ and $\hat{\lambda}_2(s) = (s(s+1)^2)^{-1}$ and their Nyquist plots are shown in Fig. 7.3. If we select an arbitrary lower limit on the nonlinearity N of $\alpha = 0.64$, the *on-axis* circle stability criterion (Theorem 6.4) yields an upper limit of $\beta = 1.54$, whereas Theorem 7.5 gives the less conservative value of $\beta = 2.63$ for closed-loop stability (Fig. 7.3).

Noting that $\hat{F}(s)$ is not strictly diagonally dominant, and so the envelope of the Gershgorin circles of $\hat{F}(s)$ centred on $\hat{f}_{11}(j\omega)$ and $\hat{f}_{22}(j\omega)$ (Fig.

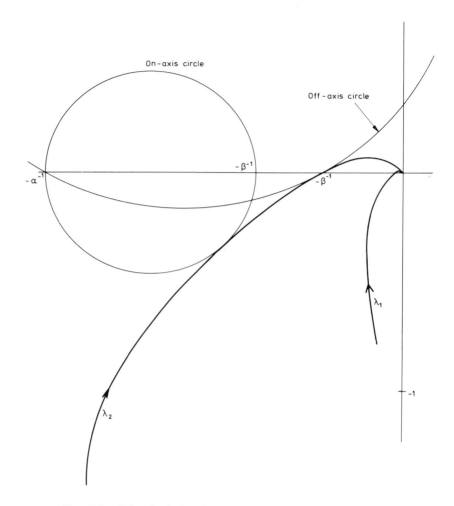

FIG. 7.3   Off-axis circle criterion based upon eigenvalue plots

7.4) will lead to far more conservative values for the upper limits for N than for the eigenloci of Fig. 7.3. Figure 7.4 shows that the off-axis circle criterion based upon Gershgorin circles is almost as good as the on-axis circle criterion based upon eigenvalue plots for a system which is marginally diagonally dominant (a considerable practical computational advantage in determining closed-loop stability).

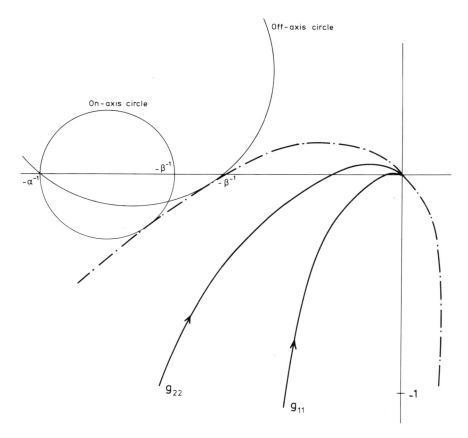

FIG. 7.4   Off-axis circle criterion based upon Gershgorin's theorem
(—·—·— Gershgorin's circle envelope)

7.2.2   The linear operator $\hat{F}(j\omega)$ is non-normal

The above graphical interpretation of Theorem 7.4 loses some of its
simplicity when the operator $\hat{F}(j\omega)$ is non-normal. Additional information
is required concerning the nature of the multiplier (its phase and frequency range etc) so that the multiplier can be located in a known sector.
Fortunately the required information concerning the multiplier can be
deduced from the eigenloci of $\hat{\Phi}(j\omega)$. The graphical interpretation of the
stability theorem is considered for two cases each dependent on the sign
of the lower bound α of the system nonlinearity.

THEOREM 7.6: OFF AXIS CIRCLE CRITERION FOR NON-NORMAL OPERATORS
Case (i) $\alpha > 0$. *The feedback system* $y = F(u - N(y))$, $u \in L_2^n$ *is* L_2^n-*stable if the eigenloci of* $\hat{\Phi}(j\omega)$, $\omega \geq 0$ *do not encircle or intersect a critical off-axis circle passing through the points* $(-b^{-1} + \gamma, 0)$ *and* $(-a^{-1} - \gamma, 0)$ *for some* $\gamma > 0$ *in the complex plane. Where* $a \triangleq p/(r + q\alpha^{-1})$, $b \triangleq (q + \xi)/(m + p\beta^{-1})$ *and* $\xi > 0$, $m > -p\beta^{-1}$, *and* $Q(F - \Phi)$ *is assumed to lie inside the sector* $S\{m, r\}$ *and* Q *is assumed to lie inside the sector* $S\{p, q\}$ *(Fig. 7.5(a))*.
Case (ii) $\alpha < 0$. *The feedback system* $y = F(u - N(y))$, $u \in L_2^n$ *is* L_2^n-*stable if the eigenloci of* $\hat{\Phi}(j\omega)$, $\omega \geq 0$ *lie entirely within a critical off-axis circle that passes through the points* $(-b^{-1} + \gamma, 0)$ *and* $(-a^{-1} - \gamma, 0)$ *for some* $\gamma > 0$ *in the complex plane. Where* $a \triangleq q/(m + q\alpha^{-1})$, $m < -q\alpha^{-1}$ *and* $b \triangleq (p + \xi)/(r + p\beta^{-1})$, $r > -p\beta^{-1}$, $\xi > 0$. *(See Fig. 7.5(b).)*

Proof To establish Theorem 7.6 it is sufficient to show that the selected values of matrices A and B guarantee that condition $s(i)$ of Theorem 7.4 is satisfied.

Now, the operator

$$E \triangleq [(I - AB^{-1})\{BN^{-1} - I + B(F - \Phi)\}^{-1} - AB^{-1}]Q^{-1} \qquad (7.16)$$

can be rewritten as

$$(I - AB^{-1})\{QBN^{-1} - Q + QB(F - \Phi)\}^{-1} - AB^{-1}Q^{-1} \qquad (7.17)$$

We now make the following assumptions:

   A(i) $Q(F - \Phi)$ is inside the sector $S\{m, r\}$
   A(ii) Q is inside the sector $S\{p, q\}$; $p \geq 0$
   A(iii) $A = aI_n$; $a \in R$
   A(iv) $B = bI_n$; $b \in R_+$

N is by definition incrementally inside the sector $S\{a, \beta\}$.
Case (i) $\alpha > 0(a > 0)$. Then QBN^{-1} is inside the sector $S\{bp\beta^{-1}, bq\alpha^{-1}\}$, $-Q$ is by definition inside the sector $S\{-q, -p\}$ and $QB(F - \Phi)$ is inside the sector $S\{bm, br\}$.
By the sum rule $QBN^{-1} - Q + QB(F - \Phi)$ is inside the sector $S\{bp\beta^{-1} - q + bm, bq\alpha^{-1} - p + br\}$.
We now make the assumption,

$$A(v)\quad pb\beta^{-1} - q + bm > 0,$$

so that $[QBN^{-1} - Q + QB(F - \Phi)]^{-1}$ is inside the sector

$$S\{(bq\alpha^{-1} - p + br)^{-1}, (bp\beta^{-1} - q - bm)^{-1}\}$$

or

$$(I - AB^{-1})(QBN^{-1} - Q + QB(F - \Phi))^{-1}$$

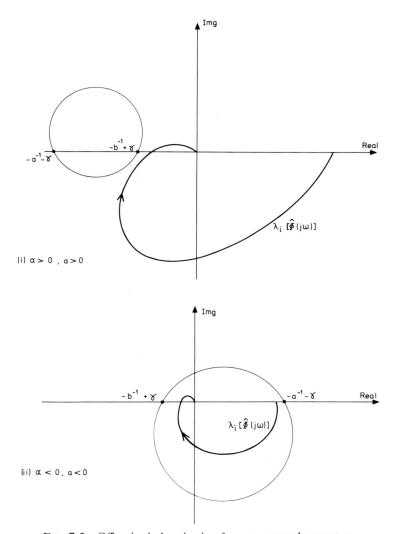

FIG. 7.5   Off-axis circle criterion for non-normal operators

is inside the sector

$$S\left\{\frac{b-a}{b(bq\alpha^{-1}-p+br)}, \frac{b-a}{b(bp\beta^{-1}-q+bm)}\right\}$$

This implies that E has a lower sector bound of $(b-a)b^{-1}(bq^{-1}\alpha-p+br)^{-1}-a(bp)^{-1}$.

To ensure that operator E is positive, it is sufficient to satisfy the following inequalities

$$(b-a)b^{-1}(bq^{-1}\alpha - p + br)^{-1} - a(bp)^{-1} \geq 0 \qquad (7.18)$$

The first inequality is satisfied if b is selected as $b = (q + \xi)/(m + p\beta^{-1})$ for $\xi > 0$ and $m > -p\beta^{-1}$. And the second inequality is satisfied by selecting $a = p/(r + q\alpha^{-1})$.

Case (ii) $\alpha < 0(a < 0)$. The analysis for the case $\alpha > 0$ was relatively straightforward. The problem is now more complex because outside sector concepts are required. A result which might appear useful in the manipulation of outside sectors is the Zames (1966, p. 234 property (v) (iii)) sum rule; unfortunately it is wrong, and numerous counter examples can be constructed. The proof fails due to the lack of symmetry of the triangle inequality. The only conditions under which this sum rule holds are if both the upper bounds are positively infinite or if both the lower bounds are negatively infinite. In this context Lemma 5.3 enables inside and outside sectors to be manipulated in a mixed manner.

Let us return to the proof of Theorem 7.6 for $\alpha < 0$.

QBN^{-1} is outside the sector $S\{bq\alpha^{-1}, bp\beta^{-1}\}$. And by Lemma 5.2 $QBN^{-1} - Q + QB(F - \Phi)$ is outside the sector $S\{bq\alpha^{-1} - q + bm, bp\beta^{-1} - p + br\}$ provided that $bp\alpha^{-1} - q + bm < bp\beta^{-1} - p + br$.

Now, introduce assumption

$$\text{A(vi)} \quad bq\alpha^{-1} - qbr < 0.$$

This implies that operator $\{QBN^{-1} - Q + QB(F - \Phi)\}^{-1}$ is *inside* the sector $S\{(bq\alpha^{-1} - q + br)^{-1}, (bp\beta^{-1} - p + br)^{-1}\}$. Therefore $(I - AB^{-1})$ $\{QBN^{-1} - Q + AB(F - \Phi)\}^{-1}$ is inside the sector

$$S\left\{\frac{b-a}{b(bq\alpha^{-1} - q + bm)}, \frac{b-a}{b(bp\beta^{-1} - p + br)}\right\}$$

which implies that the operator E has a lower sector bound of

$$(b-a)b^{-1}(bq\alpha^{-1} - q + bm)^{-1} - a(bp)^{-1}.$$

Hence the sufficient conditions for the positivity of E are:

$$(b-a)b^{-1}(bq\alpha^{-1} - q + bm)^{-1} - a(bp)^{-1} \geq 0$$
$$bq\alpha^{-1} - q + bm < 0$$
$$bp\beta^{-1} - p + br > 0$$

These inequalities are satisfied if a and b are chosen as

$$a = q(m + q\alpha^{-1})^{-1}, \qquad m < -q\alpha^{-1}$$
$$b = (p + \xi)(r + p\beta^{-1})^{-1}, \qquad \xi > 0. \qquad \square$$

7.2.3 Determination of the sectors of $Q(F-\Phi)$ and Q

For Theorem 7.6 to be of practical use, a method has to be devised to determine the sectors of $Q(F-\Phi)$ and Q. Since Q is inside the sector $S\{p, q\}, p \geq 0$, then, if $(F-\Phi)$ is inside $S\{-rp^{-1}, rq^{-1}\}$, $Q(F-\Phi)$ is inside the symmetric sector $S\{-r, r\}$. Lemma 5.5 provides a frequency domain method of determining the symmetric sector of a convolution operator; this lemma together with the following information on Q enables us to determine the sector of $Q(F-\Phi)$.

Case (i) Q is an RC multiplier, then $p = 1$, $q = \rho^{rc}$ and $c = |\theta|\,(\pi/2)^{-1}$ for θ the angle in radians between the tangent to the circle on the real axis and the real axis (Fig. 7.6).

Two further pieces of information concerning the critical circle are now required: first, the required tolerance ξ of θ in radians (allowable deviation in θ consistent with stability); second, the frequency range over which the multiplier is required to operate. This is easily determined as the smallest frequency ω_s at which the eigenvalue points $\lambda_i\{\hat{\Phi}(j\omega)\}$ ($\omega \in [\omega_s, \infty]$) are not contained in the family of off-axis circles generated as θ takes on values in the interval $[-\pi/2, 0]$. ρ and r are now chosen such that for $\omega \in (0, \omega_s]$

$$c\left|\tan^{-1}(\omega\alpha^{-1}) - \tan^{-1}(\omega(\alpha\rho^{r+c})^{-1}) - \frac{\pi}{2}\right|$$

$$+ 2c(1-c)\log\rho < \xi \tag{7.19}$$

where $\alpha > 0$, $\rho > 1$ and $r \in R_+$.

Case (ii) Q is an RC multiplier, then $p = \rho^{-rc}$, $q = 1$. θ now lies in the

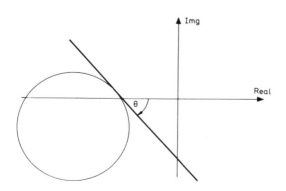

FIG. 7.6   Sector determination

interval $\left[0, \dfrac{\pi}{2}\right]$, that is, the circle centre lies above the real axis $c = \theta(\pi/2)^{-1}$ and the analysis now follows that for the RL case for determining r and c and hence ρ.

It should be noted that the conditions of Theorems 7.5 and 7.6 do not coincide when $\Phi = F$. This apparent disparity follows from the more involved approach necessary in establishing Theorem 7.6 to allow for the presence of a composite linear time operator.

Lemma 5.5 enables the general non-normal operator Theorem 7.6 to be readily implemented, although the end result will be more conservative in its stability estimates. If the computation of the eigenvalues of F is possible, a tighter result can be obtained by using the condition for operator F to be inside sector $S\{-r, r\}$ of

$$\max_{i, \ \omega \in R_+} \lambda_i (\hat{F}^*(j\omega)\hat{F}(j\omega)) \leq r^2$$

to calculate r. A more conservative set of results with the benefit of minimal computation is possible by applying Gershgorin's theorem to $\hat{\Phi}(j\omega)$ in order to obtain bounds upon its eigenvalues.

An *on-axis* circle interpretation of Theorems 7.5, 7.6 can be readily made by setting the multiplier $Q = I$ in the above.

THEOREM 7.7: F A NORMAL OPERATOR
(i) $\alpha > 0$.
The feedback system $y = F(u - N(y))$ is L_2^n-stable if the eigenloci of $\hat{F}(j\omega)$, $\omega \geq 0$ do not encircle or intersect the critical on-axis circle passing through the points $(-\alpha^{-1} - \gamma, 0)$ and $(-\beta^{-1} + \gamma, 0)$ in the complex plane for some $\gamma > 0$.
(ii) $\alpha < 0$.
The feedback system $y = F(u - N(y))$ is L_2^n-stable if the eigenloci of $\hat{F}(j\omega)$, $\omega \geq 0$ lie entirely inside a critical on-axis circle passing through the points $(-\beta^{-1} + \gamma, 0)$ and $(-\alpha^{-1} + \gamma, 0)$ for some $\gamma > 0$.

THEOREM 7.8: F A NON-NORMAL OPERATOR
(i) $\alpha > 0$.
The feedback system $y = F(u - N(y))$ is L_2^n-stable if the eigenloci of $\hat{\Phi}(j\omega)$, $\omega \geq 0$ do not encircle or intersect a critical on-axis circle passing through the points $(-b^{-1} + \gamma, 0)$ and $(-a^{-1} - \gamma, 0)$ for some $\gamma > 0$ in the complex plane. Where $a \triangleq 1/(r + \alpha^{-1})$, $b \triangleq (1 + \xi)/(m + \beta^{-1})$ and $\xi > 0$, $m + \beta^{-1} > 0$ and $(F - \Phi)$ is assumed to lie inside the sector $S\{m, r\}$.
(ii) $\alpha < 0$.
The feedback system $y = F(u - N(y))$ is L_2^n-stable if the eigenloci of $\hat{\Phi}(j\omega)$, $\omega \geq 0$ lie entirely within a critical on-axis circle that passes through points

$(-b^{-1}+\gamma, 0)$ and $(-a^{-1}-\gamma, 0)$ for some $\gamma>0$ in the complex plane. Where $a \triangleq 1/(m+\alpha^{-1})$, $m<-\alpha^{-1}$ and $b \triangleq (1+\xi)/(r+\beta^{-1})$, $r>-\beta^{-1}$, $\xi>0$.

The proofs of these theorems follows exactly that of Theorems 7.5 and 7.6 with $Q=I$, $p=1$, $q=1$ and $r=m$. These theorems are simpler to implement than either the respective off-axis circle theorems or the associated incremental gain theorem of Section 6.4 for non-normal operators F, since the norm $K(\Phi)$ of the error of approximation of F by Φ does not have to have computed in Theorem 7.8.

Example 7.2   To illustrate Theorem 7.8 consider the feedback system $y = F(u - N(y))$ with linear transfer function matrix

$$\hat{F}(s) = \frac{1}{(2s+1)} \begin{bmatrix} \dfrac{(2\cdot5s+1)}{(s+1)} & \dfrac{-(0\cdot6s+1)}{(s+1)} \\[2mm] \dfrac{-0\cdot5(s-1)}{(0\cdot5s+1)} & \dfrac{(3s+1)}{(0\cdot5s+1)} \end{bmatrix}$$

Select as an approximation operator the normal transfer functions matrix

$$\hat{\phi}(s) = \frac{1}{(2s+1)} \begin{bmatrix} \dfrac{1}{(s+1)} & 0 \\[2mm] 0 & \dfrac{1}{(0\cdot5s+1)} \end{bmatrix}$$

whose eigenvalues are obviously $\hat{\lambda}_1(s) = \{(2s+1)(s+1)\}^{-1}$ and $\hat{\lambda}_2(s) = \{(2s+1)(0\cdot5s+1)\}^{-1}$; the associated Nyquist plots are given in Fig. 7.7. Lemma 5.5 gives the symmetric sector limits of $(\hat{F} - \hat{\phi})$ as $r \leq 0\cdot707$. Typical limits on the nonlinearity $N(y)$ are: (i) for $\beta \geq \alpha > 0: \beta = 1\cdot24$, $\alpha = 0\cdot64$; (ii) for $\beta > 0 > \alpha : \beta = 3\cdot41$, $\alpha = -0\cdot59$.

A less conservative on-axis circle stability criterion can be derived if frequency-dependent sectors for the operators F and $(F-\Phi)$ are employed (See Section 5.7). Given that the operators F, $(F-\Phi)$, $\Phi \in LA_{-}^{n\times n}$ have transfer function matrices $\hat{F}(j\omega)$, $(\hat{F}(j\omega)) - \hat{\Phi}(j\omega))$, $\hat{\Phi}(j\omega)$ and that operator $(F-\Phi)$ lies inside $S\{m(j\omega), r(j\omega)\}$, for $m(j\omega)$, $r(j\omega)$ real scalars, and the normal operator Φ lies outside $S\{-\alpha^{-1}-r(j\omega), -\beta^{-1}-m(j\omega)\}$; Lemma 5.4, with the following identities, $c_1 = -\frac{1}{2}(\alpha^{-1}+r+\beta^{-1}+m)$, $r_1 = \frac{1}{2}(\alpha^{-1}+r-\beta^{-1}-m)$, $c_2 = \frac{1}{2}(r+m)$, $r_2 = -\frac{1}{2}(m-r)$ states that:

LEMMA 7.1   *If F is a stable operator such that $\hat{F}(j\omega)$ satisfies the Nyquist criterion with respect to the point $(-\frac{1}{2}(\alpha^{-1}+\beta^{-1}), 0)$ then F lies outside the sector $S\{-\alpha^{-1}, -\beta^{-1}\}$ if*

$$\|(\hat{F}(j\omega) - \hat{\Phi}(j\omega) - \frac{1}{2}(r(j\omega) + m(j\omega))I)x(j\omega)\|$$
$$\leq \frac{1}{2}(r(j\omega) - m(j\omega))\|x(j\omega)\| \tag{7.20}$$

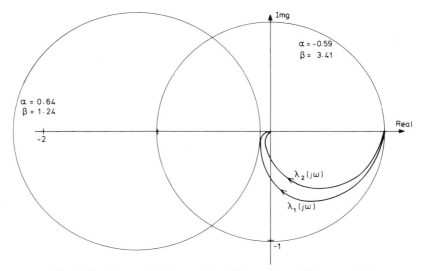

FIG. 7.7   Example 7.2, graphical illustration of Theorem 7.8

and

$$\|(\hat{\Phi}(j\omega) + \tfrac{1}{2}(\alpha^{-1} + r(j\omega) + \beta^{-1} + m(j\omega))I)x(j\omega)\|$$
$$\geq \tfrac{1}{2}(\alpha^{-1} + r(j\omega) - \beta^{-1} - m(j\omega))\|x(j\omega)\| \qquad (7.21)$$

for all $\omega \in R$ *and* $x(j\omega) \in L_2^n$.

As $\hat{\Phi}(j\omega)$ is a normal operator, a unitary matrix exists at each frequency to decompose $\hat{\Phi}(j\omega)$ into diagonal form, and so condition (7.21) can be written as

$$\|\lambda_i\{\hat{\Phi}(j\omega)\} + \tfrac{1}{2}(\alpha^{-1} + r(j\omega) + \beta^{-1} + m(j\omega))\|$$
$$\geq \tfrac{1}{2}(\alpha^{-1} + r(j\omega) - \beta^{-1} - m(j\omega)) \qquad (7.22)$$

for $i = 1, 2, \ldots, n$, and for all $\omega \in R$. Comparing this inequality with (6.42) we have the following graphical interpretation:

LEMMA 7.2   *A normal operator* $\hat{\Phi}(j\omega)$ *is outside the sector* $S\{-\alpha^{-1} - r(j\omega), -\beta^{-1} - m(j\omega)\}$ *if and only if the eigenloci* $\lambda_i\{\hat{\Phi}(j\omega)\}$, $(i = 1, 2, \ldots, n)$ *are exterior to the circle* $C[-\alpha^{-1} - r(j\omega), -\beta^{-1} - m(j\omega)]$.

Combining the conditions of Lemmas 7.1 and 7.2 it is clear that the eigenvalues of $\hat{F}(j\omega)$ are exterior to the circle $C[-\alpha^{-1}, -\beta^{-1}]$. Similarly these two lemmas taken together with Theorem 7.3 enable us to state a generalized *on-axis* circle criterion that does not involve the approximation of F by Φ.

THEOREM 7.9 $(\beta \geq \alpha > 0)$ *The feedback system* $y = F(u - N(y))$ *is* L_2^n-*stable if the eigenloci of* $\hat{\Phi}(j\omega)$, $\omega \in R$ *do not intersect nor encircle a critical on-axis circle* $C[-\alpha^{-1} - r(j\omega), -\beta^{-1} - m(j\omega)]$ *in the complex plane. Where* $m(j\omega) + \beta^{-1} > 0$ *and* $(\hat{F}(j\omega) - \hat{\Phi}(j\omega))$ *is assumed to lie inside the sector* $S\{m(j\omega), r(j\omega)\}$.

Note that Theorem 7.8 contains the above as a special case when $m = \min_\omega m(j\omega)$, $r = \max_\omega r(j\omega)$. We see that the cost in utilizing the approximation of non-normal operator F by normal Φ is an increase in the diameter of the critical circle by the sector of $(F - \Phi)$ (compare circle diameters in Theorems 7.7, 7.8 and 7.9).

An obvious corollary to Lemma 7.2 for normal operators that are inside sectors $S\{m(j\omega), r(j\omega)\}$ is:

LEMMA 7.3 *A normal operator* $\hat{\Phi}(j\omega)$ *is inside the sector* $S\{m(j\omega), r(j\omega)\}$ *if and only if the Nyquist plots of* $\lambda_i(\hat{\Phi}(j\omega))$ $(i = 1, 2, \ldots, n)$ *lie inside or on the circle* $C[m(j\omega), r(j\omega)]$.

Clearly the smallest on-axis circle $C[m(j\omega), r(j\omega)]$ that contains all the eigenvalues λ_i of $\hat{\Phi}(j\omega)$ defines the minimum sector $S\{m(j\omega), r(j\omega)\}$.

7.3 OFF-AXIS CIRCLE CRITERIA—MULTIPLIER FACTORIZATION

While the off-axis circle criterion for normal operators (Theorem 7.5) has a simple and readily implementable graphical interpretation, the equivalent result (Theorem 7.6) for non-normal operators crucially depends upon the determination of the sectors of the multiplier Q and the product of the multiplier and the degree of approximation of the linear loop operator F and some normal approximating operator Φ. The direct involvement of the sector of Q and its associated conservative estimation via Lemma 5.5, effectively reduce the practical advantages of this multivariable off-axis circle stability criterion over those of the on-axis circle criterion of Theorems 7.8 and 7.9 (also those of Section 6.4). We show in this section that by utilizing the multiplier factorization theorem of Section 5.6 for a multiplier with an RL, RC realization or Popov structure that a series of generalized multivariable off-axis circle stability criteria independent of the sector of Q can be readily generated. To accommodate non-normal linear operators, F, some aspects of optimal decomposition of F into $(F - \Phi) + \Phi$, for Φ a normal operator, are given together with conditions for estimating the minimum sector width of $(F - \Phi)$.

Consider the feedback system

$$y = F(u - N(y)) \tag{7.23}$$

that satisfies the conditions of equations (7.1) and (7.2). Utilizing the multiplier factorization theorems of (5.4) and (5.5) in the passivity Theorem 7.1 yields the following conditions for L_2^n-stability of (7.23).

$$\text{s'(i)} \quad \langle (Q_-^*)^{-1} Q_+ (I + BF)(I + AF)^{-1} x, x \rangle_T \geq 0 \tag{7.24}$$

for all $x \in L_{2e}^n$, $T \in R$, and there exists a $\delta > 0$ such that

$$\text{s'(ii)} \quad \langle (N - A)(B - N)^{-1}(Q_+)^{-1} Q_-^* x, x \rangle_T \geq \delta \|x_T\|^2 \tag{7.25}$$

for all $x \in L_{2e}^n$, $T \in R$, and Q_+, Q_-^*, $(Q_-^*)^{-1}$, $(Q_+^*)^{-1} : L_2^n \to L_2^n$.
The multiplier $Q = Q_- Q_+$ is selected such that

$$\hat{Q}_-(j\omega) = \prod_{k=0}^{r} \left(\frac{p_k - j\omega}{q_k - j\omega} \right)^{1/2} \tag{7.26}$$

$$\hat{Q}_+(j\omega) = \prod_{k=0}^{r} \left(\frac{p_k + j\omega}{q_k + j\omega} \right)^{1/2}, \qquad q_1 > p_0 > q_0 > 0 \tag{7.27}$$

which are respectively anti-causal and causal operators. This choice of multiplier, although having a real time domain description, can be made to appear as a pure complex number in the frequency domain (see also Cook, 1976) and can be realized similar to the multipliers of Zames (1966) and Cho and Narendra (1968) as either RL or RC type realizations, depending on whether Q_- and Q_+ are defined by (7.26) and (7.27) or in their inverse forms.

The nonlinear operator was defined in Section 7.1 to be incrementally inside the sector $S\{\alpha + \xi, \beta - \xi\}$, $\xi > 0$; by selecting $A = \alpha I$, $B = \beta I$ we showed by standard sector arguments in Section 7.1 that the operator $\psi = (N - A)(B - N)^{-1}$ is strictly incrementally passive. By Definitions (7.26) and (7.27) the causal multiplier $(Q_+)^{-1} Q_-^*$ is either an RL or an RC multiplier, and the composition operator $\psi(Q_+)^{-1} Q_-^*$ is causal and satisfies the strict positivity condition of (7.25) automatically via the system definitions of N and Q.

L_2^n stability of the feedback system $y = F(u - N(y))$ therefore depends only upon the satisfaction of the condition

$$\text{s'(i)} \quad \langle (Q_-^*)^{-1} Q_+ (I + BF)(I + AF)^{-1} x, x \rangle_T \geq 0, \qquad \forall x \in L_{2e}^n, \qquad \forall T \in R$$

As with condition s'(ii) all the above operators are causal and so a positivity condition may be utilized to infer the equivalent passivity condition.

LEMMA 7.4   *The passivity condition*

$$\langle (Q_-^*)^{-1}Q_+(I+BF)(I+AF)^{-1}x, x \rangle_T \geq 0, \qquad \forall x \in L_{2e}^n, \qquad \forall T \in R$$

is equivalent to

$$\langle Q_+(I+BF)(I+AF)^{-1}Q_-y, y \rangle \geq 0, \qquad \forall y \in L_2^n \qquad (7.28)$$

where

$$y = Q_-^{-1}x, \qquad x \in L_2^n \qquad (7.29)$$

Proof Since $(Q_-^*)^{-1}Q_+$ is causal, Inequality (7.24) is equivalent to

$$\langle (Q_-^*)^{-1}Q_+(I+BF)(I+AF)^{-1}x, x \rangle \geq 0, \qquad \forall x \in L_2^n$$

which in turn is equivalent to

$$\langle Q_+(I+BF)(I+AF)^{-1}x, Q_-^{-1}x \rangle \geq 0, \qquad \forall x \in L_2^n$$

Defining $y = Q_-^{-1}x$ the above becomes

$$\langle Q_+(I+BF)(I+AF)^{-1}Q_-y, y \rangle \geq 0, \qquad \forall y \in L_2^n \qquad \square$$

Provided that $(I+AF)^{-1}: L_2^n \to L_2^n$, Inequality (7.28) can be written equivalently as:

$$\langle Q_+Q_-(I+BF)x, (I+AF)x \rangle \geq 0, \qquad \forall x \in L_2^n$$

or

$$\langle Q_+Q_-(B^{-1}+F)x, (A^{-1}+F)x \rangle \geq 0, \qquad \forall x \in L_2^n \qquad (7.30)$$

provided that $\alpha \neq 0$.

By Parseval's theorem the above inequality is equivalent to:

$$Re \left\{ \int_0^\infty \langle Q_+Q_-(B^{-1}+\hat{F}(j\omega))x(j\omega), (A^{-1}+\hat{F}(j\omega))x(j\omega) \rangle_E \, d\omega \right\} \geq 0 \qquad (7.31)$$

for all $x(t) \in L_2^n$ and where $\langle x, y \rangle_E \triangleq x^*y$. A sufficient condition for Inequality (7.31) is

$$Re\{\langle Q_+Q_-(B^{-1}+\hat{F}(j\omega))x(j\omega), (A^{-1}+\hat{F}(j\omega))x(j\omega) \rangle_E\} \geq 0 \qquad (7.32)$$

for all $x(j\omega)$, $\omega \in [0, \infty]$.

Close examination of the multiplier $Q(j\omega)$ reveals that it shares the same phase characteristics as the multiplier utilized by the originators of the off-axis circle theorem (Cho and Narendra, 1968). By a suitable choice of the multipliers parameters p_i and q_i, the multiplier $Q(j\omega)$ can be made arbitrarily close to the complex number $\exp(j\theta)$ for $\omega \in [a, b]$, a subinterval of $(0, \infty)$ and a constant $\theta \in (-\pi/2, \pi/2)$. Strictly, the inverse multiplier $Q^{-1}(j\omega)$ should be considered in parallel with $Q(j\omega)$ to enable

θ to encompass all $(-\pi/2, \pi/2)$, but only a redefinition of $Q(j\omega)$ as $Q^{-1}(j\omega)$ is necessary to accommodate this requirement.

The restriction of ω to a closed subinterval of $(0, \infty)$ only produces difficulties if an off-axis disc is required in the vicinity of the frequency points $\omega = 0$ and $\omega = \infty$. This frequency constraint and its implications will be dealt with in the sequel.

The frequency inequality (7.32) can now be seen to be satisfied if the following two conditions hold:

$s_1'(i)$ $\text{Re}\, \langle \exp (j\theta)(B^{-1} + \hat{F}(j\omega))y(j\omega), (\hat{F}(j\omega) + A^{-1})y(j\omega)\rangle_E \geq 0,$

$$\forall\, y(j\omega), \qquad \forall\, \omega \in [a, b], \qquad \theta \in \left(-\frac{\pi}{2}, \frac{\pi}{2}\right) \tag{7.33}$$

$s_2'(i)$ $\text{Re}\, \langle Q_+ Q_- (B^{-1} + \hat{F}(j\omega))y(j\omega), (\hat{F}(j\omega) + A^{-1})y(j\omega)\rangle_E \geq 0,$

$$\forall\, y(j\omega), \qquad \forall\, \omega \in [0, a) \cup (b, \infty] \tag{7.34}$$

LEMMA 7.5 *The condition* $s_1'(i)$ *is equivalent to*

$$\langle (\hat{F}(j\omega) + c - jr \tan \theta)y(j\omega), (\hat{F}(j\omega) + c - jr \tan \theta)y(j\omega)\rangle_E$$

$$\geq \frac{r^2}{\cos^2 \theta} \langle y(j\omega), y(j\omega)\rangle_E, \quad (7.35)$$

For all $y(j\omega)$, *and* $\omega \in [a, b]$, $\theta \in (-\pi/2, \pi/2)$. *Where* $c = \frac{1}{2}(\alpha^{-1} + \beta^{-1})$ *and* $r = \frac{1}{2}(\alpha^{-1} - \beta^{-1})$.

Proof For the same system conditions Inequality (7.33) is equivalent to (omitting arguments etc.)

$$\text{Re}\, (\cos \theta + j \sin \theta)\{\langle \hat{F}y, \hat{F}y\rangle_E + \alpha^{-1}\beta^{-1}\langle y, y\rangle_E + \alpha^{-1}\langle \hat{F}y, y\rangle_E\} \geq 0$$

On setting $\langle y, \hat{F}y\rangle_E = \rho + j\sigma$, the above inequality becomes

$$\cos \theta\, \{\langle \hat{F}y, \hat{F}y\rangle_E + \alpha^{-1}\beta^{-1}\langle y, y\rangle_E + \rho(\beta^{-1} + \alpha^{-1})\}$$

$$+ \sin \theta(\sigma\alpha^{-1} - \sigma\beta^{-1}) \geq 0 \tag{7.36}$$

Defining $r = \frac{1}{2}(\alpha^{-1} - \beta^{-1})$ and $c = \frac{1}{2}(\alpha^{-1} + \beta^{-1})$, Inequality (7.36) simplifies on dividing throughout by $\cos \theta$ to:

$$\langle \hat{F}y, \hat{F}y\rangle_E + (c^2 - r^2)\langle y, y\rangle_E + 2c\rho + 2r\sigma \tan \theta \geq 0$$

which can be rewritten as

$$\langle \hat{F}y, \hat{F}y\rangle_E + (c - jr \tan \theta)(\rho + j\sigma) + (c + jr \tan \theta)(\rho - j\sigma)$$

$$+ \left(c^2 + r^2 \tan^2 \theta - \frac{r^2}{\cos^2 \theta}\right)\langle y, y\rangle_E \geq 0$$

or alternatively as

$$\langle \hat{F}y, \hat{F}y \rangle_E + (c - jr \tan \theta)\langle y, \hat{F}y \rangle_E + (c + jr \tan \theta)\langle \hat{F}y, y \rangle_E$$
$$+ (c^2 + r^2 \tan^2 \theta)\langle y, y \rangle_E \geq \frac{r^2}{\cos^2} \langle y, y \rangle_E$$

or equivalently as:

$$\langle (\hat{F} + c - jr \tan \theta)y, (\hat{F} + c - jr \tan \theta)y \rangle_E \geq \frac{r^2}{\cos^2 \theta} \langle y, y \rangle_E \qquad (7.37)$$

□

From Definition (5.6a) we see that Inequality (7.37) is a frequency domain *outside* sector condition on F with a complex centre $-c + jr \tan \theta$ and radius $r/\cos \theta$.

The second sufficient condition (7.34) for L_2^n-stability of the feedback system (7.23) can now be eliminated if caution is taken at the frequency limits $\omega = 0$ and $\omega = \infty$. Condition (7.34) is governed by the behaviour of

$$\text{Arg}\{Q(j\omega)\} = \sum_{k=0}^{r} \left\{ \tan^{-1}\left(\frac{\omega}{q_k}\right) - \tan^{-1}\left(\frac{\omega}{p_k}\right) \right\}$$

in the vicinity of the frequency points $\omega = 0$, $\omega = \infty$ (q_k and p_k are as defined by Cho and Narendra, 1968). Hence it can be easily shown that $\text{Arg}\{Q(j\omega)\} \to 0$ as $\omega \to 0$ or $\omega \to \infty$. The effect of condition (7.23) upon the off-axis circle criterion to be established in the sequel can be ignored provided that certain eigenvalue loci (to be defined) in an arbitrarily small region of $\omega = 0$ and $\omega = \infty$, do not intersect the family of *off-axis* discs which tend to an *on-axis* disc as $\omega \to 0$ and $\omega \to \infty$. This constraint will be assumed to be implicit in the various circle stability criteria derived in this section that depend upon the multiplier Q defined by (7.26) and (7.27).

To generate graphical stability for non-normal linear operators F, we utilize the decomposition

$$\hat{F}(j\omega) = \hat{\Phi}(j\omega) + (\hat{F} - \hat{\Phi})(j\omega), \quad \text{for} \quad \Phi \in LA_-^{n \times n} \qquad (7.38)$$

where the approximation operator Φ is normal. Before establishing the graphical interpretations of stability condition s'(i), (7.37), we define off-axis circles:

Definition 7.1   The off-axis circle $C_0[-l - \alpha^{-1}, -m - \beta^{-1}]$ is defined by drawing any desired circle C through the points $(-\alpha^{-1}, 0)$ and $(-\beta^{-1}, 0)$, the centre of the circle C_0 is then located by adding $(-\frac{1}{2}(l + m), 0)$ to the centre of C and its diameter is determined by increasing the diameter of C by $(l - m)$ (Fig. 7.8).

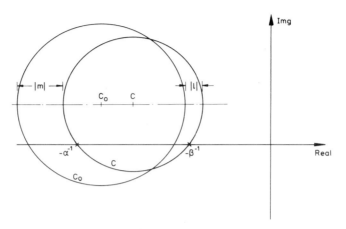

FIG. 7.8   Definition off-axis circles C_0

THEOREM 7.10   *The feedback system $y = F(u - N(y))$ is L_2^n-stable if the eigenvalue plots, $\lambda_i(\hat{\Phi}(j\omega))$ do not encircle or intersect an off-axis circle $C_0[-l - \alpha^{-1}, -m - \beta^{-1}]$, where $(F - \Phi)$ is inside the sector $S\{m, l\}$, for $\omega \geq 0$ and l and m real scalars.*

Proof   Following the same arguments used in deriving Lemma 7.1, based on the normality of $\hat{\Phi}(j\omega)$, it can be shown that $\hat{\Phi}(j\omega)$ satisfies

$$\left\|\left[\hat{\Phi}(j\omega) + \left(c + \frac{l+m}{2} - jr \tan \theta\right)I\right]x(j\omega)\right\| \geq \left\{\frac{r}{\cos \theta} + \frac{l-m}{2}\right\}\|x(j\omega)\|$$

(7.39)

for all $\omega \in [a, b]$, and $x(j\omega)$ and $\|.\|$ denotes the Euclidean vector norm. From the conditions of Theorem 7.10, $(\hat{F} - \hat{\Phi})$ satisfies the inequality

$$-\left\|\left[(\hat{F} - \hat{\Phi})(j\omega) - \frac{(l+m)}{2}I\right]x(j\omega)\right\| \geq \frac{(m-l)}{2}\|x(j\omega)\| \qquad (7.40)$$

for all $x(j\omega)$, and $\omega \in R$.

Adding Inequalities (7.39) and (7.40) and employing the triangle inequality, it can be deduced that

$$\|[\hat{F}(j\omega) + cI - jr \tan \theta]x(j\omega)\| \geq \frac{r}{\cos \theta}\|x(j\omega)\|$$

for all $\omega \in [a, b]$ and $x(j\omega)$. This is equivalent to the sufficient L_2^n-stability condition of (7.35) for the feedback system (7.23).   □

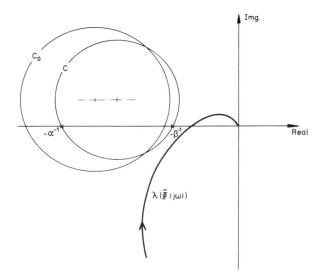

FIG. 7.9   Graphical interpretation of Theorem 7.10 (frequency independent sectors)

Theorem 7.10 is based upon a frequency-independent sector condition to establish an off-axis circle criterion for non-normal operators (Fig. 7.9). Frequency-dependent sectors (see Definitions 5.6a, 5.7a) can be readily incorporated within the same framework of Theorem 7.10:

THEOREM 7.11   *The feedback system $y = F(u - N(y))$ is L_2^n-stable if the eigenvalue plots, $\lambda(\hat{\Phi}(j\omega))$ do not encircle or intersect an off axis circle $C_0[-l(j\omega) - \alpha^{-1}, -m(j\omega) - \beta^{-1}]$, where $(\hat{F} - \hat{\Phi})$ is inside the sector $S\{m(j\omega), l(j\omega)\}$ for $\omega \geq 0$ and $m(j\omega), l(j\omega) \in R$.*

Proof   Proof follows identically to that of Theorem 7.10, except that frequency-dependent sectors are utilized (Fig. 7.10).   □

The above off-axis circle criteria offer simple geometric means of assessing closed-loop stability; unfortunately, the generality of the underlying theory is sacrificed for graphical clarity—despite the fact that the criteria are less conservative than currently known on axis circle criteria. Very general circle criteria with tighter stability bounds can be readily derived, the cost being increased analytic effort by the designer. To illustrate the non-uniqueness of the multiplier choice, a Popov-type multiplier is now selected instead of an *RL* or *RC* multiplier, thus generalizing to the multivariable setting the scalar result of Hsu and Meyer (1968).

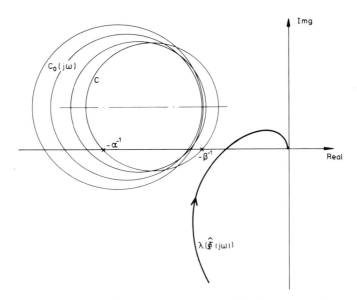

FIG. 7.10   Graphical interpretation of Theorem 7.11 (frequency dependent sectors)

By operations analogous to those outlined in the derivation of conditions (7.24) and (7.25), sufficient conditions for the L_2^n-stability of the feedback system $y = F(u - N(y))$ can be expressed as

$$s''\text{(i)} \quad \langle Q(I + BF)(I + AF)^{-1}x, x \rangle_T \geq 0$$

for all $x \in L_{2e}^n$, $T \in R$. And there exists a $\delta > 0$ such that

$$s''\text{(ii)} \quad \langle (N - A)(B - N)^{-1}Q^{-1}x, x \rangle_T \geq \delta \|x_T\|^2$$

for all $x \in L_{2e}^n$, $T \in R$, and $Q, Q^{-1}: L_2^n \to L_2^n$

By defining Q as the Popov multiplier $Q(j\omega) = (1 + j\omega q)I$, $q \geq 0$, the above condition $s''\text{(ii)}$ is automatically satisfied by standard sector arguments for $A = \alpha I$, $B = \beta I$. And so by utilizing the same derivation used in establishing Lemma 7.5 a sufficient condition for condition $s''\text{(i)}$ is

$$\|[\hat{F}(j\omega) + (c - jr \tan \theta(j\omega))]x(j\omega)\| \geq \frac{r}{\cos \theta(j\omega)} \|x(j\omega)\| \qquad (7.41)$$

for all $x(j\omega)$, $\omega \geq 0$, and $(F + A^{-1})^{-1}: L_2^n \to L_2^n$. Where c, r and $\theta(j\omega)$ are defined by $c = \frac{1}{2}(\alpha^{-1} + \beta^{-1})$, $r = \frac{1}{2}(\alpha^{-1} - \beta^{-1})$ and $\theta(j\omega) = \tan^{-1}[(q\omega)^{-1}]$.

Definition 7.2   The Popov circles $C_p[-l(j\omega) - \alpha^{-1}, -m(j\omega) - \beta^{-1}]$, are defined by the family of circles determined by selecting some $q \geq 0$ (and

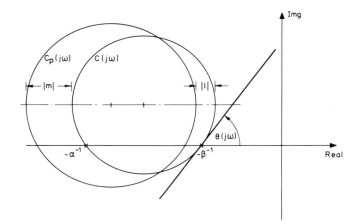

FIG. 7.11   Definition of Popov circles C_p

hence $\theta(j\omega) = \tan^{-1}[(q\omega)^{-1}])$ for $\omega \geq 0$. The Popov circles are constructed from an off-axis circle, C, drawn through the points $(-\alpha^{-1}, 0)$ and $(-\beta^{-1}, 0)$ with a tangent at the point $(-\beta^{-1}, 0)$ at an angle of $\theta(j\omega)$ to the real axis. The centre of the Popov circles C_p are located by adding $(\frac{1}{2}(m(j\omega) + l(j\omega)), 0)$ to the centre of circle C and by increasing the diameter of C by $(l(j\omega) - m(j\omega))$ for $\omega \geq 0$ (Fig. 7.11).

By analogy to Theorem 7.11 we have:

THEOREM 7.12   *The feedback system* $y = F(u - N(y))$ *is* L_2^n-*stable if the eigenvalue plots,* $\lambda(\hat{\Phi}(j\omega))$ *do not encircle or intersect the Popov circles* $C_p[-l(j\omega) - \alpha^{-1}, \ -m(j\omega) - \beta^{-1}]$ *where* $(\hat{F} - \hat{\Phi})$ *is inside the sector* $S\{m(j\omega), l(j\omega)\}$ *for* $\omega \geq 0$ *and* $m(j\omega), l(j\omega) \in R$ *(Fig. 7.12).*

To implement Theorems 7.10–7.12 a systematic mechanism for selecting the approximating normal operator Φ must be considered. To achieve stability the radius of the sector of $(\hat{F} - \hat{\Phi})$ must be minimized with respect to Φ or equivalently the matrix $(F - \Phi)$ should be sparse with small entries. To achieve this, the largest normal structured operator Φ contained within F should be selected. As already observed in Section 6.3, suitable choices for Φ are diag $(\hat{F})$, $\frac{1}{2}(\hat{F} - \hat{F}^*)$ or $\frac{1}{2}(\hat{F} + \hat{F}^*)$, or as unitary matrices.

By reversing the signs used in the proof of Lemma 7.2 we are able to state:

LEMMA   7.6   *The   normal   operator $\hat{\Phi}(j\omega)$ is   inside   the   sector* $S\{-m(j\omega), -l(j\omega)\}$ *if the circle* $C[-m(j\omega), -l(j\omega)]$ *contains all the eigenvalue plots* $\lambda_i(\hat{\Phi}(j\omega))$ $(i = 1, 2, \ldots, n)$.

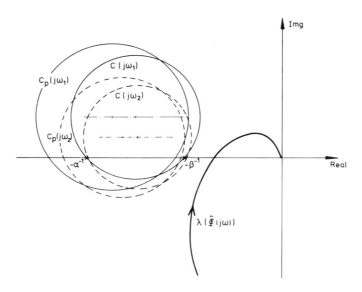

FIG. 7.12   Graphical interpretation of Theorem 7.12 (Popov circle criteria)

Clearly, then, the bounds of the smallest sector of the Hermitian matrix $\hat{\Phi}(j\omega)$ are $m(j\omega) = \min_i \{\lambda_i(\hat{\Phi}(j\omega))\}$ and $l(j\omega) = \max_i \{\lambda_i(\hat{\Phi}(j\omega))\}$. This suggests that if $(\hat{F} - \hat{\Phi})$ can be selected as Hermitian, then its smallest sector can be easily determined.

Select $\hat{\Phi}(j\omega) = \frac{1}{2}(\hat{F}(j\omega) - \hat{F}(j\omega)^*) + a(j\omega)I$ for $a \in C^1$, then

$$(\hat{F} - \hat{\Phi})(j\omega) = \frac{1}{2}(\hat{F}(j\omega) + \hat{F}(j\omega)^*) - a(j\omega)I$$

is also normal. And since the eigenvalues, $\lambda_i(j\omega)$, of the Hermitian matrix $\frac{1}{2}(\hat{F}(j\omega) + \hat{F}(j\omega)^*)$ are real, then the eigenvalues of $(\hat{F} - \hat{\Phi})(j\omega)$ are $\{\lambda_i(j\omega) - a(j\omega)\}$. So that the sector bounds of $(\hat{F} - \hat{\Phi})$ are $m(j\omega) = \min_i \lambda_i(j\omega) - a(j\omega)$ and $l(j\omega) = \max_i \lambda_i(j\omega) - a(j\omega)$. Although the sector width of $(\hat{F} - \hat{\Phi})$ is independent of $a(j\omega)$, the sector may be made symmetrical by selecting $a(j\omega) = \frac{1}{2}(\min_i \lambda_i(j\omega) + \max_i \lambda_i(j\omega))$; in this case $l(j\omega) = \frac{1}{2}(\max_i \lambda_i(j\omega) - \min_i \lambda_i(j\omega)) = \frac{1}{2}m(j\omega)$.

A more generalized technique for establishing the minimum sector $S\{m(j\omega), l(j\omega)\}$ of operator $(\hat{F} - \hat{\Phi})$ can be derived using the notion of the measure and numerical range of complex matrix defined on $LA_-^{n \times n}$.

Defining

$$\lambda^2(j\omega) \triangleq \frac{x(j\omega)^*(\hat{F}-\hat{\Phi})(j\omega)^*(\hat{F}-\hat{\Phi})(j\omega)x(j\omega)}{x(j\omega)^*x(j\omega)}, \qquad \forall x(j\omega) \neq 0.$$

(7.42)

$$\mu(j\omega) \triangleq \frac{x(j\omega)^*[(\hat{F}-\hat{\Phi})(j\omega)+(\hat{F}-\hat{\Phi})(j\omega)^*]x(j\omega)}{x(j\omega)^*x(j\omega)}, \qquad \forall x(j\omega) \neq 0.$$

It is not difficult to see that

$$\max_{x(j\omega)} \lambda^2(j\omega) \geq \mu^2(j\omega), \qquad \omega \geq 0.$$

By using the Euclidean norm interpretation of Definition 5.6a, the above definitions for $\lambda(j\omega)$ and $\mu(j\omega)$ give the alternative conditions for $(\hat{F}-\hat{\Phi})$ inside sector $S\{m(j\omega), l(j\omega)\}$ as

$$\lambda^2(j\omega) - (m(j\omega)+l(j\omega))\mu(j\omega) + m(j\omega)l(j\omega) \leq 0, \qquad \forall x(j\omega) \neq 0$$

(7.43)

Explicit determination of $m(j\omega)$ and $l(j\omega)$ from Inequality (7.43) is complicated by the fact that $\lambda(j\omega)$ and $\mu(j\omega)$ are in general maximized at different values of $x(j\omega)(\neq 0)$. However, if we let the eigenvalues of the Hermitian matrix $\frac{1}{2}[(\hat{F}-\hat{\Phi})+(\hat{F}-\hat{\Phi})^*]$ be ordered such that $\lambda_n(j\omega) > \lambda_{n-1}(j\omega) > \ldots > \lambda_i(j\omega)$, then clearly $\mu(j\omega) \in [\lambda_n(j\omega), \lambda_1(j\omega)]$ for any $x(j\omega) \neq 0$. If $\mu_m(j\omega)$ is the value for $\mu(j\omega)$which maximizes the left hand side of (7.43) when $\lambda(j\omega)$ is bounded from above by the maximum principal gain $\lambda_{mp}(j\omega)$ of $(\hat{F}-\hat{\Phi})$, then a sufficient condition to satisfy (7.43) which gives an optimum choice for sector bounds $l(j\omega)$ and $m(j\omega)$ is

$$\lambda_m^2(j\omega) - (m(j\omega)+l(j\omega))\mu_m(j\omega) + m(j\omega)l(j\omega) = 0 \qquad (7.44)$$

by minimizing the sector width

$$l(j\omega) - m(j\omega) = \frac{\lambda_{mp}^2(j\omega) + m(j\omega)^2 - 2m(j\omega)\mu_m(j\omega)}{\mu_m(j\omega) - m(j\omega)}$$

$$= \frac{\lambda_{mp}^2(j\omega) + l(j\omega)^2 - 2l(j\omega)\mu_m(j\omega)}{l(j\omega) - \mu_m(j\omega)} \qquad (7.45)$$

Minimization of the sector widths with respect to $l(j\omega)$ and $m(j\omega)$ yields

$$l(j\omega) = \mu_m(j\omega) + (\lambda_{mp}^2(j\omega) - \mu_m^2(j\omega))^{1/2} \qquad (7.46)$$

$$m(j\omega) = \mu_m(j\omega) - (\lambda_{mp}^2(j\omega) - \mu_m^2(j\omega))^{1/2} \qquad (7.47)$$

with an associated minimum sector width of $2(\lambda_{mp}^2(j\omega) - \mu_m^2(j\omega))^{1/2}$. All that remains is to select an appropriate $\mu_m(j\omega) \in [\lambda_n(j\omega), \lambda_1(j\omega)]$ to satisfy the sector condition (7.43). Three possibilities arise for the eigenvalues of

$\frac{1}{2}[(\hat{F}-\hat{\Phi})+(\hat{F}-\hat{\Phi})^*]$, (i) $\lambda_1(j\omega)>0$ (ii) $\lambda_n(j\omega)<0$ and (iii) $\lambda_1(j\omega)\lambda_n(j\omega)<0$, for $\omega \geq 0$. In each case, that value of μ_m closest to the origin gives the worst case conditioning of Inequalities (7.43), (7.44): specifically we select (i) $\mu_m(j\omega)=\lambda_1(j\omega)$ for $\lambda_1(j\omega)>0$, (ii) $\mu_m(j\omega)=\lambda_n(j\omega)$ for $\lambda_n(j\omega)<0$ and (iii) $\mu_m(j\omega)=0$ for $\lambda_1(j\omega)\lambda_n(j\omega)<0$ in Equations (7.46), (7.47) for minimum sector width of $(F-\Phi)$.

Before concluding this section we consider the special case when the approximating operator $\hat{\Phi}(j\omega)\triangleq\operatorname{diag}\{\hat{F}(j\omega)\}=\{\hat{f}_{ii}(j\omega)\}$ and the nonlinear operator is also diagonal. Some modification to Theorem 7.11 is required in this situation:

THEOREM 7.13 *If N is diagonal and lies incrementally inside the sector $S\{A+\delta I, B-\delta I\}$ for $\delta>0$, $A=\operatorname{diag}(\alpha_i)$, $B=\operatorname{diag}(\beta_i)$ and $\beta_i>\alpha_i>0$, and $(\hat{F}-\hat{\Phi})$ is inside sector $S\{M(j\omega), L(j\omega)\}$, where $M(j\omega)=\operatorname{diag}\{m_i(j\omega)\}$, $L(j\omega)=\operatorname{diag}\{l_i(j\omega)\}$; l_i, $m_i \in R$, and $\hat{\Phi}(j\omega)=\operatorname{diag}\{\hat{f}_{ii}(j\omega)\}$. Then the feedback system $y=F(u-N(y))$ is L_2^n-stable if the Nyquist plot of $\hat{f}_{ii}(j\omega)$ do not encircle or intersect an off-axis circle $C_0[-l_i(j\omega)-\alpha_i^{-1}, -m_i(j\omega)-\beta_i^{-1}]$ for $i=1,2,\ldots,n$. L and M are chosen such that $(M-L)=k(A^{-1}-B^{-1})G$, for $G\triangleq\operatorname{diag}\{(\cos\theta_i)^{-1}\}$, $\theta_i \in (-\pi/2, \pi/2)$.*

Proof Some modifications to the proofs of Theorems 7.10, 7.11 is necessary; the multiplier Q is redefined to allow differing phase for $i=1,2,\ldots,n$, whilst still remaining diagonal. Real, constant, and diagonal scaling factors are removed from the forward and feedback system operators. These operations do not invalidate the modified versions of conditions of s'(ii) (7.25) and the analagous condition to (7.24) is:

$$\langle (Q^*_+)^{-1}Q_+(B^{-1}+F)(A^{-1}+F)^{-1}x, x\rangle_T \geq 0 \qquad (7.48)$$

for all $x \in L_{2e}^n$, and $T\in R$.

Provided that $(F+A^{-1})^{-1}:L_2^n \to L_2^n$, (implicit in Theorem 7.12) a sufficient condition for (7.48) to hold is

$$\|[\hat{F}(j\omega)+C-jZ\Theta]x(j\omega)\| \geq \|ZGx(j\omega)\|$$

for all $\omega \in [a, b]$, and $x(j\omega)$. Where $\Theta\triangleq\operatorname{diag}(\tan\theta_i)$, $\theta_i \in (-\pi/2, \pi/2)$; $Z\triangleq\operatorname{diag}[\frac{1}{2}(\alpha_i^{-1}-\beta_i^{-1})]$, $C\triangleq\operatorname{diag}[\frac{1}{2}(\alpha_i^{-1}+\beta_i^{-1})]$; $G\triangleq\operatorname{diag}[(\cos\theta_i)^{-1}]$, for $i=1,2,\ldots,n$.

The operator Φ, by the conditions of Theorem 7.13, satisfies

$$\|[\hat{\Phi}(j\omega)+C+\frac{1}{2}(L+M)(j\omega)-jZ\Theta]x(j\omega)\|$$
$$\geq \|[ZG+\frac{1}{2}(L-M)(j\omega)]x(j\omega)\| \qquad (7.49)$$

for all $\omega \in [a, b]$, and $x(j\omega)$.

By assumption the operator $(F-\Phi)$ satisfies,

$$-\|[(\hat{F}-\hat{\Phi})(j\omega)-\frac{1}{2}(M+L)(j\omega)]x(j\omega)\| \geq -\|\frac{1}{2}(L-M)(j\omega)x(j\omega)\| \qquad (7.50)$$

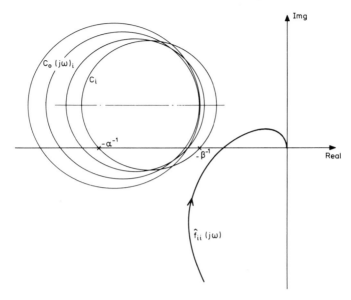

FIG. 7.13   Graphical interpretation of Theorem 7.13

Again, combining Inequalities (7.49) and (7.50) through the triangle inequality and invoking the definition $M - L = k(A^{-1} - B^{-1})G$, we conclude that

$$\|[\hat{F}(j\omega) + C - jZ\Theta]x(j\omega)\| \geq \|ZGx(j\omega)\|$$

for all $\omega \in [a, b]$, and $x(j\omega)$. This is a sufficient condition for inequality (7.48) to hold (Fig. 7.13). Analagous results to the above can be simply derived for the Popov multiplier.   □

For the special case of nonlinearities confined to the sector $S\{0, \beta\}$ the above generalizations lead to alternative Popov-type stability criteria. All the results in this section relate to direct Nyquist-type interpretations; by utilizing a conformal mapping for $\beta > \alpha > 0$, inverse Nyquist-type stability criteria can be readily derived.

   The decomposition of F into $(F - \Phi) + \Phi$ yields criteria that can easily accommodate additive perturbations ΔF in F, by just adding ΔF to the operator $(F - \Phi)$ in the above stability criteria and in the estimation of the optimum sector bounds of $(F - \Phi)$ through Inequalities (7.46) and (7.47) (see Kouvaritakis and Husband, 1981).

7.4 MULTIVARIABLE POPOV CRITERION

Consider the feedback system

$$y = F(u - GN(y)), \qquad u \in L_2^n \tag{7.51}$$

with N a nonlinear Lipschitz continuous map on L_2^n to L_2^n such that

$$\alpha_i(y_i - y_i') \le N(y)_i - N(y')_i \le \beta_i(y_i - y_i') \tag{7.52}$$

for all y, $y' \in L_2^n$ and $i = 1, 2, \ldots, n$, $N(0) = 0$.

The loop transformation theorem applied to the system (7.51) for some $N_0 \in R^{n \times n}$ gives

$$y = (I + FGN_0)^{-1}Fu - (I + FGN_0)^{-1}FG(N - N_0)(y)$$

Suppose that $G \in K(0)^{n \times n}$ but F contains some poles in the right half s-plane; the Nyquist encirclement theorem for the linear system

$$y = (I + FGN_0)^{-1}FGu = Mu$$

shows that $(I + FHN_0)^{-1}FG$ exists so that

$$y = u' - MN'(y) \tag{7.53}$$

where $u' = (I + FGN_0)^{-1}Fu$, and $N = (N - N_0)(y)$. Suppose that $N_0 = \text{diag}(\alpha_i)$, then Inequality (7.52) can be rewritten as

$$0 < N'(y)_i - N'(y')_i \le (\beta_i - \alpha_i)(y_i - y_i')$$

or

$$(\beta_i - \alpha_i)(y_i - y_i')(N'(y)_i - N'(y')_i) \ge (N'(y)_i - N'(y')_i)^2 \ge 0$$

This last inequality implies that

$$y^T N'(y) \ge N'(y)(L)^{-1}N'(y)$$

where $L = \text{diag}(\beta_i - \alpha_i)$ is a positive definite matrix.

From (7.53)

$$u' = y + MN'(y)$$

If $u \in L_2^n$, assume that u', $\dot{u}' \in L_n^2$ and that $y \in L_{2e}^n$ and let M, $DM : L_{2e}^n \to L_{2e}^n$ where $DM : x \to (d/dt)(Mx(t))$. Then

$$\dot{u}' = \dot{y} + DMN'(y)$$

If $Q \in R^{n \times n}$ is a non-singular real diagonal matrix then

$$\langle u' + Q\dot{u}'/N'(y)\rangle_T = \langle y + MN'(y) + Q\dot{y} + QDMN'(y)/N'(y)\rangle_T$$
$$\geq \langle (u' + QD)MN'(y) + L^{-1}N'(y)/N'(y)\rangle_T$$
$$- \langle Q\dot{y}/N'(y)\rangle_T$$

But

$$\langle Q\dot{y}/N'(y)\rangle_T = \int_0^T N'(y)^T Q\dot{y} \, dt$$
$$= \int_{y(0)}^{y(T)} (N'(Z))^T Q \, dz = \beta_1$$

which may be made positive by suitable choice of Q. If $Q = I$, this condition is restrictive since the path independence of $\int_0^z N(z)^T Q \, dz$ essentially requires N to be a gradient of some scalar valued function. This is always the case if $N_j(z)$ depends only on z_j, which may not be true, hence the requirement that Q be non-diagonal for a generalized N. Therefore if for some $\delta > 0$

$$\langle (u' + QD)Mx + L^{-1}x/x\rangle_T \geq \delta \|x\|_T^2 \tag{7.54}$$

then

$$\langle (u' + Q\dot{u}/x)\rangle \geq \delta \|x\|_T^2 - \beta_1 \tag{7.55}$$

and $\dot{u}'$, $u' \in L_2^n$ implies that $N'(y) \in L_2^n$; if in addition $M, DM : L_2^n \to L_2^n$, then also $y, Q\dot{y} \in L_2^n$.

The L_2^n stability criterion (7.54) is a positivity condition, which is equivalent to the requirement that the matrix $\hat{P}(\omega) = \hat{A}(j\omega) + \hat{A}^*(j\omega)$ is positive definite for all ω where $\hat{A}(j\omega) = (I + j\omega Q)\hat{M}(j\omega) + L^{-1}$ and $M = \{m_{ij}\} = (I + FGN_0)^{-1}FG$.

Note that

$$a_{ij} = (1 + j\omega q_{ii})\hat{m}_{ij}(j\omega) \qquad \text{for} \quad i \neq j$$
$$a_{ii} = (1 + j\omega q_{ii})\hat{m}_{ii}(j\omega) + (\beta_i - \alpha_i)^{-1} \quad \text{for} \quad i = j$$

then

$$p_{ij} = \begin{cases} (1 + j\omega q_{ii})\hat{m}_{ij} + (1 - j\omega q_{jj})\hat{m}_{ij}^*, & i \neq j \\ 2[\text{Re}\{(1 + j\omega q_{ii})\hat{m}_{ii}\} + (\beta_i - \alpha_i)^{-1}], & i = j \end{cases} \tag{7.56}$$

for $i, j = 1, 2, \ldots, n$.

Define the complex Popov function $\hat{m}'_{ii}(j\omega)$ by

$$\text{Re}\{\hat{m}'_{ii}(j\omega)\} = \text{Re}\{\hat{m}_{ii}(j\omega)\}$$
$$\text{Img}\{\hat{m}'_{ii}(j\omega)\} = \omega \, \text{Img}\{\hat{m}_{ii}(j\omega)\} \tag{7.57}$$

Clearly, from (7.56) if the loci of $\hat{m}'_{ii}(j\omega)$ lies to the right of the straight

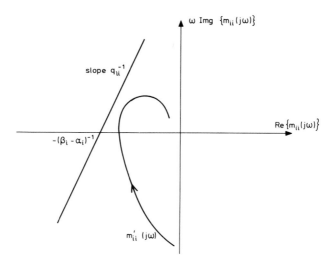

FIG. 7.14   Multivariable Popov criterion

line of scope q_{ii}^{-1} through the point $(-(\beta_i - \alpha_i)^{-1}, 0)$ then $p_{ii}(\omega)$ is positive for all ω (Fig. 7.14); this is the scalar Popov stability criterion.

Define a matrix $Z = \{z_{ij}(\omega)\}$ such that

$$z_{ij} = \begin{cases} |(1 + j\omega q_{ii})| \cdot |\hat{m}_{ij}| + |(1 + j\omega q_{jj})| \cdot |\hat{m}_{ji}| & \text{for} \quad i \neq j \\ p_{ii} & \text{for} \quad i = j \end{cases} \qquad (7.58)$$

then $|z_{ij}| \geq |p_{ij}|$ for all $\omega \in R_+$ and $i, j = 1, 2, \ldots, n$. The eigenvalues of the matrix Z are by Gershgorin's theorem contained in the union of circles centred on p_{ii} of radii $\sum\limits_{\substack{j=1 \\ j \neq i}}^{n} |z_{ij}|$ for all i. But since

$$\sum_{\substack{j=1 \\ j \neq i}}^{n} z_{ij} = \sum_{\substack{j=1 \\ j \neq i}}^{n} |z_{ij}| \geq \sum_{\substack{j=1 \\ j \neq i}}^{n} |p_{ij}|$$

the eigenvalues of P are contained within the Gershgorin circles of Z. If in addition

$$z_{ii} = p_{ii} > \sum_{\substack{j=1 \\ j \neq i}}^{n} z_{ij} = \sum_{\substack{j=1 \\ j \neq i}}^{n} |z_{ji}|$$

and is positive it follows that the eigenvalues of Z and P are positive and hence P is positive definite (a condition for L_2^n-stability of feedback system (7.51)). We are now able to state for the above definitions of q_{ij}, $\hat{m}_{ji}$ and $\hat{m}'_{ii}$

THEOREM 7.14   *The feedback system* $y = F(u - GN(y))$, $u \in L_2^n$ *is* L_2^n-*stable if the envelope of the Gershgorin circles of radii*

$$\tfrac{1}{2}\left\{|(1 + j\omega q_{ii})| \cdot \sum_{\substack{j=1 \\ j \neq i}}^{n} |\hat{m}_{ji}(j\omega)| + \sum_{\substack{j=1 \\ j \neq i}}^{n} |(1 + j\omega q_{jj})| \cdot |\hat{m}_{ji}(j\omega)|\right\} \tag{7.59}$$

centred on the Nyquist plots of $\hat{m}'_{ii}(j\omega)$ *lie to the right of the straight line of slope* q_{ii}^{-1} *through the point* $(-(\beta_i - \alpha_i)^{-1}, 0)$ *for all* i; *assuming that* $M \in K(0)^{n \times n}$.

If $q_{ii} = 0$ for all i the above multivariable Popov stability criterion is identical to Theorem 7.2 for $\alpha = 0$, based upon the incremental or passivity approach. This is not surprising, since in the above derivation a combination of the incremental and positivity approaches have been used. However, the presence of the term q_{ii} ($i = 1, 2, \ldots, n$) in the above adds another degree of flexibility and improved estimate of stability margin over that provided by the incremental gain theorem based upon Gershgorin's theorem.

In Theorem 7.14 the positive definiteness of P was assured by constructing a second and related matrix Z. However, more directly P is positive definite if

$$p_{ii} - \sum_{\substack{j=1 \\ j \neq i}}^{n} |p_{ij}| > 0 \quad \text{for} \quad i = 1, 2, \ldots, n$$

or from (7.56)

$$\text{Re}\left[(1 + j\omega q_{ii})\hat{m}_{ii} + (\beta_i - \alpha_i)^{-1}\right] - \tfrac{1}{2}\sum_{\substack{j=1 \\ j \neq i}}^{n} |p_{ij}| > 0 \tag{7.60}$$

But since

$$\sum_{\substack{j=1 \\ j \neq i}}^{n} z_{ij} \geq \sum_{\substack{j=1 \\ j \neq i}}^{n} |p_{ij}|$$

then (7.60) can be written as

$$\text{Re}\left[(1 + j\omega q_{ii})\hat{m}_{ii}(j\omega)\right] + (\beta_i - \alpha_i)^{-1} - r_i(\omega) > 0 \tag{7.61}$$

for all $\omega \in R$, $i = 1, 2, \ldots, n$, and $r_i(\omega) = \tfrac{1}{2}\sum_{j=1}^{n} |z_{ij}|$.

And so the feedback system (7.51) is L_2^n-stable if the modified Nyquist

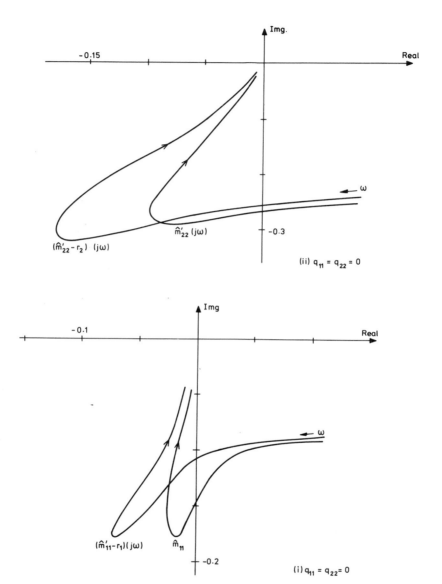

FIG. 7.15   Illustration of Popov multivariable stability criterion ($q_{11} = q_{22} = 0$)

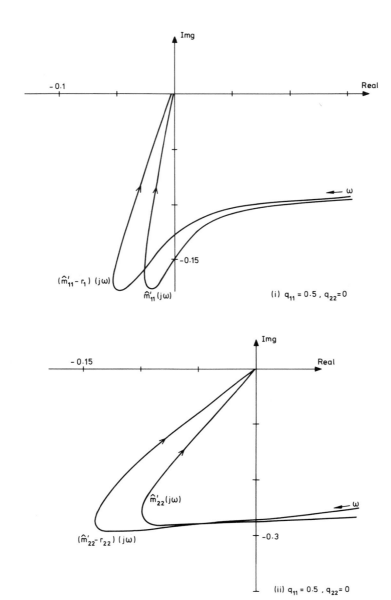

FIG. 7.16 Illustration of Popov multivariable stability criterion ($q_{11} = 0.5$, $q_{22} = 0$)

plot of $\hat{m}'_{ii}(j\omega)$ displaced by $r_i(\omega)$ in the negative direction, is to the right of the straight line of slope q_{ii}^{-1} passing through the point $(-(\beta_i - \alpha_i)^{-1}, 0)$. Also since

$$r_i(\omega) \geq \frac{1}{2} \sum_{j=1}^{n} |p_{ij}(j\omega)| \qquad (i = 1, 2, \ldots, n)$$

the above displaced loci is always contained in the Gershgorin envelope of Theorem 7.14 and hence the above direct approach is less conservative.

To establish $y, \dot{y} \in L_2^n$ the condition $(I + FGN_0)^{-1} FG \in K(0)^{n \times n}$ must hold; this is essentially a linear multivariable stability problem. If the open loop operator $\hat{F}(s) = \hat{F}_0(s) \hat{d}(s)^{-1}$ has p-poles in the right half-s plane (all contained in the monic polynomial $\hat{d}(s)$), then the multivariable Nyquist criterion shows that $(I + FGN_0)^{-1} FG \in K(0)^{n \times n}$ if the envelope of Gershgorin circles of radii $\sum_{j=1}^{n} |\{\widehat{FG}(s)\}_{ij}|$ centred on the Nyquist plots of $\{\widehat{FG}(s)\}_{ii}$ encircle the points $(-\alpha_i^{-1})$ p-times.

To implement Theorem 7.14 values for q_{ii} $(i = 1, 2, \ldots, n)$ have to be selected, these in turn influence the Popov loci and there appears to be no straightforward method of selecting the optimum value of q_{ii} for the least conservative stability limits.

Example 7.3   Consider the feedback system (7.51) with linear portion given by

$$\widehat{FG}(s) = \frac{1}{(s+1)^2(s+6)} \begin{bmatrix} (s+2) & -2 \\ -2 & (s+5) \end{bmatrix}$$

Since the diagonal elements of the matrix transfer function $\widehat{FG}(s)$ are different the Popov loci for both $\{\widehat{FG}(s)\}_{11}$ and $\{\widehat{FG}(s)\}_{22}$ have to be drawn to determine the limits on $(\beta_i - \alpha_i)$, $i = 1$, 2 for closed-loop stability. The Popov loci for $q_{11} = q_{22} = 0$ are shown in Fig. 7.15 from which $(\beta_1 - \alpha_1) = 13 \cdot 9$ and $(\beta_2 - \alpha_2) = 5 \cdot 6$, whereas for $q_{11} = 0 \cdot 5$, $q_{22} = 0$. Figure 7.16 gives the nonlinearity limits of $(\beta_1 + \alpha_1) = 250$, and $(\beta_2 - \alpha_2) = 7 \cdot 14$ for stability.

7.5 NOTES

The notion of passivity has been utilized by many workers in the determination of closed-loop system stability. The definitive papers of Zames (1966) on circle criteria established the basic systems tools which later authors (Narendra and Taylor, 1973; Desoer and Vidyasagar, 1975; and the present authors) exploited to generate increasingly generalized input-output stability criteria.

Cho and Narendra (1968) extended the earlier work of Zames (1964, 1966), Sandberg (1964) and Narendra and Goldwyn (1964) on the scalar on-axis circle criterion to a less conservative off-axis circle criterion by the use of multipliers. Interest for multivariable feedback systems has concentrated upon the on-axis circle criteria and recently Mees and Rapp (1978), Valenca and Harris (1979), Harris and Valenca (1981), Savfanov (1981), Husband and Kouvaritakis (1981), Kouvaritakis and Husband (1981) and Mees (1981) have established a variety of stability criteria for non-normal operators.

Until recently the problem of the generalization of the off-axis criterion remained unsolved. Although Cook (1976) demonstrated that an off-axis criterion based on the diagonal elements of the linear loop operator guarantees the absence of limit cycles, but the inference of stability remained elusive. However, Harris and Husband (1981) have recently established such a criterion for normal linear time-invariant operators. The generalization of the off-axis multivariable circle criterion and its implementation is given in Sections 7.2 and 7.3. Although the present authors restrict the choice of multiplier to an RL or RC realization, the authors conjecture that a much larger class of multipliers exist to satisfy an off-axis interpretation. Clearly, using the techniques of this chapter, many more graphical stability criteria can be generated for feedback systems with a particular structure (Husband and Harris, 1982).

Jury and Lee (1965), using Lyapunov stability ideas, obtained a Popov-like stability criterion for non-linear multivariable feedback systems

$$y = FN(e), \qquad e = y - u$$

with $N(\cdot) = \text{diag}\{N_i(\cdot)\}$ with sector bounds $S\{0, (\beta_i - \alpha_i)\}$. They showed that this system is stable if a real diagonal matrix Q can be found such that

$$A(s) = (I + sQ)\hat{F}(s) + K^{-1} \qquad (7.62)$$

is positive real for $K = \text{diag}(\beta_i - \alpha_i)$. This result has been extended by Moore and Anderson (1968) to have a simple graphical interpretation which is included as a special case of Theorem 7.13.

Related to Cook's (1973) work on Gershgorin banded Nyquist plots is that of Shankar and Atherton (1977), who obtained a Popov-type graphical interpretation for feedback stability, based upon the diagonal matrix Q used in the definition of the positive real matrix $A(s)$ in (7.62). In this approach the nonlinearities are confined to the sectors $N_i(e_i) \in S\{0, \beta_i\}$ for $Q = 0$; this result is identical to Cook's (1973) result for a circle criterion. More recently Mees and Atherton (1981) have extended the Popov criterion for use with Rosenbrock's (1974) diagonal dominance technique and eigenvalue methods (see Mac Farlane, 1979) for near normal linear operators. The Popov criteria are more restrictive than circle criteria, since they require the nonlinearities to be stationary; however, they are less conservative than circle criteria, since they have the added flexibility of the free variable $Q = \text{diag}\{q_{ii}\}$ and are equally simple to implement.

REFERENCES

Cho, Y. S. and Narendra, K. S. (1968). "An off-axis circle criterion for the stability of feedback systems with an monotonic nonlinearity." *IEEE Trans.* **AC–13,** 413–416.

Cook, P. A. (1973). "Modified multivariable circle theorems." *In* "Recent Mathematical Developments in Control" (Ed. D. J. Bell). Academic Press, London and New York.

Cook, P. A. (1976). "Conditions for the absence of limit cycles." *IEEE Trans.* **AC-21,** 339–345.

Desoer, C. A. and Vidyasagar, M. (1975). "Feedback Systems: Input–Output Properties". Academic Press, New York and London

Harris, C. J. and Husband R. K. (1981). "An off-axis multivariable circle stability criterion." *Proc IEE* **128,** 215–218.

Harris, C. J. and Valenca, J. M. E. (1981). "A circle stability criterion for large scale systems." IEE Conf "Control and its Applications." Warwick, March 23–26, 1981. Publ. No. 194 IEE.

Hsu, J. C. and Meyer, A. U. (1968). "Modern Control Principles and Applications." McGraw-Hill, New York.

Husband, R. K. and Harris, C. J. (1982). "Stability multipliers and the multivariable circle criteria." *Int. J. Control* **36,** 755–774.

Husband, R. K. and Kouvaritakis, B. (1981). "The Use of Sectors in the Derivation of Stability Criteria for Nonlinear Systems." OUEL Rept No. 1359/81, Oxford University.

Jury, E. I. and Lee, B. W. (1965). "The absolute stability of systems with many nonlinearities." *Automn. Remote Control* **26,** 943–961.

Kouvaritakis, B. and Husband, R. K. (1981). "A generalisation of the circle criterion." OUEL Rept No. 1355/81, Oxford University.

MacFarlane, A. G. J. (1979). "Frequency Response Methods in Control Systems." IEEE Press, Wiley, New York.

Mees, A. I. (1981). "Dynamics of Feedback Systems." Wiley, Chichester.

Mees, A. I. and Atherton, D. P. (1981). "The Popov criterion for multi-loop feedback systems." *IEEE Trans.* **AC-25,** 924–928.

Mees, A. I. and Rapp, P. E. (1978). "Stability criteria for multi-loop non-linear feedback systems." In Proc. 4th IFAC Symp. Multivariable Technological Systems (Ed. D. P. Atherton). Pergamon Press, Oxford, 183–188.

Moore, J. B. and Anderson, B. D. O. (1968). "A generalization of the Popov criterion." *J. Franklin Inst.* **285,** 488–492.

Narendra, K. S. and Goldwyn, R. M. (1964). "A geometric criterion for the stability of certain nonlinear, non-autonomous systems." *IEEE Trans.* **CT-11,** 406–408.

Narendra, K. S. and Taylor, J. H. (1973). "Frequency domain criteria for absolute stability." Academic Press, New York and London.

Rosenbrock, H. H. (1973). "Multivariable circle theorems" In "Recent Mathematical Developments in Control" (Ed. D. J. Bell). Academic Press, London and New York. 345–365.

Rosenbrock, H. H. (1974). "Computer Aided Control System Design." Academic Press, London and New York.

Sandberg, I. W. (1964). "A frequency domain condition for the stability of feedback systems containing a single time varying nonlinearity." *Bell Systems Tech. J.* **43,** 1601–1608.

Safonov, M. G. (1979). "Stability and robustness of multivariable feedback systems." MIT Press, Cambridge, Mass.

Shankar, S. and Atherton, D. P. (1977). "Graphical stability of nonlinear multivariable systems." *Int. J. Control* **25,** 375–388.

Valenca, J. M. E. and Harris, C. J. (1979). "Stability criteria for nonlinear multivariable systems." *Proc IEE* **126,** 623–627.

Zames, G. (1964): "On the stability of nonlinear time varying feedback systems." *Proc NEC* **20,** 725–730.

Zames, G. (1966). "On the input–output stability of time varying nonlinear feedback systems." *IEE Trans* **AC-11,** Pt I, 228–238, Pt II 465–475.

Zames, B, and Falb, P. L. (1968). "Stability conditions for systems with monotone and slope restricted nonlinearities." *SIAM J. Control & Optimization* **6,** 89–108.

Bibliography

Aggarwal, J. K. (1972). "Notes on nonlinear systems." Van Nostrand Reinhold, New York

Aizerman, M. A. and Gantmacher, F. R. (1964). "Absolute stability of Regulator Systems." Holden-Day, San Francisco.

Anderson, B. D. O. (1972). "The small gain theorem, the passivity theorem and their equivalence." *J. Franklin Inst.* **293**, (2), 105–115.

Araki, M. (1974). "*M*-matrices." Imperial College Tech. Rept 74/19.

Atherton, D. P. (1975) "Nonlinear Control Engineering." Van Nostrand Reinhold, New York.

Atherton, D. P. and Dorrah, H. T. (1980). "A survey on nonlinear oscillations." *Int. J. Control* **31**, 1040–1105.

Atherton, D. P. (1981) "Stability of Nonlinear Systems." Wiley, Chichester.

Banks, S. P. and Collingwood, P. C. (1979). "Stability of nonlinearly interconnected systems and the small gain theorem." *Int. J. Control* **30**, 901–917.

Barman, J. F. (1973) "Well posedness of feedback systems and singular perturbations." Ph.D. Thesis, University of California, Berkeley.

Barker, R. A. and Vakharia, D. J. (1970). "Input–output stability of linear time invariant systems." *IEEE Trans.* **AC-15**, 316–319.

Bergen, A. R., Iwens, R. P. and Rault, A. J. (1966). "On input–output stability of nonlinear feedback systems." *IEEE Trans.* **AC-11**, 742–745.

Bergen, A. R. and Sapiro, M. A. (1967) "The parabola test for absolute stability." *Trans. IEEE* **AC–12**, 312–314.

Blight, J. D. and McChamroch, N. H. (1975) "Graphical stability criteria for large scale nonlinear multiloop systems." Proc IFAC 6th Triennial World Congress, Boston, Paper 44.5

Bohn, E. V. (1962). "Design and synthesis methods for a class of multivariable feedback control systems based on single variable methods." *AIEE Trans.* **81**, 109–115.

Brockett, R. W. and Willems, J. L. (1965). "Frequency domain stability criteria." *IEEE Trans.* **AC-10**, Pt I No. 3, Pt II No. 4.

Brockett, R. W. (1966). "The status of stability theory for deterministic systems." *IEEE Trans.* **AC-11**, 596–607.

Brockett, R. W. and Willems, J. L. (1965). "Frequency domain stability criteria." Parts I, II. *IEEE Trans.* **AC-10**, 225–261, 407–413.

Brockett, R. W. and Lee, H. B. (1967). "frequency domain instability criteria for time varying and nonlinear systems." *Proc. IEEE* **55,** 604–618.

Browder, F. E. (1963) "The solvability of nonlinear functional equations." *Duke Math. J.* **30,** 557–560.

Callier, F. M. and Desoer, C. A. (1972). "A graphical test for checking the stability of a linear time invariant feedback system." *IEEE Trans.* **AC-17,** 773–780.

Callier, F. M. and Desoer, C. A. (1974). "L_p stability $(1 < p < \infty)$ of multivariable nonlinear time varying feedback systems that are open loop unstable." *Int. J. Control* **19,** 65–72.

Chen, C. T. (1968). "L^p-stability of linear time varying feedback systems." *J. SIAM Control* **6,** 186–193.

Cook, P. A. (1973). "Stability of linear constant multivariable systems." *Proc. IEE* **120,** 1557.

Cook, P. A. (1974). "Nyquist plot methods of investigating multivariable feedback systems." Proc. IFAC Multivariable Tech. Syst., Manchester, Paper S-28.

Cook, P. A. (1975). "Circle criteria for stability in Hilbert space." *SIAM J. Control & Optimization* **13,** 593–610.

Davis, J. H. (1972). "Encirclement conditions for stability and instability of feedback systems with delays." *Int. J. Control* **15,** 793–799.

Davis, J. H. (1972). "Fredholm operators, encirclements and stability criteria." *J. SIAM Control* **10,** 608–622.

Desoer, C. A. (1964). "A generalization of Popov's criterion." *IEEE Trans.* **AC–10,** (2), 182–184.

Desoer, C. A. (1970). "Notes for a Second Course on Linear Systems." Van Nostrand Reinhold, New York.

Desoer, C. A. and Callier, F. M. (1972). "Convolution feedback systems." *SIAM J. Control* **10,** 737–746.

Desoer, C. A. and Chan, W. S. (1975). "The feedback interconnection of lumped parameter time invariant systems." *J. Franklin Inst.* **300,** 335–351.

Dewey, A. G. (1967). "Frequency domain stability criteria for nonlinear multivariable systems." *Int. J. Control* **5,** 77–84.

Dewey, A. G. and Jury, E. I. (1966). "A stability inequality for a class of nonlinear feedback systems." *IEEE Trans.* **AC-11,** 54–62.

Estrade, R. F. and Desoer, C. A. (1971). "Passivity and stability of systems with a state representation." *Int. J. Control* **13,** (1), 1–26.

Freeman, E. A. (1973). "Stability of linear constant multivariable systems: Contraction mapping approach". *Proc. IEE* **120,** 3, 379–384.

Fuller, A. T. (1975). "Frequency criteria for the absence of periodic modes." *Automn. Remote Control* **28,** 1776–1780.

Gelb, A. and Van der Velde, W. E: (1968) "Multiple input describing functions and nonlinear system design." McGraw Hill, New York.

Gray, J. O. and Taylor P. M. (1976) "The computer aided design of multivariable nonlinear control systems using frequency domain techniques." IFAC/IFIP Symp. Software for Computer Control. pp. 213–219.

Gray, J. O. and Taylor, P. M. (1977) "Frequency response methods in the design of multivariable nonlinear feedback systems." Proc. IFAC Symp. Multivariable Tech. Syst. Fredericton, pp. 225–232.

Haddad, E. K. (1972). "New criteria for bounded input–bounded output and asymptotic stability of nonlinear systems." Proc. IFAC Paris. Paper 32.2.

Harris, C. J. (1975). "Sufficient conditions for the non-oscillation of non-linear pulse controlled systems." *Proc. IEE* **122**, 193–196.

Harris, C. J. (1975). "Frequency stability criteria for nonlinear stochastic systems." *Int. J. Systems Sci.* **6**, 579–589.

Harris, C. J. (1981). "A note on the generalized Nyquist criterion." *IEEE Trans.* **AC-26** (2), 611.

Harris, C. J. and Billings, S. A. (1981). "Self Tuning and Adaptive Control." Peter Peregrinus, London.

Holtzmann, J. M. (1968). "A local bounded input bounded output condition for nonlinear feedback systems." *IEEE Trans.* **AC-13**, 585–587.

Hsu, C. H. and Chen, C. T. (1968). "A proof of the stability of multivariable systems." *Proc. IEEE* **56**(11), 2061–2062.

Hyseyin, O. (1973). "On the circle criterion." *Int. J. Control* **18**, 9–16.

Hyseyin, O. (1973). "On the Popov criterion." *Int. J. Control* **17**, 1137–1142.

Jury, E. I. (1974). "Inners and Stability of Dynamical Systems." Wiley, New York.

Kavanagh, R. J. (1958). "Multivariable control system synthesis." *Trans. AIEE* **77** (part 2), 425–429.

Lighthill, M. J. and Mees, A. I. (1973). "Stability of nonlinear feedback systems." *In* "Recent Mathematical Develop in Control." (Ed. D. J. Bell), 1–20. Academic Press, London and New York.

Lindgren, A. and Pinkos, R. F. (1966). "Stability of symmetric nonlinear multivariable systems." *J. Franklin Inst.* **282**, 92–101.

MacFarlane, A. G. J. (1979). "The development of frequency–response methods in automatic control." *IEEE Trans.* **AC-24**, 250–265.

MacFarlane, A. G. J. (1970). "Return-difference and return-ratio matrices and their uses in analysis and design of multivariable feedback control systems." *Proc. IEE* **117**, 2037–2049.

McGee, J. B. and MacLellan, G. D. S. (1968) "Stability of nonlinear multivariable control systems." *Proc IEE* **115**, 590–591.

McClamrod, N. H. and Ianculescu, G. D. (1975) "Global stability of two linearly interconnected nonlinear systems." *IEEE Trans.* **AC-20**, 678–682.

Mees, A. I. (1973). "Describing functions, circle criteria and multiple loop feedback systems." *Proc. IEE* **120** (1), 126–130.

Naumov, B. N. and Tsypkin, Y. Z. (1964) "A frequency criterion for absolute process stability in nonlinear automatic control systems." *Automn. Remote Control* **25**, 1027–1037.

Noldus, E. J. (1973). "Instability of feedback systems containing several time varying nonlinear amplifiers." *Proc. JACC*, 870–875.

Noldus, E. J. (1973). "Criterion for unbounded motion by positive operator methods." *Int. J. Control* **18**, 289–296.

Nyquist, H. (1932). "Regeneration Theory." *Bell Syst. Tech. J.* **2**, 126–147.

O'Shea, R. P. (1966). "A combined frequency–time domain criterion for autonomous linear systems." *IEEE Trans.* **AC-11,** 3.

Paley, R. E. A. C. and Wiener, N. (1934). "Fourier transforms." *Amer. Math. Soc. Coll. Publ.* **XIX,** New Providence 1934.

Partovi, S. and Nahi, E. H. (1969). "Absolute stability of dynamic systems containing nonlinear functions of several state variables." *Automatica* **5**, 465–473.

Popov, V. M. (1962). "Absolute stability of nonlinear control systems of automatic control." *Automn. Remote Control* **22,** 857–858.

Postlethwaite, I. (1975). "A generalized inverse Nyquist stability criterion." *Int. J. Control* **26,** 677–695.

Ramani, N. and Atherton, D. P. (1974). "Stability of nonlinear multivariable systems." Proc. IFAC Symp. Multivariable Tech. Syst., Manchester, Paper S10.

Ramani, N. and Atherton, D. P. (1975). "A note on the stability and eigenvalues of $G(s)$." *Int. J. Control* **22,** 701–704.

Ramarajan, S. and Thathachar, M. A. L. (1972). "L^2-stability of time varying systems with global conditions on the time varying gain." *Int. J. Syst. Sci.* **3,** 385–384.

Rootenberg, J. and Oso, J. M. (1971). "On cross-coupling and stability in nonlinear control systems." *IEE Trans.* **AC-16,** 73–75.

Rootenberg, J. and Wal, R. (1973). "Frequency criterion for the absence of limit cycles in nonlinear systems." *IEEE Trans.* **AC-18,** 64–65.

Rosenvasser, E. N. (1963). "The absolute stability of nonlinear systems." *Automn. Remote Control* **24,** 283–291.

Saeks, R. (1970). "Causality in Hilbert spaces." *SIAM Review* **12,** 357–383.

Saeks, R. (1973). "Resolution Space, Operator, Systems". Springer Verlag, New York.

Sandberg, I. W.(1965). "Conditions for the causality of nonlinear operators defined on a function space." *Q. Appl. Math.* **23,** 87–91.

Sandberg, I. W. (1965). "Some stability results related to those of V. M. Popov." *Bell Syst. Tech. J.* **46,** 2133–2148.

Sandberg, I. W. (1965) "An observation concerning the application of the contraction mapping fixed point theorem and a result concerning the norm boundedness of solutions of nonlinear functional equations." *Bell Syst. Tech. J.* **44,** 1809–1812.

Sandberg, I. E. (1965). "A note on the application of the contraction mapping fixed point theorem to a class of nonlinear functional equations." *SIAM Rev.* **7,** 199–204.

Sandberg, I. W. (1966). "On generalizations and extensions of the Popov criterion." *IEEE Trans.* **CT-13,** 1.

Srinath, M. B., Thathachar, M. A. L. and Ramapriyan, H. K. (1968). "Absolute stability of systems with multiple nonlinearities." *Int. J. Control* **7,** 365–375.

Sundareshan, M. K. and Thathacher, M. A. L. (1973). "Generalized factorizability conditions for stability multipliers." *IEEE Trans.* **AC-18,** 183–184.

Tokumaru, H. and Saito, N. (1965). "On the absolute stability of automatic control systems with many nonlinear characteristics." *Mem. Fac. Engng Kyoto Univ.* **27,** 347–379.

Uronen, P. and Jutila, E. A. A. (1972). "Stability via the theorem of Gershgorin." *Int. J. Control* **16,** 1057–1061.

Viswanadham, N. and Deekshatulu, B. L. (1966). "Stability analysis of nonlinear multivariable control systems." *Int. J. Control* **5,** 369–375.

Valenca, J. M. E. and Harris, C. J. (1979) "A Nyquist type criterion for the stability of multivariable linear systems." 17th IEEE Conf. Decision and Control, San Diego, California, USA.

Valenca, J. M. E. and Harris C. J. (1981). "Representacoa de multiplicadores em espacos L_p." VIII Journadas Luso-Espanholas de Matematic, Coibra, Portugal.

Valenca, J. M. E. and Harris, C. J. (1981) "Os espacos X_p." Ibid.

Vidyasagar, M. (1972). "L_p-stability of time varying linear feedback systems." *IEEE Trans* **AC-17,** 412–414.

Vidyasagar, M. (1972). "Input–output stability of a broad class of linear time invariant multivariable feedback systems." *SIAM J. Control* **10,** 203–209.

Vidyasagar, M. (1972). "Some applications of the spectral radius concept to nonlinear feedback stability." *IEEE Trans.* **CT-19,** 608–615.

Willems, J. C. (1971). "The generation of Liapunov functions for input–output stable systems." *SIAM J. Control* **9,** 105–134.

Wu, M. Y. and Desoer, C. A. (1969). "L_p-stability $(1 \leq p \leq \infty)$ of nonlinear time varying feedback systems." *SIAM J. Control* **7**(2), 356–364.

Yakubovitch, V. A. (1970). "Absolute stability of nonlinear control systems." Part 1, *Automatika Telemehk* **31**(12); Part 2 (1971) Ibid; **32**(6).

Zames, G. and Falb, P. L. (1967). "On the stability of systems with monotonic and odd monotonic nonlinearities." *IEEE Trans.* **AC-12,** 221–223.

Subject Index